Reagan and the World

REAGAN AND THE WORLD

LEADERSHIP AND NATIONAL SECURITY, 1981–1989

EDITED BY

BRADLEY LYNN COLEMAN AND KYLE LONGLEY

FOREWORD BY

JACK MATLOCK JR.

UNIVERSITY PRESS OF KENTUCKY

Paperback edition 2018

Scholarly publisher for the Commonwealth,
serving Bellarmine University, Berea College, Centre College of Kentucky, Eastern Kentucky University, The Filson Historical Society, Georgetown College, Kentucky Historical Society, Kentucky State University, Morehead State University, Murray State University, Northern Kentucky University, Transylvania University, University of Kentucky, University of Louisville, and Western Kentucky University.

Editorial and Sales Offices: The University Press of Kentucky
663 South Limestone Street, Lexington, Kentucky 40508-4008
www.kentuckypress.com

Library of Congress Cataloging-in-Publication Data

Names: Coleman Bradley Lynn 1973- editor. | Longley Kyle editor.
Title: Reagan and the world : leadership and national security 1981-1989 / edited by Bradley Lynn Coleman and Kyle Longley ; foreword by Jack Matlock Jr.
Description: Lexington Kentucky : The University Press of Kentucky 2017. | Series: Studies in conflict diplomacy and peace | Includes index.
Identifiers: LCCN 20170108051 ISBN 9780813169378 (hardcover : alk. paper) ISBN 9780813169385 (pdf) | ISBN 9780813169392 (epub)
Subjects: LCSH: United States—Foreign relations—1981-1989. | Reagan Ronald—Influence.
Classification: LCC E876 .R39283 2017 | DDC 973.927092—dc23
LC record available at https://lccn.loc.gov/2017010805

ISBN 978-0-8131-7554-6 (pbk. : alk. paper)

This book is printed on acid-free paper meeting the requirements of the American National Standard for Permanence in Paper for Printed Library Materials.

∞

Manufactured in the United States of America.

Member of the Association of University Presses

For John A. Adams,
in recognition of his support
for military history and strategic analysis
at the Virginia Military Institute

Contents

Foreword

In November 1985, just before Ronald Reagan left Washington to meet Soviet leader Mikhail Gorbachev for the first time, the president wrote out his thoughts about Gorbachev and the forthcoming meeting on a yellow legal pad. His secretary typed what he wrote and returned it to the president. Reagan made some handwritten corrections on the typescript. National Security Assistant Robert "Bud" McFarlane handed the memo to me as we boarded Air Force One for Geneva. "If the President got anything wrong," McFarlane advised, "we will have a chance to brief him in Geneva and set him straight."

McFarlane's request for corrective comment, if needed, did not surprise me. From the time the meeting with the Soviet leader had been announced, Reagan had spent several hours each week studying the Soviet Union and learning about its new leader. He took our briefings and papers seriously, frequently making comments such as "Thanks for pointing this out. I had a general notion but didn't know enough to be confident." When we challenged something that he had said or written—as we did when he repeated "quotations" from Vladimir Lenin that could not be verified—he would thank us.

When it came to his memo on Gorbachev, no correction was necessary. He had changed the only statement we would have challenged. He had originally written, "Our recent PFIAB [President's Foreign Intelligence Advisory Board] study makes it plain the Soviets are planning a war. They would like to win without it and their chances of doing that depend on being so prepared we could be faced with a surrender or die ultimatum." In his revision, he bracketed for removal the phrase "planning a war" and edited the sentence to read: "They would like to win by being so much better prepared we could be faced with a surrender or die ultimatum."

Other comments were relevant not only to the Geneva meeting but also to US foreign policy in general. Take human rights, for example. For Ronald Reagan, improving respect for human rights was one of the foremost goals of his foreign policy. Nevertheless, he questioned the way we were dealing with the issue. He wrote: "I am sorry we are somewhat publicly on record about human rights. Front page stories that we are banging away at them on their human rights abuses will get us some cheers from the bleachers but it won't help those who are being abused. Indeed, it could wind up hurting them."

Reagan then quoted former president Richard Nixon, who had described to him how he took up the question of Jewish emigration from the Soviet Union only after signing the arms-control agreements in 1972. Nixon asked Soviet leader Leonid Brezhnev to permit an increase in emigration to ensure ratification of the agreement. Jewish emigration rose from six hundred a year before Nixon took office to thirty-five thousand following the agreement. But then "the Jackson–Vanik Amendment was passed [by Congress,] which made Jewish emigration a public condition for most favored nation treatment. That year the number of Jews allowed to emigrate was cut in half and today the number is down to a trickle." Reagan added that Nixon had "expressed optimism that I might accomplish what he did in 1972, but only if I didn't force Gorbachev to eat crow and embarrass him publicly." Reagan emphasized: "We must always remember our main goal and his need to show his strength to the Soviet gang back in the Kremlin."

From this point on, President Reagan and Secretary of State George P. Shultz dealt privately with human rights issues. Before long, they established regular consultations with senior Soviet officials. These conversations produced rapid results once the Soviet leader recognized that better protection of human rights was an essential component of his perestroika (restructuring) reform. Reagan and Shultz avoided claiming credit for the improvement in Soviet human rights, recognizing that doing so would harm, not help, the victims of abuse.

In the memo regarding the Geneva meeting, Reagan identified the three key issues in US-Soviet relations: "The security issues like arms control, the regional areas of conflict and the prevalent suspicion and hostility between us." It was clear to him that without trust there could be little improvement in US-Soviet relations and that, given the distrust that did prevail, trust could only be built over time as small steps led to greater confidence. Reagan subsequently latched on to the Russian proverb "Doveryai, no proveryai" (Trust but verify). This point of view was directed as much at skeptics in his own administration, who argued that the Soviet leaders could not be trusted, as it was to Gorbachev and the Soviet leadership. As it turned out, Gorbachev agreed to the most comprehensive verification procedures specialists could devise, and Soviet officials carried out the agreements to the letter.

Reagan was not thinking of concluding treaties merely for their own sake. In fact, he recognized the danger of papering over real problems with toothless or ambiguous agreements. He was a firm believer in dealing from strength. He remarked in his memo on the Geneva meeting that "another of our goals probably stated to Gorbachev in private should be that failure to come to a solid, verifiable arms reduction agreement will leave no alternative except an arms race and there is no way that we will allow them to win such a race." Nevertheless, he set fair goals for the use of American strength, instructing negotiators not to seek unilateral advantage but to find solutions that fit both countries' peaceful interests.

As for the choice between fair arms-reduction agreements and an arms race that the Soviets would lose, by February 1987 Gorbachev got the point. From that time, he lectured the Politburo on the need to reduce arms unilaterally because the Soviet Union had overbuilt its offensive capacity, creating anxiety in the United States and western Europe. According to Gorbachev adviser Anatoly Chernyaev, the Soviet leader explained the need for reductions by observing that the Western military-industrial complex would trap them in an arms race that the Soviet Union would lose. In December that year, Reagan and Gorbachev signed the Intermediate-Range Nuclear Forces Treaty, which eliminated in both countries' arsenals a whole category of nuclear weapons, with agreed on-site inspection to guarantee compliance.

In concluding his memo, Reagan gave a final piece of wise advice. "But let there be no talk of winners and losers. Even if we think we won, to say so would set us back in view of their inherent inferiority complex."

From my perspective, the attitudes Reagan expressed in regard to Gorbachev and the Soviet Union prevailed in his dealings with others. Although firm in defending American interests, he always tried to understand the position of his Soviet adversaries. He hoped to find ways to accommodate their legitimate, peaceful interests. He understood that lasting agreements had to be beneficial to both sides and therefore that seeking one-sided advantages or crowing about victory was likely to do more harm than good.

Contemporary international security problems resemble in many ways the challenges of the 1980s. For this reason, the Reagan presidency remains vital to our understanding of global affairs, offering lessons on style and substance for national security professionals in the twenty-first century. We should also consider his goals and objectives. Importantly, Reagan wanted a world without nuclear weapons, a dream he shared with Mikhail Gorbachev. Their efforts greatly reduced the nuclear danger, but current US and Russian arsenals remain the largest in the world, and the prospect for further reduction have dimmed with the revival of Cold War rhetoric in US-Russian relations. Our current generation of strategists must pay more attention to the reasons why Reagan and Gorbachev tried to eliminate nuclear weapons—and find ways to get the United States and other countries back on course.

This book, edited by Bradley Lynn Coleman and Kyle Longley, will educate and inform students and scholars of the Reagan presidency. The essays will also help guide current and future generations of presidential advisers. The contributors are among the most thoughtful scholars of international security affairs. They describe and analyze important aspects of the Reagan period and highlight opportunities for additional research. This collection is a timely addition to the literature on a topic of enduring importance, helping us move beyond "talk of winners and losers" and toward a deeper understanding of the final decade of the Cold War.

—Jack Matlock Jr., former US ambassador
to the Soviet Union (1987–1991),
special assistant to the president for
national security affairs (1983–1986), and
US ambassador to Czechoslovakia (1981–1983)

Abbreviations

CDU	Christian Democratic Union
CIA	Central Intelligence Agency
contra	counterrevolutionary
CPD	Committee on the Present Danger
CSU	Christian Social Union (Germany)
DoD	US Department of Defense
FDP	Free Democratic Party (Germany)
FOIA	Freedom of Information Act
GE	General Electric
HASC	House Armed Services Committee
H.R.	House Resolution
IBWC	International Boundary and Water Commission
IDF	Israeli Defense Forces
INF	intermediate-range nuclear forces
INF Treaty	Intermediate-Range Nuclear Forces Treaty
JCS	Joint Chiefs of Staff
KGB	Committee for State Security (Soviet Union)
LAF	Lebanese Armed Forces
MAD	mutually assured destruction
MDR	Mandatory Declassification Review
MIA	missing in action
MNF	multinational force (Lebanon)
NATO	North Atlantic Treaty Organization
NSC	US National Security Council
NSDD	National Security Decision Directive
NSPG	National Security Planning Group
NSSD	National Security Study Directive
OJCS	Organization of the Joint Chiefs of Staff (Joint Staff)
OMB	Office of Management and Budget

OPEC	Organization of the Petroleum Exporting Countries
PLO	Palestine Liberation Organization
POW	prisoner of war
PRC	People's Republic of China
RG	record group
SALT	Strategic Arms Limitation Treaty/Talks (Treaty between the United States of America and the Union of Soviet Socialist Republics on the Limitation of Strategic Offensive Arms)
SASC	US Senate Armed Services Committee
SDI	Strategic Defense Initiative (Star Wars)
SPD	Social Democratic Party (Germany)
TOW	tube-launched, optically tracked, wire-guided antitank missile
UN	United Nations
USBR	US Bureau of Reclamation

Introduction

Bradley Lynn Coleman and Kyle Longley

President Ronald Reagan traveled to the Soviet Union in May 1988. He personally delivered the Intermediate-Range Nuclear Forces Treaty, recently ratified by the US Senate, to the Soviet secretary general, Mikhail Gorbachev. The two men also discussed the status of ongoing strategic nuclear arms negotiations and other topics of shared interest. Yet the importance of the Moscow summit did not really concern treaties or agreements. The enduring legacy of Reagan's visit instead involved his engagement with Soviet citizens.

In Moscow, the president mingled with tourists in Red Square, dined with Soviet artists and athletes, and attended the ballet. Then, on May 31, Reagan spoke to six hundred students at Gorbachev's alma mater, the prestigious Moscow State University. "Your generation is living in one of the most exciting, hopeful times in Soviet history," Reagan observed.[1] In his prepared remarks, the president talked about Hollywood films, the US government, and the information revolution. He then took questions from the students.

"It was surreal and illuminating," Svetlana Savranskaya, a senior at Moscow State University remembered. "For those [of us] in attendance," she added, "the Cold War ended on May 31, 1988. . . . We understood that the smiling man who spoke about things close to our hearts, like human rights, would not push the button" to unleash a US nuclear attack on the Soviet Union. President Reagan, "the leader of our archenemy," proved to be "human, engaging, and enthusiastic" about building a real partnership with the Soviet Union. On the stage at Moscow State University, she concluded, Reagan demolished the "wall of mistrust" that divided the Soviet and American people.[2]

In early 2013, the John A. Adams '71 Center for Military History and

Strategic Analysis—a specialized element of the Virginia Military Institute (VMI) focused on the Cold War—launched a project to explore and promote the military history of the Reagan era. Sparked by the ongoing declassification of Reagan administration records, the endeavor included a dissertation grant, essay contest, oral history interviews, and public lectures. With partners across the VMI community and country, the center also organized a three-day conference on Reagan in Lexington, Virginia. Svetlana Savranskaya, now a senior research fellow at George Washington University, joined dozens of established historians, national security professionals, and Reagan administration officials for the event.

Conceived four years ago, this book on leadership and national security is an important piece of the center's Reagan initiative. Over the past thirty years, writers have devoted considerable attention to the Reagan presidency. Early critics such as Walter LaFeber and Michael Rogin portrayed Reagan as a dangerous warmonger and his presidency as plagued with mismanagement, misconduct, and foreign-policy failures.[3] In response, Reagan supporters, including Peter Schweizer and William Pemberton, described Reagan as the triumphant hero of the American century. The president, they concluded, had renewed American strength and "won" the Cold War against communism.[4] Raymond Garthoff and others—including many of the historians featured in this book—have recently produced more-balanced descriptions of the Reagan administration, blending Reagan's accomplishments and shortcomings into a more coherent and accurate portrayal of the president.[5] Engaging newly released archival documents, this book advances the recent trend in the literature on the Reagan presidency, broadening our understanding of this essential period in the history of international security relations.

The dynamics of the Reagan administration present challenges to students of the past. Indeed, there were two Ronald Reagans making national security policy during his presidency. One Reagan pushed a massive military buildup, supported the overthrow of totalitarian regimes, and advocated for the expansion of democracy and capitalism. The other Reagan worked to abolish nuclear weapons, engage adversaries, and promote human rights. Historians must disentangle Reagan's words and deeds. The gap between his rhetoric and actions often leaves students searching for the real Reagan. In addition, his chaotic, often confusing management style—compounded by the presence of six national security advisers at the White House in just eight years—makes it difficult to locate the administration's position on any given issue.

An additional challenge lies in Reagan's complex relationship with George H. W. Bush, a political opponent in the Republican Party who became his vice president. The Cold War, according to Bush, had not ended by the time of his inauguration as forty-first president of the United States in January 1989. Bush inherited, among other problems, a crushing national deficit and rapidly changing international order. During his desperate campaign for reelection in 1992, President Bush claimed that the United States won the Cold War against the Soviet Union. Making the assertion, he hoped to gain a political advantage against Democratic Party presidential nominee William J. Clinton. Later, Republic Party neoconservatives such as Dick Cheney and Donald Rumsfeld seized on this concept, interpreting and presenting Reagan in ways that justified their own assertive brand of American internationalism in the Middle East and beyond.

Organized in four parts, this book reflects the complexity of the Reagan presidency. The first part focuses on Reagan and the US national security establishment. In chapter 1, US Department of State historian James Graham Wilson examines the president's engagement with the Soviet Union. Wilson argues that President Reagan's willingness to engage adversaries—over many of his advisers' objections—"proved an indispensable component of the final decade of the Cold War." In chapter 2, Beth A. Fischer explores the president's position on nuclear weapons. A pathbreaking scholar of the Reagan presidency, Fischer presents Reagan's commitment to the elimination of nuclear weapons as a deeply held moral conviction. Ronald J. Granieri, a senior fellow at the Foreign Policy Research Institute, evaluates Reagan's controversial secretary of defense, Caspar Weinberger, in chapter 3. In doing so, Granieri offers valuable insight into the organization and function of the national security establishment during the Reagan presidency. In chapter 4, James R. Locher III shifts the narrative to Capitol Hill with coverage of the Goldwater–Nichols Department of Defense Reorganization Act of 1986. Over the opposition of the president, secretary of defense, and Joint Chiefs of Staff, the landmark legislation enhanced the unity of the US Armed Forces, strengthened civilian control of the military, and generated structural reforms across the defense community. The legislation, Locher shows, was a triumph of courageous, values-based bipartisan leadership by Arizona Republican Barry Goldwater and Georgia Democrat Sam Nunn.

Part 2 covers US relations with the Soviet Union and Europe. In chapter 5, the influential British scholar Archie Brown argues that Gorbachev, not Reagan, was the indispensable international actor of the 1980s. An emeritus professor at Oxford University, Brown confirms that Reagan's military buildup and hard-line anti-Soviet rhetoric strengthened the Kremlin's determination to compete with the United States during the early 1980s. After 1985, Gorbachev's willingness to engage Reagan produced a negotiated end to the Cold War. In chapter 6, James Cooper, a senior lecturer at Oxford Brookes University, analyzes the "special relationship" between Reagan and Margaret Thatcher. The US president and British prime minister shared ideological convictions—notably a passionate disdain for communism—but often "downgraded" their partnership to advance personal goals. In chapter 7, University of Virginia professor William I. Hitchcock examines US-French relations during the Reagan presidency. Reagan and President François Mitterrand held conflicting ideological views but forged an important partnership based on pragmatic interest and a shared sense of history. In his essay "Navigating Choppy Waters," David F. Patton of Connecticut College explores US-German relations during the final decade of the Cold War. At the center of the Cold War in Europe, West Germans, active agents of their own experience, successfully shaped their relationship with the United States to achieve their national goals and objectives, notably the reunification of Germany.

Part 3 explores US relations with Asia, Latin America, and the Middle East. In chapter 9, University of Arizona professor Michael Schaller traces the transformation of Reagan's attitudes toward Communist China and Vietnam. Over time, Reagan abandoned his strident rhetoric toward the former US adversaries in favor of a more moderate, constructive posture. Kyle Longley of Arizona State University treats US policy toward Central America in chapter 10. Reagan's "obsession" with the region resulted in a series of bad decisions that nearly brought down the Reagan White House. Staying focused on the Americas, Evan R. Ward investigates US-Mexican environmental relations during the Reagan years in chapter 11. A professor at Brigham Young University, Ward shows how the Reagan administration productively used bilateral forums to address Mexican-

American water issues during the 1980s. Ward challenges readers to integrate environmental topics into the history of US foreign relations. In chapter 12, Charles F. Brower IV, professor at the Virginia Military Institute and former US Army aide to President Reagan, describes and analyzes US policy toward Lebanon. "President Reagan," Brower concludes, was "a stranger in a dangerous land."

In addition to the essays printed in this volume, the Adams Center project generated other significant scholarship on the Reagan presidency. Importantly, six additional articles, written with Adams Center support since 2013, offer valuable information and analysis on the Reagan era, and all are available on the Adams Center's website (www.vmi.edu/adamscenter). In the first, renowned journalist and Reagan biographer Lou Cannon shares his personal insights on the president's leadership in the essay "Freedom Man." Alan Dobson, now an honorary professor at St. Andrews University, dissects Reagan's management style in an essay titled "Reagan's Strategies and Policies." Svetlana Savranskaya covers the Reagan–Gorbachev summits—including insightful treatment of the president's 1988 visit to Moscow—in her paper "Bringing Down the Walls." The two leading scholars of the Red Army, David Glantz and Jacob Kipp, examine Soviet conventional and nuclear policy during the 1980s. Finally, James Hentz, the head of VMI's Department of International Studies and Political Science, treats US policy toward southern Africa during the Cold War in "Reading History Forward."

The authors featured in this book stand on the forefront of Reagan scholarship. Even so, students and scholars must do more work on the Reagan presidency. Every month, employees of the National Archives and Records Administration declassify and release additional US government records generated during the Reagan years. The continued flow of new sources promises to refine and challenge our understanding of Reagan. This collection therefore includes an essay by Ryan Carpenter, a doctoral candidate at the Catholic University of America actively engaged in research on the national security policy of the 1980s. His essay, "Researching Reagan," surveys key memoir and manuscript sources on the Reagan presidency. Carpenter also identifies important topics for further research, subjects not covered here, including US policy toward Afghanistan, covert operations, and counter illicit trafficking during the Reagan years.

The essays published here and online significantly advance our under-

Admiral James G. Stavridis, US Navy (ret.), addresses the Reagan conference audience at the Virginia Military Institute, November 3, 2014. The former North Atlantic Treaty Organization commander called on attendees to build bridges, not walls, to promote US national security in the twenty-first century. (Courtesy of the John A. Adams '71 Center for Military History and Strategic Analysis)

standing of leadership and national security during the Reagan presidency. Together, they provide readers with a greater understanding of the complexity of the Reagan years. The writers differ, of course, on their interpretation of President Reagan's leadership and other aspects of national security affairs during the 1980s. The president's courageous engagement with Gorbachev, for example, clashed with his obstructionist approach to Costa Rican president Oscar Arias's peace initiative in Central America. Scholars focused on relations between the United States and Europe present Reagan more favorably than those examining American relations with the developing world. Here and elsewhere, Reagan responded to different situations in different ways across time and space. For students of the period, this complexity only enhances his appeal as a scholarly subject.

The publication of this book marks the end of the Adams Center project to better understand the enduring legacy of the Reagan presidency. It is also a launching point for the next generation of scholars and national security professionals. At the Virginia Military Institute in November 2014, former North Atlantic Treaty Organization commander Admiral James G. Stavridis, US Navy (ret.), talked about the linkages between twentieth- and twenty-first-century international security. "Twentieth century national security was all about building walls," he observed, and the results proved "cataclysmic"—two world wars and a Cold War. Walls did not provide security for the United States; twenty-first-century leaders therefore need to find another approach to national defense. "Walls are not security, we have to find ways to build bridges—play the long game—to create real security" for the United States, Stavridis proposed.[6] The Reagan presidency, as this book shows, offers a template for building those bridges but also reveals the risks associated with perpetuating an outdated national security mindset.

Notes

1. "Moscow Summit; Excerpts from the President's Talk to Artists and Students," *New York Times,* June 1, 1988.

2. Svetlana Savranskaya, "Bringing Down the Walls: Reagan and Gorbachev," paper presented at "The Enduring Legacy: Leadership and National Security during the Ronald Reagan Era," November 3–4, 2014, John A. Adams '71 Center for Military History and Strategic Analysis, Virginia Military Institute, Lexington, VA, 10–11, at http://www.vmi.edu/adamscenter.

3. Walter LaFeber, *Inevitable Revolutions: The United States and Central America* (New York: Norton, 1985); William Leogrande, *Our Own Backyard: The United States and Central America* (Chapel Hill: University of North Carolina Press, 1998); Michael Rogin, *The Movie: And Other Episodes of Political Demagoguery* (Berkeley: University of California Press, 1988); and Frances Fitzgerald, *Way Out There in the Blue: Reagan, Star Wars, and the End of the Cold War* (New York: Simon and Schuster, 2001).

4. Peter Schweizer, *Victory: The Reagan Administration's Secret Strategy That Hastened the Collapse of the Soviet Union* (New York: Atlantic Monthly Press, 1996) and *Reagan's War: The Epic Story of His Forty-Year Struggle and Final Triumph over Communism* (New York: Anchor, 2003); William E. Pemberton, *Exit with Honor: The Life and Presidency of Ronald Reagan* (Armonk, NY: M. E. Sharpe, 1997); Ronald Reagan, *Reagan, in His Own Hand: The Writings of Ronald Reagan That Reveal His Revolutionary Vision for America,* ed. Kiron Skinner, Annelise Anderson, and Martin Anderson (New York: Free Press, 2001); and Edward Lynch, *The Cold War's Last Battlefield: Reagan, the Soviets, and Central America* (New York: Global Academic, 2013).

5. Raymond L. Garthoff, *The Great Transition: American-Soviet Relations and the End of the Cold War* (Washington, DC: Brookings Institution Press, 1994); Beth A. Fischer, *The Reagan Reversal: Foreign Policy and the End of the Cold War* (Columbia: University of Missouri Press, 1997); and Michael Schaller, *Right Turn: American Life in the Reagan–Bush Era, 1980–1992* (New York: Oxford University Press, 2006).

6. James G. Stavridis, keynote presentation at "The Enduring Legacy."

Part 1

Ronald Reagan and the National Security Establishment

1

Ronald Reagan's Engagement and the Cold War

James Graham Wilson

There are two private moments leading up to Ronald Reagan's White House years that illustrate his sense of mission. "Why are you doing this, Ron? Why do you want to be President?" Stuart Spencer, a longtime associate, asked Reagan during the campaign against President Jimmy Carter in 1980. "To end the Cold War," was his answer. How did he plan to do that? "I'm not sure, but there has got to be a way," Reagan insisted.[1] On another occasion, the former governor told his future national security adviser, Richard Allen, that his overall approach to the Soviets was not complicated: "We win; they lose."[2] These moments foreshadowed presidential rhetoric familiar now to everyone. At Westminster, England, in June 1982, Reagan extolled "the march of freedom and democracy which will leave Marxism-Leninism on the ash-heap of history as it has left other tyrannies which stifle the freedom and muzzle the self-expression of the people."[3] The following spring he called the Soviet Union an "evil empire."[4] Four years after that, standing in front of the Brandenburg Gate in West Berlin, he proclaimed: "General Secretary Gorbachev, if you seek peace, if you seek prosperity for the Soviet Union and Eastern Europe, if you seek liberalization: Come here to this gate! Mr. Gorbachev, open this gate! Mr. Gorbachev, tear down this wall!"[5]

Twenty-five years after the collapse of the Berlin Wall and the end of the Cold War, these statements elicit broader questions. Did Reagan construct and execute a grand strategy to win the Cold War? Did his thinking toward the Soviet Union change over time? Would another US president—such as Jimmy Carter or George H. W. Bush—have pursued the same policies after the arrival of Mikhail Gorbachev in 1985? No matter how one answers these questions, there is now a presumption of greatness about Reagan. Americans from across a wide political spectrum associate the memory of the fall of the Berlin Wall with Reagan's speech at the Brandenburg Gate on June 12, 1987—even though Reagan was not president on November 9, 1989, when the wall actually came down, and Gorbachev gave no order that fateful evening.

Reagan was indeed a key figure in the story of the end of the Cold War.[6] His greatest contribution, however, was his willingness to *engage* the Cold War adversary. Strategies of engagement on the part of President Reagan and his administration preceded the arrival of Gorbachev on the scene in March 1985. The ascent of Secretary of State George P. Shultz from July 1982 to January 1985 empowered Reagan's instincts to negotiate with the Soviets in spite of his fervent anticommunism and inherent skepticism about whether the Soviets could ever be trusted. So, too, did the arrival of Jack Matlock, the top Soviet adviser on the National Security Council (NSC) staff from the summer of 1983 on, who crafted a four-part framework for diplomacy with the Soviets. Progress was halting, as hard-liners such as Secretary of Defense Caspar W. Weinberger resisted such efforts, and the president refrained from intervening to settle personal and policy disputes among his team. Reagan's subsequent engagement with Gorbachev led him to think in terms grander than anyone might have expected: he seized on the prospect of sharing Strategic Defense Initiative (SDI) technology with the Soviet Union to make certain that both sides stuck to a blockbuster deal on nuclear arms to reduce arsenals eventually to zero.

Reagan and Communism

Ideology and faith were key components in the life of Ronald Reagan, which ran parallel to the life of the Soviet Union. Born in Tampico, Illinois, on February 6, 1911, Reagan was the son of Nelle Clyde Wilson Reagan, who had only recently been baptized into the Disciples of Christ Church, and Jack Reagan, a disappointing, alcoholic father who would move the family ten times over the next decade. The Reagan family eventually settled in Dixon, one hundred miles west of Chicago, where Reagan spent his teenage years as a lead in school plays and a lifeguard who notched seventy-seven rescues over the course of six summers. Young Reagan, who went by the nickname "Dutch" after his father remarked that he resembled a "fat Dutchman," asked to be baptized into his mother's church after reading Harold Bell Wright's novel *The Printer of Udell's: A Story of the Middle West* (1902). He learned from Ben Cleaver, his family's pastor and the father of his first girlfriend, about the "atheistic doctrines" on which communism rested and how the world "must look [to America] for its emancipation from the most heartless spiritual despotism ever."[7]

In 1928, Reagan followed Margaret Cleaver ninety miles south to Eureka College, a Disciples affiliation. The two were engaged upon graduation in 1932, yet the engagement did not last. "As fond as she was of Dutch, she thought he lacked interest in the wider world," writes biographer Jacob Weisberg.[8] Reagan headed into the world of radio, becoming a successful sports announcer first in Davenport and then in Des Moines, Iowa. Already a self-made man in spite of the Great Depression, Reagan aspired higher. A screen test for Warner Brothers in 1936 eventually landed him a contract that would make him a film star.

Reagan was forever after associated with the role of George Gipp in *Knute Rockne—All American* (1940) and was most proud of his performance in *Kings Row* (1942).[9] He also played a leading role in the film *Brother Rat* (1938), a comical depiction of cadet antics at the Virginia Military Institute. His stint in the First Motion Picture Unit of the US Army Air Forces included acting in and narrating recruitment and training films. He explained why America was fighting in World War II and what for. After his discharge in September 1945, Reagan found more opportunities for activism than the lead acting roles to which he aspired. His ascent to the presidency of the Screen Actors' Guild coincided with an era of ugly labor strife in Hollywood. On one occasion, he received a telephone call threatening disfigurement if he did not support a union strike sponsored by Communist fronts. Reagan regarded this strike as something much larger than a local dispute. World War II demonstrated that ideology had consequences; it appeared that communism was the new fascism. As he saw it, ideology transcended national identity—Nazis who committed atrocities, for instance, were entities apart from Germans. In his testimony before the House Un-American Activities Committee, he basically said that Communists were not real Americans, so from his perspective there was nothing un-American about naming names.

In presidential elections, Reagan voted for Franklin D. Roosevelt four times and then for Harry S. Truman in 1948. He remained a registered Democrat even as he supported Dwight D. Eisenhower in 1952 and 1956 and aligned himself with modern American conservatism. His education in retail politics during this period was remarkable. Hired by General Electric (GE) to host a television theater and hold meetings showing off its new consumer products, Reagan was also selling the American dream.[10] He hosted town-hall meetings, a task for which he crafted a standard speech that elucidated all-American, capitalist values in the face of what he saw as the expansion of government and the specter of international communism.

"You and I have a rendezvous with destiny," Reagan proclaimed in his advertisement for Barry Goldwater's faltering presidential campaign in 1964. "We will preserve for our children this, the last best hope of man on Earth, or we will sentence them to take the first step in a thousand years of darkness."[11] Reagan's political ambitions were high. After winning the California governorship two years later, he briefly pursued the Republican presidential nomination in 1968. He criticized Richard Nixon's foreign policies—especially toward Vietnam, the Soviet Union, and the People's Republic of China—while also compromising with the opposition in the California legislature. "Anytime I can get 70 percent of what I'm asking for out of a hostile legislative body, I'll take it," he told aide Peter Hannaford. "I figure that it will work well enough for me to go back later and get a little more of it here and a little more of it there."[12]

Reagan very nearly defeated Gerald Ford in the Republican primary of 1976 and eliminated the term *détente* from the sitting president's political vocabulary after castigating his foreign policies on the eve of the North Carolina primary. That year marked the bicentennial celebration of the founding of the United States; in an impromptu speech at the Republican National Convention, the former governor described a letter for a time capsule to be opened on the three hundredth anniversary of the independence of the United States in 2076. "Whether [Americans] have the freedoms that we have known up until now will depend on what we do here," he said. "Will they look back with appreciation and say, 'Thank God for those people in 1976 who headed off that loss of freedom, who kept us now 100 years later free, who kept our world from nuclear destruction?'"[13]

In other words, Reagan was arguing, America was engaged in a struggle between freedom and communism that had the potential to end in nuclear annihilation. Yet however eloquently stated in 1964 and 1976, Reagan's vision for the future did not address the fate of people in the rest of the world. *Americans* were to remain free in 2076, but what about the inhabitants of the Soviet Union or the citizens of leftist regimes in eastern Europe, Latin America, Asia, and Africa? Did America's preservation of peace and freedom require liberating the Communist world? Or could America achieve its goal while coexisting alongside that world?

Reagan would have responded to these questions in two ways. On the one hand, communism was a disease to be eradicated. Americans required "frequent vaccination to guard against being infected until the day when this health threat will be eliminated as we eliminated the black plague," Reagan declared in a radio address in May 1975.[14] A divided world could not survive "half-slave, half-free," he wrote to a supporter while on the campaign trail in 1980. "We must also keep alive the idea that the conquered nations—the captive nations—of the Soviet Union must regain their freedom."[15]

On the other hand, Reagan believed in "peace through strength." "America has never gotten into a war because it was too strong," he used to tell his supporters. An important and often overlooked influence on him was his second wife, Nancy Davis Reagan, who later recalled, "For years it had troubled me that my husband was always being portrayed by his opponent as a warmonger, simply because he believed, quite properly, in strengthening our defenses."[16]

"Peace through strength" did not mean liberating humanity but rather restoring the US strategic advantage that had existed prior to the Cuban Missile Crisis. "When John F. Kennedy demanded the withdrawal of Soviet missiles from Cuba and the tension mounted, it was Nikita Khrushchev who backed down, and there was no war," Reagan said in 1980. "Our nuclear superiority over the Soviets was about 8 to 1."[17] Indeed, conservatives and neoconservative Democrats such as Scoop Jackson insisted that the Soviets had not only caught up with the United States during the Brezhnev era but had surpassed it. Détente had not failed to curb Soviet meddling in the Third World, and strategic arms control had not stopped the Kremlin from deploying SS-20 intermediate-range missiles as well as a new generation of intercontinental ballistic missiles and strategic bombers that could knock out US ground-based-missile silos. Reagan and his colleagues on the Committee on the Present Danger in the late 1970s opposed the Treaty between the United States of America and the Union of Soviet Socialist Republics on the Limitation of Strategic Offensive Arms (Strategic Arms Limitation Treaty, SALT) II because they believed it locked in these Soviet advantages.

Reagan subscribed to both "peace through strength" and a "crusade for freedom." This assessment of the Soviet Union held contradictions. "Peace through strength" cast the Soviets as incredibly strong. In his radio speeches following the presidential primary in 1976—many of which he drafted himself—Reagan cited Soviet capabilities to fight and win a nuclear war. "Crusade for freedom" cast the Soviets as inherently weak: its economy was on the brink of collapse, and there was no real point in negotiating with it because the Kremlin had never lived up to its end of any bargain. When Jimmy Carter prevailed in November, Reagan returned to his ranch in California and prepared to run again four years later. He castigated Carter for his commitment to signing SALT II, insisting that the president of the United States ought to be able to broker a better deal. Privately, the former governor was dubious whether any deal was possible. "I don't really trust the Soviets," Reagan wrote to a friend in April 1980, "and I don't really believe that they will really join us in a legitimate limitation of arms agreement."[18]

President Reagan and the Soviet Union, January 1981–July 1982

In January 1981, Reagan entered the White House with a fundamental ambivalence about how to approach the Soviet Union. He predicted recovery but also acknowledged relative declines on the part of the United States and its allies. Indeed, the global economy grew very little between 1971 and 1982. After a miraculous recovery from 1945 on, the economies of most West European countries were sputtering at the end of the 1960s. The need to stabilize and retool the economies of the World War II aggressors tested the victors' commitment to free trade and open competition. In the United States, goods produced in Japan and West Germany crowded out those produced at home. In large swaths of the South and the Rust Belt stretching from New York to Ohio and Michigan, manufacturing jobs disappeared. The oil embargo by the Organization of the Petroleum Exporting Countries (OPEC) because of US support for Israel during the Arab–Israeli conflict in October 1973 closed the spigot on the flow of cheap oil that had fueled the recovery of international capitalism after the Great Depression and World War II. The rise of OPEC called into question the notion of a coalition of great powers that could impose political and economic order on their terms. The embargo caused tremendous angst. "Can Capitalism Survive?" read a cover of *Time* in 1975. "Is Capitalism Working?" read a slightly less ominous cover in 1980.[19]

Reagan's former employer, GE, exemplified capitalism's stagnation. A legacy of the iconic inventor Thomas Edison, GE produced power turbines, jet engines, locomotives, televisions, microwaves, and lightbulbs. Despite pioneering innovations such as a CT scan in the 1970s, however, GE ambled through a decade in which the Dow Jones Industrial Average closed at 785.57 on January 2, 1970, and 785.75 on January 2, 1980. Shortly after Reagan gave his Inaugural Address in late January 1981, in which he declared that "government is not the solution to our problem; government is the problem,"[20] Jack Welch took the helm of GE. Welch's unstated message was that the problem at the company was too many jobs. "Neutron Jack," as he was quickly dubbed, left the machines intact and operational and dispatched the humans—just like the "enhanced radiation weapon," or neutron bomb.

America would recover, of course, and one of the key long-term decisions that helped was Paul Volcker's interest-rate hikes, which tamed inflation but did no political favors for Jimmy Carter at the end of his term or for Ronald Reagan in his first years in office. American workers' real wages dropped more than 10 percent from 1978 to 1982, and during the recession of 1981–1982 US unemployment figures approached 11 percent.[21]

In the spring of 1981, Reagan was confident that his economic stimulus from tax cuts and ratcheted-up defense spending would reinvigorate the American economy. But he did not believe America was operating from a position of economic and military strength when it came to dealing with the Soviets. Indeed, the two top administration priorities in 1981 were to cut taxes and to ramp up defense spending. It was not at all clear at the start of that year that Reagan would even take an active role in foreign policy. Certainly, it was not clear to his own secretary of state, the assertive Alexander Haig, who expected to be the "vicar . . . of foreign policy."[22]

Nevertheless, Reagan reached out to his Soviet counterparts, beginning with a letter to Leonid Brezhnev shortly after John Hinckley's assassination attempt on March 30. The president reminded the Soviet leader of their introduction in California a decade earlier: "When we met I asked if you were aware that the hopes and aspirations of millions and millions of people throughout the world were dependent on the decisions that would be reached in your meetings [with Richard Nixon]," after which "you took my hand in both of yours and assured me that you were aware of that and that you were dedicated with all your heart and mind to fulfilling those hopes and dreams." Now was the time to act upon this pledge to help foster peace, Reagan urged. "It is in this spirit, in the spirit of helping the people of both our nations," the president went on to write, "that I have lifted the grain embargo. Perhaps this decision will contribute to creating the circumstances which will lead to the meaningful and constructive dialogue which will assist us in fulfilling our joint obligation to find lasting peace."[23] Reagan followed up with subsequent letters that fall and amid the imposition of martial law in Poland that December. By the spring of 1982, he hoped for a potential summit with Brezhnev—or at least a meeting on the sidelines of the upcoming United Nations Conference on Disarmament in New York City.

In other words, Reagan wanted to engage the Soviets from the very start of his administration, even as he embarked upon a military buildup and told the British Parliament in June 1982 about "the march of freedom and democracy which would leave Marxism-Leninism on the ash-heap of history as it has left other tyrannies which stifle the freedom and muzzle the self-expression of the people."[24] Yet it also confounded him that Soviet leaders would not respond more constructively to private letters he sent in between tough public statements. Hard-liners such as Caspar Weinberger, William Casey, and William Clark, who had known the president a long time, discouraged Reagan's entreaties to Soviet leaders. They clashed with Secretary of State Al Haig, who, bombast notwithstanding, was more attuned to trans-Atlantic partners' concerns. Reagan rarely gave clear orders, and he did not intervene to halt the bickering among his top advisers. In the fall of 1981, the president called up a respected Washington journalist to deny that personnel changes were to be expected. Alexander Haig was "the best Sec. of State we've had in a long time," the president recorded in his diary after the call.[25] He summoned his secretary of state and national security adviser and ordered "a halt to the sniping."[26] This was about as clear as he got.

Shultz's Engagement; Reagan's Engagement

By July 1982, Al Haig had alienated everyone in the administration and lost the president's confidence. He was replaced by George Shultz, a highly respected veteran of the Nixon administration. Shultz was not a traditional diplomat, but he was a skilled and patient negotiator. He loved telling the story of his first political crisis, a labor dispute left over from Lyndon Johnson's presidency. Johnson had invoked the Labor Management Relations (Taft-Hartley) Act of 1947 to stop the strike for eighty days, and the Supreme Court had upheld his decision. As the new secretary of labor, Shultz inherited the problem once the eighty days were up. "I have a strategy for how to handle this strike," Shultz recalled telling Nixon. "Let the pressures produced by the strike cause the union and management to settle it themselves through the collective bargaining process."[27] Patience worked; that was the lesson Shultz wanted to apply to the Cold War. "Coming into office as secretary of state at a time when we were confronted with tremendous problems," he later explained, "the economist in me asked, 'Where are we trying to go, and what kind of strategy should we employ to get there?' recognizing that results would often be a long time in coming."[28]

Al Haig had been a moderate compared to most of the officials surrounding Reagan, but he also blamed Moscow for abetting the Baader-Meinhof gang in their attempt to kill him when he was supreme allied commander of the North Atlantic Treaty Organization. Whereas Haig was a cold warrior who had fought Communists in Korea and Vietnam, Shultz had encountered Communists from a different perspective. As secretary of the Treasury, he had traveled to Moscow and Leningrad, where he was shown remnants of the nine-hundred-day siege by the Nazis during World War II. "I had learned something of the human dimension to the Soviet Union," Shultz later wrote. "I also learned that the Soviets were tough negotiators but that you could negotiate successfully with them."

Their diplomats were smart and unflappable. "I respected them not only as able negotiators but as people who could make a deal and stick to it."[29]

Shultz wanted to engage his Soviet counterpart, Andrei Gromyko, however obstinate the longtime Soviet foreign minister could be. From July 1982 to January 1985, Shultz's engagement became Reagan's engagement and vice versa. With the assistance of the new Soviet specialist on the NSC, Jack Matlock, who replaced Richard Pipes, Shultz helped rationalize Reagan's conflicting impulses so that engagement was placed at the forefront. Unlike previous administrations, the Reagan team set human rights in the Soviet Union as a central cone of negotiations.

The formal Soviet strategy of the administration was National Security Decision Directive 75 (NSDD-75), "US Relations with the USSR," which Reagan signed on January 17, 1983. NSDD-75 articulated three basic goals:

> To contain and over time reverse Soviet expansionism by competing effectively on a sustained basis with the Soviet Union in all international arenas—particularly in the overall military balance and geographical regions of priority concern to the United States. This will remain the primary focus of U.S. policy toward the USSR.
>
> To promote, within the narrow limits available to us, the process of change in the Soviet Union toward a more pluralistic political and economic system in which the power of the privileged ruling elite is gradually reduced. The U.S. recognizes that Soviet aggressiveness has deep roots in the internal system, and that relations with the USSR should therefore take into account whether or not they help to strengthen this system and its capacity to engage in aggression.
>
> To engage the Soviet Union in negotiations to attempt to reach agreements which protect and enhance U.S. interests and which are consistent with the principle of strict reciprocity and mutual interest. This is important when the Soviet Union is in the midst of a process of political succession.[30]

Here was a distinction between NSDD-75 and previous declaratory strategies concerning the Soviet Union: "To promote, within the narrow limits available to us, the process of change in the Soviet Union toward a more pluralistic political and economic system in which the power of the privileged ruling elite is gradually reduced." Saying it and doing it were two different things. On January 19, 1983, two days after Reagan had signed off on NSDD-75, Shultz sent the president his vision of a way forward, a memorandum titled "U.S.-Soviet Relations in 1983." Instead of containing and reversing Soviet expansionism through military and economic pressure, it called for countering the "new Soviet activism by starting an intensified dialogue with Moscow" on the basis of realism and mutual interests.[31]

Shultz devised a plan to get Reagan to do what the president had long sought: engage directly with a high-ranking Soviet official. Anatoly Dobrynin, the Soviet ambassador to the United States, was well suited for this role. A resident of Washington, DC, for twenty years, Dobrynin possessed a cosmopolitan outlook and a gregarious demeanor. He had over the years established friendships with Bobby Kennedy and Henry Kissinger. He did not spout the rhetoric of international class conflict and the eventual triumph of communism. A few days before February 15, 1983, Shultz hatched a scheme to accompany Dobrynin to the White House to meet with the president. National Security Adviser William Clark called the secretary of state to express his disapproval of the meeting (he had already shared his misgivings with their mutual boss), but his objections went unheeded. Shultz believed that Reagan's direct participation in the US-Soviet dialogue accorded with the president's impulses to negotiate arms reductions in spite of hard-liners' objections and that "the efforts of the staff at the NSC to keep [Reagan] out," he later recalled, "were beginning to break down."[32]

"We talked for 2 hours," Reagan wrote in his diary after meeting Dobrynin. "Sometimes we got pretty nose to nose. I told him I wanted George [Shultz] to be a channel for direct contact with [General Secretary Yuri] Andropov—no bureaucracy involved." Reagan also broached the subject of the Soviet Pentecostals who were living in the basement of the US embassy in Moscow. If the Soviets would allow them to leave unharmed, the president promised not to grandstand.[33] "George tells me that after they left [the White House] the Ambassador said 'this could be an historic moment.'"[34]

Shultz's actions infuriated top advisers, who had been around Reagan far longer. "Mr. President, if our plans for the Soviets (or any other issue in my area of responsibility) are not coordinated with Cap [Caspar Weinberger] and Bill [Casey] and Jeanne [Kirkpatrick], we will fail," Clark wrote to Reagan in a handwritten letter in March.[35] Several acrimonious meetings followed. The next month Reagan confided in his diary: "Some of the N.S.C. staff are too hard line & don't think any approach should be made to the Soviets. I think I'm hard-line & will never appease but I do want to try & let them see there is a better world if they'll show by deed they want to get along with the free world."[36]

On June 15, 1983, Shultz testified in front of the Senate Foreign Relations Committee. "In the past two years this nation . . . has made a fundamental commitment to restoring its military and economic power and moral and spiritual strength," he declared. "And, having begun to rebuild our strength, we now seek to engage the Soviet leaders in a constructive dialogue through which we hope to find political solutions to outstanding issues." There were clear and understandable sources of tension, Shultz went on to say. "But we are not so deterministic as to believe that geopolitics and ideological competition must ineluctably lead to permanent and dangerous confrontation."[37] As long as the president did not stake too much political capital on achieving a deal—as his predecessors had done—he could avoid the pitfalls of unforeseen events. Expectations needed to be kept in check. Strength and realism would guide America's dialogue with the Soviet Union. Human rights should be discussed. So should Soviet behavior in Afghanistan, but their withdrawal was not a precondition for an arms agreement. Point by point, Shultz articulated the four-part framework—bilateral relations, regional matters, arms control, and human rights.

Although the Soviets walked out of arms negotiations in Geneva at the end of 1983, Shultz and Matlock prepared for them to return. The two men wanted to establish a firmer relationship that could not be switched on and off, that included human rights, and that moved away from the linkage of unrelated problems. Matlock started Saturday morning seminars for NSC principals to refine US policies on the Soviet Union and to establish long-term priorities that did not include destroying the Soviet Union. He drafted a speech for Reagan to deliver in January 1984, in which the president spoke of an Ivan and Anya and Jim and Sally meeting in a diner.[38] In NSC meetings later on that year, Secretary of Defense Caspar Weinberger opposed efforts to restart arms negotiations. The priority, to him, was to identify new potential strategic imbalances and attempt to resolve them.

Even after his smashing reelection that November, however, Reagan was reluctant to take actions to harmonize his national security team. "A long meeting with Sec. Shultz," he recorded in his diary on November 14, 1984. "We have trouble. Cap & Bill Casey have views contrary to George's on S. Am., the Middle East & our arms negotiations. It's so out of hand George sounds like he wants out. I cant [*sic*] let that happen. Actually George is carrying out my policy. I'm going to meet with Cap & Bill & lay it out to them. Wont [*sic*] be fun but has to be done."[39] As with Haig and Allen, Reagan ultimately shied away from confronting individuals subordinate to him—and even from issuing clear orders. Around this time, White House Chief of Staff James A. Baker III and Secretary of the Treasury Donald Regan informed the president they had decided to switch jobs. This passive managerial style helped enable the Iran-Contra shenanigans, revelations about which nearly ground the Reagan presidency to a halt for two years. In the meantime, Shultz, to head off sniping from the Pentagon about what he might have offered Gromyko, assembled a large US delegation that included Assistant Secretary of Defense Richard Perle, a known skeptic of nuclear agreements. To the surprise of Shultz and others who traveled to Geneva in January 1985 to work out the details of the Nuclear and Space Arms Talks, set to commence that March, the message they heard from the Soviet delegation was that the goal ultimately should be zero nuclear weapons.

Reagan, Shultz, and Gorbachev

It took four years of diplomacy on the part of Reagan, Shultz, and Gorbachev to move the United States, the Soviet Union, and the world closer to zero nuclear weapons. In mid-1985, a year and a half after Reagan gave his speech about Ivan and Anya and Jim and Sally, Reagan and Gorbachev took on the roles of Ivan and Jim meeting in a diner. Gorbachev was the single most important individual in bringing about the end of the Cold War because he accepted strategic sufficiency and allowed East Germany and eastern Europe to withdraw peacefully from the Soviet orbit; in January 1986, he foreshadowed dramatic changes by publicly calling for the abolition of nuclear weapons by the year 2000.

Reagan shared Gorbachev's goal of abolishing nuclear weapons. But SDI was essential for that to happen. Critics got the president wrong when it came to the system they derided as "Star Wars." In fact, SDI was the central component of his grand vision of a world without nuclear weapons. "The president stressed that he was prepared, once any of our SDI programs proved out," read the minutes of an NSC meeting on September 20, 1985, "to then announce to the world that integrating these weapons in our respective arsenals would put international relations on a more stable footing." "In fact," the president went on to say, "this could even lead to a complete elimination of nuclear weapons. We must be prepared to tell the world that we were ready to consult and negotiate on integrating these weapons into a new defense philosophy, and to state openly that we were ready to internationalize these systems."[40]

Reagan grew even more passionate about sharing SDI after engaging the Soviet leader, Mikhail Gorbachev, in Geneva in November 1985. "We should remember the principle of sharing SDI at the deployment stage," the president told his team on February 3, 1986. "As we continue to develop SDI we need to find a way for SDI to be a protector for all—perhaps the concept of a 'common trigger' where some international group, perhaps the [United Nations], could deploy SDI against anyone who threatened use of nuclear weapons. Every state could have this guarantee."[41]

No US leader but Ronald Reagan could have gotten away with saying these things. Who could conceive of a more extraordinary thing than an American president sharing a nuclear shield with the Soviet Union? Someone who wanted to vest America's national security in the United Nations, perhaps, while the world embarked upon eliminating nuclear weapons. Reagan proposed doing the first, hinted strongly at the second, and contemplated these schemes just three years after calling the Soviet Union an "evil empire."

"I do not understand the reasoning behind your conclusion that only a country preparing a disarming first strike would be interested in defenses against ballistic missiles," Reagan wrote Gorbachev on February 16, 1986. The United States had never borne ill toward anyone, the president insisted. After World War II, the United States had not sought to expand its territory when it had the power to do so. In every letter to Soviet leaders and in each meeting with them, Reagan repeated this example of how the United States had disarmed and acted defensively after World War II.[42]

In his meetings with Gorbachev in Reykjavik in October 1986, Reagan laid out his plan. Both sides would begin reducing nuclear stockpiles. The United States would pursue SDI with the intent to share it with the Soviet Union. The defensive system would provide insurance so that both sides would stick to their commitments. Then, after both sides had dismantled their nuclear arsenals, they would keep SDI to protect themselves from a madman such as Libya's Muammar Gaddafi should he ever get the bomb. Gorbachev rejected this proposal; several months later, however, he agreed to "delink" SDI from an INF Treaty. Hard-liners around the president regarded Gorbachev's decision as a consequence of the leverage SDI provided. Reagan saw it as an opportunity to keep pressing for his supremely ambitious plan. "Why can't we agree now that if we get to a point where we want to deploy we will simply make all the information available about each other's systems so that we can both have defenses?" the president asked his national security team on September 8, 1987. "I don't believe that we could ever do that," Secretary of Defense Weinberger responded.[43]

Ultimately, Reagan's conception of what SDI could achieve surely *was* a dream. It was a combination of the promise of American technological wizardry and the conviction of an eternal optimist. Reagan trusted that his counterpart in the Kremlin would not press the button; as he repeated to Gorbachev to the point of annoyance, he intended to "trust but verify." Although his critics derided SDI as making nuclear war less unthinkable, SDI assisted Reagan in overcoming his skepticism of whether bargains with the Soviets could ever be sustained.

Reagan and the End of the Cold War

In December 1987, Reagan and Gorbachev signed a treaty to eliminate intermediate-range nuclear forces. The Washington Summit, where the two leaders signed the INF Treaty, was not the president's finest performance. Reagan was perhaps too focused on convincing Gorbachev to accept the logic of SDI to grasp that the Soviet leader was walking back from previous intransigence on the scope and duration of restrictions on testing it. The signing of the INF Treaty was an unprecedented achievement in arms control in that it got rid of an entire class of missiles; still, the president aspired toward an even-greater agreement to reduce strategic

President Ronald Reagan greets a Soviet boy while touring Red Square on May 31, 1988. The president engaged students, artists, and athletes during his visit to Moscow. (Courtesy of the Ronald Reagan Presidential Library)

nuclear weapons before he left office. He instructed his team on February 9, 1988, "The bottom line is you've got to go for the gold."[44] That summer, standing in the middle of Red Square, Reagan said that the epithet *evil empire* had referred to "another time, another era."[45]

"We meant to change a nation," Reagan said in his Farewell Address to the Nation on January 11, 1989, "and instead, we changed a world."[46] The "we" referred to the American people, yet it was even more inclusive than that. Reagan believed that the Soviet Union was embracing the principles of freedom of speech, respect for human dignity, and right of property. The legacy of his engagement with the Soviets, therefore, was not "we won; they lost." The Cold War was not yet over when he and George Shultz left office. The Berlin Wall remained standing, Germany was still divided, and eastern Europe continued to be under Moscow's control. Gorbachev made the key decision to accept strategic sufficiency, but Reagan set the terms for the big strategic debates. A triptych on nuclear arms negotiations in the 1980s would feature Gorbachev and Reagan; the panels would be titled "Strategic Arms Reductions," "Strategic Defense," and the "Zero Option." Had Reagan not defeated Carter in November 1980 or had he not survived the assassination attempt the following March, Gorbachev would still have become the general secretary of the Communist Party in 1985. Yet there would have been neither SDI nor Reykjavik. And likely no INF Treaty.

Most importantly, absent Reagan there would not have been the stark contrast between the "evil empire" and "another time, another era." The latter statement reduced substantially the Soviet perception of the United States as a threat in advance of a year of miracles in Poland, East Germany, and Czechoslovakia. Gorbachev was the key variable in this transformation; however, Shultz and Matlock's reconfiguration of US policies toward the Soviet Union preceded his arrival. They emboldened the president's instincts to sit down with the adversary. Reagan's engagement proved an indispensable component of the final decade of the Cold War. Whether he had a grand strategy for victory or not neither enhances nor detracts from his achievements.

Notes

The views expressed here are those of the author and do not necessarily reflect those of the US Department of State or the US government.

1. Stuart Spencer, quoted in Thomas C. Reed, *At the Abyss: An Insider's History of the Cold War* (New York: Presidio Press and Ballantine Books, 2004), 234.

2. Richard Allen, interview, May 28, 2002, Ronald Reagan Oral History Project, Presidential Oral History Program, Miller Center of Public Affairs, University of Virginia, Charlottesville, at http://millercenter.org/president/reagan/oralhistory/richard-allen.

3. Ronald Reagan, "Address to Members of the British Parliament," June 8, 1982, at http://www.reagan.utexas.edu/archives/speeches/1982/60882a.htm.

4. Ronald Reagan, remarks at the Annual Convention of the National Association of Evangelicals, Orlando, Florida, March 8, 1983, at http://www.reagan.utexas.edu/archives/speeches/1983/30883b.htm.

5. Ronald Reagan, remarks on East–West relations at the Brandenburg Gate in West Berlin, June 12, 1987, at http://www.reagan.utexas.edu/archives/speeches/1987/061287d.htm.

6. James Graham Wilson, *The Triumph of Improvisation: Gorbachev's Adaptability, Reagan's Engagement, and the End of the Cold War* (Ithaca, NY: Cornell University Press, 2014).

7. Paul Kengor, *God and Ronald Reagan: A Spiritual Life* (New York: Harper, 2004), 34.

8. Jacob Weisberg, *Ronald Reagan* (New York: Holt, 2016), 16.

9. Ronald Reagan, with Richard Hubler, *Where's the Rest of Me?* (New York: Duell, Sloan, and Pearce, 1965), 103. Reagan titled his first autobiography after his most memorable line in *Kings Row,* which he described as "the finest picture I've ever been in."

10. See Thomas W. Evans, *The Education of Ronald Reagan: The General Electric Years and the Untold Story of His Conversion to Conservatism* (New York: Columbia University Press, 2008).

11. Ronald Reagan, "A Time for Choosing," October 27, 1964, at http://www.reagan.utexas.edu/archives/reference/timechoosing.html.

12. Quoted in Peter D. Hannaford, interview, in *Leadership in the Reagan Presidency, Part II: Eleven Intimate Perspectives*, ed. Kenneth W. Thompson (Lanham, MD: University Press of America, 1993), 155.

13. Ronald Reagan, "Will They Say We Kept Them Free?" August 19, 1976, at http://www.reagan.utexas.edu/archives/reference/8.19.76.html.

14. Ronald Reagan, "Communism, the Disease," radio broadcast, May 1975, in Ronald Reagan, *Reagan, in His Own Hand: The Writings of Ronald Reagan That Reveal His Revolutionary Vision for America,* ed. Kiron K. Skinner, Annelise Anderson, and Martin Anderson (New York: Free Press, 2001), 11–12.

15. Ronald Reagan to Severin Palydowycz, June 1980, in Ronald Reagan, *Reagan: A Life in Letters,* ed. Kiron K. Skinner, Annelise Anderson, and Martin Anderson (New York: Free Press, 2003), 374–75.

16. Nancy Reagan, *My Turn* (New York: Random House, 1989), 63.

17. Ronald Reagan, "PEACE," August 18, 1980, in *Reagan, in His Own Hand,* 482.

18. Ronald Reagan to Charles Burton Marshall, April 8, 1980, in *Reagan: A Life in Letters,* 398–99.

19. See "Can Capitalism Survive?" *Time,* July 14, 1975, cover, and "Is Capitalism Working?" *Time,* April 21, 1980, cover.

20. Ronald Reagan, "Inaugural Address," January 20, 1981, at http://www.presidency.ucsb.edu/ws/?pid=43130.

21. Jeffry A. Frieden, *Global Capitalism: Its Fall and Rise in the Twentieth Century* (New York: Norton, 2006), 373.

22. Quoted in George Church, Dean Brelis, and Gregory Wierzynski, "Alexander Haig: The Vicar Takes Charge," *Time,* March 16, 1981.

23. President Reagan to Soviet General Secretary Brezhnev, n.d., in *Foreign Relations of the United States, 1981–1988* (hereafter *FRUS, 1981–1988*), vol. 3: *Soviet Union, January 1981–January 1983,* ed. James Graham Wilson (Washington, DC: US Government Printing Office, 2016), document 46, at https://history.state.gov/historicaldocuments/frus1981-88v03/d46.

24. Ronald Reagan, "Address to Members of the British Parliament," June 8, 1982, at http://www.reagan.utexas.edu/archives/speeches/1982/60882a.htm.

25. Diary entry for November 1, 1981, in Ronald Reagan, *The Reagan Diaries,* ed. Douglas Brinkley (New York: HarperCollins, 2007), 47.

26. Diary entry for November 5, 1981, in ibid.

27. George P. Shultz, *Turmoil and Triumph: My Years as Secretary of State* (New York: Scribner's, 1993), 30.

28. Ibid., 31.

29. Ibid., 119.

30. NSDD-75, "US Relations with the USSR," in *FRUS, 1981–1988,* 3: document 260, at https://history.state.gov/historicaldocuments/frus1981-88v03/d260.

31. Shultz, *Turmoil and Triumph,* 162.

32. Ibid., 164.

33. Ronald Reagan, *An American Life: The Autobiography* (New York: Simon and Schuster, 1990), 558.

34. Diary entry for February 15, 1983, in Reagan, *Reagan Diaries,* 131.

35. William Clark to Ronald Reagan, handwritten note, March 1983, William Clark Files, Ronald Reagan Presidential Library, Simi Valley, CA.

36. Diary entry for April 6, 1983, in Reagan, *Reagan Diaries,* 142.

37. "Secretary Shultz's Statement before the Senate Foreign Relations Committee," June 15, 1983, *Department of State Bulletin* 83 (July 1983): 66.

38. Ronald Reagan, "Address to the Nation and Other Countries on United States–Soviet Relations," January 16, 1984, at http://www.reagan.utexas.edu/archives/speeches/1984/11684a.htm.

39. Diary entry for November 14, 1984, in Reagan, *Reagan Diaries,* 277.

40. NSC Meeting, September 20, 1985, Executive Secretariat, NSC: National Security Council Meeting Files, Box 91303, Ronald Reagan Presidential Library.

41. National Security Planning Group Meeting, February 3, 1986, Executive Secretariat, NSC: National Security Planning Group Files, Box 91308, Ronald Reagan Presidential Library.

42. Ronald Reagan to Mikhail Gorbachev, February 16, 1986, at http://www.thereaganfiles.com/19860216.pdf.

43. National Security Planning Group Meeting, September 8, 1987, minutes, at http://www.thereaganfiles.com/870908.pdf.

44. Ibid.

45. Quoted in "Editorial Note," in *FRUS, 1981–1988,* vol. 6: *Soviet Union, October 1986–January 1989,* ed. James Graham Wilson (Washington, DC: US Government Printing Office, 2016), document 155, at https://history.state.gov/historicaldocuments/frus1981-88v06/d155.

46. Ronald Reagan, "Farewell Address to the Nation," January 11, 1989, at http://www.reagan.utexas.edu/archives/speeches/1989/011189i.htm.

2

A Question of Morality

Ronald Reagan and Nuclear Weapons

Beth A. Fischer

> A leader takes people where they want to go. A great leader takes people where they don't necessarily want to go, but ought to be.
>
> —Rosalynn Carter

When President Ronald Reagan entered office in 1981, the prevailing nuclear doctrine was mutually assured destruction (MAD). The central idea of MAD was that both superpowers were deterred from launching a nuclear attack on the other by the fact that neither side had defenses. If one were to attack, the other could retaliate, and both would be obliterated. A first strike would prove suicidal, therefore deterring a would-be aggressor. MAD required both sides to have large nuclear arsenals on hair-trigger alert. It was necessary to have enough nuclear weapons to be able to survive a first strike and to promptly retaliate in kind.

Foreign-policy experts insisted that this precarious vulnerability had kept the peace since the end of World War II. The only reason the superpowers had not gone to war against each other, they believed, was the threat of nuclear retaliation. Vulnerability to nuclear annihilation had led to a period of relative peace.

Owing to the paucity of information about decision making in the Kremlin, it was impossible to determine if these assumptions were accurate. Would Moscow expand or attack if the United States did not have a large and resilient nuclear arsenal? No one knew for sure. The situation was akin to the old joke about the salesman selling elephant repellant in North Dakota. "But there are no elephants here!" a potential customer scoffs. "See! It works!" the salesman confidently replies. MAD—the foundation of American strategic doctrine—was not based on vast quantities of data from a wide range of high-quality sources. It was based on an assumption: Moscow sought to attack the West, and US nuclear arsenals, combined with the Soviet Union's lack of defenses, had deterred it from doing so. This was the gospel, accepted as an article of faith within the foreign-policy community.

President Reagan rejected this gospel. He believed that both MAD and nuclear weapons were morally reprehensible. As a consequence, nuclear weapons should be abolished. "For forty years nuclear weapons had kept the world under a shadow of terror," the president asserted. "[MAD] was the craziest thing I ever heard of. . . . We were a push button away from oblivion."[1] The superpowers needed to move beyond MAD to a world free from the ongoing threat of nuclear annihilation.

Throughout his presidency, Reagan challenged the experts, his advisers, his allies, and his conservative supporters to go not "where they want[ed] to go" but rather to where the president believed we "ought to be": a nuclear-free world. Reagan's quest to abolish nuclear weapons upended the conventional understanding of "security" and formed the basis on which the Cold War ended. Thus, it is President Reagan's most enduring legacy.

Reagan's Opposition to MAD

President Reagan opposed MAD for many reasons, some of them practical, many of them ethical. For one thing, he abhorred the fact that nuclear weapons targeted innocent civilians. "By the time the 1980s rolled around we were placing our entire faith in a weapon whose *fundamental target was the civilian population,*" he wrote in his memoirs. "A nuclear war is aimed at people, no matter how often military men like to say, 'No, we only aim to hit other missiles.'"[2]

Moreover, Reagan believed his greatest responsibility as president was to protect the American people. Continuing to forego defenses against a nuclear attack violated this sacred obligation.

In addition, as a practical matter, nuclear weapons were so destructive that victory was not possible. "For the first time in history, man had the power to destroy mankind itself," Reagan observed. "A war between the superpowers would incinerate much of the world and leave what was left of it uninhabitable forever."[3] In such a world, "peace" entailed nothing more than the never-ending threat of nuclear annihilation. Reagan likened this situation to "two westerners standing in a saloon aiming their guns at each other's head—permanently."[4]

Such a peace was also disturbingly precarious; MAD required large arsenals on hair-trigger alert. According to the doctrine's logic, if an aggressor launched a nuclear attack, the target would need to respond in kind almost immediately. "Everything would happen so fast that I wondered how much planning or reason could be applied in such a crisis," Reagan worried, noting that missiles launched from Soviet submarines could reach the White House in six minutes. "*Six minutes* to decide how to respond to a blip on a radar scope and decide whether to unleash Armageddon! How could anyone apply reason at a time like that?"[5]

Moreover, such a situation increased the probability of an accident. Communications systems can fail, Reagan knew, as can safety measures. During a crisis, panic or misunderstanding might lead to an unintended missile launch. The Soviet downing of Korean Air Lines Flight 007 in September 1983 had underscored the probability of both human and systems error. "If mistakes could be made by a [Soviet] fighter pilot, what about a similar miscalculation by the commander of a missile launch crew?" Reagan asked.[6] The president spoke repeatedly with his advisers regarding his concerns about an accidental nuclear Armageddon. Reagan was "genuinely alarmed that the world could get out of control," National Security Adviser Robert "Bud" McFarlane has recalled. "He genuinely understood that systems can fail and he saw a responsibility to think beyond established doctrine."[7] Mutually assured destruction was simply too amoral and too fragile to be the basis of global security, Reagan reasoned. It depended on "no slip-ups, no madmen, no unmanageable crises, no mistakes—forever."[8]

Nuclear weapons themselves had become the enemy, President Reagan believed. The overwhelming stockpiles, the destructive capacity, the hair-trigger alert, and the never-ending threat of nuclear annihilation all constituted the fundamental threat to global security. Ronald Reagan hated communism, but he hated MAD even more. Communism was a dumb idea, but MAD was a potentially catastrophic one.

As a consequence, Reagan sought to move beyond MAD. He sought to fundamentally change the way people thought about security, nuclear weapons, and strategic doctrine. Most of his advisers did not care to reconceptualize security, nor did his allies or fellow conservatives. But Reagan—in conjunction with Mikhail Gorbachev—took them not "where they want[ed] to go" but where he believed the world "ought to be."

Reagan's Strategy to Move beyond MAD

Reagan's first step in moving beyond MAD was to reduce and eventually to eliminate nuclear weapons. "No *one* could win a nuclear war," the president insisted. "Yet as long as nuclear weapons were in existence, there would always be risks they would be used, and once the first nuclear weapon was unleashed, who knew where it would end? My dream, then, became a world free of nuclear weapons. . . . [F]or the eight years I was president I never let my dream of a nuclear-free world fade from my mind."[9] Reagan called for the reduction of nuclear stockpiles during his very first press conference, and by March 1982 he was publicly calling for their complete abolition. According to one study, Reagan advocated for the elimination of nuclear weapons 150 times during his presidency—90 of which preceded Gorbachev's rise to power.[10]

Reagan's quest to eliminate nuclear weapons was radical for the time. The prevailing approach to arms control—as enshrined in the Strategic Arms Limitation Treaty (SALT)—was to limit the rate at which nuclear arsenals could grow. The objective was not to reduce stockpiles but rather to manage their growth. The assumption was that nuclear weapons were necessary to maintain peace. The most radical proposal at the time was the nuclear freeze movement, which sought to freeze superpower arsenals at their current levels. Reagan opposed this proposal not only because it threatened to institutionalize what he believed to be a Soviet advantage but also, more importantly, because it did nothing to remove the threat of nuclear annihilation.

The Strategic Defense Initiative (SDI) was the second step in moving beyond MAD. Unveiled in March 1983, SDI was a research program aimed at building a space-based defensive system against a nuclear attack. As commander in chief, Reagan believed that continuing to forego defenses would be both illogical and immoral. "Every offensive weapon ever invented by man has resulted in the creation of a defense against it," he observed. "[Wasn't] it possible in this age of technology that we could invent a defensive weapon that could intercept nuclear weapons and destroy them as they emerged from their silos?"[11] A defensive system would not only protect innocent civilians from an intentional attack by the Soviet Union but also guard against accidental missile launches and "madmen" who might seek to blackmail the United States.

It was necessary but insufficient to reduce nuclear weapons, Reagan believed. Even if nuclear arsenals were reduced by 90 percent, security would still be achieved through a "balance of terror," in which both sides were vulnerable to nuclear annihilation. "If the Soviet Union will join with us in our effort to achieve major arms reductions, we will have succeeded in stabilizing the nuclear balance," he explained in an address to the nation in March 1983. "Nevertheless, it will still be necessary to rely on the specter of retaliation, on mutual threat. And that's a sad commentary on the human condition." The president asked: "Wouldn't it be better to save lives than to avenge them? . . . What if free people could live secure in the knowledge that their security did not rest upon the threat of instant US retaliation to deter a Soviet attack, that we could intercept and destroy strategic ballistic missiles before they reached our own soil or that of our allies." The time had come "to break out of a future that relies solely on offensive retaliation for our security," the president urged. "I've become more and more deeply convinced that the human spirit must be capable of rising above dealing with other nations and human beings by threatening their existence."[12]

President Reagan saw SDI as part and parcel of his quest to eliminate nuclear weapons. His reasoning was simple: if the United States were to have defenses, Soviet nuclear weapons would become useless. And if *both* superpowers were to have defenses, the weapons would become obsolete. Thus, they could be eliminated.

As a consequence, President Reagan repeatedly offered to share SDI technology with the Soviets. During the Geneva summit in late 1983 and the Reykjavik meeting in late 1986 as well as in letters to Soviet leaders, the president repeatedly offered to share SDI technology to pave the way for the elimination of nuclear weapons.[13] Soviet leaders doubted his sincerity, however. It seemed preposterous that the man who had called the Soviet Union the "evil empire" and who had embarked on a costly military buildup would voluntarily transfer such cutting-edge military technology. The Soviets found Reagan's offers to be insincere and profoundly irritating. "Excuse me, Mr. President," Gorbachev interrupted during one session of the Reykjavik summit meeting, "but I do not take your idea of sharing SDI seriously. You don't want to share even petroleum equipment, automatic machine tools or equipment for dairies, while sharing SDI would be a second American revolution. And revolutions do not occur all that often. Let's be realistic and pragmatic. That's more reliable."[14]

The Strategic Defense Initiative also appealed to Reagan's penchant for heroic stories in which good prevails over evil. As he saw it, SDI would "save lives rather than avenge them."[15] It promised to protect civilians; it would end the ongoing threat of nuclear annihilation; and it would enable the complete abolition of nuclear weapons. Moreover, US resources would be invested in protection rather than destruction. Reagan would save humanity by replacing mutually assured destruction with mutually assured survival.

Paradoxically, the third element of Reagan's quest to eliminate nuclear arms was the military buildup. Although President Jimmy Carter had initiated an increase in US forces, the Reagan administration ushered in the largest peacetime military buildup in US history. The objectives were threefold. The short-term goal was to catch up with the Soviet Union. Reagan officials erroneously believed that the United States had fallen behind in the arms race—or was about to fall behind—resulting in what they called a "window of vulnerability." The second aim was to deter Soviet expansionism. Officials reasoned—again, mistakenly—that the Soviet Union had invaded Afghanistan in 1979 because the United States had appeared weak. Renewed American strength would prevent future adventurism. The ultimate objective of the buildup, however, was to persuade Moscow to enter into arms-reduction talks. Reagan officials erroneously calculated that the Kremlin would not agree to reduce its weapons until confronted by an adversary of equal strength and resolve. Thus, the ultimate objective of the buildup was to pressure the Kremlin into drawing down its nuclear arsenal.

Reagan explained his reasoning in November 1982. "Some may question what modernizing our military has to do with peace," he acknowledged.

> A secure force keeps others from threatening us, and that keeps the peace. And just as important, it also increases the prospects of reaching significant arms reductions with the Soviets, and that's what we really want. The United States wants deep cuts in the world's arsenal of weapons, but unless we demonstrate the will to rebuild our strength and restore the military balance, the Soviets, since they're so far ahead, have little incentive to negotiate with us. Let me repeat the point because it goes to the heart of our policies. Unless we demonstrate the will to rebuild our strength, the Soviets have little incentive to negotiate.[16]

Although it seemed paradoxical, Reagan hoped the buildup would ultimately lead to arms reductions. "I wanted to go to the negotiating table [with the Soviet Union] and end the madness of the MAD policy," Reagan explained later in his memoirs, "but to do that I knew America first had to upgrade its military capabilities so that we would be able to negotiate with the Soviets from a position of *strength,* not weakness."[17] As Secretary of State George P. Shultz explained to the Senate Foreign Relations Committee in 1983, "Strength and realism can deter war, but only direct dialogue and negotiation can open the path toward lasting peace."[18]

Opposition to Reagan's Ideas

But Reagan was leading in a direction that many foreign-policy experts and allies did not want to go. The president's advisers believed his ideas about the elimination of nuclear weapons and SDI were fanciful, if not downright dangerous. They could tolerate his calls for the reduction of nuclear weapons but felt that completely eliminating them was out of the question. Abolishing nuclear weapons would undermine MAD. There would be nothing to deter the Soviets from expanding or attacking. As Reagan's longtime friend and adviser Martin Anderson has recalled, "The conventional wisdom on nuclear weapons was very clear during the late 1970s. Virtually no one at the time thought seriously that there was a chance of any reduction in nuclear missiles. And when Reagan began to talk privately of a dream he had when someday we might live in a world free of all nuclear missiles, well, we just smiled."[19] Many of Reagan's advisers did not take him seriously at first. The president was not an arms-control expert or a foreign-policy specialist. He articulated his views in very simple, accessible language that at times led others to conclude that the ideas themselves were simplistic or lacking in substance. In addition, his grasp of basic facts about nuclear weapons could be tenuous. At times, he confused different types of weaponry, offered questionable facts, and as late as 1983 indicated that he did not know that the Soviets relied primarily on land-based intercontinental ballistic missiles for their defense.[20] In retrospect, Reagan may have garbled these facts because he thought they were beside the point. His objective was to reduce and eventually eliminate nuclear weapons. Everything else was a detail.

At the time, however, Reagan's halting grasp of arms control and his fanciful talk about a nuclear-free world and space-based defenses did not inspire confidence in his advisers or allies. For many, the president was a foreign-policy dilettante who needed to be educated about the virtues of MAD. Although no one was enthralled with the idea of a never-ending threat of nuclear annihilation, most thought it was the least-bad avenue to peace. MAD had prevented the Cold War from becoming hot.

Secretary of State Shultz, who normally deferred to the president's directives, counseled Reagan to abandon his calls for the elimination of nuclear weapons. "I told the president that I shared his dissatisfaction with our dependence on the threat of nuclear annihilation as the means for keeping the peace. But nuclear weapons cannot be un-invented," he recalled later. In 1984, Shultz advised Reagan that "the present structure of deterrence and of our alliances depends on nuclear weapons and the best approach is to work for large reductions in nuclear arsenals." Shultz lamented that he "made no real impact" on the president, however. "He stuck with his own deeply held view of where we should be heading."[21]

Foreign-policy advisers removed from Reagan's letters and speeches, as best they could, any passages that called for the elimination of nuclear weapons. For example, early in his presidency Reagan penned a letter to Soviet leader Leonid Brezhnev that discussed his desire for a nonnuclear world. Secretary of State Alexander Haig was appalled. "[I was] astonished at [the president's] attitude when I measured it against the backdrop of what he was saying publicly, and what was attributed to him as a classic cold warrior," he recounted to Reagan biographer Lou Cannon. In Haig's view, the president appeared embarrassingly naive.[22] He advised the president in no uncertain terms to forego the letter. Reagan complied.

In another instance in the spring of 1982, when Reagan read a column by Ann Landers in which a citizen expressed fears about an impending nuclear war, he decided to write a letter to Landers. A nuclear war is "unthinkable," he wrote, which is why "we must have a true verifiable reduction [in nuclear arsenals] leading to the eventual elimination of all such weapons." National Security Council (NSC) staff quickly struck the reference to abolishing nuclear weapons. Reagan conceded and signed a version that called only for the reduction of nuclear arsenals.[23]

George Shultz described the speechwriting process as "an agony of pulling and hauling" in which foreign-policy bureaucrats deleted language calling for a nonnuclear world and the president reinserted it. At times, the secretary of state had to step in. "Every meeting I go to the president talks about abolishing nuclear weapons," Shultz admonished his staff. "I cannot get it through your heads that the man is serious."[24]

Conservative Republicans, who strongly supported Reagan's strident anticommunism, were appalled by his calls to eliminate nuclear weapons. "Reagan had a totally naïve view against nuclear weapons, which I saw time and again," recounted Kenneth Adelman, director of the Arms Control and Disarmament Agency from 1983 to 1987. "All of us who were conservative thought that when [President] Carter said, 'I want to eliminate nuclear weapons,' that was the stupidest thing we'd ever heard. We all made fun of it. And then we had our hero who says things really more extreme than Carter ever does, and he's unstoppable in doing it."[25] Conservative opinion makers such as George Will and Charles Krauthammer publicly lambasted the president for nearly agreeing to eliminate nuclear weapons during the Reykjavik summit in 1986, and conservative interest groups conveyed their disapproval privately.[26] Reagan's performance in Reykjavik prompted Richard Nixon and Henry Kissinger—who had been estranged from each other for more than a decade—to join forces to denounce the idea of a nonnuclear world. Eliminating nuclear weapons could provoke the "most profound crisis" in the history of the North Atlantic Treaty Organization (NATO) alliance, they warned. "Any Western leader who indulges in the Soviets' disingenuous fantasies of a nuclear-free world courts unimaginable perils."[27]

NATO allies were equally concerned about a nonnuclear world. Superpower relations were extraordinarily tense in the early 1980s. The allies counted on the US nuclear arsenal sitting on the Soviet Union's doorstep to deter a Soviet attack on western Europe. British prime minister Margaret Thatcher, Reagan's close friend, was especially wary of talk about eliminating nuclear weapons. "Next year we will have had peace in Europe for forty years," she told the president during a meeting in December 1984. "That is a very long period of peace. We are going to have to live with [MAD] for a considerable period of time," she insisted. Reagan replied, "I don't think there's any morality in that at all."[28]

Reagan's advisers were even less enthralled with SDI.[29] Before the project was unveiled, it had been a closely guarded secret, which alienated those who were not in the inner circle. Astonishingly, Shultz did not find out about the program until two days prior to Reagan's announcement, and even the secretary of defense, Caspar W. Weinberger, had to learn about it through unofficial channels.[30] None of the leading members of Congress had been consulted, nor had close allies such as Canada and Britain.

But that was not the crux of the problem. There was a litany of other complaints. The necessary science and technology did not exist. It would be unbearably costly. Reagan was making sweeping claims without evidence. It violated the Anti–Ballistic Missile Treaty of 1972, which had outlawed ballistic missile defense. And most concerning of all, it would be dangerously destabilizing: if deployed, SDI would enable the United States to launch a nuclear attack against the Soviet Union without fear of reprisal. The United States would be protected against a retaliatory strike, thus upending MAD. As a consequence, both allies and the Soviets would perceive SDI as offensive in nature. US allies were already skittish about the threat of war, and SDI raised questions about the defense of Europe. The project might prompt Moscow to launch a preemptive strike against the United States or its allies before the system was deployed or to engage in a buildup so as to overwhelm the system. SDI also threatened to launch an arms race in space. "To say that there was 'opposition' to the plan does not really convey the torrent of fury and scorn that was released by the president's proposal," Weinberger observed later.[31]

With the exception of Weinberger, who not only shared Reagan's antipathy for MAD but also relished the $26 billion windfall that the SDI program would bring to his department, Reagan's advisers opposed SDI. But they soon realized they would be unable to dissuade the president from pursuing the project. Thus, they grudgingly went along. Perhaps the program could be bargained away in exchange for deep reductions in the Soviet arsenal, they reasoned.

But the president was adamant that SDI would not be used as a bargaining chip. SDI was a critical component in his quest to abolish nuclear weapons. It would enable him to save lives rather than avenge them. Such goals were too lofty to be traded away. "A certain amount of mythology grew up around the Strategic Defense Initiative," the president reflected in his memoirs. "One of them was that I had proposed the idea to produce a bargaining chip for use in getting the Soviets to reduce their weaponry. I've had to tell the Soviet leaders a hundred times that the SDI was not a bargaining chip. I've told them I'd share it with others willing to give up their nuclear missiles."[32]

Although Reagan's advisers were reluctantly willing to go along with the president's pet project, none of them could abide his desire to share SDI technology with the Soviets. Even Weinberger admitted that the idea "scared the pants off me."[33] "President Reagan was not only a true believer in SDI, he was definitely a true believer in sharing," Jack Matlock, former US ambassador to the Soviet Union, explained in 1993. "This was something that most of the bureaucracy, virtually the entire bureaucracy . . . said we can't do." Matlock recalled that when he was on the NSC staff, he drafted a presidential letter to the Kremlin in July 1986. Reagan wanted to insert a section proposing to share SDI technology with the Soviets, but the original draft contained no such offer. As Matlock recalls,

> I sent the draft in, and [Reagan] changed it. He changed the section and made a very strong commitment to sharing . . . the research. I checked this out and all the experts said, "We can't do that." So I changed it back and sent it to him. It went back to him four times. And finally, he called me in, and he said, "Jack, is this my letter?" And I said, "Yes, sir, Mr. President." He said, "This is what I want to say." And I said, "Look, Mr. President, everybody tells me we can't do that." And he said, "Damn it, it is my letter, that's what I am going to do." And well, that's the letter he sent.[34]

Reagan continued to push the idea of sharing SDI. During an NSC meeting in September 1987, he was uncharacteristically emphatic. "Why can't we agree now that if we get to a point where we want to deploy [SDI] we will simply make all the information available [to the Soviets] . . . so that we can both have defenses?" Reagan pleaded. "I don't believe we can ever do that," Weinberger retorted. General Robert T. Herres, the vice chairman of the Joint Chiefs of Staff, interjected, "Mr. President, there is a great risk in exchanging technical data. Much of our technology is easily convertible to other purposes and into an offensive area." Kenneth Adelman added, "Mr. President, that would be the most massive technical transfer the western world has ever known." The conversation turned to other matters, but Reagan was insistent. "There has to be an answer to all these questions because some day people are going to ask why we didn't do something now about getting rid of nuclear weapons. You know, I've been reading my Bible and the description of the Armageddon talks about destruction, I believe, of many cities and we absolutely need to avoid that. We need to do something now." National Security Adviser Frank Carlucci agreed: "We certainly need to avoid Armageddon." "The answer is SDI," Weinberger added.[35]

By 1987, Reagan was growing frustrated. Moscow was not taking seriously his offers to share SDI technology, and Gorbachev continued to insist that the program had to be restricted before an arms-reduction treaty could be signed. So the president came up with another plan: placing SDI under international control. Such an approach would have many benefits, Reagan reasoned. It would make defenses available to all nations, thus enhancing global security. It would get around the problem of mistrust. And it addressed the problem posed by the Kremlin's insistence that arms reductions could not proceed until Reagan made concessions on SDI. If SDI were transferred to an international body, the president believed, the path would be cleared for an arms-reduction treaty.[36]

Administration officials were not mollified. The allies would not buy it, they argued, and the Soviets would try to gain control of the international body overseeing SDI.[37] Despite Reagan's enthusiasm for the proposal, his officials were able to bury it by assigning a committee to look into the matter.[38]

Gorbachev as Partner

Reagan's vision of a nuclear-free world met resistance throughout North American and West European capitals. Only one other world leader sought the elimination of nuclear weapons: Mikhail Gorbachev.

When Gorbachev became general secretary of the Soviet Union in March 1985, he sought to revitalize the Soviet economy. In order to do so, he needed to reduce military spending and to invest more heavily in consumer goods and technology. To reduce military spending, he needed to end the arms race. Thus, Gorbachev sought to improve relations with the West.

Like many of his fellow reformers, Gorbachev believed nuclear weapons were of little value. The primary purpose of these costly weapons was to deter an attack by the United States, but such an event was improbable. The weapons were therefore useless. Reform-minded military officials argued that the Soviet Union's bloated arsenals were worse than useless; they were counterproductive because they appeared threatening to the West, which prompted a US buildup, which in turn undermined Soviet security. Military reformers argued that the Soviet Union should drastically reduce its arsenal and in particular focus on divesting itself of its offensive weapons. The focus would be on what the Soviets called "non-provocative defense."[39] The West would feel less threatened, thus opening the door for reductions in the US arsenal. The Soviet Union would paradoxically increase its security by reducing its nuclear stockpile.

Thus, for economic and strategic reasons Moscow sought to drastically reduce, if not eliminate, its nuclear arsenal.[40] In the spring of 1986, the Soviet commitment to nuclear disarmament increased dramatically. The explosion at the Chernobyl nuclear power plant on April 26 shook the Soviets to their core: the threat of nuclear annihilation no longer seemed abstract. Ridding the world of nuclear weapons became a moral imperative. Chernobyl was "the equivalent of [Gorbachev's] personal Cuban missile crisis [*sic*]," Gorbachev's adviser and spokesperson Andrei Grachev has recalled. "Before 26 April his intention to propose a curb on the arms race along with a radical reduction of nuclear weapons was mostly based on economic and security concerns, while after Chernobyl his attitude towards nuclear weapons transformed into a psychological aversion, a moral rejection bringing him in this respect closer to Reagan. The fight for a non-nuclear world . . . became a personal challenge."[41]

It took years for the two leaders to appreciate the depth of each other's commitment to nuclear disarmament. Decades of mistrust inhibited progress toward eliminating nuclear weapons. However, the Reykjavik summit in October 1986 proved to be a watershed. Toward the close of

Soviet general secretary Mikhail Gorbachev and US president Ronald Reagan at the Hofdi House in Reykjavik, Iceland, October 11, 1986. Reagan and Gorbachev wanted to abolish nuclear weapons. (Courtesy of the Ronald Reagan Presidential Library)

the difficult meetings, exhausted and frustrated, Gorbachev proposed to eliminate all nuclear weapons. Reagan jumped on the idea and agreed. But a historic turning point was not to be. Gorbachev then added that such an agreement would be contingent upon restrictions on SDI, which Reagan refused. The summit ended acrimoniously, but upon further reflection each leader saw the lost agreement as a defining moment. Each understood that the other was sincere in his desire to rid the world of the threat of nuclear annihilation. It was this shared dream that formed the foundation of their partnership to end the Cold War.

Morality, Leadership, and the Shadow of Terror

In *The Better Angels of Our Nature,* Steven Pinker provides a sweeping account of the decline in violence over the second millennia of the common era.[42] War, homicides, and torture have declined precipitously as the modern state system has arisen and democratic values have spread across the globe. Practices and ideas that had long been simply facts of life—

colonization, beheadings, child labor—ultimately became abhorrent. The view arose that these practices crossed a line demarcating that which is ethical from that which is not. With Gorbachev's help, President Reagan nudged the idea of mutually assured destruction over this line. When Reagan took office in 1981, MAD was the conventional wisdom; experts believed nuclear weapons had successfully deterred a superpower war and were therefore necessary for global security. Thirty years later the idea of eliminating nuclear weapons has entered the mainstream. Political leaders, military officials, and security experts across the world support the idea of abolishing nuclear weapons—including former Reagan officials and officials from the former Soviet Union.[43] Ronald Reagan and Mikhail Gorbachev were pivotal in moving this idea from the realm of the preposterous to the realm of the possible.

For Reagan, abandoning MAD was a moral imperative. It was not a geostrategic initiative; it was not a matter of winning an arms race or gaining strategic advantage. Nor was it about economics, although a case could certainly be made that the nuclear arms race had been nonsensically costly. Abandoning MAD was not a political issue, either. Reagan was not catering to a public clamoring for the elimination of nuclear weapons. Few Americans seriously entertained such an idea, and the most radical vision at the time was simply to freeze the growth of nuclear arsenals. For Reagan, moving beyond MAD cut to the core of what it meant to be a decent human being and a strong leader. Abandoning MAD was about ushering in a more humane and more stable era of global security.

President Reagan took the foreign-policy establishment not "where [it] want[ed] to go" but rather where he believed it "ought to be." His views about national security were radical for the time. "Peace," he believed, must be something more than the mere absence of nuclear war. "Security" had to be more substantive than a never-ending threat of nuclear Armageddon. Nuclear stockpiles and mutually assured destruction posed the greatest threat to humanity.

It is hard to underestimate the challenge posed by Reagan's task. A foreign-policy novice, he was surrounded by advisers, allies, and fellow conservatives who strongly opposed his views. Moreover, he was seeking to reconceptualize security during the height of the Cold War. The president began calling for the elimination of nuclear weapons years before Mikhail Gorbachev came to power, at a time when Soviet leaders were spouting their traditional ideological epithets. Remarkably, the president was able to put aside his own strident anticommunism so as to pursue a more secure, more humane world. Reagan had to overcome his advisers, his supporters, his allies, and his own convictions about communism to pursue a nonnuclear world.

"Our people look to us for leadership, and nobody can provide it if we don't," the president wrote to Gorbachev in November 1985. "But we won't be very effective leaders unless we can rise above the specific but secondary concerns that preoccupy our respective bureaucracies and give our governments a strong push in the right direction."[44]

Reagan's decision to focus on the superpowers' mutual interest in abolishing nuclear arms was pivotal. Gorbachev shared this dream. The two leaders had many differences, but on this one issue they had a sense of shared purpose. Just as importantly, neither leader could accomplish this task alone. Each was dependent on the other. Cooperation was essential. As Gorbachev told the Politburo on April 3, 1986, "Despite all the contradictions in our relations [with the United States], the reality is such that we cannot do anything without them, and they cannot do anything without us. We live on the same planet. We will not be able to preserve peace without America."[45] It was this mutual desire to end the threat of nuclear annihilation—and this inherent inability to accomplish this goal alone—that was the basis on which Reagan and Gorbachev built a more cooperative relationship. President Reagan's most enduring legacy is his quest to abolish nuclear weapons, which enabled the peaceful resolution of the Cold War. It is his antinuclearism—not his anticommunism—that distinguishes Reagan as an exceptional twentieth-century leader.

Notes

1. Ronald Reagan, *An American Life: The Autobiography* (New York: Simon and Schuster, 1990), 13.

2. Ibid., 549, italics in original. For more on Reagan's antinuclearism, see Martin Anderson and Annelise Anderson, *Reagan's Secret War: The Untold Story of His Fight to Save the World from Nuclear Disaster* (New York: Crown, 2009); Paul Lettow, *Ronald Reagan and His Quest to Abolish Nuclear Weapons* (New York: Random House, 2005); and Beth A. Fischer, *Reagan Reversal: Foreign Policy and the End of the Cold War* (Columbia: University of Missouri Press, 1997), 77–79, 102–56.

3. Reagan, *An American Life,* 258. See also Ronald Reagan, interview by NHK

Television, November 11, 1983, in *Public Papers of the Presidents of the United States: Ronald Reagan, 1983,* book 2: *July 2 to December 31, 1983* (Washington, DC: US Government Printing Office, 1984), 1582.

4. Reagan, *An American Life,* 547.

5. Ibid., 257, italics in original.

6. Ibid., 584.

7. Robert McFarlane, remarks at "Understanding the End of the Cold War, 1980–87: An Oral History Conference," Brown University, May 7–10, 1998, 144.

8. Ronald Reagan, remarks to the Institute for Foreign Policy Analysis, March 14, 1988, American Presidency Project, at http://www.presidency.ucsb.edu/ws/?pid=35547#axzz1nhyn0pZ8.

9. Reagan, *An American Life,* 550, italics in original; see also 265.

10. Anderson and Anderson, *Reagan's Secret War,* 93–94.

11. Reagan, *An American Life,* 547.

12. Ronald Reagan, "Address to the Nation," March 23, 1983, *Weekly Compilation of Presidential Documents* (*WCPD*) 19 (1983): 447.

13. For example, see "Question-and-Answer Session with Reporters," March 29, 1983, in Reagan, *Public Papers of the President of the United States: Ronald Reagan, 1983,* book 2, 463–70, and transcripts from NSC meetings in Jason Saltoun-Ebin, ed., *The Reagan Files: Inside the National Security Council* (N.p.: CreateSpace, 2010), 349–422, italics added.

14. Mikhail Gorbachev, remarks, Reykjavik summit meeting, October 11, 1986, afternoon session, transcript supplied at the conference "Understanding the End of the Cold War," document 37, 6. See also Aleksandr Bessmertnykh, remarks at "A Retrospective on the End of the Cold War," Oral History Conference, Woodrow Wilson School of Public and International Affairs, Princeton University, February 26–27, 1993, Session II, 95.

15. Reagan, *An American Life,* 550.

16. Ronald Reagan, "Address to the Nation on Arms Reduction and Deterrence," November 22, 1982, *WCPD* 18 (1982): 1519. See also Secretary of State George Shultz, "US-Soviet Relations in the Context of US Foreign Policy," remarks before the Senate Foreign Relations Committee, June 15, 1983, in *American Foreign Policy: Current Documents, 1983* (Washington, DC: US Government Printing Office, 1985), 508.

17. Reagan, *An American Life,* 13–14, italics in original.

18. Shultz, "US-Soviet Relations in the Context of US Foreign Policy," 508.

19. Martin Anderson, *Revolution* (New York: Harcourt Brace Jovanovich, 1987), 73.

20. Lou Cannon, *President Reagan: The Role of a Lifetime* (New York: Simon and Schuster, 1991), 291.

21. George P. Shultz, *Turmoil and Triumph: My Years as Secretary of State* (New York: Scribner's, 1993), 466.

22. Quoted in Cannon, *President Reagan,* 301.

23. As recounted in Chester J. Pach Jr., "Sticking to His Guns: Reagan and National Security," in *The Reagan Presidency: Pragmatic Conservatism and Its Legacies,* ed. W. Elliot Brownlee and Hugh Davis Graham (Lawrence: University Press of Kansas, 2003), 103.

24. Shultz, *Turmoil and Triumph,* 466.

25. Kenneth Adelman, interview, September 30, 2003, Ronald Reagan Oral History Project, Presidential Oral History Program, Miller Center of Public Affairs, University of Virginia, Charlottesville.

26. James Mann, *The Rebellion of Ronald Reagan* (New York: Viking, 2009), 47–51.

27. Richard Nixon and Henry Kissinger, "A Real Peace," *National Review* 39 (May 22, 1987): 32.

28. Both Thatcher and Reagan quoted in Shultz, *Turmoil and Triumph,* 509.

29. For more on officials' reactions to SDI, see Shultz, *Turmoil and Triumph,* 246–64; Caspar Weinberger, *Fighting for Peace: Seven Critical Years in the Pentagon* (New York: Time Warner, 1990), 291–329; and Anderson, *Revolution,* 80–99.

30. Bill Clark and Ed Meese surreptitiously briefed Weinberger on the SDI project (Weinberger, *Fighting for Peace,* 305).

31. Ibid., 308.

32. Reagan, *An American Life,* 547–48.

33. NSC Meeting, February 10, 1987, transcript in Saltoun-Ebin, *The Reagan Files,* 370.

34. Jack Matlock, remarks at the conference "A Retrospective on the End of the Cold War," Session II, 81–82.

35. NSC Meeting, September 8, 1987, transcript in Saltoun-Ebin, *The Reagan Files,* 385–87.

36. NSC Meeting on Arms Control and SDI, February 10, 1987, transcript in Saltoun-Ebin, *The Reagan Files,* 366–68, 371.

37. Ibid., 365–72.

38. The Arms Control Support Group conducted a study called THRESHER RAIN, which looked into the idea of transferring SDI to an international body. See ibid., 367.

39. This doctrine was also called "sufficient defense" or "reasonable sufficiency." For example, see Aleksei Arbatov, "Parity and Reasonable Sufficiency," *International Affairs* 10 (1988): 75–87, and "How Much Defense Is Sufficient?" *International Affairs* 4 (1989): 31–44, and Makhmut Gareyev, "The Revised Soviet Military Doctrine," *Bulletin of the Atomic Scientists,* December 1988, 30–34.

40. In January 1986, Gorbachev called for the elimination of nuclear arsenals by the year 2000. In 1987, Moscow accepted the Reagan administration's proposal to eliminate all intermediate-range nuclear forces in Europe and had agreed in principle to a 50 percent reduction in strategic arms. The Intermediate-Range Nuclear Forces Treaty was signed in December 1987, and the Strategic Arms Reduction Treaty was signed on July 31, 1991, coming into force on December 5, 1994.

41. Andrei Grachev, *Gorbachev's Gamble: Soviet Foreign Policy and the End of the Cold War* (Cambridge: Polity Press, 2008), 81.

42. Steven Pinker, *The Better Angels of Our Nature: Why Violence Has Declined* (New York: Penguin, 2011).

43. For example, see the Global Zero website at http://www.globalzero.org.

44. Ronald Reagan to Mikhail Gorbachev, handwritten letter, November 28, 1985, in Saltoun-Ebin, *The Reagan Files,* 286–90.

45. From Anatoly Chernyaev's notes from a Politburo session, April 3, 1986, supplied at the conference "Understanding the End of the Cold War," document 20.

3

Beyond Cap the Foil

Caspar Weinberger and the Reagan-Era Defense Buildup

Ronald J. Granieri

On December 1, 1980, President-elect Ronald Reagan called his former California budget director and current head of his transition team's budget-control task force, Caspar Willard Weinberger. According to Weinberger's memory, Reagan began that call: "I know you have a full and very exciting and very rich life. . . . And I want to spoil the whole thing by asking you to serve as Secretary of Defense."[1]

Thus began a collaboration that altered the course of US history and security policy. Reagan and Weinberger presided over the largest peacetime defense buildup in that history. Although the combination of reduced international tensions and the pressures of budget deficits led to modest declines in defense expenditures after 1985, the Reagan defense budgets created a new normal that persisted through the following decades and colored the historical understanding of Reagan's presidency. Critics charge, "Reagan and his foreign policy advisers came into office on a wave of hyperbole about the Soviet threat designed to rally the American public to support a major military buildup."[2] Supporters unsurprisingly frame the issue differently, claiming that Reagan "reversed the long-term decline in support of our military forces."[3] Weinberger himself claimed the administration's main priority was to "restore our deterrent capability," which had allegedly eroded during the 1970s.[4]

However one characterizes the administration's priorities, the simple numbers reveal the significance of the buildup that Weinberger managed for Reagan. Between 1981 and 1987, the Reagan administration spent more than $1.5 trillion on defense, more than doubling the annual budget of the Department of Defense (DoD).[5] Although general growth in federal spending kept defense relatively modest as a share of the total budget (growing from 23.2 percent of the total in fiscal year 1981 to 28.1 percent in fiscal year 1987 and declining thereafter) and economic growth held down defense's share of total gross domestic product (hovering around 6 percent), the total numbers were eye-catching.[6] Reagan had campaigned on the need for fiscal responsibility but did not allow budgetary concerns to place limits on defense policy, at least not initially. The decision to pursue the buildup even as deficits widened reflected the deepest priorities of his administration.[7]

The very intensity of the political dispute about the buildup has often hindered reasoned historical analysis of the people who shaped it. Contemporary critics were sure that the buildup would lead to fiscal if not literal catastrophe and portrayed Reagan and Weinberger as either fools or nuclear-obsessed knaves. The alarmism of such works as *With Enough Shovels* by Robert Scheer, which concluded that Reagan and Weinberger's defense policy "greatly underestimates . . . the very real likelihood that it will lead to a very real catastrophe," as well as the more measured pessimism of *Deadly Gambits* by Strobe Talbott reflected conventional wisdom in the early 1980s and its revulsion against Reagan's alleged abandonment of the arms-control consensus.[8] Both reactions seem rather quaint in light of subsequent events, in which Armageddon stubbornly refused to happen and the Cold War reached its peaceful conclusion. Nevertheless, long-term deficits and debt remain a troubling legacy of the Reagan years. Meanwhile, there is a growing shelf of books that claim the buildup directly led to the collapse of the Soviet Union and the peaceful conclusion to the Cold War, ascribing to Reagan a strategic vision bordering on prescience and dismissing any criticisms as irrelevant in the face of the historical triumph.[9]

Either vision is problematic when taken to its extreme. Whether the Reagan buildup led to victory in the Cold War or was a heavy anchor on the future of the US economy, however, no one can doubt its significance. Any president coming into office in 1981 would probably have increased the defense budget in some ways—indeed, Jimmy Carter did precisely that in his last year in office and intended to continue on that path. Nevertheless, the scope and speed of the Reagan defense program depended on the policy preferences and the ideological commitment of Reagan's closest advisers, especially Secretary of Defense Weinberger. That fact makes a clearer historical understanding of the motivations behind the Reagan buildup essential for anyone who wants to understand the late Cold War era.

Despite his critical role in that story, however, Caspar Weinberger has not been treated well by most historians of the Reagan era. Although he spent most of his nearly seven years at the Pentagon in the center of controversy and was involved in every major policy decision of the era, he never completely escaped the partisan pigeonhole, which reduced his scholarly appeal. In office and in the two decades between his departure from office in 1988 and his death in 2006, Weinberger cultivated his image as a defender of US security and his connections with the political Right. Through public appearances and interviews, his work with *Forbes* magazine, and publications such as his book *The Next War* (1996),[10] Weinberger criticized the budget cuts of the Bush and Clinton administrations and championed continued higher levels of defense spending. For strong Reaganites, therefore, Weinberger never ceased to be valued and popular.

Weinberger's reputation within the larger political and historical literature has been much less positive. In the eyes of most observers then and now, Weinberger was primarily the hard-line foil for his long-term colleague in government and the private sector, Secretary of State George P. Shultz. Scholarship on Reagan has experienced a renaissance in the twenty-first century, moving beyond partisan clichés to offer a more nuanced understanding of his role in breaking the ice with the Soviets and hastening the end of the Cold War. Despite that appreciation, or perhaps because of it, Weinberger has been even more marginalized, lumped together with other conservatives, hard-liners, and hawks (in the literature, these terms appear both synonymous and interchangeable, occasionally spiced with the anachronistic cognomen *neoconservative*) such as William Casey, director of the Central Intelligence Agency (CIA). Their stock has fallen as Reagan's has risen. During the 1980s and throughout the 1990s, writers were content to dismiss Reagan as an unreconstructed and unreflective hawk. Now that the president has been rehabilitated, those same writers and their successors have consigned those advisers whom Reagan himself chose and trusted to the outer historical darkness.[11]

Two examples especially illustrate this approach. Don Oberdorfer, who wrote one of the first full-scale chronicles of the Reagan administration's role in the end of the Cold War, drew on his experience as a diplomatic correspondent for the *Washington Post.* Thus, he relied heavily on access to and interviews with Secretary of State Shultz but conducted only one interview with Weinberger, so the results are predictable. In Oberdorfer's telling, the "hard-liners" are largely irrelevant to the story except when it is narratively necessary to mention them in order to highlight Shultz and Reagan's wisdom. Oberdorfer gives Weinberger his due as a loyal friend to Reagan but makes no real effort to analyze the defense secretary's role in US policy making. Weinberger instead pops up at regular intervals as the villain whose "intransigence" blocked the secretary of state's efforts "at every turn."[12]

James Mann's recent book, *The Rebellion of Ronald Reagan* (2009), which offers a revisionist account on the end of the Cold War by emphasizing Reagan's heartfelt support for détente, writes Weinberger out of the story altogether. *Rebellion* has seven index entries for Weinberger, all pointing to text that virtually repeats the (unexamined) assertion that he was "relentlessly anti-Soviet."[13] In Mann's relentlessly Whiggish history, the greatness of Reagan and Mikhail Gorbachev, assisted by Shultz, is revealed in their resistance against conservatives in both of their countries. Nowhere does Mann make any effort to analyze the specific role that Weinberger played in the developments leading up to Reagan's alleged rebellion or even the basis for Weinberger's (and Reagan's) hawkish anticommunism.[14]

The point here is not that Weinberger was always right or that he needs to be redeemed for the sake of some reflexive balance. He was indeed strongly hawkish on many questions and did eventually lose influence to Shultz when it came to arms-control diplomacy. He also tended to hold to his positions rather than seek negotiations, which made him a particularly tenacious defender of the buildup he had been brought in to oversee and saw him sidelined as political pressures forced changes upon the administration.

There, however, is the rub. Conservatives in the 1980s often spoke of the baleful influence of moderate White House and State Department advisers who somehow threatened to obstruct "the real Reagan," or at least the Reagan they believed to be the most real. These complaints led Reagan speechwriter Aram Bakshian to comment sarcastically that the conservative refrain "let Reagan be Reagan" really meant "let me be Reagan."[15] Those conservatives failed to appreciate how advisers such as James A. Baker III, Michael Deaver, and George Schulz represented authentic parts of Reagan's complicated personality and preferences. They refused to admit that the alleged moderates' success was not some trick but a reflection of their connection with part of Reagan.

In an ironic inversion, recent Reagan revisionists, having "discovered" that Reagan was really a dove all along, now claim that the hawks were dangerous interlopers and foreign bodies. Neither extreme case is true. Reagan had both Weinberger and Shultz on his team because he wanted both of them there; both represented part of his intentions. In the run-up to the elections in 1984, when tensions between the State Department and the DoD were running particularly high—Shultz had told Reagan he would have to choose between him and Weinberger after the election—Reagan told his National Security Adviser Robert McFarlane that he trusted Shultz but Weinberger was his friend. He did not want either to leave, so McFarlane would have to "reconcile" their positions.[16]

That one exchange is proof of how hard it was to work for Ronald Reagan and especially to be his national security adviser—which is a topic for another essay. But it is also an authentic reflection of Reagan's complex relationship with his advisers and indeed of the complexity of his policies. Reagan sincerely believed that the purpose of a hard-line policy was to bring the Soviets to talk and then to negotiate from a position of strength. In that pursuit, Caspar Weinberger, who provided the strength, was as important as George Shultz, who eventually led the talks. It is worth noting as well that Shultz consistently defended the Pentagon budget, a point he makes in his own memoirs. Even if he won fewer bureaucratic battles as the years wore on, Weinberger was never irrelevant to the Reagan administration's foreign and security policy. He was more than simply a foil for the "good guys." He was an active participant in every important debate within the administration even if he did not always carry the day. When he departed the cabinet in November 1987, he was behind only Robert McNamara as the longest-serving secretary of defense. Both his policies and his management style shaped the department through his tenure in office and beyond. His historical importance therefore deserves closer examination than it has heretofore received.

Weinberger's Background

Who was Caspar Weinberger? He was a California lawyer and a lifelong Republican, a graduate of Harvard College (class of 1938) and Harvard Law School (class of 1941). Commissioned as a US Army officer during World War II, he served on General Douglas MacArthur's staff in Australia and New Guinea before beginning a legal career in his native San Francisco in 1945. A career in Republican electoral politics ended in 1958 after three successful terms in the state legislature and a failed run for the Republican nomination for attorney general, but he eventually rose to be chairman of the state party in 1964 while also serving as a newspaper columnist and radio and television talk show host. Initially connected to the liberal northern wing of the California Republican Party, he was pushed aside by the ascendant conservatives from the south when Ronald Reagan was elected governor in 1966, who kept Reagan from appointing him as finance director despite high-level endorsements. After a year in which the state budget deficit ballooned, however, Reagan ended up firing his budget director and calling on Weinberger after all.[17] Within a year, through rigorous spending cuts and tax increases, Weinberger helped balance the budget and produce a surplus, which Reagan returned to state residents as tax rebates in time to ride to a landslide reelection in 1970.

By that point, Weinberger had left Sacramento for Washington, where he worked his way up the Nixon administration. Beginning as head of the Federal Trade Commission in 1969, he became deputy director (under George Shultz) and then director of the Office of Management and Budget (OMB). In those positions, he cemented his reputation as an able manager and a stringent budget hawk, a reputation reinforced when he became secretary of Health, Education, and Welfare in 1973. His two years at the head of the nation's largest civilian bureaucracy earned him the moniker "Cap the Knife." Untainted by the Watergate scandal, he held that position into the Ford administration, not stepping down until 1975.[18] He returned to San Francisco as vice president and chief counsel of the international construction firm Bechtel, where he again served under George Shultz, who had become president of the firm. He remained active in a variety of civic and political organizations and often traveled abroad on business. He also maintained his connection to Republican candidates. Although he was only tangentially connected to the Reagan campaign in 1976, he was more active in 1980, leading to his inclusion in the transition team and his return to Washington as defense secretary.

The National Security Establishment

Personal relationships between presidents and secretaries of defense have varied over the years. The nature of the position during the Cold War guaranteed that a secretary of defense would always be an important and visible member of the president's team, but not all secretaries arrived at the Pentagon already enjoying a strong relationship with the president, and not all have been taken deeply into a president's confidence. Some of them were chosen specifically because of their ability and willingness to tend to the bureaucratic details and stay out of public-policy discussions. A secretary who combines the institutional advantages of his position with a previously existing professional and personal relationship with the president and who is also broadly knowledgeable about both foreign affairs and Washington bureaucracy is in a very strong position to influence policy. Weinberger enjoyed all of those advantages when he entered office in January 1981.

Having been Reagan's finance director in California made him one of the very few secretaries of defense to have previously served the president in a different cabinet-level capacity. Weinberger's connection to Reagan was that much stronger because both he and Reagan looked back upon their time together in Sacramento as a great success. Even after Weinberger left California for Washington, he maintained his connection to the Reagan team, offering regular reports to his former colleagues to help them adjust to federal initiatives.[19] In the letter he wrote to Reagan accepting his appointment as defense secretary, he asserted, "The years I worked with you in Sacramento are among the happiest in my life, and I am eager to start again."[20]

Weinberger expressed both professional respect and personal affection for Reagan. Contrary to what critical biographers and disgruntled former staff members have written and said, Weinberger claimed Reagan was no mystery to him. Although in his own memoirs he could not avoid the usual banal and semimystical references to "the electric and electrifying nature of the President's smile," Weinberger asserted that the "various myths about President Reagan and his 'detached, unengaged style'" and his "lack of knowledge or direction" were "spawned mainly by people who did not know him and who had not worked with him." Those negative images "differ[ed] grossly from the facts as I had long known them." Reagan "had a well-formed philosophy, formed by a great deal of reading and a great deal of study," and "was really just like what you saw."[21] He told Reagan biographer Lou Cannon that Reagan "was underestimated by 'serious people' in Washington because they were totally unused to a president who is light-hearted and serene, secure within himself, a happy man who wants to have all the people in the room that he's meeting with happy, too, and wants to have his countrymen happy and serene."[22] That optimism was one source of Reagan's preference for "debate and discussion" among staff members with contrasting views: he "had an ultimate sort of sunny belief in the idea that people could be brought around to be convinced as he was," even as he rarely made decisions on the spot.[23]

Weinberger entered his position with a sense of momentum, advanced by virtue of a personal relationship with the president based on a sense of shared principles and goals. Even when in later years Reagan's decisions began to tilt against his defense secretary, their relationship endured, to some colleagues' frustration. Michael Deaver, for example, also known for his own loyalty to Reagan, describes being sent by White House colleagues to urge Weinberger to ask the president for defense cuts. "I remember [James] Baker asked me to go over and see Cap, because if Cap told Reagan he could give it up, some of it, Reagan would have done it. But it was like talking to Reagan. . . . Cap said, 'If the President tells me to do this, I'll do it.' 'No, I'm asking you to tell the President.' 'Well, I can't.'"[24]

Weinberger's secure position also allowed him to choose a team of advisers with whom he enjoyed very close cooperation. The most important was Frank Carlucci, who had been Weinberger's deputy at the Department of Health, Education, and Welfare, whom Weinberger selected as his first deputy secretary of defense. Decades later Carlucci praised their "extraordinarily good working relationship." He acknowledged that he, General Counsel William H. Taft IV, and military assistant General Colin Powell "were probably the only three people in the Pentagon that could get Cap to change his mind. Cap, as you know, is very tenacious."[25]

Ironically, Weinberger's choice of Carlucci initially earned him significant criticism from conservatives in Congress and the media. In part, the criticism stemmed from the fact that Carlucci had worked for the CIA under Jimmy Carter and Stansfield Turner. Even more germane was conservatives' disappointment that their preferred candidate was passed over. William Van Cleave, a defense intellectual connected to groups such as the Committee on the Present Danger and the famously hawkish Team B as well as chair of Reagan's Defense Transition Team, had his eye on the post and powerful patrons behind him. Weinberger, however, was cold to the idea of working with Van Cleave. According to observers at the time, Van Cleave and his associates focused especially strongly on rapid modernization of the US nuclear arsenal as part of a program of "quick fixes" in the DoD. This attitude clashed with the prevailing views among the military leadership as well as with Weinberger and Reagan's belief that a conventional buildup had at least equal if not superior priority to nuclear issues. Although Weinberger was well aware of the political support behind Van Cleave, he was unimpressed by the Defense Transition Team's work and was confident enough in his own judgment and the president's support to shock conservatives by abruptly dismissing Van Cleave and his team just before Christmas 1980. Calling their work "uneven," he denounced the team for "having an agenda of its own," making it "not useful to me in developing the President's program." In contrast, he argued that the outgoing secretary of defense, Harold Brown, and his staff were "extremely helpful."[26]

Weinberger's ties to Reagan helped him deal with the unconventional arrangements in the Reagan White House, which were the source of much frustration and internecine conflict. The experience of previous administrations in the Cold War period had encouraged the development of certain structures in the national security establishment. The National Security Act of 1947, amended in 1949, created the DoD to integrate activities among the US armed services, instituted an independent US Air Force, and established the CIA. The legislation also provided for the creation of a permanent National Security Council (NSC), based in the White House, which included the secretaries of state, defense, and treasury as well as representatives of the military and intelligence services.[27] Different administrations after 1947 shaped the details of these arrangements according to the individual presidents' desires and their relations with their staff, but the bias over the years had been toward centralizing decision making in the White House. The Nixon administration had taken this development to its ultimate conclusion, vesting influence especially in the national security adviser (Henry Kissinger), whose management of the NSC and close cooperation with the president were often at the expense of the cabinet secretaries.[28] Nixon had also relied heavily on his White House chief of staff, H. R. Haldeman, to control communications between the White House and the rest of the bureaucracy. Overall, this extreme centralization in the White House had suited Nixon's view of the president's role, which led to important breakthroughs such as the opening to China, but it also had baleful effects that revealed themselves in the Watergate scandal, which led to Nixon's resignation. Because of competition between the White House/NSC, State, DoD, and the CIA, leaving it to the president to settle disputes had become common in American politics by the time Reagan came into office.

Reagan's efforts to manage these seemingly inevitable rivalries within the national security establishment were complicated by personal as well as structural rivalries. In an effort both to reward loyalty and to guarantee smooth management, Reagan had decided to make George H. W. Bush protégé James Baker III White House chief of staff while also appointing conservative stalwart Edwin Meese as counselor to the president, with cabinet rank. Although the arrangement made sense for personal reasons, it was organizationally problematic and created tensions in the years to come. The relationship between Baker and Meese was made even more complicated by a third figure, Deputy Chief of Staff Michael Deaver. A close friend of the Reagans, Deaver assumed control over the scheduling and the presentation of a White House famous for its mastery of symbolism. Through Reagan's first term, these three powerful individuals, known to the press as the "troika," were supposed to pull together to manage the administration, but each jockeyed for influence and used the administration's various agencies as well as the media in their constant search for advantage.

Playing a subordinate role within the White House was the assistant to the president for national security affairs, Richard V. Allen. Assigning him this role was a conscious decision by the Reagan team. Having seen the mischief that came from having a national security adviser usurp the powers of the secretary of state under Nixon and Carter, the Reagan administration decided that the national security adviser would be reduced to a staff and advisory role, responsible for coordinating the paper flow rather than being a source of new policy ideas. This new conception received concrete reinforcement in two significant ways. First, Allen did not report directly to the president but rather to Meese, sharply limiting his access. Second, the national security adviser's office was moved from its Kissinger-era location near the Oval Office (which went to Chief of Staff Baker) to the White House basement.[29]

These decisions proved fateful for the Reagan administration. Despite his initial agreement, Allen quickly chafed under his subordinate role. Considered a lightweight by foreign-policy professionals and too much of a conservative ideologue by Baker and Deaver, Allen lost out in one of the administration's first major shakeups. Outmaneuvered by his rivals and victim of a minor scandal involving a misplaced honorarium for Nancy Reagan, he resigned in early 1982. Recognizing his original mistake, Reagan agreed that Allen's successor, William Clark (another close Reagan friend and adviser from Sacramento), would have direct access to the president. Nevertheless, Allen's departure made him the first of a total of six national security advisers over Reagan's eight years in office. Although some of his successors, such as Clark, enjoyed greater access, and others, such as Frank Carlucci and Colin Powell, displayed considerable political and bureaucratic skill, the revolving door in the White House basement made the NSC and the national security adviser uncertain players in the administration. Even Baker admitted that "President Reagan was an extraordinarily successful two-term president . . . but he was never really able to enjoy a smoothly functioning national security apparatus."[30]

The multiplayer game of access to the president initially worked in Weinberger's favor. Weinberger enjoyed good personal relations with Meese and was on good terms with both Allen and Deaver. Baker and Weinberger had a respectful relationship, though tensions emerged as they tangled over the political implications of the DoD budget and the electoral significance of détente with the Soviets. Weinberger had the closest ties with Clark, whom he considered "a thoroughly decent, completely honest man, totally devoted to the cause of Mr. Reagan's success."[31] The two worked very closely together during Clark's eighteen-month tenure at the NSC, which represented the apogee of Weinberger's influence within the administration.

Weinberger's most controversial relationship was with the State Department, where strong personality clashes exacerbated structural tensions. Baker, who had a front-row seat, commented later, "The intramural bickering and fighting between State and Defense was [*sic*] terrible right from the beginning."[32] Weinberger had been included on the short list of candidates for secretary of state. Reagan's first choice, however, was retired general Alexander M. Haig. Although Reagan and Haig barely knew each other, Haig's work in the Nixon administration, combined with his subsequent experience as supreme allied commander in Europe, gave him an international profile far above that of Reagan's other foreign-policy advisers. Haig was an impressive, accomplished figure, known among friends and staff for his sense of humor and charm. But he could also be prickly in defending his position and privileges. Weinberger ironically described him as "constitutionally unable to present an argument without an enormous amount of passion and intensity, heavily overlaid with a deep suspicion of the competence and motives of anyone who did not share his opinions."[33]

Haig's eighteen months at Foggy Bottom proved to be a trial for all concerned. The wrong note was struck on Inauguration Day, when Haig visited the White House with the draft of a document (National Security Decision Directive 1) that delineated the responsibilities of all of the members of the president's foreign-policy team, with the secretary of state expressly given the position of *primus sine pares*. Remembering no doubt how the Nixon White House and Kissinger's NSC had undermined Secretary of State William P. Rogers, Haig was determined that his fate would be different. He thought he had an ally in Allen and had also shown a preliminary draft of the document to Weinberger. When Haig entered the White House to meet with Baker, Meese, Deaver, Weinberger, and Allen (all still in their formal attire from the inaugural festivities), however, he found that none was in any hurry to approve the document. Carlucci remembers seeing a draft and telling Weinberger, "'Cap, that's a disaster. You can't do that.' . . . Cap went back and said that, and the problems began." After a brief and (for Haig) frustrating discussion, Meese agreed to take the draft under advisement. That document remained unratified, to Haig's mounting anger.[34] Press reports soon circulated about rivalries within the national security establishment. In such circumstances, a lesser man might have sought allies, but that was not Haig's way. Carlucci suggested Haig and Weinberger meet weekly for breakfast to coordinate policy, but "most of the breakfasts Al would spend complaining about the goddam bastards in the White House."[35] Haig saw Weinberger as a rival and a threat, which inhibited making common cause against the White House. He also expressed frustration that Weinberger made statements about foreign policy that poached on State Department turf.[36]

Haig departed the cabinet in June 1982. His replacement was a familiar face for Weinberger, George P. Shultz. Shultz had been Weinberger's boss at OMB and again at Bechtel, and the two men had worked together successfully for more than a decade by the time they met again around Reagan's cabinet table. Once Shultz joined the administration, however, he and Weinberger were almost continually at odds. Part of this tension was due to policy disagreements, but there was also a personal, psychological dimension to it. Before 1982, Shultz had always been Weinberger's superior. In the Reagan cabinet, however, they were equals. There were also fundamental differences between Shultz, a labor economist and believer in discussion and negotiation, and the aggressive corporate lawyer Weinberger. Their approaches had clashed at Bechtel. Shultz's inclination when faced with class-action lawsuits was to seek settlements. Weinberger, however, worried about precedents and concessions to "legal blackmail. . . . So generally I would recommend that we fight rather than yield, but invariably George would want to settle." At OMB, Weinberger was also frustrated by Shultz's unwillingness to share his opinions, which left his deputy trying to represent the office without clear guidance.[37] Shultz for his part disparaged Weinberger's typical strategy, which was to "take a position and never change. He seemed to feel that the outcome, even if it differed from his position, would likely move further in his direction when he was difficult and intransigent. In many a battle, this technique served him well. But over time, as more and more people understood the technique, its effectiveness waned, and Cap's capacity to be part of final solutions declined."[38]

Navigating internal Reagan administration rivalries was at least as difficult as policy making in the world of the 1980s. Weinberger proved to be one of the more durable participants in that many-sided contest, for better or worse.

Weinberger and the Defense Budget

Weinberger's primary policy responsibility was the defense buildup, and, as he wrote to Reagan at the end of 1980, he accepted with enthusiasm the "awesome set of responsibilities, particularly at a time when I think we are so urgently in need of a major and rapid strengthening of all our defense forces."[39] Managing relations with Congress and the public, however, was increasingly difficult. Reagan successfully used the defense buildup to create his electoral coalition, especially to win over southern Democrats, helping to orchestrate the gradual Republican takeover of southern politics over the decades to come. But that did not mean that his defense secretary was necessarily popular on Capitol Hill. Weinberger's tendency to dogmatism, his resistance to adjustments to the budget, and, perhaps most of all, his tendency to stick to his script in his testimony and not give an inch until absolutely necessary (which sarcastic staff members called "taping") made him a difficult witness for the many congressional committees before which he testified. Even a positive profile by Rowland Evans and Robert Novak in 1981 referred to him as "maddeningly resolute."[40]

Weinberger faced a rather anomalous situation. Congress, like the electorate as a whole, was initially positively disposed toward the buildup for its own reasons, but that willingness had an expiration date. Weinberger admitted that "the tolerance of the Congress for increasing defense spending was wearing thin the first month, and it kept wearing thinner and thinner as we went on." Expressing frustration that members often accused him of overstating threats in order to gain increases, especially when the threats did not materialize, he sarcastically told an interviewer many years later, "It was roughly the question of, 'You didn't have a fire, so why do you need fire insurance?'"[41]

As Weinberger pushed relentlessly for bigger budgets in the face of growing resistance, his positive qualities—tenacity, focus on detail, ability to stay on message—threatened to become significant political liabilities for the administration. His image suffered as a result. In moments of frustration, he pointed out "that when we wanted to increase our defense budget, it took enormous effort . . . but in the USSR when three or four men in the Kremlin were able to make that decision, it went into effect immediately." This problematic and provocative statement led one senator to comment, "Mr. Secretary, you sound envious." At which point, Weinberger hastened to add that he was "not the least envious" and that he had used the contrast to explain how the Soviets had managed their rapid buildup through the 1970s.[42]

A first glance suggests a contradiction between Weinberger's careers at

OMB and DoD. It is certainly true that at OMB Weinberger was not afraid to cut Pentagon spending. In a meeting of the Defense Program Review Committee in August 1971, the chairman of the Joint Chiefs of Staff, Admiral Thomas Moorer, seconded by Henry Kissinger, worried whether the United States could live up to its international commitments if planned cuts went through. When OMB director Shultz left the meeting after an outburst from Moorer, Weinberger offered a blunt, pragmatic rebuttal. Asserting the president's commitment to budgetary control, he concluded: "72% of the budget is uncontrollable and 28% controllable, of which 70% is defense. No one is out to get Defense, but that is the only area we can look at without asking Congress to make laws that we can't realistically expect them to make."[43] Such statements built the legend of Cap the Knife.

Reagan played on that legend at first, declaring to an audience shortly after his inauguration: "I can assure you that Cap is going to do a lot of trimming over there in Defense to make sure the American taxpayer is getting more bang for every buck that is spent. I've even heard that there was a sigh of relief in several other departments when it was learned that Cap-the-Knife was going to Defense, and not to those other departments."[44] Weinberger was more circumspect, claiming that he was not a budget cutter for its own sake but rather was trying to "budget according to needs" while also recognizing "that not all government spending is of equal importance or necessity."[45]

Weinberger displayed his priorities even before he was confirmed as secretary of defense. In the final report of the Budget Control Task Force in January 1981, Weinberger noted that the original plan to cut $13 billion to get that fiscal year's baseline down to $620 billion was no longer sufficient. Estimates of outlays for 1981 had already risen from $633 billion to $661 billion, which meant that any plan to get down to $620 billion required more than $40 billion in cuts to a budget whose fiscal year had already begun. Weinberger advocated deeper cuts and offered a list of proposals to get as close to the target as possible. At the same time, he took for granted that a defense supplemental increase of $14 billion would remain in place. "As you know," he declared in a memo referring to the report,

> our present plans include substantial increases in Defense spending over the previously set base line in the next five years. We

> will, of course, do everything possible to reduce the net effect of these increases by identifying and putting into effect as many savings as possible that will not reduce the growing and needed real strength of our Armed forces. But unless we make clear that at the same time we are also planning, urging, and seriously intending to adopt massive reductions in planned non-defense spending over a period of several years, the inflationary expectations for the future will continue unbroken and a generally resigned attitude that again it will be "business as usual in Washington" will, in my opinion, lead to more inflation and serious disillusionment of the public with the new Administration.

Weinberger instead called for an "electrifying signal," proposing that all department heads develop plans for 10 percent cuts to outlays for 1981. He admitted that making these cuts would be politically difficult but concluded, "It is not just balance which is important; it is balance at substantially reduced expenditure levels that can help the most with inflation and, perhaps even more important, can reduce the size, power and intrusiveness of our government." Ironically, the memo also ended with great praise for the incoming OMB director, David Stockman, and a call for colleagues to help Stockman build on his "splendid start" with the budget.[46]

Reagan and Weinberger's desire to limit the size of government ended at the Pentagon. Even Richard Nixon, whose advice both men prized, was not able to shake this attitude. In late 1980, Nixon wrote to both Reagan and Weinberger. To Reagan, Nixon argued that the Pentagon "should not be a sacred cow" and urged an immediate 10 percent cut. Nixon also congratulated Weinberger on his appointment in a warm handwritten letter, assuring "Dear Cap" that "of all your important government positions I am sure you will find SecDef the most challenging and (despite inadequate pay) the most rewarding." At the same time, he urged Weinberger to "be generous on the hardware and tough on the software." Repeating that the DoD should not be a sacred cow, he concluded, "You will find more briefcase carriers and loafers in the Pentagon than you had even in [the Department of Health, Education, and Welfare]."[47] Weinberger thanked Nixon for his "very thoughtful note" and agreed, "We do need increased expenditures of a highly effective nature."

He also hoped to be able to "make some other savings by careful review of all of the other activities of the department."[48]

In large part because of such performances, David Stockman entered into his job as Reagan's OMB director hopeful that Weinberger would be an ally in the struggle to cut spending, both out of general intellectual sympathy and because Weinberger knew the OMB job so well. The budget-cutting wunderkind from Michigan was young enough to be Weinberger's son and initially looked up to Cap the Knife as a potential ally. If their relationship ever could be described in familial terms, however, it was more like that between Laius and Oedipus. Once they began disagreeing about the size and shape of the defense budget, policy disagreement quickly led to personal estrangement. As Stockman lost battle after battle over the defense budget, he attacked conservatives for failing to live up to their fiscal promises. He reserved special criticism for those whom he felt should have known better, such as Weinberger. In his bitter memoirs, Stockman accused Weinberger of betraying his principles, adding the snarky comment that "Cap the Knife had become Cap the Shovel."[49]

Weinberger saw Stockman as an unreliable partner who never stopped trying to undermine the defense budget. His references to Stockman in his memoirs betray both frustration and a whiff of condescension. He describes Stockman as "very bright, basically quite knowledgeable about budgetary matters; a quick study with a rather glib and authoritative way of answering questions or making his points. . . . Particularly troubling was that he was most positive when he did not yet quite have his facts straight."[50]

It is tempting to attribute Weinberger's apparent conversion to expedience or to the lack of defining principles. To make such an assumption, however, misses an important point in his character. The contrast between his actions at OMB and at the Pentagon reflects the very different priorities of those agencies and of the people who put him there. Weinberger's defining characteristic, as writers such as Lou Cannon have noted, was that he was a lawyer. To take that analysis a step further, he was not the kind of lawyer who viewed every conversation as a negotiation but rather the kind who was at heart "the ultimate advocate . . . shrewd, articulate, and extremely stubborn . . . [in using] his legal skills to champion whatever client he represented at the moment."[51] Thus, he had recognized what Nixon wanted when he appointed him to head OMB and the Department of Health, Education, and Welfare, just as he knew what Reagan wanted when he installed Weinberger at the Pentagon with the charge to rebuild America's allegedly neglected defenses.

Broadly committed to Reagan's vision of restoring US defenses, Weinberger admitted in retrospect that he did not know a "damned thing" about the details of defense policy at the start. He told one interviewer, "I had to learn as much as I could as quickly as I could. I treated it roughly like a law suit and trial that I would have to conduct and simply immersed myself in it completely."[52] It certainly helped that Weinberger's outlook corresponded to that of Reagan and other conservatives, who did not consider the Pentagon when they railed against excessive government spending. But most of all his outlook reflected his basic approach to his work. "Cap, you don't offer suggestions, you just take positions," Shultz allegedly complained at one contentious White House discussion. Weinberger's response was a shrug.[53]

Weinberger and Foreign Policy

Weinberger had firm opinions on foreign relations, as one might expect from someone who had hoped to be secretary of state. But simply dismissing those opinions as "hard-line" underestimates the variety of opinions within the conservative policy establishment in the 1980s. Weinberger's positions are not so easily pigeonholed: sometimes he was among the more conservative voices in the administration; sometimes he advocated significant and creative changes in policy. A brief sketch of specific positions can help us appreciate the complexity beneath the caricature.

Weinberger was a strong advocate of the Atlantic alliance and especially of the Anglo-American special relationship. He was often frustrated by the failure of America's North Atlantic Treaty Organization (NATO) allies to live up to their commitments to spend up to agreed-upon budget targets. He also joined with other members of the administration to criticize European plans to help the Soviet Union build new pipelines to bring natural gas from Siberia to western European markets. The pipeline debate crossed partisan lines. British Conservative Margaret Thatcher was as committed to the project as German Social Democrat Helmut Schmidt, each of whom saw economic advantages to it. They found support within the Reagan administration from Alexander Haig, who claimed that fighting the pipeline created unnecessary problems in the alliance, and from Secretary of Commerce Malcolm Baldridge, who represented American business interests that wanted part of the lucrative work. Weinberger feared that the project would allow the Soviets access to Western technology that could improve their defenses and that European countries' dependence on Siberian gas could give Moscow political leverage over them. In this case, he and CIA director William J. Casey could indeed be identified on the hardest line in the debate, though his concerns about Russian leverage over European politics have proven sadly prescient.

In Middle East policy, however, Weinberger advocated creative changes. His ties to Bechtel had helped him cultivate relationships with the ruling elites in Saudi Arabia, and he was a fervent advocate of improving American relations with the kingdom and with the Arab world more broadly. Most famously during a trip to the region in early 1982, Weinberger raised eyebrows when he told the press that the United States "needed more than one friend in the Middle East." He expressed that sentiment both in private and in public and even in meetings with representatives of America's other important friend in the Middle East, Israel. Weinberger's relationship with Israel was famously frosty because neither Prime Minister Menachem Begin nor Defense Minister Ariel Sharon trusted his judgment. They held it against him that he had been a strong advocate of the deal that delivered Airborne Warning and Control System radar planes and extra equipment for F-15 fighters to Saudi Arabia in 1981. Weinberger also worked to undermine the Israelis' plans to use US funds to build their own fighter plane (the LAVI), pushing them to continue purchasing F-15s and F-16s instead.[54] Many Israeli officials and American supporters of Israel accused him of being anti-Israel, if not anti-Semitic. Indeed, thanks to his last name, Weinberger received a steady stream of vitriolic correspondence from constituents who claimed he was a self-hating Jew or a traitor to his people or both. Weinberger took such attacks in stride and consistently argued that better relations with the states of the region would serve the security interests of both the United States and its ally Israel.

The Reagan administration's policies toward the Middle East were much more nuanced than many administrations before or since, and those nuances reflect in part the influence of Weinberger and other Republican Arabists. Weinberger and CIA director Casey especially worked the connection with Saudi Arabia as part of a broader strategy to drive down the price of oil by the mid-1980s. Lower oil prices removed both significant inflationary pressures from a US economy that had been battered by the oil shocks of the 1970s and an important prop for a Soviet economy that depended on oil to earn hard currency overseas, thus serving the Reagan administration's larger anti-Soviet strategy.[55] This strategic view of the Middle East required controversial compromises with the rulers in Riyadh, but it certainly was more nuanced and deft than anything suggested by such reductive terms as *hard-line* and *hawkish.*

In other diplomatic areas as well, Weinberger proved to be cautious and conservative rather than aggressive. Concerned about the rise of Iranian radicalism (a position no doubt reinforced by his contacts with the Saudis), he advocated pro-Iraqi neutrality in the ongoing Iran–Iraq War. He also rejected Robert McFarlane's plans to appeal to mythical moderates in Iran through arms sales, a position that put Weinberger at odds with both the NSC and the Israelis, who were at that time themselves strongly pro-Iranian.[56] In that one area, Weinberger made common cause with Shultz because both of them opposed the policy that led to the Iran-Contra scandal. Weinberger's opposition to the trading of arms for hostages did not, however, spare him from receiving an indictment from Special Prosecutor Lawrence Walsh. Because the Pentagon was formally responsible for transferring HAWK missiles to Iran, Walsh convinced a grand jury to indict Weinberger for misleading Congress on the transactions. Only after the "nightmare year" of 1992 ended with a pardon from President George H. W. Bush was Weinberger freed from the legal consequences of a policy he had neither proposed nor supported.[57]

On the question of committing American troops to combat roles abroad in the service of diplomatic goals, Weinberger was, if anything, a soft-liner and a reluctant warrior. The purpose of the Reagan buildup, he argued, was to deter the Soviets on the global chessboard, not to dispatch American forces piecemeal to deal with regional flare-ups. The most famous example of Weinberger's opposition to military interventions was in Lebanon, where he opposed sending peacekeeping forces in 1982, only to lose out to State Department insistence. Weinberger objected that a lightly armed force at the Beirut airport would achieve no military pur-

Secretary of Defense Caspar Weinberger (*standing*) with President Reagan, Vice President George H. W. Bush, Secretary of State George Shultz, and others in the White House Situation Room after the bombing of the marine barracks in Beirut, Lebanon, on October 23, 1983. A key architect of US national security policy during the Reagan presidency, Weinberger served as secretary of defense from 1981 to 1987. (Courtesy of the Ronald Reagan Presidential Library)

pose and simply be a magnet for attacks. After he was proven right in October 1983, when a car bomb killed more than two hundred marines as they slept in their barracks, Weinberger decided to make a public statement of his views. In a speech to the National Press Club in November 1984, he unveiled what he called "the Weinberger Doctrine," a catalog of six conditions for American use of force abroad that included a clear mission, sufficient force, and both congressional and public approval.[58]

Weinberger wanted to avoid politically divisive and potentially catastrophic interventions. His assistant, Colin Powell, credits the Weinberger Doctrine as the first draft of what is more famously called the Powell Doctrine, a model for restraint in the use of military force. It is especially worth noting here that when it came to dispatching forces overseas and seeking military solutions to diplomatic problems during the Reagan years, the primary impetus came not from alleged hard-liners at the Pentagon but from the civilian desk warriors at Foggy Bottom and the West

Wing. Sometimes those most intimately acquainted with the construction of military forces are the most careful about squandering them.

Weinberger and Arms Control

A final point to consider in this assessment of Weinberger's role in the Reagan administration is his contribution to the Reagan record on arms control, which is as complicated and surprising as the president himself and has been a centerpiece of the Reagan revisionism of the past decade. Although a critic of détente in the 1970s, Reagan was also at heart a nuclear abolitionist. He attacked arms-control agreements such as the Strategic Arms Limitation Talks II from both the left (he believed it wrong merely to limit future growth of stockpiles, preferring to negotiate on reducing existing forces) and the right (he was convinced that the Soviets "cheated" or "fudged" on the limitations).[59] His repeatedly stated goal was to pursue agreements that reduced actual stockpiles, even if that meant avoiding interim agreements.

During much of Reagan's public career, however, this abolitionist element in his thinking never got much public traction. Critics ignored or derided his sentiments. Even his fans generally preferred the image of Reagan the hard-liner. Historical reality, however, has created problems for both the fans and the critics. Those who suggested in 1976, 1980, and 1984 that Reagan's antediluvian attitudes toward arms control guaranteed stalemate in East–West relations and perhaps even threatened the future of all life on earth were proven wrong when Reagan ended up participating in negotiations with Mikhail Gorbachev that not only eliminated intermediate-range nuclear weapons but also reduced strategic arms on the way to the end of the Cold War. Meanwhile, those who want to portray Reagan as a visionary who never wavered in his pursuit of victory over nuclear weapons, communism, and the Cold War (not necessarily in that order) are faced with the fact that Reagan administration policies and rhetoric did change over time. They also tend to forget how many conservative firebrands who now pray regularly before the Reagan shrine denounced Reagan's second-term arms-control negotiations. Reagan's liberal critics try to account for progress after 1985 by ritually repeating "Gorbachev, Gorbachev" or by insisting that Reagan, aided by a few carefully chosen sensible heroes (usually Secretary of State Shultz), fundamentally changed direction.[60] Reagan fans just elide any changes in their attempt to emphasize continuities.[61]

The more scholars actually separate themselves from their personal predilections and study the documents, however, the more they reach the sensible conclusion that the end of the Cold War depended on a combination of principles and tactical flexibility, making it a "triumph of improvisation," to steal a phrase from a brilliant recent work by James Graham Wilson.[62]

To focus on an example of a historical development that continues to be controversial and misunderstood at the same time, consider the origins and consequences of the Reagan administration's embrace of the so-called zero option—the idea that instead of negotiating mutually agreed-upon levels of a particular weapon (in this case, intermediate- and short-range nuclear missiles stationed in Europe), the goal should be the elimination of such weapons altogether. From the moment Reagan announced this policy in a National Press Club speech in November 1981 until he and Gorbachev signed the Intermediate-Range Nuclear Forces Treaty six years later, debate raged over whether the zero option was a sincerely held and legitimate negotiating strategy or merely a dodge to avoid negotiations at all. Viewed from a safe historical distance, it appears that the zero option was both: it was a bold stroke and a firm negotiating position; a dodge calculated to manage the political complications of the Reagan coalition and a sincerely held goal. To admit that the zero option was both sincere and bogus is not to insult historical memory or to impugn the motives of historical actors. Rather, it merely reflects the messy reality of events and the often surprising ways that ideas and circumstances interact.

Even as scholars have become more comfortable with the idea of Reagan embracing arms control, however, they remain committed to a narrative in which his hard-line advisers tried to stop him. In so doing, these scholars miss one of the most important elements of the narrative—that it was the hard-liner Weinberger who was the first and most insistent enthusiast for the zero option. The administration's commitment to closing the "window of vulnerability" through significant increases in the defense budget corresponded to the administration's hard-line image, even though Reagan also claimed that the ultimate goal was to be strong enough to bring the Soviets to the negotiating table for real reductions. Squaring this circle exposed tensions within the Reagan national security team, but not along the lines suggested by a simple hard-line/soft-line dichotomy. Weinberger claims that his European colleagues introduced him to the zero option during NATO defense ministerial meetings in the spring and summer of 1981. Although he professed initial skepticism, he eventual embraced the idea, arguing that it would allow the West to test Soviet sincerity and to build up its own strength while holding out the prospect of real change in the future. When he presented the idea to Reagan, the president immediately saw its benefits. It appealed to his preferences for simple solutions and his distaste for details and also reduced arms control to its basic elements.

After Reagan made the zero option the centerpiece of his first major arms-control address, before the National Press Club in November 1981, most observers did not know how to react. NBC correspondent Marvin Kalb asked Weinberger confusedly, "Have you always been secret doves?" His question highlights the combination of bemused disbelief and cynicism the zero option inspired in many observers. Weinberger responded unflappably that he did not "see any change from dove to hawk . . . or anything of that kind at all. I see a perfectly clear evolution of a policy which the President enunciated many times last year . . . to arm and regain the strength of the United States so that we can enter into effective negotiating discussions."[63]

The process may have been clear to Weinberger and Reagan, but for an arms-control community that valued incremental progress Reagan's approach appeared frighteningly outside the mainstream. Secretary of State Haig, no slouch when it came to standing firm against the Soviets, was appalled by the zero option because he felt it left no room for negotiation. Even after Reagan made the zero option official policy, Haig and other experts, such as Arms Control and Disarmament Agency chief Eugene Rostow and the chief arms negotiator Paul Nitze, were never completely comfortable with it. Haig and Rostow pushed for some modifications from zero in an effort to advance negotiations. Nitze's "walk in the woods" with his Soviet opposite number in 1982 was the most famous attempt by arms-control thinkers to develop alternatives to zero. Meanwhile, others, such as Rostow's successor, Ken Adelman, embraced the zero option precisely because it made an agreement more difficult.[64]

There eventually would be a treaty based on "global zero," eliminating an entire class of weapons. It was not an easy or direct road, but one does not have to be a Reagan acolyte to realize that its ultimate destination depended on the president's determination to cling to his abolitionist goal, even as he allowed his advisers to work out the tactical details. The Reagan administration was at heart a coalition of various types of conservatives, and Reagan held it together well enough, even as it suffered significant strains during the second term.[65] The Intermediate-Range Nuclear Forces Treaty was a triumph precisely because it satisfied so many of the elements of that coalition. Many observers, however, saw it only as a simple struggle between arms-control advocates and hard-liners, even trying to argue that resistance against the treaty had inspired Weinberger's resignation in November 1987. Weinberger retorts in his memoirs that such an attitude on his part would have been "ironic, because I had proposed the treaty in the first place."[66]

Reagan's arms-control record is indeed ironic, providing results very different from those predicted by most outside observers. His success, though, is due not to any providential intercession but to the surprisingly skillful way that Reagan and those he trusted balanced principles and process. Ronald Reagan was an antinuclear hawk, which is different from an advocate of disarmament and also different from what we usually consider a hard-liner. The antinuclear hawk vision added important long-term idealism to what would otherwise sound and look like simple rejectionism as he refused to enter into smaller-scale incremental agreements. Those members of the administration such as Weinberger who were able to appreciate that paradox and work within it proved to be more successful. Reagan aide Annelise Anderson argues that George Shultz—like Haig more conventionally conservative in his thinking—considered Reagan's antinuclear position to be "nuts." Nevertheless, the pragmatic Shultz warned his staff, "You better get used to it because that's what he thinks."[67] Shultz's tactical skill allowed him to be much more successful than his martial predecessor. Weinberger realized this about Reagan much earlier, advocating the zero option from the start and tenaciously advocating for the defense increases that he and Reagan considered the necessary precondition for successful negotiations. Shultz eventually found a way to channel Reagan's enthusiasm for arms reduction in the direction of opening talks with the Soviets, though the nature of the subsequent talks was not always his to control.

Beyond Cap the Foil

One cannot understand the Reagan record on arms control or the larger trajectory of Reagan's foreign and security policy without appreciating the power of his sincerely held yet contradictory convictions or how those apparently conflicting impulses were reflected and shared by key actors within his administration, such as Caspar Weinberger.

Weinberger entered the Pentagon as something of a blank slate on national security issues, though he shared conventional Republican internationalist views, including a skeptical relationship to détente and suspicion of the Soviets. Weinberger also enjoyed the full confidence of a president who had ridden to office promising to build up America's defenses. As Weinberger had done in his legal work, he embraced his client's priorities and defended them tenaciously. His client appreciated the effort. *Pace* the Reagan revisionists, Weinberger's actions and arguments were as genuine a reflection of Reagan's priorities as those of the celebrated moderates. Neither rubber stamp nor merely a foil for the other leading men in the administration, Caspar Weinberger was one of the key architects of the Reagan administration's national security policy and thus deserves his share of the credit and responsibility for how it turned out.

Notes

1. Quoted in Caspar Weinberger, *Fighting for Peace: My Seven Years at the Pentagon* (New York: Warner Books, 1992), 14. See also Caspar Weinberger, interview, November 19, 2002, Ronald Reagan Oral History Project, Presidential Oral History Program, Miller Center of Public Affairs, University of Virginia, Charlottesville; materials from this project are hereafter referred to as "Miller Center Oral History" (MCOH).

2. Frances FitzGerald, *Way Out There in the Blue: Reagan, Star Wars, and the End of the Cold War* (New York: Simon and Schuster, 2000), 16.

3. Edwin Meese, *With Reagan* (Washington, DC: Regnery Gateway, 1992), 17.

4. Weinberger, MCOH interview, 17.

5. Caspar W. Weinberger, *Annual Report to Congress, Fiscal Year 1988/89* (Washington, DC: US Government Printing Office, 1987), 86.

6. Ibid., 93–95. See also the chart in Meese, *With Reagan,* 177.

7. Lou Cannon, *President Reagan: The Role of a Lifetime* (New York: PublicAffairs, 2001), 5–10.

8. Robert Scheer, *With Enough Shovels: Reagan, Bush, and Nuclear War* (New York: Random House, 1982), 122; Strobe Talbott, *Deadly Gambits: The Reagan Administration and the Stalemate in Nuclear Arms Control* (New York: Knopf, 1984).

9. See especially Peter Schweizer, *Victory: The Reagan Administration's Secret Strategy That Hastened the End of the Cold War* (New York: Atlantic Monthly Books, 1994) and *Reagan's War: The Epic Story of His Forty-Year Struggle and Final Triumph over Communism* (New York: Anchor, 2003).

10. Caspar W. Weinberger and Peter Schweitzer, *The Next War* (New York: Regnery, 1996).

11. FitzGerald, *Way Out There in the Blue;* Beth A. Fisher, *The Reagan Reversal: Foreign Policy and the End of the Cold War* (Columbia: University of Missouri Press, 1997).

12. Don Oberdorfer, *From the Cold War to the New Era* (Baltimore: Johns Hopkins University Press, 2001), 35, 98–99, 172.

13. James Mann, *The Rebellion of Ronald Reagan* (New York: Penguin, 2009), 32, 38, 216, 248, 255. The other references merely mention Weinberger's name.

14. Ibid., 173–76.

15. Aram Bakshian Jr., MCOH interview, January 14, 2002, 31, 42.

16. Robert C. McFarlane, with Zofia Smardz, *Special Trust* (New York: Cadell and Davies, 1994), passim.

17. Caspar Weinberger, *In the Arena* (Washington, DC: Regnery, 2001), 151–53; Stuart Spencer, MCOH interview, November 15–16, 2001, 18–19; Michael Deaver, MCOH interview, September 12, 2002, 8.

18. Weinberger, *In the Arena,* 204–52.

19. Peter Hannaford, MCOH interview, January 10, 2003, 33.

20. Caspar Weinberger to Ronald Reagan, December 16, 1980, Folder 3, Weinberger Papers I: 573, Library of Congress (LOC), Washington, DC.

21. Weinberger, *Fighting for Peace,* 10–11; Weinberger, MCOH interview, 32.

22. Quoted in Cannon, *President Reagan,* 148.

23. Weinberger, MCOH interview, 33.

24. Deaver, MCOH interview, 53–54.

25. Frank Carlucci, MCOH interview, August 28, 2001, 14–15.

26. *Congressional Quarterly (CQ) Almanac 1981* (Washington, DC: CQ Press, 1981), 191–92; Caspar Weinberger, briefing papers, MCOH, 1–2; William Van Cleave to Weinberger, December 19, 1980, with attachments, Folder 1, Weinberger Papers I: 572, LOC; Defense Policy Briefing Book, June 30, 1980, Folder 3, Weinberger Papers I: 572, LOC; Weinberger, *Fighting for Peace,* 41 n.; Len Colodny and Tom Schachtman, *The Forty Years War: The Rise and Fall of the Neocons; From Nixon to Obama* (New York: HarperPerennial, 2009), 294. See also Weinberger to Anne Armstrong, December 30, 1980, responding to Armstrong to Weinberger, December 16, 1980, Folder 2, Weinberger Papers I: 573, LOC.

27. See David Rothkopf, *Running the World: The Inside Story of the National Security Council and the Architects of American Power* (New York: PublicAffairs, 2006), as well as Steven L. Rearden, *The Formative Years, 1947–1950,* vol. 1 of *Sec-*

retaries of Defense Historical Series, ed. Office of the Secretary of Defense Historical Office (Washington, DC: US Government Printing Office, 1984).

28. For a recent discussion of this development from the perspective of Nixon's secretary of defense, see Richard A. Hunt, *Melvin Laird and the Foundation of the Post-Vietnam Military, 1969–1973,* vol. 7 of *Secretaries of Defense Historical Series,* ed. Office of the Secretary of Defense Historical Office (Washington, DC: US Government Printing Office, 2015).

29. Richard Pipes, *Vixi: Memoirs of a Non-belonger* (New Haven, CT: Yale University Press, 2003), 144–53; Alexander M. Haig, *Caveat: Realism, Reagan, and Foreign Policy* (New York: Macmillan, 1984), 85.

30. James Baker, oral history, n.d., transcript, Office of the Secretary of Defense Oral History Program, 4.

31. Weinberger, *In the Arena,* 149.

32. Baker, oral history, Office of the Secretary of Defense Oral History Program, 4–5.

33. Weinberger, *Fighting for Peace,* 29.

34. Carlucci, MCOH interview, 13; Caspar Weinberger, "Memorandum for the Record: Meeting Held on January 20, 1981, Ed Meese's Office," Folder 5, Weinberger Papers I: 573, LOC; Haig, *Caveat,* 52–55, 64, 75–77, 83–85; Cannon, *President Reagan,* 161.

35. Carlucci, MCOH interview, 13–14.

36. Haig, *Caveat,* 77, 86–88.

37. Weinberger, *In the Arena,* 197, 259.

38. George P. Shultz, *Turmoil and Triumph: My Years as Secretary of State* (New York: Scribner's, 1993), 144.

39. Weinberger to Reagan, December 16, 1980, Folder 3, Weinberger Papers I: 573, LOC.

40. Rowland Evans and Robert Novak, "He Makes America Strong," *Readers' Digest,* June 1981, 131, clipping included in Mrs. Jerome J. Klipka to Weinberger, June 21, 1985, Folder 3, Weinberger Papers I: 596, LOC; see also Weinberger to Klipka, June 28, 1985, Folder 3, Weinberger Papers I: 596, LOC.

41. Weinberger, MCOH interview, 12.

42. Ibid., 24.

43. Defense Program Review Committee meeting, August 5, 1971, minutes, in memo to Henry Kissinger, August 10, 1971, Kissinger Transcripts, Document 319, 10–11, Digital National Security Archive, at http://search.proquest.com/dnsa.

44. Ronald Reagan, remarks to the Mid-winter Congressional Conference of the National League of Cities, March 1, 1981, in *Public Papers of the President of the United States: Ronald Reagan, 1981, January 20 to December 31, 1981* (Washington, DC: US Government Printing Office, 1982), 179–80. The record notes "laughter," but whether that laughter was derisive, one cannot say.

45. Weinberger, *Fighting for Peace,* 40.

46. Weinberger to Reagan, memo, January 7, 1981, Folder 5, Weinberger Papers I:

573, LOC, referencing the OMB Position Paper, 4–6. See also Spending Control Task Force to Reagan, November 7, 1980, in Weinberger to Milton Friedman et al., November 11, 1980, Folder 1: "Spending Control Task Force," Weinberger Papers I: 574, LOC.

47. Richard Nixon to Reagan, November 17, 1980, in Cannon, *President Reagan,* 70; Nixon to Weinberger, December 15, 1980, Folder 2: "Ideas/Suggestions 3," Weinberger Papers I: 573, LOC.

48. Weinberger to Nixon, December 31, 1980, Folder 2: "Ideas/Suggestions 3," Weinberger Papers I: 573, LOC.

49. David Stockman, *The Triumph of Politics: The Inside Story of the Reagan Revolution* (New York: Avon Books, 1987), 301.

50. Weinberger, *Fighting for Peace,* 48–49.

51. Cannon, *President Reagan,* 132.

52. Weinberger, MCOH interview, 11.

53. Robert McFarlane, oral history interview, November 1, 1989, MC 162, Box 2, Folder 22, Don Oberdorfer Collection, Princeton University Library, Princeton, NJ.

54. Dov Zakheim, *Flight of the LAVI* (London: Brassey's, 1996).

55. Schweizer, *Victory;* see also the discussion of oil in Stephen Kotkin, *Armageddon Averted: The Soviet Collapse, 1970–2000* (New York: Oxford University Press, 2001), 10–17.

56. Weinberger's contempt for McFarlane (a contempt heartily reciprocated) is apparent in *Fighting for Peace,* 353–85.

57. Weinberger, *In the Arena,* 347–71.

58. Caspar Weinberger, "The Uses of Military Power," speech to the National Press Club, November 28, 1984, in *Fighting for Peace,* 433–45.

59. Diary entries for January 29 and June 3 and 4, 1985, in Ronald Reagan, *The Reagan Diaries,* ed. Douglas Brinkley (New York: HarperCollins, 2007), 297, 332.

60. See, for example, James Mann, *The Rebellion of Ronald Reagan* (New York: Penguin, 2009).

61. See, for example, Schweizer, *Reagan's War.*

62. James Graham Wilson, *The Triumph of Improvisation: Gorbachev's Adaptability, Reagan's Engagement, and the End of the Cold War* (Ithaca, NY: Cornell University Press, 2014).

63. Caspar Weinberger, interviewed by Marvin Kalb, *Meet the Press,* NBC, November 22, 1981, in *Public Statements of Caspar W. Weinberger, Secretary of Defense,* 5 vols. (Washington, DC: Historical Office, Office of the Secretary of Defense, 1981–1987), 5:3427.

64. Ken Adelman, MCOH interview, September 30, 2003, 36–37.

65. See William F. Buckley Jr. to Reagan, October 18, 1987, included in William F. Buckley Jr., *The Reagan I Knew* (New York: Basic Books, 2008), 204–7.

66. Weinberger, *Fighting for Peace,* 347.

67. Quoted in Annelise Anderson, MCOH interview, December 17, 2002, 56–57.

4

Transformative Leadership on Capitol Hill

The Goldwater–Nichols Defense Reorganization Act

James R. Locher III

> Of all the kinds of leadership that require exceptional political skill, leadership of reform movements must be among the most exacting.
> —James MacGregor Burns, *Leadership*

Many experts rank the Goldwater–Nichols Department of Defense Reorganization Act of 1986 as the greatest transformation of the US military establishment since the National Security Act of 1947.[1] This landmark legislation overcame decades of service independence and separateness to create a highly integrated and capable military establishment. Secretary of Defense William J. Perry praised the act as "perhaps the most important defense legislation since World War II."[2] Joint Chiefs of Staff (JCS) vice chairman Admiral William A. Owens described the Goldwater–Nichols Act as "the watershed event for the military since the second [*sic*] World War."[3] Many other secretaries of defense, JCS chairmen and vice chairmen, and warfighting commanders have similarly cited the act's enduring significance.

Differing from nearly all legislation, the Goldwater–Nichols Act did not originate as a proposal from the president. It was a congressional initiative from start to finish, enacted over the opposition of Department of Defense (DoD) leaders and their powerful allies. This was not the normal order of producing legislation in Washington. Since 1937, when President Franklin D. Roosevelt declared, “It is the duty of the president to propose and it is the privilege of the Congress to dispose,”[4] the president had become the nearly exclusive initiator of major legislation. How was it possible for Congress on its own and over Pentagon objections to lead historic reforms of the military establishment?

The Setting

The defense reorganization battle started in early 1982 shortly after President Ronald Reagan had initiated a major buildup of the defense budget and military capabilities. He came to office pledging to strengthen national defense, reversing President Jimmy Carter’s budget cuts. More than defense spending was down. American opinion of the US military had reached a low point by the early 1980s. Following the defeat in Vietnam, the failed Iran hostages rescue mission, and the Soviet invasion of Afghanistan, only 29.9 percent of the US public expressed a “great deal of confidence” in the US military.[5] To those knowledgeable about military affairs, other operational failures or setbacks—such as North Korean naval vessels’ seizure of the USS *Pueblo*, a US intelligence-gathering ship, in 1968 and the disjointed response by US forces to the Khmer Rouge capture of the American cargo ship *Mayaguez* in 1975—had increased the level of concern.

Weak central authority had plagued the DoD since its creation. The department’s unifying elements—secretary of defense, JCS chairman, and unified (now called combatant) commanders—were underpowered. The real clout remained with the services—army, navy, air force, and Marine Corps. The services had helped erect in law and regulation a system of defense organization that preserved their independence and prerogatives. These organizational arrangements were, however, misaligned with modern warfare’s requirement for a highly integrated effort. President Dwight D. Eisenhower articulated this need in a message to Congress in 1958: “Separate ground, sea, and air warfare is gone forever. If ever again we should be involved in war, we will fight it in all elements, with all services, as one single concentrated effort. Peacetime preparatory and organizational activity must conform to this fact. Strategic and tactical planning must be completely unified, combat forces organized into unified commands, each equipped with the most efficient weapons systems that science can develop, singly led and prepared to fight as one, regardless of service."[6] Eisenhower's arguments did not persuade the services or Capitol Hill.

Since the struggle over military unification in the immediate post–World War II era, an alliance between the services and Congress had blocked initiatives from presidents to create a more unified military establishment. This powerful alliance had weakened President Harry S. Truman's defense organization proposals in 1947. Of the resulting National Security Act, Eisenhower later said, "The three service departments were but loosely joined. The entire structure . . . was little more than a weak confederation of sovereign military units. Few powers were vested in the new secretary of defense. All others were reserved to three separated executive [military] departments."[7] Truman in 1949 and Eisenhower in 1953 and 1958 secured modest improvements to defense organization, principally strengthening the position of secretary of defense. But Congress balked at changes that would threaten control by the services.

For the next three decades, presidents did not request and Congress did not enact significant statutory changes to Pentagon organization. Although the service-dominated structure repeatedly demonstrated its flaws, administrations studied but did not propose reforms. The inability of Eisenhower—a war hero with great military prestige and influence—to overcome opposition to defense reform had convinced others not to challenge the service–Congress alliance.

Prospects for reform of defense organization looked particularly bleak in early 1982. The formidable union between the services and Congress remained intact. Moreover, Reagan's secretary of defense, Caspar W. Weinberger, not wanting talk of organizational ills to undercut his budget-building efforts, aligned himself with the services' antireform stance. Because Weinberger and Reagan were close friends, it was unlikely that the president would become pro-reform. So even the two traditional sources of pressure for greater military integration—the president and the secretary of defense—were antireform or inactive.

Despite this bleak outlook, in February 1982 a sitting JCS chairman, air force general David C. Jones, impelled by the failed hostage rescue mission in Iran, boldly appealed for Congress to fix the broken JCS system. During testimony before a closed hearing of the House Armed Services Committee (HASC), Jones proclaimed, "It is not sufficient to have just resources, dollars and weapon systems; we must also have an organization which will allow us to develop the proper strategy, necessary planning, and the full warfighting capability. We do not have an adequate organizational structure today."[8] This call for reform ignited a fierce struggle between the Pentagon and Congress that would last four years and 241 days—a period longer than World War II. Highly displeased with Jones's testimony, the DoD firmly staked out its opposition to organizational changes.

Early Action in the House

Thanks to the knowledge and perseverance of Archie D. "Arch" Barrett, a professional staff member and retired air force colonel, the HASC Investigations Subcommittee undertook an examination of the JCS organizational issues raised by General Jones. In August 1982, under the leadership of its chairman, Congressman Richard C. "Dick" White (D–TX), the Investigations Subcommittee succeeded in gaining HASC and House approval of the modest Joint Chiefs of Staff Reorganization Bill, House of Representatives (H.R.) 6954, during that session of Congress. Most important among H.R. 6954's ten provisions were ones that would permit the JCS chairman to provide military advice "in his own right," create a deputy chairman position, and place the Joint Staff solely under the chairman's management. Despite swift action on H.R. 6954, little interest or commitment to the bill existed in the HASC. According to a senior staff member, the bill was permitted to go forward because members thought "nothing is going to happen. They just figured it would die some other way. The HASC did not regard it as a serious issue."[9] They were right. Without a companion bill in the Senate, the House legislation died when the Ninety-Seventh Congress adjourned at the end of 1982. In addition, its champion, Congressman White, retired from the House.

In the Ninety-Eighth Congress, Congressman Bill Nichols (D–AL), who had lost a leg in combat during World War II, became the new chairman of the Investigations Subcommittee. He initially pursued JCS reorganization because it was unfinished business. His subcommittee formulated a stronger bill, designated H.R. 3718, than the one approved in 1982. It passed the HASC after being considered for ten minutes, and the House approved it by voice vote on October 17, 1983. A few more subcommittee members had shown interest in 1983, but most considered JCS reorganization "to be one of the least understood, least interesting, most boring, and politically unrewarding issues the subcommittee could address."[10]

Even Nichols did not see JCS reorganization as his issue; to him, it was unfinished Dick White work. Six days after the House vote, his view changed dramatically. On October 23, 1983, a tragic terrorist bombing in Beirut, Lebanon, leveled the four-story barracks of US marine peacekeepers and killed 241 servicemen, including a constituent of the Alabama congressman. Just twenty-eight days earlier, Nichols had visited the marines in Beirut as part of an HASC delegation. The bombing and deaths rocked Nichols and made him an ardent believer in the need to fix the joint system.

Dithering in the Senate

The Senate Armed Services Committee (SASC) entered the reorganization fray in June 1983 when its chairman, John Tower (R–TX), initiated a series of hearings on the DoD's structure, organization, and decision-making procedures. Unlike HASC efforts, which focused solely on JCS reorganization, SASC hearings would look at eight major dimensions of defense organization: Office of the Secretary of Defense, Organization of the Joint Chiefs of Staff (OJCS), military departments, unified commands, budget process, acquisition process, interagency relations, and congressional review and oversight. A textbook on organization inspired this comprehensive approach: "An organization is not a mechanical system in which one part can be changed without a concomitant effect on the other parts. Rather, an organizational system shares with biological systems the property of intense interdependence of parts such that a change in one part has an impact on others."[11]

Given the SASC members' limited knowledge about defense organization, Tower agreed to staff preparation of a comprehensive report on the various organizational issues. For more than forty years, conflicting studies and testimony on principles for organizing the US military establishment had created great uncertainty on needed directions. The staff study sought to analyze these differing views as objectively as possible. Given the workload involved, the entire committee staff and many military legislative assistants in the committee members' offices engaged in the research and analysis.

Tower entered these hearings with much different expectations than General Jones or HASC reformers. Based on meetings with retired marine lieutenant general Victor H. "Brute" Krulak, Tower believed that there needed to be a move "away from centralization." This would make the services even more powerful and diminish the authority of integrating officials and offices. Tower had served in the navy during World War II and still held the rank of senior chief boatswain's mate in the Naval Reserve. He remained closely connected to the sea service. Beyond his navy loyalties, Tower saw this inquiry as a chance to strengthen his credentials for secretary of defense, a job he had long coveted. If he were able to implement Krulak's ideas, the services were likely to lend their support to his candidacy for the top Pentagon post. Krulak's ideas conflicted with four decades of evidence. As Eisenhower had noted, the DoD remained a loose confederation at a time when its warfighting components needed to be tightly integrated. Tower's inquiry was misdirected and ill fated.[12]

As the hearings progressed, Tower came to understand that the Pentagon needed something quite different from Krulak's anachronistic ideas. The inquiry and accompanying staff study had, however, generated interest and momentum. Tower had also made promises of progress to Senator Sam Nunn (D–GA), the SASC's ranking Democrat, and to Congressman Nichols and his HASC colleagues. The committee chairman could not abandon the inquiry; he had to figure out how to slow roll it until his planned retirement at the end of 1984. Tower still wanted to be secretary of defense, but he saw the path to that job would be served by opposing defense reorganization, not by supporting it.

When Tower's committee failed in either 1983 or 1984 to produce a companion bill to the House's JCS reorganization bill, Nichols forced the issue. He attached H.R. 3718, the JCS reorganization bill passed by the House in 1983, to the defense authorization bill, the two committees' principal annual legislation. This move would compel the SASC–HASC conference committee, formed to resolve differences between the Senate and House bills, to address JCS reorganization. For this conference, it was the SASC's turn to provide the chairman. Tower deftly used this position to control the action. Despite Nichols's pleas, Tower delayed the conference committee's consideration of the JCS reorganization bill until the very last issue at 1:00 a.m. The exhausted conferees supported a few modest JCS reforms but were not prepared to try to overcome Tower's determined opposition. The conference approved only two significant provisions: giving the chairman the responsibility of deciding when the JCS would decide issues and of selecting Joint Staff officers from among the most outstanding service officers.

Tower's opposition to defense reorganization pleased the DoD. Pentagon leaders had earlier decided to focus their efforts on defeating defense reorganization in the SASC. Controlled by Democrats, the House was less susceptible to pressures from a Republican administration, and it had already easily passed two JCS reorganization bills. The Republican-controlled Senate was much more likely to be persuaded, especially by the White House. The SASC became and remained the principal battleground in the defense reorganization fight. The HASC, especially Congressman Nichols, had played an important role in keeping the issue alive, advancing key ideas, and weakening the service–Congress alliance. It would continue to be an important partner to the SASC, but party politics relegated it to playing a supporting role. Defense reorganization was going to be won or lost in the SASC.

By the end of 1984, nearly three years had passed since General Jones's call for action, and little had been accomplished. Jones had retired and been replaced as JCS chairman by army general John W. "Jack" Vessey Jr., a reform opponent. The top Pentagon civilian and military leadership was now unified in opposition to JCS or defense reorganization, and Congress was stalemated on the issue. Many believed that the window for making changes had passed. They were soon surprised.

Goldwater–Nunn Partnership

In January 1985, Senator Barry Goldwater (R–AZ), the Republican candidate for president in 1964 and founder of the modern conservative political movement, replaced Tower as SASC chairman. Goldwater had celebrity status in military circles, especially in the air force, where he had reached the rank of major general in the Air Force Reserve before retiring in 1967. His career had shown him to be opinionated, independent, and unpredictable. These characteristics came to the forefront as he started his chairmanship. To great Pentagon concern, the seventy-six-year-old Goldwater decided to make defense reorganization his top priority during the Ninety-Ninth Congress, which would be the last two of his thirty years in the Senate.

Goldwater determined that this controversial issue needed to be pursued on a bipartisan basis. He proposed to Senator Nunn, still the ranking Democrat, that they work on defense reorganization as equal partners. Goldwater recalled that in starting this effort he had "wanted to establish two things—equality and trust."[13] He and Nunn created a four-member bipartisan staff that would report to both of them. They consulted closely on every step and "became comfortable communicating openly and candidly with each other."[14] The SASC chairman and the ranking Democrat established a gold standard for bipartisan collaboration. Goldwater explained that his bipartisan roots went back to his entry into politics: "Arizona was a strong Democratic state—had a lot of counties that were 100 percent Democratic. I was a Republican, and I had to get elected."[15] Nunn also had a strong bipartisan reputation, saying, "I never accomplished anything without the help of someone from the other party."[16] The Goldwater–Nunn partnership proved to be the second most important development in the defense reorganization battle; only Jones's appeal for reform ranked as more consequential.

Goldwater and Nunn had a daunting challenge in front of them. Only two or three other senators on the nineteen-member SASC then favored reorganization. Nearly every member maintained a close connection with one or more services, either because they had worn a uniform, many during World War II, or because important military bases were located or defense hardware was purchased in their state. Overcoming these close ties would not be easy.

Another stumbling block arose from the members' continued lack of knowledge on defense organization and modern organizational practice. Because the committee's agenda focused on defense policy and budgets, it did not expose members to the interworking of the Pentagon. The lack of knowledge made members susceptible to superficial appeals by the services. Goldwater and Nunn realized this is what had happened in 1947 when Congress listened to the navy's and Marine Corps' arguments that a more integrated military would lead to a Prussian-style General Staff and thus threaten the republic.

The strenuous opposition to defense reform by the nation's top military officers represented another monumental challenge. The task of overruling a unanimous JCS on a topic outside of Congress's area of expertise would give many legislators pause. The vast network of military associations, such as the Navy League and Air Force Association, and veterans groups, such as the Veterans of Foreign Wars, would support the Pentagon's opposition. Their lobbying, newspaper editorials, and letter-writing campaigns would reinforce antireform positions on Capitol Hill.

Goldwater and Nunn's leadership would be pivotal in overcoming these many obstacles. Goldwater understood the magnitude of the challenge: "When Nunn and I began to make our move, I wouldn't have bet more than a sawbuck on our chances of success. History and tradition were against us. Yet I had made up my mind that I would not retire from the Senate without giving reorganization my best shot."[17] As the two senators began to work together, their opponents came to understand the importance of their partnership and made every effort, including disinformation campaigns, to break it.

Leadership Values and Character

In many respects, Goldwater and Nunn were quite different. The Arizona Republican operated by his astute instincts; the Georgia Democrat relied on hard work and superior knowledge. Goldwater was bold; Nunn was cautious. Goldwater was the gunslinger; Nunn, the deliberate statesman. They divided the work to maximize their different strengths. Goldwater shaped the major reform thrusts and protected the effort from the unending attacks by the Pentagon and its allies. Using his cerebral skills, Nunn zeroed in on detailed analyses and solutions. Both played critical roles: "Goldwater emerged as the moral force behind reorganization, and Nunn became the intellectual force. Nunn's contribution made the senators' work profound; Goldwater's made it possible."[18]

Although Goldwater and Nunn differed in many respects, they had highly congruent leadership values and character. A key common value was their career-long dedication to serving the nation. Working on defense reorganization, they focused solely on the national interest. There was no personal agenda, no party agenda, no constituent agenda—only service to the nation. Describing Nunn's devotion to national service, Senator John W. Warner (R–VA) later said, "His approach to national security issues has been guided by one fundamental criteria: What Sam Nunn believes is in the best interest of the United States of America."[19]

The two senators were also known for their integrity, honesty, and trustworthiness. Of Goldwater, the *Washington Post* reported, "His reputation for personal integrity was unblemished." As evidence, the paper cited his role in Nixon's resignation: "At the height of the Watergate crisis, when the Republicans in Congress needed someone to tell President Richard M. Nixon he should resign, they chose Mr. Goldwater."[20] Nixon resigned the day after meeting with Goldwater. Both Goldwater and Nunn had earned a reputation for moral leadership and could be counted on to do the right thing. Leadership guru James MacGregor Burns writes of the importance of this value in reform efforts: "Reform leadership by definition usually implies moral leadership, and this imposes a special burden. It means that reformers must not follow improper means in trying to achieve moral ends, on the ground that the means can taint and pervert the ends."[21]

Another Goldwater and Nunn value was treating others with dignity and respect. Even in the heat of political battle, their courtesy and fair-minded approach were constants. Goldwater observed, "To disagree, one doesn't have to be disagreeable."[22] The aging Republican and rising Democrat were also committed to excellence in their work. They set high standards for themselves and their organizations. Nunn was viewed as having "a deeply personal compulsion to learn."[23]

Trust and loyalty were also important to the two senators. Goldwater declared, "Loyalty is the most important virtue in politics."[24] Nunn "devoted himself to building long-term personal relationships with his colleagues in the Senate."[25] They worked hard to earn each other's trust, resulting in an extraordinary level of that feeling. Nunn observed, "Goldwater developed more trust in me than anybody else on the committee."[26] The SASC chairman said, "In going into this battle, I placed absolute trust in Nunn. He never disappointed me, not once. With Sam, I'd take on the devil in hell."[27]

Goldwater and Nunn's colleagues and subordinates fully understood these values because the two men's behavior consistently exemplified them. Their values-based leadership created an environment for open dialogue and productive engagements among committee members with highly divergent and strongly held views. It also freed staff members to focus on their work on a controversial subject without the need to worry about how they would be treated. As a recent study has concluded, "Values-driven organizations are the most successful organizations on the planet."[28] In 1985–1986, Goldwater and Nunn created a values-driven organization that provided the basis for historic success.

In discussing reform and revolutionary leaders, Burns observes that such leadership "demands commitment, persistence, courage, perhaps selflessness and even self-abnegation."[29] The two senators' character fulfilled each of these leadership demands. Their commitment never wavered despite unending pressure. Goldwater reported being lobbied incessantly by antireform officers, both active and retired, many of them his good friends.[30] He and Nunn had to endure for two years in their struggle to overcome the formidable obstacles. Goldwater was not known for persistence on legislative matters; he preferred to evangelize by giving straight-shooting speeches rather than by grinding away in a long-term crusade. Nevertheless, on defense reorganization, he persisted.

The chairman and the ranking Democrat exhibited extraordinary courage in taking on this historic effort. As his career was coming to an end, Goldwater was risking his relationship with his beloved military. As Capitol Hill's rising star on defense matters, Nunn also incurred considerable risk: a defeat on this high-profile issue would considerably dim his star. Goldwater and Nunn were also selfless. No political or personal benefits would accompany a victory on defense reorganization. It was a good-government issue with great upsides for the nation if successful and great downsides for the two senators if defeated.

Beyond possessing the character traits of good leaders, Goldwater and Nunn were visionary leaders. They had a clear picture of how a unified military establishment would perform. Their ability to visualize and articulate an achievable and desirable future for the Pentagon contributed importantly to formulating coherent fixes and attracting commitment from others. The two senators also played a key role in confronting reality. Pentagon leaders were in denial about the mismatch of organizational capabilities and operational and administrative requirements. Far too much nostalgia for a bygone era existed in the military establishment. Goldwater and Nunn defined the truth of organizational dysfunction and thereby clearly established the starting point for change. The chairman and ranking Democrat also possessed political-management skills, which would be imperative in preparing a path for their fractured committee to formulate and approve a far-reaching defense reorganization bill.

Problems in Defense Organization

The SASC staff had made considerable progress on its defense organization study by the time Goldwater and Nunn were forming their partnership. The study gave highest priority to identifying problems and their causes. In organizational analyses, problems and causes often receive limited attention in the headlong pursuit of solutions. Although this tendency is derided as "solutions in search of a problem," it is usually the norm. Without rigorous identification of problems, symptoms rather than underlying ills become the targets of reform. The resulting solutions produce great turbulence but do not fix problems. The staff study of defense organization avoided this fate by painstaking analysis of problems, their causes, and their consequences.

When released in October 1985, the staff study, titled *Defense Organization: The Need for Change,* revealed crippling deficiencies in the DoD. Foremost was limited mission integration at the policy-making level. The study used the term *mission integration* to describe "the integration of the distinct military capabilities of the four services to prepare for and conduct effective unified operations in fulfilling major U.S. military missions." It viewed mission integration to be the DoD's principal organizational goal. It found the organizations in the DoD's Washington headquarters to be "excessively focused on functional areas, such as manpower, research and development, and installations and logistics." This focus had led to organizational activities that prioritized functional efficiency at the expense of a focus on "major missions and their objectives and strategy."[31]

A second major problem centered on the imbalance between service and joint interests. *Defense Organization* concluded, "The Military Departments and Services exercise power and influence which are completely out of proportion to their statutorily assigned duties."[32] The services dominated the JCS and unified commands. They also worked together to oppose the secretary of defense and his civilian staff, leading to fractious civil–military disputes on major issues.

A related problem centered on the inadequacy of military advice. During World War II and thereafter, the JCS operated on the principle of unanimity—that the chiefs would achieve complete agreement before forwarding a recommendation to civilian authority. Reaching agreement required finding the lowest common denominator that would accommodate each service's position. Ambassador Robert W. Komer observed, "Because of the way it operates, the JCS system is the prisoner of the services which comprise [*sic*] it."[33] The watered-down advice had little utility. The staff study found that "the institutional views of the JCS . . . do not offer clear, meaningful recommendations on issues affecting more than one service." It cited a statement by General Jones: "The corporate advice provided by the Joint Chiefs of Staff is not crisp, timely, very useful or very influential." The study also included a harsher assessment by former secretary of defense James R. Schlesinger: "The proffered advice is generally irrelevant, normally unread, and almost always disregarded."[34]

Given the weakness of joint institutions, it is not surprising that military officers did not want to serve in the OJCS or unified command headquarters. The staff study identified a problem with the inadequate qualifications possessed by joint-duty officers.[35] Of the OJCS staff (now Joint Staff), the study reported: "For the most part, officers do not want OJCS assignments, are pressured or monitored for loyalty by their services while serving in the OJCS; are not prepared by either education or experience to perform their joint duties; and serve for only a relatively short period once they have learned their jobs."[36] Military officers desired service assignments that were much more career enhancing, and so they avoided the risks of a joint assignment.

Defense Organization examined the problems of the unified commands in great depth. It found an imbalance between the authority and responsibility of the unified commanders. The study judged that the commanders' authority "remains extremely limited." It cited weak authority over service components, limited influence over resources, and little ability to promote greater unification within their commands. The study quoted from the *Blue Ribbon Defense Panel Report* of 1970: "'Unification' of either command or of the forces is more cosmetic than substantive."[37] In 1984, noted Harvard scholar Samuel P. Huntington declared, "Unified commands are not really commands, and they certainly aren't unified."[38]

The study also found the unified commands to be plagued by confused and cumbersome operational chains of command. It reported, "The appropriate relationship between operational commanders and those above them in the chain of command are very uncertain." The staff study cited three reasons for this problem: (1) unclear statutes on the role of the secretary of defense; (2) an ambiguous Pentagon directive on the role of the JCS; and (3) the de facto influence that the service chiefs retained over unified commands headed by an officer from their service.[39]

Turning to DoD management processes, *Defense Organization* judged strategic planning to be ineffective. It was often said of the Pentagon's Planning, Programming, and Budgeting System that "the first 'P' is silent." Ambassador Komer observed, "The reality is best characterized as a piecemeal, irregular, highly informal process, largely driven by cumulative program decisions influenced more by budget constraints and consequent inter-service competition than by notion of U.S. strategic priorities."[40] Programming and budgeting dominated DoD activity. The staff study concluded, "Too much of the time and attention of DoD and its senior civilian and military officials is consumed by resource decisions. This has led to insufficient attention to strategic planning, operational matters, and execution of policy and resource decisions."[41]

Concerning the military departments, the staff study identified numerous problems, foremost being confusion concerning the service secretaries' roles. In the great debate in 1947 over creation of a single military establishment, there was "a failure to determine what role the service secretaries should play in a unified Department of Defense. . . . Their relationship to the secretary of defense . . . was never precisely defined." Among numerous deficiencies caused by this confusion, one was an effort to provide for the service secretaries' independence from the secretary of defense.[42]

A second military department problem was the existence of two top headquarters staffs in the army and air force and three in the navy: the secretariat and military headquarters staff. This was a carryover from World War II when the secretary and his secretariat handled all business matters and the chief of staff and his military staff worked directly with the president on the war effort. After the war, both staffs were retained despite the fact that they then had a common mission, a retention that led to unnecessary staff layers and duplication of effort.[43]

Defense Organization's chapter on congressional review and oversight generated the greatest interest among SASC members because they were living these problems every day. Key among these problems was how the budget process dominated the agenda at the expense of other legislative tasks. Equally concerning was "the steady and dramatic increase in congressional involvement in the annual defense budget submission," leading to congressional micromanagement of defense programs.[44]

In all, *Defense Organization* identified 34 problems and 118 causes, examined 144 alternative solutions, and offered 91 recommendations.

Principles and Process

Goldwater and Nunn were convinced that the staff study's analysis was on target. They had to find a way to persuade their committee colleagues of the validity of its ideas. In formulating their approach, the two senators established four operating principles. First, defense reorganization had to be undertaken on a bipartisan basis. This topic was too complicated and emotional to also bear the burdens of party politics. Becoming a political issue would doom defense reorganization. Second, every effort should be made to cooperate with the White House and Pentagon. Passing the legislation would be just half of the reorganization effort; the other half would be implementation. This second half would require good-faith undertakings by the executive branch. To make such efforts more likely, the two senators were determined to avoid unnecessary disputes. They also continually went out of their way to speak about the long-term nature of the problems, thereby seeking to avoid criticism of sitting defense officials.

A third principle envisioned addressing defense reorganization in as honest and objective manner as possible. Last, Goldwater and Nunn wanted to have a full, open debate of the issues. They wanted every idea and concern to be expressed and examined no matter how long it took. A letter from the two senators to Secretary Weinberger on February 4, 1985, reflected these principles: "It is our sincere hope . . . to work closely with you in an objective analysis of potential improvements. . . . You should be assured that the committee's study is not a criticism of you, of any other official of the Department of Defense, or of this administration."[45]

As Goldwater and Nunn began their work on defense reorganization, they made two key decisions. First, they determined to make the staff study the centerpiece of the committee's examination of defense organization, and so they directed a more vigorous study effort. The two senators spent the next four months working closely with the staff on its study. The second decision would create the nine-member Task Force on Defense Organization, which they waited until May 1985 to form. In line with their desire for bipartisanship and equality, Goldwater and Nunn cochaired the task force. Four Republicans joined Goldwater: Senators Bill Cohen (ME), Dan Quayle (IN), Pete Wilson (CA), and Phil Gramm (TX). Nunn selected three Democrats: Senators Carl Levin (MI), Ted Kennedy (MA), and Jeff Bingaman (NM).

When the Senate was in session, the task force met once a week from mid-June through early October to discuss a chapter of the staff study or to meet with former military officers or defense officials. Attendance was extraordinarily high; no one wanted to miss a moment of the consideration of this contentious issue. As the task force began its work, Quayle, Wilson, and Gramm took antireform stances and supported Pentagon arguments. The Democrats were more open on the issue but quite cautious and looking for reassurance before overruling the Pentagon. Bingaman revealed this concern when he said the staff study's "arguments and proposals appear sound, but all the generals and admirals across the river in the Pentagon are against this."[46]

As the task force was conducting its early sessions, a potentially important development occurred. On June 17, Reagan established the President's Blue Ribbon Commission on Defense Management. National Security Adviser Robert C. "Bud" McFarlane had outmaneuvered Weinberger in gaining the president's support for a commission to examine the full range of defense reorganization issues in parallel with the work being done by the SASC and HASC. David Packard, cofounder of the Hewlett-Packard Company and former deputy defense secretary, chaired the sixteen-member commission, which soon became known as the Packard Commission. The membership appeared to tilt slightly toward reform and included four pro-reform experts: retired army general Paul Gorman, William J. Perry, retired air force lieutenant general Brent Scowcroft, and R. James Woolsey. Most notably, creation of the commission shifted the executive branch's responsibility for considering defense reorganization from the Pentagon to the Packard Commission.

Goldwater and Nunn were quite pleased by the commission's creation. They now had someone in the executive branch with whom they could work. They quickly established and maintained a fruitful dialogue with Packard and other commissioners.

Early in task force meetings, members established set positions on the staff study's analysis. The difficulty of achieving a thoughtful debate of the issues surprised Goldwater and Nunn. The task force instead "engaged in static, exhausting trench warfare. Barrages of arguments, research, and analysis did not alter frontline positions."[47]

In September, after assessing the stalemate on the task force, Goldwater and Nunn recognized that they "were facing the same powerful parochial interests that had defeated Truman and Eisenhower."[48] They were forced to adopt a more innovative strategy. They settled on a two-part course of action: (1) enlarge the battlefield beyond government by capturing the media's attention and (2) sequester the task force in a weekend retreat with prominent former officials and scholars in an effort to expand and strengthen their support for defense reform.

In executing the first part of the strategy in October, Goldwater and Nunn jointly gave six speeches on the Senate floor, highlighting the best analysis from *Defense Organization.* These speeches by what one newspaper called a "bipartisan juggernaut on Capitol Hill"[49] succeeded in grabbing the media's attention and led to articles in all major newspapers and news magazines. Many reporters quoted sentences from a Goldwater speech: "The system is broken and it must be fixed. The reorganization of the Department of Defense may be the most important thing that Congress does in my lifetime. It will be the most important thing I do in mine."[50] The *New York Times* summarized the speeches: "The two senators accused the military of endangering the nation's defense and squandering its assets with interservice bickering."[51] Media reporting on defense reorganization served many purposes. It opened the issue to wider public debate and subjected Pentagon performance and arguments to more scrutiny. Media commentary also put a favorable light on Goldwater and Nunn's work. Last, it helped to inform all senators of the coming issue, especially the ten SASC members who did not serve on the Task Force on Defense Organization.

Goldwater and Nunn scheduled the retreat for the first weekend in October 1985 at Fort A. P. Hill, an army base about seventy miles from Washington. Nine senators were joined by fifteen experts, including two former secretaries of defense, two former JCS chairmen, and two members of the Packard Commission: former senator Nicholas F. Brady (R–NJ) and General Paul Gorman. The outside experts leaned in favor of reform, but Goldwater and Nunn ensured that opposing views were well represented. Simply because the attending senators were sequestered for two full days, their understanding of the issues as presented in the staff study was greatly improved, especially by their formal and informal discussions with seasoned experts. More task force members soon supported reorganization, and even opponents supported some ideas, especially the strengthening of the unified commanders. Goldwater and Nunn judged the retreat to be "an overwhelming success."[52] Years later Goldwater assessed the retreat "as the pivotal moment during which the pendulum began to swing in the right direction."[53]

Next on Goldwater and Nunn's agenda were eleven hearings with government and private witnesses. The first hearing, held on October 16, 1985, featured public release of the study *Defense Organization: The Need for Change.* The three professional staff members who wrote the report testified.[54] Goldwater and Nunn understood the importance of this first public presentation of the report's analysis. In their judgment, the hearing's outcome would determine success or failure. Nunn expressed their objective, "We want the report to rally support from outside government and to frame the debate inside government."[55] Media coverage of the hearing was extensive. Every major private and public television network filmed the action, and print reporters packed the press tables. SASC members' opening statements and grueling questions showed that the committee was still fractured on defense reorganization. But the ideas in the staff study were clearly communicated and well defended. Media reporting was pro-reform. This initial hearing gave momentum to Goldwater and Nunn's efforts.

Goldwater and Nunn instructed the witnesses for the next ten hearings to base their testimony on the staff study. To provide time for them to examine the study, the committee paused for four weeks. When the committee reconvened, Secretary Weinberger testified. He refused to admit that problems existed. His stonewalling stance caused many members to "write off DoD as a meaningful participant in the reform process."[56] As the hearings progressed, the testimony from chief Pentagon antagonists—the service secretaries and chiefs—was weak. By comparison, pro-reform testimony from retired senior officials and military officers was more thoughtful and insightful. As the hearings progressed, Goldwater and Nunn shifted from a defensive to an offensive posture. They were winning the battle of public testimony, but the only battle that really counted was the one to gain committee approval of a reorganization bill. That battle would be joined in the new year.

After the hearings ended, Goldwater and Nunn directed the committee staff to prepare a defense reorganization bill based on the recommendations of the staff study as informed by testimony and other discussions. The SASC met on the morning of February 4, 1986, to begin consideration of this bill. As the senators gathered, Goldwater and Nunn had only a one-vote margin, with ten senators in favor of or leaning in favor of reorganization and nine senators still opposed. Thirteen months of hard work by the committee chairman and the ranking Democrat had thus produced only the narrowest of margins. Goldwater could count on only two other Republican senators: Strom Thurmond (R–SC) and Bill Cohen. Nunn had gathered the support of six other Democrats; only Senators John Stennis (D–MS) and John Glenn (D–OH) remained opposed. Stennis stood with the navy; Pascagoula Shipyards, where navy ships were built, ranked as the single-largest employer in Mississippi. As a former marine, Glenn firmly defended Marine Corps positions. Given the intense lobbying from the Pentagon and its many supporters, Goldwater and Nunn's ability to sustain ten pro-reform votes was not a certainty. If the Pentagon could persuade just one member, with the eighty-three-year-old Thurmond a likely target, to switch to an antireform stance, Goldwater and Nunn's efforts would be crippled.

Markup of the bill required fourteen grueling sessions over thirty days. The senators on the SASC debated every provision, offering a staggering total of more than 140 written and oral amendments. This was double the number of amendments normally offered during the committee's markup of the defense authorization bill that approved the entire defense budget. As the debate progressed, two pro-reform senators—Cohen and Levin—played important roles, serving as de facto deputies to Goldwater and Nunn. Both of them lawyers, Cohen and Levin were highly intellectual and grasped the complexities of organizational issues.

For the first two weeks of markup, the battle lines remained unchanged: ten senators in favor and nine opposed. As the antireformers began to realize that they could not secure a tenth vote, they set their sights on maintaining a ten–nine vote and then working to derail this weakly supported bill on the Senate floor.

The operating principles that Goldwater and Nunn had established for the committee's defense reorganization work proved highly beneficial, especially their "commitment to a patient, fair, everyone-gets-to-be-heard process."[57] The chairman and ranking Democrat honored every request for more research, more analysis, more alternatives, a briefing, and gathering of an opinion from a defense official or military officer. Senator John Warner, a former navy secretary who led the opposition, commented favorably on Goldwater and Nunn's approach: "At no time did the distinguished chairman or ranking minority member deny me any privilege under the procedures of the committee to make known my views and the views of those senators working with me." Senator Levin said that Goldwater "chaired the committee in a nonpartisan way; he has done it in the fairest way I have ever seen a chairman conduct the committee."[58]

Goldwater and Nunn's decision to ensure a robust debate proved critical. Arguments in favor of reform proved to be much more credible; antireform positions were increasingly shown to be superficial and indefensible. As the markup entered its third week, the first antireformer switched sides: Republican Phil Gramm joined the pro-reform camp. Others slowly followed him. When Goldwater and Nunn had thirteen or fourteen votes in favor, the opposition collapsed.

Although the overall outcome was clear, the committee still worked carefully through every provision. As it was nearing the end of its consideration of the bill, Goldwater and Nunn slowed the pace to provide an opportunity to hear from the Packard Commission. That session occurred on February 28, 1986, the day the commission delivered its report to the president. At the meeting, Packard delighted Goldwater and Nunn when he said, "The portions of the commission's report dealing with defense organization and the committee's bill are consistent and mutually supportive."[59] This statement reassured many committee members and provided a rationale for some to adopt a pro-reform stance. On March 6, the committee met to vote on approving the bill. Surprisingly, all nineteen senators voted in favor of the bill despite the fact that three or four of them remained displeased with the outcome.

The final two steps in the legislative process proved to be anticlimatic after the dramatic process of marking up the bill. The full Senate devoted the entire day of May 7 to considering the bill. No significant changes were made. The last amendment, which Nunn offered in a magnanimous gesture, named the bill for Goldwater. The Senate approved the bill ninety-five to zero. The HASC now had to catch up to the SASC. It needed to expand its JCS reorganization bill to match the broader defense reorganization bill passed by the Senate.

After the House passed a companion bill named after Congressman Nichols, the SASC–HASC conference committee met on August 12 and concluded its work on September 11. Goldwater served as the conference chairman, Nichols as vice chairman. Goldwater asked the conferees to adhere to four principles: "Focus on the genuine needs of U.S. national security. . . . [C]arefully consider each issue and hear all points of view. . . . [E]ach provision should rise or fall on its own merits. . . . [E]nsure that the provisions of law are not so detailed or specific that they cannot be adapted to the needs of the unforeseen future."[60] The Senate and House bills had similar objectives, but their provisions differed on how to achieve them. The bills contained more than two hundred substantive differences and more than a thousand significant wording differences. Resolving these differences and determining the best approaches for the military establishment was demanding work. The final compromise made was the easiest: titling the bill the Goldwater–Nichols Act. On September 15 and 16, the Senate and House passed the conference committee report and sent the bill to President Reagan for signature.

Elements of the Pentagon urged a presidential veto, but Reagan signed the bill on October 1—the last day of the ten days, not counting Sundays, provided in the Constitution for the president to act on a bill. Given the Pentagon's negative attitude, the White House did not arrange a signing ceremony despite the historic nature of the legislation.

Objectives, Provisions, and Assessment

After more than four years of legislative work, what did the Goldwater–Nichols Act prescribe? Totaling eighty-five pages of legal text, it made thousands of changes to Title 10 of the United States Code, which governs the US Armed Forces. Although the act addressed both the DoD's administrative and operational dimensions, it prioritized fixing operational matters. The law's overall thrust sought to balance joint and service interests. In doing so, it pursued nine objectives.[61] Key among these objectives was to strengthen civilian authority. Although several provisions advanced this objective, one sentence in the report accompanying the bill left no doubt as to the secretary of defense's authority: "The secretary has sole and ultimate power within the Department of Defense on any matter on which the secretary chooses to act."[62]

A second objective sought to improve military advice. Some of the most far-reaching provisions of the Goldwater–Nichols Act addressed this objective. First, the JCS chairman was made the principal military adviser to the president, secretary of defense, and National Security Council. Second, the duties previously performed by the corporate JCS and new duties were assigned to the chairman. Third, the chairman was given a vice chairman to assist him or her. Last, the chairman was assigned full control over the Joint Staff, a role previously performed by all five JCS members.

The Goldwater–Nichols Act's third and fourth objectives addressed the unified commands. It sought to place clear responsibility on unified commanders for accomplishment of assigned missions and to ensure that the authority of unified commanders was commensurate with their responsibility. The act eliminated all confusion on the operational chain of command by mandating that it run from the president to the secretary of defense to the unified commander. The act also prescribed authority for unified commanders modeled on authority traditionally given to service unit commanders. It authorized each unified commander to give authoritative direction, prescribe the internal chain of command, organize his or her command and forces, employ forces, assign command functions to subordinate commanders, coordinate and approve aspects of administration and support, select and suspend subordinates, and convene courts-martial.

Four principal provisions sought to achieve the Goldwater–Nichols Act's objective of increasing attention to strategy formulation and contingency planning. First, it required the president to submit annually a report on national security strategy. Second, it required the JCS chairman to prepare fiscally constrained strategic plans, replacing the pie-in-the-sky, no-fiscal-constraints plans previously developed. Third, it instructed the secretary of defense to prepare policy guidance for the preparation and review of contingency plans. The fourth provision required civilian assistance to the secretary of defense in his review of contingency plans, a task that the secretary had previously performed alone.

To achieve the sixth objective of providing for more efficient use of resources, the Goldwater–Nichols Act assigned six resource-related duties to the JCS chairman. Importantly, the chairman was to advise the secretary of defense on the resource priorities of the unified commanders and assess whether program and budget submissions of defense components conformed to strategic plans and unified command priorities.

Improving management of joint officers was the Goldwater–Nichols Act's seventh objective. In Title IV, the Joint Officer Personnel Policy, the act established procedures for the selection, education, assignment, and promotion of joint officers. A key provision required service in a joint assignment prior to promotion to general or flag rank.

To enhance the effectiveness of military operations, the Goldwater–Nichols Act relied on the authority it had given to each unified commander to ensure unity of command in both peacetime and wartime. It also gave the JCS chairman the tasks of developing joint doctrine and joint training policies.

The act's ninth objective to improve DoD management sought to address numerous deficiencies, including excessive supervisory spans of control, unnecessary staff layers and duplication of effort, growth in headquarters staffs, poor supervision of defense agencies, and an unclear division of work among defense components.

As with all major transformations, not every objective has been fully achieved. Objectives on the operational side—joint advice, chain of command, authority of combatant commanders, joint officer policies, and effectiveness of military operations—have achieved much of what was hoped for. Strengthening civilian authority and improving attention to strategy formulation and contingency planning have seen important improvements. Key efforts on the administrative side—providing for more effective use of resources and improving DoD management—have been major disappointments. Nevertheless, the Goldwater–Nichols Act has profoundly improved DoD performance. In early 2013, Secretary of Defense Chuck Hagel agreed with this assessment: "The success of our Armed Forces since the enactment of the Goldwater–Nichols Act amply demonstrates that the Act has enhanced the ability of our Armed Forces to defend our nation and to operate successfully as joint forces under our combatant commanders."[63]

"Leadership is the key to 99 percent of all successful efforts," observed Erskine Bowles, businessman and White House chief of staff for the Clinton administration.[64] His statement clearly applies to the triumphant outcome of the defense reorganization struggle in the mid-1980s. Many leaders contributed to this historic, Congress-led process, including General David Jones, Congressman Bill Nichols, Bud McFarlane, and David Packard, to name a few. But Barry Goldwater and Sam Nunn stand at the front of this line. What was it about their leadership that made the impossible possible? It was their values and character. Those personal attributes attracted the commitment of others, inspired courage and sacrifice, and aroused great intensity and passion for this noble cause. Among impressive results, the Goldwater–Nichols Act's transformation of the DoD enabled the fielding of the most proficient joint warfighting force in the world. Repeated battlefield successes evidence this unmatched prowess. All of this would not have been achievable without the leadership provided by two giants of the US Senate: Barry Goldwater and Sam Nunn.

Notes

1. See, for example, Douglas C. Lovelace Jr., *Unification of the United States Armed Forces: Implementing the 1986 Department of Defense Reorganization Act* (Carlisle, PA: Strategic Studies Institute, 1996), iii.

2. William J. Perry, speech honoring Senator Sam Nunn, the Pentagon, July 12, 1996, 2, James R. Locher III Papers, Special Collections, National Defense University Library, Washington, DC.

3. William A. Owens, "'Jointness' Is His Job," *Government Executive,* April 1995, 61.

4. Franklin D. Roosevelt, press conference, July 23, 1937, Press Conferences of President Franklin D. Roosevelt, 1933–1945, Series 1, Folders 382–86, Franklin D. Roosevelt Presidential Library and Museum, Hyde Park, NY.

5. Tom W. Smith and Jaesok Son, *General Social Survey 2012 Final Report: Trends in Public Attitudes about Confidence in Institutions* (Chicago: University of Chicago Press, 2013), 2, 15.

6. Dwight D. Eisenhower, "Message to Congress," April 3, 1958, in *The Department of Defense: Documents on Establishment and Organization, 1949–1978,*

ed. Alice C. Cole, Alfred Goldberg, Samuel A. Tucker, and Rudolph A. Winnacker (Washington, DC: Office of the Secretary of Defense, 1978), 175.

7. Ibid., 177.

8. General David C. Jones, testimony, US House of Representatives, Committee on Armed Services, *Military Posture and H.R. 5968: Hearings before the Committee on Armed Services,* part 1: *Military Posture,* 97th Cong., 2nd sess., February 3, 1982, HASC no. 97-33, 337.

9. Quoted in James R. Locher III, *Victory on the Potomac: The Goldwater–Nichols Act Unifies the Pentagon* (College Station: Texas A&M University Press, 2002), 78.

10. Ibid., 112.

11. Paul R. Lawrence and Jay W. Lorsch, *Developing Organizations: Diagnosis and Action* (Reading, MA: Addison-Wesley, 1969), 10–11.

12. Locher, *Victory on the Potomac,* 113–15.

13. Barry M. Goldwater, with Jack Casserly, *Goldwater* (New York: Doubleday, 1988), 342.

14. Locher, *Victory on the Potomac,* 231.

15. Barry M. Goldwater, interviewed by the author, May 8, 1995, Scottsdale, Arizona.

16. Quoted in Bob Schieffer, "Sam Nunn's Legacy of Bipartisanship," *CBS News,* March 20, 2011.

17. Goldwater, *Goldwater,* 340.

18. Locher, *Victory on the Potomac,* 233.

19. 142, no. 141, Cong. Rec. S12299 (October 3, 1996).

20. Bart Barnes, "Barry Goldwater, GOP Hero, Dies," *Washington Post,* May 30, 1998.

21. James MacGregor Burns, *Leadership* (New York: Harper and Row, 1978), 170.

22. Goldwater, *Goldwater,* 49.

23. Steve Coll, "Sam Nunn, Insider from the Deep Southland; the Georgia Senator, Building Bridges and Forging a Power Base in the 'Club,'" *Washington Post,* February 18, 1986.

24. Goldwater, *Goldwater,* 27.

25. Coll, "Sam Nunn."

26. Sam Nunn, interviewed by the author, July 14, 1995, Washington, DC.

27. Goldwater, *Goldwater,* 342.

28. Richard Barrett, "Unleashing Human Potential for Performance and Profit," n.d., 1, at http://documents.routledge-interactive.s3.amazonaws.com/9780415815031/Unleashing_Human_Potential_Paper.pdf.

29. Burns, *Leadership,* 169.

30. Locher, *Victory on the Potomac,* 225.

31. US Senate, Committee on Armed Services, *Defense Organization: The Need for Change: Staff Report to the Committee on Armed Services,* 99th Cong., 1st sess., Committee Print, S. Prt. 99-86 (Washington, DC: US Government Printing Office, October 16, 1985), 2–3.

32. Ibid., 3.

33. Quoted in ibid., 173.

34. Both Jones and Schlesinger quoted in ibid., 5.

35. Prior to 1986, Title 10 of the United States Code limited the Joint Staff to four hundred members. OJCS was a larger umbrella organization of which the Joint Staff was a part.

36. US Senate, Committee on Armed Services, *Defense Organization,* 181.

37. Ibid., 6.

38. Samuel P. Huntington, "Defense Organization and Military Strategy," *Public Interest,* Spring 1984, 24.

39. US Senate, Committee on Armed Services, *Defense Organization,* 303.

40. Quoted in ibid., 494–95.

41. Ibid., 7.

42. Ibid., 417, 420.

43. Ibid., 427.

44. Ibid., 591.

45. Barry Goldwater and Sam Nunn to Caspar W. Weinberger, February 4, 1985, Official Files of the Senate Armed Services Committee, 98th Cong., Goldwater–Nichols Reorganization, Boxes 1902–49, National Archives and Records Administration, Center for Legislative Archives, Washington, DC.

46. Quoted in Locher, *Victory on the Potomac,* 318.

47. Ibid., 299.

48. Ibid., 319.

49. George C. Wilson, "Military Reform to Be Unveiled; Sens. Goldwater and Nunn to Direct Bipartisan Effort," *Washington Post,* October 15, 1985.

50. Quoted in ibid.

51. Bill Keller, "2 Key Senators Join in Assault on the Military," *New York Times,* October 6, 1985.

52. Locher, *Victory on the Potomac,* 343.

53. Goldwater interview, May 8, 1995.

54. The three staff members were James R. Locher III, Jeffrey H. Smith, and Richard D. Finn Jr.

55. Quoted in Locher, *Victory on the Potomac,* 357.

56. Ibid., 377.

57. Ibid., 407.

58. Senator Warner and Senator Levin speaking on the Department of Defense Reorganization Act of 1986, S. 2295, 99th Cong., 2d sess., 132, no. 60, Cong. Rec. S5481, S5500 (May 7, 1986).

59. Quoted in Locher, *Victory on the Potomac,* 410.

60. Senator Barry Goldwater, chairman, Committee on Armed Services, opening statement for the Conference Committee Meeting, August 13, 1986, Official Files of the Senate Armed Services Committee, 98th Cong., Goldwater–Nichols

Reorganization, Boxes 1902–49, Center for Legislative Archives, National Archives and Records Administration.

61. Goldwater–Nichols Department of Defense Reorganization Act of 1986, Pub. L. 99-433, sec. 3.

62. The report that accompanied the bill is *Goldwater–Nichols Department of Defense Act,* 99th Cong., 2nd sess., September 12, 1986, Report 99-824, quote on 101.

63. "Advance Policy Questions for the Honorable Chuck Hagel," pursuant to Hagel's nomination as secretary of defense in 2013, at http://www.armed-services.senate.gov/imo/media/doc/Hagel%2001-31-13.pdf.

64. Erskine Bowles, quoted in John F. Harris, "Chief of Staff Considers Governor's Race," *Washington Post,* August 13, 1998.

Part 2

The Soviet Union and Europe

5

Gorbachev, Perestroika, and the End of the Cold War

Archie Brown

Ronald Reagan's first term was not marked by foreign-policy successes. In particular, the Cold War got colder, and US relations with the Soviet Union were as fraught as they had been at any time since the Cuban Missile Crisis in 1962. Yet March 11, 1985, turned out to be a fortunate day for President Reagan—and for a great many other people, especially in eastern Europe. On that day, Mikhail Gorbachev, at fifty-four the youngest member of the Politburo, succeeded Konstantin Chernenko as general secretary of the Soviet Communist Party.

Reagan overlapped with as many as four Soviet leaders. Prior to Gorbachev, there had been Leonid Brezhnev, Yuri Andropov, and Konstantin Chernenko, but as Reagan complained, they "kept dying on me."[1] He met none of them while they were alive, and he did not attend their funerals. There was a joke that went the rounds in Moscow in 1984 shortly after Andropov's funeral and the choice of his ailing and wheezing successor, the seventy-two-year-old Chernenko. The story had Mrs. Thatcher phoning Reagan and saying, "You should have come for the funeral, Ron. They did it very well. I'm definitely coming back next year." And come back she did (although Reagan again stayed away) just thirteen months later, for Chernenko's burial and for the opportunity, which she seized, to renew her acquaintance with Gorbachev, whom she had welcomed to Britain three months earlier. At that time, December 1984, Gorbachev was number two in the Soviet hierarchy and the likeliest successor to Chernenko, although there could be many a slip between cup and lip in Soviet politics.

It is sometimes suggested that the Soviet leadership chose Gorbachev because he was seen as a "soft-liner" and because of the policies pursued by the Reagan administration.[2] There is not, however, a shred of evidence to support that contention. The formerly top-secret Soviet documents that became available to Western researchers in the post-Communist era show the Soviet reaction to the US military buildup in general and the Strategic Defense Initiative (SDI) in particular (as well as to Reagan's stepped-up anti-Soviet rhetoric) to have been the usual one: a commitment to tightening discipline domestically and to building yet more missiles. In March 1983, Reagan officially launched the SDI project; that same month the president referred to the Soviet Union as an "evil empire."[3] The transcripts of meetings of the Politburo—the highest policy-making body of the Communist Party—from that year show a hardening rather than a softening of Soviet resolve in the light of what the leaders collectively saw as a heightened threat from the United States. When at the end of May 1983 the Politburo addressed what it considered to be an enhanced threat emanating from the United States and its allies (especially the decision to deploy Pershing II and Cruise missiles), it came up with a four-pronged response: (1) to maintain to the full the Soviet Union's own armaments program; (2) to strive to improve relations with both China and Japan; (3) to convene a meeting of the leaderships of the Communist states of eastern Europe to establish a common line on foreign policy and to maintain a united front; and (4) to intensify both international and domestic propaganda against the Reagan administration's "anti-Soviet fabrications."[4]

Among the Politburo members, Gorbachev did not have any particular responsibility for foreign policy until after the death of Andropov in February 1984. Nevertheless, he shared his colleagues' extremely critical view of the Reagan administration's policies. To a greater extent than the others, however, he was sensitive to the dangers inherent in the Cold War, including the risk of nuclear war erupting by accident—through technical malfunction or miscalculation. Gorbachev accepted that neither side wanted nuclear war—to have done so would have carried irrationality to the point of madness—but the danger of it occurring by mischance was one he took very seriously.[5] That became all the more of a hazard at a time of heightened international tension, such as existed during the first Reagan administration. Gorbachev did not, however, air his private views in the Politburo or dissociate himself in any way from current Soviet foreign and defense policy until he had secured the highest office within the system. Had he done so, instead of rising to become the general secretary of the Central Committee of the Communist Party and hence the de facto leader of the Soviet Union, his rapid upward political mobility would have come to a shuddering halt.

What was seen in Moscow in 1983 as increasing belligerence from Washington raised more general concerns within the Committee for State Security (better known as the KGB) and the Soviet political and military establishment that the United States might even be contemplating a nuclear strike against the Soviet Union. A Western military exercise was actually altered to remove the possibility of its being seen as a cover or preparation for a real nuclear strike on Russia. Oleg Gordievski, the KGB officer who was a double agent working for the British secret service, MI6, conveyed to the West those genuine concerns in Moscow. The North Atlantic Treaty Organization (NATO) exercise Able Archer in November 1983 "simulated a crisis designed to lead to nuclear conflict," and it was intended to bring in senior Western ministers as active participants.[6] The British foreign secretary, Sir Geoffrey Howe, later noted: "Gordievski left us in no doubt of the extraordinary but genuine Russian fear of real-life nuclear strike. NATO deliberately changed some aspects of the exercise so as to leave the Soviets in no doubt that it was only an exercise. Gordievski's own reports to his nominal masters reinforced the message, and the crisis passed."[7] This was, though, a very dangerous state of affairs, for the United States and Europe no less than for the Soviet Union. If the Soviet leadership had become convinced that the United States was about to launch a nuclear attack on Russia, they would have been strongly tempted to get their own surprise attack in first. So both sides had an interest in reducing tension because a cold peace was vastly preferable to nuclear holocaust. But if it were true, as it surely was, that nobody during the Cold War was likely to be elected president of the United States if he were deemed to be soft in relation to the Soviet Union, it was even more true that no one could become *Soviet* leader through advocating a concessionary foreign policy or by saying anything that might be seen as undermining the Soviet military-industrial complex. So Gorbachev, speaking in the Politburo in the years before he became Soviet leader, said nothing that would lead his colleagues to believe that he was going to change Soviet foreign policy or to suspect that he could possibly be in any way a "soft-liner."

Indeed, the main speech proposing him as Soviet leader, both in the Politburo and at the Central Committee meeting that formally elected him as general secretary, was delivered by Andrei Gromyko, who had been Soviet foreign minister since 1957 and had been an increasingly important architect as well as implementer of Soviet foreign policy throughout that period. Gorbachev was subsequently to distance himself from this standard Soviet policy, but not until he had attained the most powerful post within the Soviet system. Gromyko enthusiastically extolled Gorbachev's attributes and qualifications for the top job in his speech commending him to the Central Committee. In the course of it, he stressed that Gorbachev "always defends the point of view that the holy of holies for us all is to struggle for peace and to maintain our defense at the necessary level."[8]

Of course, a reference to the "struggle for peace" was not in any sense a harbinger of the kind of the kind of foreign policy Gorbachev was to go on to pursue. Even at its most belligerent or when it was taking over the countries of eastern and central Europe just after the end of the Second World War, the Soviet Union was always rhetorically engaged in a "struggle for peace." Indeed, there was a Soviet joke in Brezhnev's time in which the question was asked of the mythical Radio Armenia: "Will there be a world war?" After a long pause, the answer came: "No. There will be no war. But there will be such a struggle for peace that not a single stone will be left standing."

Support for Gorbachev at the time of the leadership vacancy was of no avail in helping Gromyko to continue to wield great influence on the content and conduct of Soviet foreign policy. Gromyko was perfectly happy to be moved from the Foreign Ministry to the post of titular head of state—chairman of the Presidium of the Supreme Soviet. He had believed, however, that his successor as foreign minister would be one of his own protégés, thus facilitating continuity of policy and respect for his authority. Gorbachev instead surprised the entire Soviet establishment by appointing a neophyte in international affairs, Georgian Communist Party first secretary Eduard Shevardnadze, who went on to establish productive and even friendly working relations with his American counterparts—first George P. Shultz and subsequently James A. Baker III. The appointment of Shevardnadze was just one element, albeit an important part, in Gorbachev's replacement of the entire top tier of the Soviet foreign-policy-making elite within the first year of his general secretaryship. Although Gorbachev's recruitment in February 1986 of Anatoly Chernyaev to be his chief foreign-policy aide and adviser on international policy did not cause anything like the same stir as the nomination of Shevardnadze had done, it was also a crucial appointment. Occupying a more behind-the-scenes role, Chernyaev, who favored far-reaching change of Soviet foreign policy, became Gorbachev's principal speechwriter in that sphere and had ample opportunity to influence him.

Gorbachev and the Communist Party

As long ago as June 1979, six years before Gorbachev became Soviet leader, the person who was his closest friend, Zdeněk Mlynář, a leading Czech reformist Communist (who was expelled from the Communist Party of Czechoslovakia after the Soviet invasion put an end to the Prague Spring of 1968), described Gorbachev as "open-minded, intelligent, and anti-Stalinist."[9] Nobody else in the Soviet top leadership team, headed at that time by Brezhnev, could have been portrayed in those terms. Gorbachev was then the most junior member—a secretary of the Central Committee with responsibility for agriculture but not yet even a candidate member of the Politburo. Of the three characteristics Mlynář mentioned, nothing was more important than Gorbachev's *relatively open mind*—indeed, a *remarkably* open mind for someone who had risen to power through the Communist Party apparatus. That is really a key to understanding the Soviet perestroika *and* the transformation of Soviet foreign policy in the Gorbachev era.

There was a constituency for change within the Soviet Union at the time of Chernenko's death, but such change could have occurred in more than one direction. It was easy to agree that it was time to get the country moving again, for economic growth had been in long-term decline. But there were many different views on the kind of change that was needed. The Communist Party of the Soviet Union was both a vanguard party and a mass party. As a matter of policy, it had within its ranks about one in ten of the country's working population. A popular misconception in the West was that these party members, either as a result of conviction or brainwashing, were single-mindedly united. The Western mass media, looking for alternative views to those associated with Communist orthodoxy, directed their attention away from the ruling party and on to the small band of brave dissidents who were overt critics of Soviet domestic or foreign policy.

The Communist Party leadership itself promoted the image of unbreakable unity within its ranks, but the reality was very different. Behind the monolithic façade that the party attempted, with some success, to present to its own people and the outside world, it in fact contained people of the most diverse views: Russian nationalists, neo-Stalinists, social democrats, economic liberals, Marxist–Leninist dogmatists, political and social conservatives, and a great many careerists. Careful analysis would uncover the very different tendencies within the party even before the reforms of the Gorbachev era. To the extent that the divergent views got into Soviet publications (as distinct from being voiced in private conversation), they had to be couched in careful language that required some decoding. Yet even within the bureaucratic apparatus of the Central Committee of the Communist Party, different tendencies could be discerned. There were people who seriously wished to pursue vastly better relations with the West, but there were also Russian nationalists, Marxist–Leninist dogmatists, and Stalinists who were suspicious even of the limited détente of the 1970s and who favored a harder line both internally and externally.[10]

Within the hierarchical Communist system, where power was concentrated at the apex of the structure, the top leader's—that is, the general secretary's—beliefs, values, and leadership style could make a vast difference. Brezhnev, who led the Soviet Union for almost two decades, presided over an essentially conservative Communist regime. Domestic innovation was stifled, dissent severely repressed, and military expenditure was accorded a high priority as the leadership set great store on remaining one of the world's two superpowers. With Gorbachev's ascent to power, all of the diverse groupings and tendencies that had led a furtive and subdued life within the multimillion-member Communist Party were initially encouraged, for a broadening of the limits of discussion meant that they all could more openly articulate their particular viewpoints. The party leader's authority, however, was such that he was able to encourage and even empower particular groups and tendencies and put others on the defensive. It was soon the party intellectuals with some sympathy for social democracy and the liberals who could take most comfort from Gorbachev's policies and pronouncements in the domestic sphere. In foreign policy, those who were serious about seeking better East–West relations and reducing the influence of the military-industrial sector drew most encouragement from Gorbachev.

It is often remarked that much that happened during the period of less than seven years in which Gorbachev occupied the Kremlin was far removed from what he envisaged at the outset. That is unquestionably true. Some of what occurred, above all the dissolution of the Soviet state, was utterly remote from what he expected or wanted. His reforms had many unintended consequences. Nevertheless, to compare Gorbachev's opinions in 1985 with political outcomes five or six years later and to conclude that the dramatic change owed little to the general secretary would be extremely misleading. For the greater part of the perestroika era, Gorbachev was the most radical reformer within the Politburo as well as the most authoritative. He was often the initiator—and still more often the facilitator—of a host of enhanced freedoms that emerged in the Soviet Union in the second half of the 1980s. Gorbachev's thinking evolved during his time as Soviet leader, and he moved from being a reformer of the existing Soviet system to a *systemic transformer,* someone who was prepared to change the fundamentals of the political system at home and to transform Soviet foreign policy no less radically.[11]

Misunderstanding Gorbachev

One of the most egregious misunderstandings of Gorbachev was that he never really changed. That was the view of some of the leading figures in the Reagan administration, notably Defense Secretary Caspar W. Weinberger, although it was *not* the view of Secretary of State George Shultz, whose judgement, in the final analysis, President Reagan fortunately preferred to that of Weinberger. Nor was it the view of Jack Matlock, who was Reagan's best-informed adviser, initially as the Soviet expert on the National Security Council and subsequently as an unusually influential US ambassador to Moscow from 1987 to 1991.[12] In an interview for the Hoover Institution Oral History of the Cold War Project in October 1998, Weinberger said that Gorbachev's only contribution was to recognize that the Soviet Union "couldn't win a war," adding, "I don't think he ever changed his philosophy. He talked a lot about perestroika, glasnost, all of those things, but he never really changed."[13]

That is just about as misleading a remark about Gorbachev as it is possible to find, for it misses all the essential points. The respects in which Gorbachev did not change were that he remained highly intelligent, flexible, and, crucially, open-minded. But precisely because of that flexibility and open-mindedness, he changed his understanding even of those concepts he began with and used throughout his general secretaryship. Thus, the Russian word *perestroika,* which means "reconstruction," was initially a synonym for reform of the Soviet system, especially economic reform, at a time when the very word *reforma* was taboo, as it had been from early in the Brezhnev era. But under the umbrella of the rather neutral term *perestroika,* Gorbachev radicalized the political agenda, and perestroika came to stand for root-and-branch political reform amounting to a transformation of the political system.

Similarly, the Russian term *glasnost,* meaning "openness" or "transparency," began as advocacy of a somewhat more open dialogue between the Soviet party–state and its citizens, with more information given to the public, and over a very few years it developed into something almost synonymous with freedom of speech and publication. By the later 1980s, official Soviet publishing houses were printing in huge editions literary works that prior to the Gorbachev era would have landed their possessors subject to arrest if a single copy of the book or article, whether in a printed edition published abroad or in *samizdat* typescript (underground dissident publication), were found in their possession. Spectacular examples included the publication of George Orwell's novels *Animal Farm* (1945) and *Nineteen Eighty-Four* (1949) and the works of Alexander Solzhenitsyn, among them *The Gulag Archipelago,* published abroad in 1973 to the outrage of the Soviet authorities but not in the Soviet Union until 1989. Its appearance in the West in 1973 had led to Solzhenitsyn being denounced as a traitor, subsequently deprived of his Soviet citizenship, and then forcibly expelled from his beloved Russia. In the second half of the 1980s, the publication of works in Moscow that called into question the very foundations of the Soviet system should have made clear to any alert observer that something quite remarkable was taking place.

Yet there were those in the West who were so steeped in Cold War assumptions that they did not recognize that from 1987 on a serious domestic liberalization, accompanied by far-reaching foreign-policy change, was under way. Robert Gates, who was both deputy director of the US Central Intelligence Agency and a Soviet specialist, continued to argue, after the evidence to the contrary was becoming increasingly apparent, that "Gorbachev still had the same goals as his predecessors."[14] Jack Matlock, reporting this argument, notes the friction it caused with the State Department and observes: "Shultz did not conceal his anger at what he considered Bob Gates's stubborn refusal to see the changes in Soviet policy. He feared that Reagan would be swayed by the pessimistic intelligence analysis. He need not have worried. Reagan, like Shultz, would base his judgment on his interactions with Gorbachev and Shevardnadze."[15]

Did Reagan's Hard Line Force Soviet Surrender?

There are two very popular arguments as to why Gorbachev embarked on far-reaching reform that are at best profound oversimplifications or at worst flatly wrong. The first such contention is that the military balance of power had so turned against the Soviet Union as a result of the Reagan administration's policies that the Soviet leadership had no option but to liberalize and to seek accommodation with the United States. The second is that the Soviet economy was in such dire straits that the regime had no alternative but to turn to reform.

The facts are that the East–West imbalance was much more to the advantage of the West in earlier postwar decades than it was by the time Gorbachev entered the Kremlin. Western countries in general and the United States in particular were far stronger militarily vis-à-vis the Soviet Union in the 1940s, 1950s, and the 1960s than they were by the 1980s, the Soviet Union having achieved a rough military parity with the United States from the early 1970s on. Those earlier decades were, however, a time of Communist expansion—certainly not years in which the Soviet Union was calling a halt to the Cold War because it lagged behind the United States militarily. If you have the military power to wipe your potential adversary off the face of the earth, the fact that this adversary may have more sophisticated technology is not necessarily going to be decisive.

Even Ronald Reagan, a great optimist about SDI, later repeated in his memoirs something he had written in his diary on March 23, 1983: that the defensive weapons he believed would make nuclear missiles obsolete might take at least twenty years to develop.[16] Historically, when the Soviet Union felt threatened by a hardening of the Western line, encompassing substantially increased military expenditure, this perception strengthened the hardest-liners within the Soviet Union and led to correspondingly stepped-up military preparations there. That, indeed, is what happened during the first Reagan administration and when Gorbachev's three immediate predecessors overlapped with Reagan. Quite specifically, it was what happened in 1983 in response to SDI and the policies of Reagan's first term. Writing of the reaction in Moscow in the first half of the 1980s to the policies emanating from Washington, Anatoly Dobrynin, the long-serving Soviet ambassador to the United States (who, under Gorbachev's leadership, became for a time the head of the International Department of the Communist Party's Central Committee), noted in his memoirs: "The impact of Reagan's hard-line policy on the internal debates in the Kremlin and on the evolution of the Soviet leadership was exactly the opposite from the one intended by Washington. It strengthened those in the Politburo, the Central Committee, and the security apparatus who had been pressing for a mirror-image of Reagan's own policy. Ronald Reagan managed to create a solid front of hostility among our leaders. Nobody trusted him. Any of his proposals almost automatically were considered with suspicion. This unique situation in our relations threatened dangerous consequences."[17] Yet, all that notwithstanding, Reagan was in a number of respects to become a good partner for Gorbachev. An important plus in this relationship was the strength of Reagan's standing in Washington. He had convincingly won a second term in the White House, and his fervent anti-Communist credentials, dating back to his Hollywood days, afforded him political protection. Those factors, together with the policies he had pursued and the rhetoric he had deployed since becoming president, meant it was difficult to make stick any accusations that he had become soft on the Soviet Union. There was no lack, however, of prominent American critics of the Intermediate-Range Nuclear Forces (INF) Treaty, which would remove Soviet and American intermediate-range nuclear weapons from Europe, when Reagan and Gorbachev were about to sign it in December 1987. Former secretaries of state Henry Kissinger and Alexander Haig were among those who criticized the treaty, as did Senator Bob Dole (KS), the Republican leader in the Senate.[18] Yet the zero option had been a long-standing Reagan policy, which the Soviet leadership had dismissed out of hand when the American president proposed it early in his first term. As Jack Matlock observes, "It was a striking irony that many of the persons objecting to the INF Treaty had been original supporters of the zero option. Apparently, in their eyes, the zero option was useful only so long as the Soviet Union rejected it."[19]

American and European public opinion had, however, welcomed the improvement in East–West relations and held Gorbachev in high esteem. In a major British television opinion poll in 1989, he emerged as "statesman of the decade" and winner of the Hope for the Future Award. At the end of that same year, he was *Time* magazine's "man of the decade."[20] In 1990, he was awarded the Nobel Peace Prize. None of this adulation was to prevent Gorbachev's domestic standing from deteriorating rapidly in 1990–1991. Even in 1987, Gorbachev also faced domestic criticism for the concessions made in the lead-up to the signing of the INF Treaty, although that criticism was more muted and behind the scenes in the Soviet Union at that time than was the disapproval of Reagan in Washington and much less hostile than Gorbachev's opponents were to become in the last two years of his leadership. In 1987–1988, Reagan and Gorbachev had no difficulty in facing down their domestic critics. At that time, the traditional deference accorded the party leader in the Soviet Union still worked in Gorbachev's favor. An American president, however, who had in the past taken a less tough line on the Soviet Union than Reagan had might have felt more obliged to concede ground to influential Washington critics. Reagan, as Jack Matlock and George Shultz have stressed, wanted to negotiate from strength, but he *did wish to negotiate* with the Soviet leadership, if only he could find a partner with whom it were possible to "do business," in Margaret Thatcher's words.[21] He found such a person in Gorbachev, a general secretary like no other in Soviet history.

This Soviet leader who took office in March 1985 had a different mindset from Brezhnev, Andropov, and Chernenko, and he shared Reagan's detestation of nuclear weapons. Gorbachev's concern about the nuclear threat was intensified by the accident at Chernobyl in 1986, when human error at one nuclear power station caused widespread radioactive contamination. If an accident at a power station could cause such devastation—and the damage done by the Chernobyl accident was the equivalent of the explosive power of just a single nuclear warhead—the consequences of nuclear war did not bear thinking about.[22] Both Gorbachev and Reagan were sincere in their desire to outlaw nuclear weapons. They had different ideas on how to go about this, but it was probably the most important policy objective they held in common, even though it was an aspiration that many in their own administrations did not believe to be realistic.

Was Perestroika Economically Determined?

The other frequently advanced but incorrect explanation for the change in the Soviet Union after 1985, touched on earlier in this essay, is the idea that relative economic decline *forced* the launch of perestroika. Of course, Gorbachev was concerned and was far from alone in the Soviet Union in being concerned about the country's technological backwardness in many areas and about the long-term slowdown in the rate of economic growth. That slowdown was one of the stimuli to policy innovation, but it did not imply the kind of political reform or change of foreign policy that Gorbachev went on to embrace. Indeed, the economic determinist argument that sees perestroika as an inevitable consequence of the failures of the planned economy falls at the first hurdle. It does not explain why Gorbachev gave priority to political over economic reform. It is at odds with his hesitation to move beyond cautious and rather minor concessions to the market and unwillingness to embrace a more fully fledged market economy.

There were, of course, strong institutional opponents of any such movement in the Soviet Union, and to take on that resistance would have been chancy. But Gorbachev took greater risks in removing many of the traditional levers of power held by Communist Party officials and in curtailing the prerogatives of the office of general secretary by introducing contested elections for a legislature with real power. Chinese Communist leaders have been very fearful of and highly resistant to that kind of *political* reform, but they have introduced the type of marketizing *economic* reform that Gorbachev might have been expected to attempt to implement if the economy had occupied the highest position on his agenda. In fact, he confessed in an article published twenty-five years after the launch of perestroika that "in the heat of political battles we lost sight of the economy, and people never forgave us for the shortages of everyday items and the lines for essential goods."[23]

Gorbachev's top priorities were political reform at home and an end to the Cold War. The two policies went hand in hand, for as the Soviet system became freer by the month, this change vastly improved the atmosphere in which meetings with Western leaders took place, and domestic political reform was, of course, accompanied by "new thinking" on Soviet foreign and defense policy. Among the new liberties were the development of freedom of speech and increasingly of publication; freedom of religious observation and the end of the persecution of churches; freedom of communication across frontiers, including freedom to travel and an end to the jamming of foreign broadcasts; and ideological freedom (with Marxism–Leninism dethroned from its position as the one indisputable body of doctrine and replaced by a commitment to pluralism and free intellectual inquiry). The new freedoms facilitated the development of civil society, so that although perestroika began as a revolution from above, the new toleration and novel liberties within a very few years generated strong and diverse pressures from below.

In foreign policy, the most fundamental change that Gorbachev made was encapsulated in his declaration that the people of every country had the right to decide for themselves what kind of political and economic system they wished to live in. He made that statement at the Nineteenth Conference of the Communist Party in June 1988.[24] It received rather more attention in the outside world when he repeated it in his speech to the United Nations in New York in December of the same year.[25] Even then, the "freedom of choice" part of the speech received less attention than the "hard news" of Soviet troop withdrawals from eastern Europe, as Gorbachev's English-language interpreter, Pavel Palazchenko, noted in his memoirs.[26]

Yet it is possible to see everything that happened in 1989, with the peoples of eastern and central Europe casting aside their Communist rulers and achieving independence from Soviet tutelage, as a consequence of their taking Gorbachev at his word. And what is important in that context is that he did keep his word. Naturally, he would have preferred to see radically reformed eastern European countries maintain a warm relationship with a reformed Soviet Union, but this was not what happened. However, not a shot was fired by a Soviet soldier as European Communist rulers were ousted, not even in the especially sensitive case of East Germany during the massive demonstrations of 1989 or when German unification was peacefully negotiated and achieved in 1990.

Of all Soviet leaders, Gorbachev was the most skeptical of military solutions to political problems. In that context, he had wanted from the outset of his leadership to get Soviet troops out of Afghanistan, but he encountered the problem that other leaders, including American and British, have faced after essentially failed foreign interventions: how to explain to their own people, especially the mothers and fathers of soldiers who died in these wars, that the sacrifices they made were largely in vain. Nevertheless, by 1987 a firm decision to withdraw all Soviet troops from Afghanistan by February 1989 was taken, and that deadline was met.

Underpinning Soviet foreign policy of the perestroika years was a fundamental reevaluation of world politics, which Gorbachev encouraged and embraced. He rejected the notion of East–West relations as a zero-sum game and moved far beyond the old Soviet attachment to "peaceful coexistence" and the ideological struggle Soviet leaders insisted was part and parcel of it. Gorbachev instead endorsed the idea that there were universal values and universal interests. In doing so, he had already by 1988, with Reagan still in the White House and by now more of a partner rather than an adversary, removed the ideological justifications for the Cold War. In 1989, when Gorbachev's actions and nonactions corresponded with his words, the Cold War ended on the ground.

Notes

1. Quoted in Lou Cannon, *President Reagan: The Role of a Lifetime* (New York: PublicAffairs, 2000), 258.

2. See, for example, Richard Pipes, "Misinterpreting the Cold War: The Hardliners Had It Right," *Foreign Affairs* 74, no. 1 (1995): 154–60.

3. Ronald Reagan, remarks at the Annual Convention of the National Association of Evangelicals in Orlando, Florida, March 8, 1983, at http://www.reagan.utexas.edu/archives/speeches/1983/30883b.htm.

4. "Zasedanie Politbyuro TsK KPSS, 31 maya 1983 goda," Fond 89, Reel 1.1003, Opis 42, File 53, Hoover Institution Archives, Palo Alto, CA.

5. Mikhail Gorbachev, *Ponyat' perestroyku . . . pochemu eto vazhno seychas* (Moscow: Al'pina, 2006), 29.

6. Geoffrey Howe, *Conflict of Loyalty* (London: Macmillan, 1994), 350.

7. Ibid.

8. *Materialy vneocherednogo plenuma tsentral'nogo komiteta KPSS 11 marta 1985 goda* (Moscow: Politizdat, 1985), 8.

9. In private conversation with the author, June 1979. See Archie Brown, intro-

duction to a dialogue between Gorbachev and Mlynář in which they reflect on their experience and the evolution of their beliefs, in Mikhail Gorbachev and Zdenek Mlynář, *Conversations with Gorbachev: On Perestroika, the Prague Spring, and the Crossroads of Socialism,* trans. George Shiver (New York: Columbia University Press, 2002), vii–xxiii.

10. For Western analyses of the variety of views within the Soviet Communist Party in the post-Stalin but pre-perestroika period, see, for example, Archie Brown, "Political Power and the Soviet State," in *The State in Socialist Society,* ed. Neil Harding (London: Macmillan, 1984), 51–103, and Brown, *Seven Years That Changed the World: Perestroika in Perspective* (Oxford: Oxford University Press, 2007), 157–89; Yitzhak Brudny, *Reinventing Russia: Russian Nationalism and the Soviet State, 1953–1991* (Cambridge, MA: Harvard University Press, 1998); Jeffrey T. Checkel, *Ideas and International Political Change: Soviet/Russian Behavior and the End of the Cold War* (New Haven, CT: Yale University Press, 1997); Robert D. English, *Russia and the Idea of the West: Gorbachev, Intellectuals, and the End of the Cold War* (New York: Columbia University Press, 2000); Matthew Evangelista, *Unarmed Forces: The Transnational Movement to End the Cold War* (Ithaca, NY: Cornell University Press, 1999); Ronald J. Hill, *Soviet Politics, Political Science, and Reform* (White Plains, NY: Wiley, 1980); Neil Malcolm, *Soviet Political Scientists and American Politics* (London: Macmillan, 1984); and Julie M. Newton, *Russia, France, and the Idea of Europe* (London: Palgrave Macmillan, 2003). For an early and remarkably broad-ranging account of the hitherto taboo views and analyses of Soviet society (to be found within the Communist Party itself) that began to be expressed openly in large-circulation publications in the perestroika era, see Alec Nove, *Glasnost in Action: Cultural Renaissance in Russia* (Boston: Unwin Hyman, 1989). On foreign-policy disagreements within the Soviet Union and on the importance of both ideational innovation and leadership change to bringing an end to the Cold War, see Richard K. Herrmann and Richard Ned Lebow, eds., *Ending the Cold War: Interpretations, Causation, and the Study of International Relations* (New York: Palgrave Macmillan, 2004).

11. Archie Brown, "Did Gorbachev as General Secretary Become a Social Democrat?" *Europe–Asia Studies* 65, no. 2 (2013): 198–220; Anatoly Chernyaev, *My Six Years with Gorbachev,* trans. and ed. Robert English and Elizabeth Tucker (University Park: Pennsylvania State University Press, 2000); and Andrei Grachev, *Gorbachev's Gamble: Soviet Foreign Policy and the End of the Cold War* (Cambridge: Polity Press, 2008).

12. See George P. Shultz, *Turmoil and Triumph: My Years as Secretary of State* (New York: Scribner's, 1993); Jack F. Matlock Jr., *Autopsy on an Empire: The American Ambassador's Account of the Collapse of the Soviet Union* (New York: Random House, 1995), and *Reagan and Gorbachev: How the Cold War Ended* (New York: Random House, 2004).

13. Caspar Weinberger, interview, October 20, 1998, transcript, 7, Hoover Institution Oral History of the Cold War Project, Hoover Institution Archives.

14. Matlock, *Reagan and Gorbachev,* 269.

15. Ibid., 270.

16. Ronald Reagan, *An American Life: The Autobiography* (New York: Simon and Schuster, 1990), 571. In his diary entry for March 23, 1983, Reagan observed of the televised address he had made earlier that evening, "I did the bulk of the speech on why our arms build up was necessary & then finished with a call to the Science community to join me in research starting now to develop a defensive weapon that would render nuclear missiles obsolete. I made no optimistic forecasts—said it might take 20 yrs. or more but we had to do it. I felt good" (in Ronald Reagan, *The Reagan Diaries,* vol. 1: *January 1981–October 1985,* unabridged ed., ed. Douglas Brinkley [New York: HarperCollins, 2009], 209).

17. Anatoly Dobrynin, *In Confidence: Moscow's Ambassador to America's Six Cold War Presidents (1962–1986)* (New York: Random House, 1995), 482.

18. Matlock, *Reagan and Gorbachev,* 275.

19. Ibid.

20. Mark Sandle, *Gorbachev: Man of the Twentieth Century?* (London: Hodder Education, 2008), 122.

21. After her first meeting with Mikhail Gorbachev three months *before* he became general secretary of the Soviet Communist Party, Margaret Thatcher told BBC political editor John Cole: "I like Mr Gorbachev. We can do business together" (Margaret Thatcher, interview for BBC, December 17, 1984, at http://www.margaretthatcher.org/speeches/displaydocument.asp?docid=105592).

22. Shultz, *Turmoil and Triumph,* 724.

23. Mikhail Gorbachev, "Perestroika Lost," *New York Times,* March 14, 2010.

24. Mikhail Gorbachev, "O khode realizatsii resheniy XXVII s"ezda KPSS v zadachakh po uglubleniyu perestroyki: Doklad na XIX Vsesoyuznoy konferentsii KPSS 28 iyunya 1988 goda," in *Izbrannye rechi i stat'i,* vol. 6 (Moscow: Politizdat, 1989), 347.

25. Mikhail Gorbachev, "Vystuplenie v organizatsii Ob'edinennykh natsii," in *Izbrannye rechi i stat'i,* vol. 7 (Moscow: Politizdat, 1990), 189.

26. Pavel Palazchenko, *My Years with Gorbachev and Shevardnadze: The Memoir of a Soviet Interpreter* (University Park: Pennsylvania State University Press, 1997), 370. Palazchenko cites remarks in support of this observation made by George Shultz at a Princeton conference in 1993.

6

For Better and for Worse

Ronald Reagan's Relationship with Margaret Thatcher, 1981–1983

James Cooper

Margaret Thatcher and Ronald Reagan were elected to office as prime minister of the United Kingdom and president of the United States in 1979 and 1980, respectively. Their electoral successes can be attributed to the economic problems and the international instability of the 1970s. With the collapse of détente and increasing Cold War tension, Reagan and Thatcher saw an overlapping of their international interests. Furthermore, both pledged to reverse their respective countries' economic decline through a combination of incentive-based, monetarist, and free-market solutions.[1] Before gaining power, Reagan and Thatcher met twice, in London in 1975 and 1978. Unfortunately, no record of these meetings is available. Of that first meeting, Reagan recalled in his memoirs: "I'd planned on spending only a few minutes with Margaret Thatcher but we ended up talking for almost two hours. . . . [W]e were soul mates when it came to reducing governments and expanding economic freedom."[2]

For their proponents, Reagan and Thatcher reduced the excesses of government intervention that had problematized their respective economies since the 1930s response to the Great Depression and to action taken during and following the Second World War. Supporters also celebrate the relationship between two cold warriors that brought the "evil empire" to the negotiating table and did the necessary business with Mikhail Gorbachev to win the Cold War. Indeed, Thatcher's enthusiasm for Mikhail Gorbachev as a man whom she could "do business with" should he lead the Soviet Union underlined Reagan's similar optimism about him.[3] All of this was concurrent to saving the Falklands from Argentinian aggression and standing up to terrorism. Those less disposed to the Reagan–Thatcher partnership claim that they were effectively in cahoots, leading the New Right as they widened the gulf between rich and poor, busted the labor unions, and were prepared to risk destroying the world in a nuclear war in order to save it from the menace of global communism. For instance, Thatcher's enthusiastic agreement to US deployment of cruise missiles on British military bases prompted a significant revival in the Campaign for Nuclear Disarmament in the United Kingdom. Yet she did not abandon the United States. Thatcher was determined that Britain should play a leading role in the North Atlantic Treaty Organization (NATO) and welcomed the opportunity to challenge the campaign's claims. Amid these contrasting and partisan views, Reagan and Thatcher were clear in their mutual admiration. In the *National Review* in 1988, Reagan argued that "the British spirit of enterprise, which had transformed the world in Queen Victoria's day, seemed to have been put to sleep. . . . Margaret Thatcher changed all that."[4] That same year the president wrote in his diary: "She really is a great stateswoman."[5] Writing in her memoirs in 1993, Thatcher observed: "Ronald Reagan's election was of immediate and fundamental importance, because it demonstrated that the United States, the greatest force for liberty that the world has ever known, was about to reassert a self-confidant leadership in world affairs. . . . I regarded it as my duty to do everything I could to reinforce and further President Reagan's bold strategy to win the Cold War which the West had been slowly but surely losing."[6]

Any study of the relationship between Reagan and Thatcher must be contextualized by the notion of the Anglo-American "special relationship." There is much historiographical debate as to the extent that Anglo-American relations can be viewed as "special." This characterization is based on the defining features of the relationship: common values, a shared history, personal connections, and overlapping national interests.[7] The "special relationship" between Reagan and Thatcher as well as their apparent commonality in domestic and foreign policies have been feted in works of higher journalism.[8] However, this consensus is increas-

Prime Minister Margaret Thatcher and President Ronald Reagan at the White House, February 26, 1981. Self-interest shaped the Anglo-American "special relationship" during the Reagan years. (Courtesy of the Ronald Reagan Presidential Library)

ingly the focus of historians who are challenging the previously held consensus of a transatlantic, New Right mutual-appreciation society in the 1980s.[9] This essay explores the political and pragmatic nature of the "special relationship," with a particular focus on Reagan's first three years as president—the period for which a significant number of documents are now available.[10] It identifies the extent to which Reagan and Thatcher's relationship represents the triumph of a philosophical bond and common cultural connections or, in contrast, simply an interest-led association that also offered mutual utility and political cover for a New Right agenda at home and cold warrior foreign policies. Three case studies provide the means to answer this question. The first focuses on Thatcher's initial meeting with Reagan shortly after the beginning of his presidency. The second and third focus on national security issues, namely the Falklands War of 1982 and the American intervention in Grenada in 1983.

February 1981

The first meeting between Reagan and Thatcher as world leaders in February 1981 was ostensibly about demonstrating a commonality in domestic policy and closeness in foreign policy. On the surface, Thatcher's official visit to the United States, February 25 to 28, was an exercise in reaffirming the "special relationship." Moreover, it was also an opportunity for two conservative leaders to show a united front, which would afford them political cover as they wrestled with economic problems at home and communism abroad. However, behind that unity was a much more complicated picture, representing independent political motivations and wrapped up in the high politics of Anglo-American relations.[11] Indeed, the first telephone discussion between President Reagan and Prime Minister Thatcher, on the occasion of Reagan's first inauguration, foreshadowed the politics of this meeting:

> PR: Nancy and I are specially looking forward to welcoming you to Washington next month. . . . I look forward to talking to you on international issues as well, as well as the economic problems we face.
>
> PM: The newspapers are saying mostly that President Reagan must avoid Mrs Thatcher's mistakes so I must brief you on the mistakes.

PR: I don't think I have to worry about that. I have just been watching and I know you have got such an uphill battle there but my goodness you've been staying there in the front line without rest or recreation.

PM: Well you know it makes it worth it when you are fighting for things we are fighting for[;] then we have to give everything we've got.

PR: We will lend strength to each other.

PM: We will.[12]

Despite Reagan's solidarity with Thatcher, the prime minister's economic policy received a great deal of public criticism from members of the Reagan administration and in the American press. Nevertheless, Thatcher expected that the president would wish to ensure a cohesive foreign- and defense-policy agenda.[13] The British government believed that the new administration would view the prime minister as "an ally whom they much respect and with whose Government they feel they have much in common."[14] Given a shared cold warrior philosophy, which Thatcher herself was keen to encourage, and a recession at home, Thatcher sought to strengthen Reagan's apparent favorable opinion of her economic agenda.[15]

The Reagan administration was concerned by the performance of the British economy. The reasons for this concern were twofold. First, just when the administration was advocating the case for its economic package to Congress, in particular the parallel reductions in taxation and spending, it was determined to ensure that Reaganism would not be likened to Thatcherism, which was widely viewed to be the cause of Britain's economic struggles. In late February 1981, Martin Anderson, an economic adviser, circulated a memorandum to senior White House staff that offered "a brief description between [*sic*] the economic program implemented in England by Prime Minister Thatcher and the economic program proposed by President Reagan." The briefing admitted that the Conservative Party entered office in 1979 "with much the same rhetoric that surrounds the Reagan Administration's economic program" but emphasized that "the substance of these programs has been very different."[16] Alexander Haig, the US secretary of state (1981–1982), briefed Reagan that he should expect Thatcher to discuss the British economy.[17] However, the second reason, in contrast to Anderson's overtly political concern, is represented by Haig's interest in Thatcherism, which was based on a belief that Thatcher's economic fortunes—and, accordingly, her political future—were vital to US national security. Haig informed the president that the United States "benefited from Mrs. Thatcher's pro-American, anti-Soviet instincts. She believes in a politically active, outward-looking Britain. Her cooperation is limited, however, by a deteriorating economic situation." Therefore, Haig warned, American interests would be undermined if Thatcher were unable to reverse Britain's economic fortunes: "Mrs. Thatcher's political future may be tied to the economy. Elections must be held by Spring 1984. The Labor [*sic*] opposition is embroiled in a left-right struggle over party policies and leadership. The policies being expounded by the left, which is ascendant, would seriously detract from the UK's role in NATO."[18]

Haig's concern for the administration's relationship with Thatcher was therefore based on promoting US interests. Thus, for Haig, the Reagan–Thatcher relationship was functionalist: interests, not sentiment, were driving his foreign-policy advice to the president. The administration's doubts about Thatcher's economic program followed other longstanding concerns within Republican circles about Britain's economic performance generally and as a consequence about its reliability as an ally to the United States. For instance, in January 1975 Henry Kissinger, the secretary of state (1973–1977), had told President Gerald Ford that "Britain is a tragedy—it has sunk to begging, borrowing, stealing until North Sea oil comes in."[19]

In addition to the connection between the British economy and the fate of the "special relationship," political cover was the focus of Thatcher's visit. For instance, Philip Geyelin, writing in the *Washington Post,* argued that the president needed "Thatcher's reinforcement for his economic designs" and "enthusiasm for the . . . tough line on the global Soviet threat." Geyelin added that Thatcher would benefit "from Reagan's endorsement of her profoundly unpopular economic policies."[20] Thatcher's arrival at the White House was marked by a degree of flourish and pomp to suggest that the two leaders would provide the political cover that each craved. On February 26, after referring to their previous meetings in 1975 and 1978, Reagan promoted a common agenda for their time in office: "You have said that we enter into a decade fraught with danger, and so we have. . . . Britain and America will stand side by side."[21]

In response, the prime minister confidently declared: "Mr. President, the natural bond of interest between our two countries is strengthened by the common approach which you and I have to our national problems. . . . We're both trying to set free the energies of our people."[22] Even as Thatcher arrived at the White House and talked with the president, however, her economic program was criticized a short walk away on Capitol Hill. Donald T. Regan, the treasury secretary (1981–1985), was vehement in his criticism of Thatcherism. In his testimony to a congressional committee, Regan sought to distance the Reagan administration's economic package from Thatcherism.[23] The White House worsened the situation by distributing Anderson's memorandum and holding an explanatory briefing during which Murray Weidenbaum, the new chairman of the Council of Economic Advisers, reinforced Regan's observations.[24] Compounding administration concerns for the British economy in general were clearly doubts about Thatcher's ability to implement the correct—and necessary—formula for reform. Therefore, just as Thatcher was trying to establish a close relationship with the president and promote a commonality in their domestic agendas, members of the Reagan administration were distancing his policies from those of his guest and undermining the Thatcher government in the process—regardless of Haig's concerns as to what a weakened Thatcher government would mean for US interests.

Despite the embarrassment caused by his own administration, Reagan's personal warmth toward Thatcher helped ensure that she was able to claim that the visit had been successful. James Brady, the White House press secretary, told American reporters: "It was difficult to pry them away from each other at the end."[25] On returning to Britain, Thatcher reported to Parliament: "The reception given to us in Washington was warm and generous, testifying to the health of the Anglo-American relationship and also to the excellent understanding that President Reagan and I had established even before either of us assumed our present responsibilities."[26]

Yet Thatcher's opponents did not ignore her difficulties. For instance, taking full advantage of his political position, Michael Foot, the Labour Party leader and leader of the opposition (1980–1983), responded to the prime minister's statement in Parliament by arguing, "In the United States the prime minister gave several homilies on our domestic affairs, but does she appreciate that the most friendly advice that she could have given to the United States was not to follow her example?"[27] Likewise, despite Reagan's public confidence in Thatcher, Britain's economic difficulties meant that his administration was concerned for the prime minister's political future. In July 1981, Richard V. Allen, the national security adviser at the time (1981–1982), informed Reagan that there was "troubling political, social and economic drift" in Britain and that Thatcher had "lost her grip on the political rudder." There was much concern as to what the situation would mean for US interests: as Allen cautioned, the Labour Party "could prove harmful to our security interests even if [it were] reduced to a splinter group." He argued: "With no British leader seeming to have a clear idea of where or how to go, some political turbulence is likely, with adverse effect on the country's reliability as a U.S. ally."[28] The apparent early lessons of Thatcherism continued to haunt Reagan's economic agenda as well. Alan H. Meltzer, writing in the *New York Times* in August 1981, reported that Reagan's opponents warned: "Reaganomics will produce Thatcheritis."[29]

The meeting between Reagan and Thatcher in February 1981 demonstrated that domestic interests trumped sentimental objectives and statements about the "special relationship." Thatcher sought to use the visit as political cover for difficult economic circumstances in Britain by claiming that Reagan's election and agenda essentially endorsed her own. In contrast, despite Reagan's generous public statements, his administration was concerned by how—and, crucially, for how long—Thatcher would be able to support US interests abroad. Similarly, that her government's economic policy was failing ensured that the Reagan administration disputed any commonality between Thatcher's economic program and Reagan's proposed cuts to tax and spending because the comparison threatened his domestic ambitions. One caveat to heed here is that the US and British economies were different and defined by their own institutional, financial, and political arrangements.[30] However, it is clear that behind the celebrated "special relationship," politics and self-interest were at play.

The Falklands, 1982

The outbreak of the Falklands/Malvinas War on April 2, 1982, saw the Reagan administration keen to see an end to the conflict as soon as possible given that it was a war between a regional ally and a global ally. Reagan commented in his diary on April 6: "Fairly quiet day except in the

So. Atlantic. The Royal Navy is sailing toward to the Falklands Islands to oust Argentina. Both sides want our help. I'm leaving Al Haig home from Barbados to cope with it. We have to find some way to get them to back off."[31] The Falklands War divided the Reagan administration. Some officials, such as Jean Kirkpatrick, the US ambassador to the United Nations (1981–1985), were anxious that the US government should not break ranks with the anti-Communist regime in Argentina. Reagan had dispatched Haig, determined to broker a peaceful outcome, to London and Buenos Aires in an unsuccessful attempt to secure a negotiated settlement. At the same time, however, Secretary of Defense Caspar W. Weinberger (1981–1987) helped ensure that the British received copies of US intelligence reports on the situation. Furthermore, the British were afforded access to the American base on Ascension Island, a British territory.[32] In his diary, Nicholas Henderson, the British ambassador to the United States (1979–1982), noted that Haig wanted the British to allow "the Argentinians to find a way out, short of total humiliation." For Henderson, Haig's stance was the result of American public and government opinion: "Given the post-Vietnam sentiment in the USA, their dislike of colonialism and their wish to get on good terms with Latin America, we had been very lucky that they came down on our side."[33] The division of opinion within the Reagan administration suggests internal argument as to which ally best represented US interests and should therefore be prioritized: Argentina was a non-Communist country in what the administration considered a potentially troublesome region, whereas Thatcher was a reliable US global ally in the Cold War, which was a key consideration due to Britain's role in NATO and in the deployment of Pershing and Cruise missiles.

In 1982, the Falkland Islands—or at least two of the inhabited islands out of the total 780—were home to 1,800 people. The islands were four hundred miles away from Argentina, which had claimed sovereignty since the nineteenth century, and eight thousand miles from Britain. Given the islands' lack of obvious economic and strategic advantages, successive British governments had quietly attempted to discuss sovereignty over the Falklands with Argentina, much to the islanders' chagrin and opposition. Needing a quick upsurge in popular support to remain in power, General Leopoldo Galtieria, around four months into his leadership of the military junta that had ruled Argentina since 1976, ordered the invasion of East Falklands on April 2, 1982. The junta did not expect a war over the Falklands, and initially neither did the British, at least in some quarters. After all, in 1982 British defense and foreign policy revolved around the "Troubles" in Northern Ireland, the reemerging global threat of the Soviet Union, and, according to the very limited British intelligence in Latin America, the Guatemalan threat to Belize, which was greater than that of Argentina toward the Falklands.[34] However, that Thatcher staked her premiership on the conflict is best explained by the reaction from Admiral Sir Henry Loach, the First Sea Lord: "If we muck around, if we pussyfoot, if we don't move very fast and are not entirely successful . . . we shall be living in a different country whose word will count for little."[35] Ultimately, after seventy-four days of fighting, Argentina surrendered on June 14, 1982.[36]

The Reagan–Thatcher dimension to the Falklands War concerns the prime minister's determination to secure the president's personal support for British action in the Falklands. Writing to the president on April 16, 1982, in the context of Haig's diplomatic efforts, she stated, "Our aim is to avoid conflict. But it is essential that America, our closest friend and ally, should share with us a common perception of the fundamental issues of democracy and freedom which are at stake, as I am sure you do."[37] The complexity of the situation for the Reagan administration is best summarized by Haig's remarks at a National Security Council (NSC) meeting on April 30: "There are growing pressures at home and abroad to support Britain. At the same time, we need to work with Argentina and keep the American community in Argentina protected. Moreover, if this pro-American government falls in Buenos Aires, it may well be replaced by a Left-wing, Peronist regime. Therefore, the Secretary said, we need to be careful in how we raise our tilt." At the end of the meeting, Reagan noted "that it would be nice if, after all these years, the U.N. could accomplish something as constructive as averting war between the U.K. and Argentina."[38] Reagan clearly wanted the conflict to end as quickly as possible so as not to have to choose sides, so he tried to strike a careful balance between the politics of Anglo-American relations and the Cold War. Although the president would later acknowledge that the United States provided Thatcher "with whatever aid we could," he initially hoped to convince Thatcher of the importance of some concession to the Argentinians owing to his fears that if the junta lost power, Argentina would become unstable and allow potentially others with less-desirable ideological influences to take power. However, Reagan ultimately sympathized with Thatcher's reluctance to make concessions given the war's cost in terms of British "blood and treasure."[39]

Reagan delivered his famous Westminster Speech on June 8, 1982, during the closing days of the Falklands War.[40] Reagan noted in his diary that he was the first American president ever to address what he termed as a "Joint session" of the British Parliament.[41] And in his memoirs, he recalled that the purpose of his Westminster speech was to demonstrate that he "wasn't flirting with doomsday" by speaking out frankly against the Soviet Union. Reagan was determined to explain how "democracies were up against an expansionist powerhouse that was trying all over the world to peddle its system, yet we who had the system of government that *worked* were doing nothing to sell our vision of freedom."[42] In her own memoirs, Thatcher later described Reagan's speech as "remarkable." She argued that at the Palace of Westminster, Reagan "marked a decisive stage in the battle of ideas which he and I wished to wage against socialism, above all the socialism of the Soviet Union."[43] In his speech, Reagan argued that despite the need for caution, the West's ultimate objective must be to seek freedom for all people; Westerners should "be staunch in our conviction that freedom is not the sole prerogative of a lucky few, but the inalienable and universal right of all human beings." The president called for "a major effort to secure the best—a crusade for freedom that will engage the faith and fortitude of the next generation. For the sake of peace and justice, let us move toward a world in which all people are at last free to determine their own destiny."[44]

The *Daily Mail,* a British right-wing newspaper, stated that as much as "Reagan's eyes crinkle with charm and his tone is courteous," his message "was as uncompromising as the Rocky Mountains."[45] However, for the British press more broadly, the key passage was his support for Britain over the Falklands:

> On a distant island in the South Atlantic young men are fighting for Britain. And yes, voices have been raised protesting their sacrifice for lumps of rock and earth so far away. But those young men aren't fighting for mere real estate. They fight for a cause—for the belief that armed aggression must not be allowed to succeed, and

> the people must participate in the decisions of government—the decisions of government under the rule of law. If there had been firmer support for that principle some forty-five years ago, perhaps our generation wouldn't have suffered the bloodletting of World War II.[46]

Ian Atkin, political editor for the *Guardian,* a left-of-center British newspaper, observed how Thatcher had "won what she most wanted and most urgently from President Reagan's historical visit to Westminster and Whitehall—a ringing declaration of American support for the broad objective of Britain's stand in the Falkland Islands[,] which effectively obliterated the increasing obvious differences between Whitehall and Washington over the future of the islands."[47] A *Guardian* leader observed that "Mrs Thatcher glowed" following Reagan's support over the Falklands.[48] Robert Porter, political correspondent for the *Daily Mail,* likewise noted that Reagan's words were "a tremendous morale booster to Mrs Thatcher after the UN muddle last week" over whether the United States was totally supporting Britain.[49] The *Daily Express,* also a conservative newspaper, opined, "[Reagan] said what needed to be said and what his audience and the country wanted to hear."[50] A leader in the *Daily Telegraph* commented, "Mr. Reagan's words yesterday were especially welcome. In a speech which was dominated by the theme of the ultimate triumph of democracy and freedom over the forces of oppression and evil, the President singled out Britain's resistance to Argentine aggression as an object lesson. . . . Unequivocally, without qualification, he said that British forces in the South Atlantic were fighting for the principles which are dearest to his heart—the cause of liberty and democracy."[51] However, there was an element of cynicism in the British press. Indeed, the press also duly noted the political reality and importance of presidential tours in terms of the American electorate. The *Guardian*'s leader reported that Reagan's aides admitted how an important aspect of the president's European tour was to be seen to be acting as "a World Statesman on the small screens in Dallas and Detroit."[52] The *Daily Express* agreed and claimed that Reagan "was addressing his fellow countrymen as much as ourselves."[53] The president's endorsement of British action in the Falklands was equally noted in the American coverage of his Westminster Speech. R. W. Apple Jr., reporting for the *New York Times,* noted that

Reagan's "brief comment" on the Falklands War was what "most deeply stirred his audience."[54] Lou Cannon informed readers of the *Washington Post* how "the president," before he had finished his last sentence in support of the British soldiers in the Falklands, "was stopped by a rising murmur of approval, punctuated with shouts of 'Hear, hear,' that welled from his audience and became a cheer."[55]

The Westminster Speech was a clear example of Reagan outlining foreign-policy objectives. However, his public endorsement of Thatcher's action in the Falklands was particularly important given US interests in Latin America and vital to Thatcher's international credibility in responding to Argentina's action. Thatcher's victory in the Falklands granted her a timely and emphatic success and helped secure her victory in the general election in 1983. Reagan's support for Thatcher in 1982 was therefore crucial not just to her international policy but also to her domestic successes. More generally, it demonstrated the domestic focus of national security concerns. Despite being the scene for one of Reagan's major speeches about the Cold War, the British response revolved around its own immediate national security interests, namely the Falklands War.

Grenada, 1983

Grenada, an eastern Caribbean island and member of the British Commonwealth, population 100,000 in 1983, became a point of antagonism between Reagan and Thatcher. The US intervention in Grenada was indicative of the overriding prioritization of the president's agenda, even compared to his "special relationship" with the British prime minister. On October 16, 1983, an extreme, hard-line Marxist group within the Grenada government staged a violent coup, murdered Maurice Bishop, the prime minister, at which point his deputy, Bernard Coard, seized power. Coard's regime was a short one: he was executed three days later, and a military government under General Hudson Austin was established. The Reagan administration was alarmed by these developments. The president feared that Grenada could become another Cuba. The administration deemed that the East Caribbean region was a crucial front in the Cold War. Following an appeal for US military action from Grenada's neighbors in the Organization of Eastern Caribbean States, Reagan ordered an invasion.[56]

The Thatcher government did not share American concerns that the coup would automatically lead to instability in the region. Sir Geoffrey Howe, the British foreign secretary (1983–1989), epitomized this disinterest in the region; he later admitted that before the US invasion he had hardly even heard of Grenada. In the period between the coup and Reagan's decision to order military action, Thatcher's government was not involved in the arrangements for a US invasion of a member of the British Commonwealth: Howe even told the House of Commons that there was no reason to expect US action.[57]

As a courtesy, Reagan had asked Thatcher for her thoughts about the possibility of US military intervention. The prime minister argued that it would be an error, but sensing that Reagan was planning action anyway, she decided to telephone the president in order to offer him her counsel. On October 24, Reagan was called away from a meeting with congressional leaders, the chairman of the Joint Chiefs of Staff, Secretary of State George P. Shultz (1982–1989), and Secretary of Defense Weinberger to speak with Thatcher. The conversation was apparently one-sided, with the prime minister dominating proceedings. Reagan was heard saying, "Margaret . . . but Margaret . . . ." When the conversation was finished, Reagan reported back to those waiting for him: "Mrs Thatcher has strong reservations about this."[58] Despite Thatcher's opinion, he did not change his mind. In his diary, he wrote: "She was upset & doesn't think we should do it. I couldn't tell her it had started."[59] Despite lamenting the situation in his diary, Reagan had willfully misled the prime minister.

In an attempt to restore himself in Thatcher's good graces, Reagan telephoned the prime minister on October 26, 1983. Thatcher's opening remarks lacked the warmth that she typically reserved for the president: "Hello, Margaret Thatcher here." In an attempt to utilize his Hollywood charm, Reagan joked, comparing himself to a cowboy who was expecting a difficult conversation upon returning home: "If I were there, Margaret . . . I'd thrown my hat in the door before I came in." Yet Reagan received the cold shoulder, with Thatcher simply responding, "There's no need to do that." The president subsequently offered a rambling, meandering account of the decision to invade Grenada, including blaming the secrecy on fears of a leak on his side of the Atlantic. Unlike in her usual manner, Thatcher did not interrupt Reagan, thus betraying her anger and frustration. She eventually lost her patience. After Reagan explained that he wanted the United States to help Grenada return to the constitution that the British had left it and had since been suspended following the coup, Thatcher simply replied that the newly ousted government had already suspended the constitution in 1979. Despite the president's apology for any embarrassment he had caused his ally, Thatcher was keen to end the conversation in good time.[60] The audio of the conversation suggests that Thatcher was grateful for Reagan's call, which was an indication of the president's desire to apologize to his ally. Nevertheless, even though she readily agreed with Reagan about the dangers of leaks, she clearly felt that the president had embarrassed her.[61] Indeed, despite her claims to sharing philosophical beliefs and a close political friendship with Reagan, she must have recognized—if she never had before—that as far as the United States went, Reagan's interests would always supersede her own. Given the obvious nature of the balance of power in Anglo-American relations, there was seemingly little that Thatcher could do to change the situation or publicly and explicitly demonstrate her discontent in the future.

The disagreement was undoubtedly a source of tension between the two administrations. In his memoir, Shultz, who was a robust proponent of the military action, recalled: "President Reagan and I felt that she was just plain wrong. He had supported her in the Falklands. He felt he was absolutely right about Grenada. She didn't share his judgment at all. He was deeply disappointed."[62] When a senior member of the British Parliament later asked Reagan why he had not told Thatcher about the invasion ahead of time, the president replied, "Because I didn't want her to say no."[63] This incident was humiliating for Thatcher. Her political opponents and the British press were vitriolic. Neil Kinnock, the leader of the Labour Party and the opposition (1983–1992) at the time, told the prime minister in the House of Commons that "the relationship that was said to exist between the right hon. Lady and the President turned out to be not so special." He added: "In the chaos and humiliation of the Grenada affair, will the right hon. Lady [*sic*] at least take the opportunity of adopting a new deportment in world affairs and, as a consequence, demonstrate a greater independence in furthering British interests and working for peace throughout the world?" Thatcher's response summarized the reality of the event and the power relationship in Anglo-American relations: "When two nations are friends each owes the other its own judgment. That does not mean that the other in either case is compelled to accept it."[64] Yet she was able to voice her critique, and on this occasion it was very public indeed. The prime minister told a BBC World Service interview on October 30, 1983, "We in the Western democracies use our force to defend our way of life. We do not use it to walk into independent sovereign territories. . . . If you're going to pronounce a new law that wherever communism reigns against the will of the people, even though it's happened internally, there the USA shall enter, then we are going to have really terrible wars in the world."[65] Nevertheless, it was clear that despite Thatcher's claims to a "special relationship" with Reagan, her interests were subject to being overridden by the president's priorities. Likewise, just as Thatcher sought to further her own political credentials through the "special relationship," she was subject to criticism and mockery when that relationship did not work in her favor.

The claims that there is an Anglo-American "special relationship" and that the United States and United Kingdom pursue individual national interests are not mutually exclusive. The "specialness" of Anglo-American relations can revolve around common values, concerns, interests, and personal chemistry. But, ultimately, the individual demands of national security and economic interest will challenge any commonality of mission at home and abroad. This was the case even with the much-feted relationship between Reagan and Thatcher. The president and prime minister undoubtedly enjoyed a close relationship and shared a mutual admiration. However, it is clear that their "special relationship" was also a political partnership between two pragmatic politicians, with each partner determined to serve an independent agenda shaped by political circumstances and national institutions. They provided each other with political cover when they could, but the two administrations were not afraid to break ranks when they concluded it served their best interests to do so.

Reagan and Thatcher had common concerns. Both wanted to defeat socialism at home and communism abroad and to roll back government intervention in the economy. However, beneath a commonality in philosophy, they were subject to differences in politics and policy and were willing to use these differences to further their own agendas. Commentators and opponents recognized this reality. Thus, the Reagan–Thatcher relationship was special when it suited but likewise was often downgraded as required. For better and for worse, theirs was a marriage of philosophical love and to a greater extent of political convenience. Common and individual interests triumphed over political principles, no matter how strongly these two leaders professed allegiance to those ideals.

Notes

I thank the John Adams '71 Center for Military History and Strategic Analysis at the Virginia Military Institute and am grateful to my colleagues for their comments on a draft of this essay, in particular Alan Dobson, Rob Havers, and Thomas Robb.

1. There is a vast literature about the economic decline. For the American case, a key work is M. A. Bernstein and D. E. Adler, eds., *Understanding American Economic Decline* (Cambridge: Cambridge University Press, 1994). For the British case, see, for instance, Andrew Gamble, *Britain in Decline: Economic Policy, Political Strategy, and the British State,* 4th ed. (London: Palgrave Macmillan, 1994), and Richard English and Michael Kenny, eds., *Rethinking British Decline* (Basingstoke, UK: Macmillan, 2000), 1–22.

2. Ronald Reagan, *An American Life: The Autobiography* (London: Simon and Schuster, 1990), 204.

3. For Reagan, Thatcher, and Gorbachev, see Richard Aldous, *Reagan & Thatcher: The Difficult Relationship* (London: Hutchinson, 2012), 171–76, 197. The "do business quote" comes from Margaret Thatcher, interview, BBC, December 17, 1984, at http://www.margaretthatcher.org/speeches/displaydocument.asp?docid=105592.

4. Ronald Reagan, "Margaret Thatcher and the Revival of the West," *National Review,* May 19, 1989, 21.

5. Diary entry for Wednesday, November 16, 1988, in Ronald Reagan, *The Reagan Diaries,* ed. Douglas Brinkley (New York: HarperCollins, 2007), 667.

6. Margaret Thatcher, *The Downing Street Years* (London: Harper Collins, 1993), 156–57.

7. There is a vast historiography about the "special relationship." See, for instance, Alan P. Dobson, *Anglo-American Relations in the Twentieth Century: Of Friendship, Conflict, and the Rise and Decline of Superpowers* (London: Routledge, 1995); Jonathan Colman, *A "Special Relationship"? Harold Wilson, Lyndon B. Johnson, and Anglo-American Relations "at the Summit," 1964–68* (Manchester, UK: Manchester University Press, 2004); John Dumbrell, *A Special Relationship: Anglo-American Relations from the Cold War to Iraq,* 2nd ed. (Basingstoke, UK: Palgrave Macmillan, 2006); Alan Dobson and Steve Marsh, eds., *Anglo-American Relations: Contemporary Perspectives* (London: Routledge, 2012); and Thomas Robb, *A Strained Partnership? US-UK Relations in the Era of Detente, 1969–77* (Manchester, UK: Manchester University Press, 2013).

8. See Geoffrey Smith, *Reagan and Thatcher* (London: Bodley Head, 1990); John O'Sullivan, *The President, the Pope, and the Prime Minister* (Washington, DC:

Regnery, 2006); and Nicholas Wapshott, *Ronald Reagan and Margaret Thatcher: A Political Marriage* (London: Sentinel, 2007).

9. See Aldous, *Reagan & Thatcher,* and James Cooper, *Margaret Thatcher and Ronald Reagan: A Very Political Special Relationship* (Basingstoke, UK: Palgrave, 2012).

10. The documents cited in this essay are just a sample of those that can be discussed. For an introductory overview of this period, see Wapshott, *Ronald Reagan and Margaret Thatcher,* 126–208.

11. For a more detailed account of this first meeting between Reagan and Thatcher, see James Cooper, "'I Must Brief You on the Mistakes': When Ronald Reagan Met Margaret Thatcher, February 25–28, 1981," *Journal of Policy History* 25, no. 2 (2014): 274–97.

12. Margaret Thatcher and Ronald Reagan, telephone conversation number 10, Wednesday, January 21, 1981, at http://www.margaretthatcher.org/document/114254. PR is "president," and PM is "prime minister."

13. Steering Brief, Brief by Foreign and Commonwealth Office, February 19, 1981, Prime Minister's Visit to the United States, February 25–28, 1981, Foreign and Commonwealth Office 82/1110, "Prime Ministers [*sic*] Visit to the US: Briefing," National Archives of the United Kingdom, Kew, Richmond.

14. Ibid.

15. Brief by Foreign and Commonwealth Office, United States Internal Political and Economic Scene, February 19, 1981, Prime Minister's Visit to the United States, February 25–28, 1981, Foreign and Commonwealth Office 82/1110, "Prime Ministers [*sic*] Visit to the US: Briefing."

16. Martin Anderson to senior White House staff, memo, "Reaganism and Thatcherism," February 26, 1981, at http://www.margaretthatcher.org/document/111729.

17. Alexander Haig to Ronald Reagan, "Visit of Prime Minister Thatcher," Briefing Book, re: visit of British Prime Minister Thatcher, February 25–28, 1981, Binder 1/2, Box 91434 (RAC 1), Executive Secretariat, NSC: VIP Visits, Ronald Reagan Presidential Library, Simi Valley, CA.

18. Ibid.

19. Henry Kissinger, conversation with President Gerald Ford, Wednesday, January 8, 1975, at http://www.margaretthatcher.org/archive/displaydocument.asp?docid=110510.

20. Philip Geyelin, "In Thatcher's Tracks," *Washington Post,* February 24, 1981.

21. Ronald Reagan, remarks at the welcoming ceremony for Prime Minister Margaret Thatcher of the United Kingdom, February 26, 1981, at http://www.reagan.utexas.edu/archives/speeches/1981/22681b.htm.

22. Margaret Thatcher, remarks upon arriving at the White House, February 26, 1981, at http://www.margaretthatcher.org/document/104576.

23. Donald Regan, criticism of Mrs. Thatcher's economic policy, transcript attached to Sir Kenneth Couzens KCB, Overseas Finance, Her Majesty's Treasury,

to Mr. Beryl Sprinkel, Under Secretary Designate, Monetary Affairs, US Treasury, March 3, 1981, at http://www.margaretthatcher.org/document/114256.

24. Anthony Holden, "The Sweet Smell of Summitry Goes Sour," *Observer*, March 1, 1981.

25. Quoted in Don Oberdorfer, "Anglo Accord: U.S.-British Accord Proclaimed 'On All Major Strategic Issues'; U.S. Proclaims Basic Agreement 'On All Strategic Issues,'" *Washington Post,* March 1, 1981.

26. Margaret Thatcher, statement, House of Commons, March 2, 1981, at http://www.margaretthatcher.org/document/104585.

27. Michael Foot, response to Thatcher's statement, House of Commons, March 2, 1981, at http://www.margaretthatcher.org/document/104585.

28. Richard V. Allen to President Ronald Reagan, memo, "Britain Drifts," July 31, 1981, at http://www.margaretthatcher.org/archive/displaydocument.asp?docid=110522.

29. Allan H. Meltzer, "Economic Scene; Policy in the USA and Britain," *New York Times,* August 7, 1981.

30. On the differences between the US and British economies, see, for instance, Cooper, *Margaret Thatcher and Ronald Reagan.*

31. Diary entry for April 6, 1982, in Reagan, *The Reagan Diaries,* 78.

32. Richard Vinen, *Thatcher's Britain: The Politics and Social Upheaval of the 1980s* (London: Simon and Schuster, 2009), 142.

33. Diary entry for May 30–31, 1982, in Nicholas Henderson, *Mandarin: The Diaries of Nicholas Henderson* (London: Weidenfeld and Nicolson, 1994), 467–68.

34. Vinen, *Thatcher's Britain,* 134–38.

35. Quoted in ibid., 139.

36. For a history of the Falklands War, see, for instance, Lawrence Freedman, *The Official History of the Falklands Campaign* (London: Routledge, 2005), and Stephen Badsey, Rob Havers, and Mark Grove, eds., *The Falklands Conflict Twenty Years On: Lessons for the Future* (New York: Frank Cass, 2005).

37. Margaret Thatcher to Ronald Reagan, message, April 16, 1982, at http://www.margaretthatcher.org/document/122860.

38. NSC meeting, April 30, 1982, minutes, Archive (Reagan Library), Margaret Thatcher Foundation, at http://www.margaretthatcher.org/document/114329.

39. Reagan, *An American Life,* 359–60.

40. Both Reagan and Thatcher enjoyed the rare distinction of addressing each other's respective political institutions. Reagan was invited to address members of the British Parliament at the Palace of Westminster in June 1982. See Ronald Reagan, "Address to Members of the British Parliament, June 8, 1982," Public Papers of President Ronald W. Reagan, Reagan Presidential Library, at http://www.reagan.utexas.edu/archives/speeches/1982/60882a.htm, and Robert C. Rowland and John M. Jones, *Reagan at Westminster: Foreshadowing the End of the Cold War* (College Station: Texas A&M University Press, 2010). Thatcher later addressed a joint meeting of the US Congress in February 1985. See Margaret Thatcher, "Speech to Joint Houses

of Congress," February 20, 1985, at http://www.margaretthatcher.org/document/105968. These speeches provided an opportunity for Reagan and Thatcher to support each other's agenda—again, in both domestic and international policy.

41. Diary entry for Wednesday, June 2, 1982, in Reagan, *The Reagan Diaries,* 88.

42. Reagan, *An American Life,* 555.

43. Thatcher, *Downing Street Years,* 258.

44. Reagan, "Address to Members of the British Parliament, Palace of Westminster."

45. "A Great Performer and True Believer" (comment), *Daily Mail,* June 9, 1982.

46. Reagan, "Address to Members of the British Parliament, Palace of Westminster."

47. Ian Atkin, "Thatcher Stands Firm with New Reagan Support," *Guardian,* June 9, 1982.

48. "America Sweet and Sour," *Guardian,* June 9, 1987.

49. Robert Porter, "We Support You," *Daily Mail,* June 9, 1982.

50. "Reagan's Rhetoric" (opinion), *Daily Express,* June 9, 1982.

51. "The President's Beliefs," *Daily Telegraph,* June 9, 1982.

52. "America Sweet and Sour."

53. "Reagan's Rhetoric."

54. R. W. Apple Jr., "President Urges Global Crusade for Democracy," *New York Times,* June 9, 1982.

55. Lou Cannon, "President Calls for 'Crusade'; Reagan Proposes Plan to Counter Soviet Challenge," *Washington Post,* June 9, 1982.

56. Aldous, *Reagan & Thatcher,* 144; John Campbell, *Margaret Thatcher,* vol. 2: *The Iron Lady* (London: Vintage, 2008), 273.

57. Aldous, *Reagan & Thatcher,* 145.

58. Ibid., 146–48.

59. Diary entry for Monday, October 24, 1983, in Reagan, *The Reagan Diaries,* 190.

60. Aldous, *Reagan & Thatcher,* 151–53. For the full transcript of the conversation, see "Reagan Phone Call to Thatcher," October 26, 1983, at http://www.margaretthatcher.org/document/109426.

61. Ronald Reagan to Margaret Thatcher, telephone call, October 26, 1983, audio version, at http://www.margaretthatcher.org/document/145250.

62. George Shultz, *Turmoil and Triumph: My Years as Secretary of State* (New York: Scribner's, 1993), 340.

63. Quoted in Aldous, *Reagan & Thatcher,* 154.

64. UK House of Commons, PQs, October 27, 1983, at http://www.margaretthatcher.org/document/105459.

65. Quoted in Aldous, *Reagan & Thatcher,* 145. Thatcher made this statement during a phone-in program on the BBC World Service, October 30, 1983, at http://www.margaretthatcher.org/document/110628.

7

The Sense of History

Ronald Reagan and François Mitterrand

William I. Hitchcock

Over the course of the Reagan years, relations between France and the United States were surprisingly close—more so perhaps than at any time since the 1950s. Surprising because the chief executives of these two nations were ideological opposites and because their countries had a long history of friction, disagreement, and mutual exasperation. Add to this the basic power asymmetry—during the Reagan years the United States looked to Britain as its most steadfast European ally and to Germany as its most strategically important. In the eyes of US officials, France limped along as a distant third. Yet in the 1980s something happened to pull these two nations into a close partnership. The notable Franco-American convergence of the early 1980s, this chapter argues, had a great deal to do with "the sense of history" that the two leaders, Ronald Reagan and François Mitterrand, shared. In particular, both men had developed a deep loathing of communism and a distrust of the Soviet Union that went back many decades for each leader. Whatever their political philosophies, both had no illusions about the Soviet Union; both were opponents of détente; and both felt that only by sticking together could the Western countries hope to bring about the containment of Soviet aggression and even the end of the division of Europe itself. Both men sensed which way history was moving: toward the principles of freedom, democracy, and liberty and away from the totalitarian schemes of the Communist bloc. Although the two men continued to have many differences on issues of economic policy, security matters, and support for Third World regimes, they were able to overcome many of these disputes because of their remarkable ideological affinity.[1]

From the outset, it would be hard to imagine two more dissimilar men as Ronald Reagan and François Mitterrand. Reagan, once a Democrat, began his career as a moderately successful screen actor, though he showed a flair for politics while serving as the strongly anti-Communist president of the Screen Actors Guild in the 1950s. He turned to national politics in 1964 when he spoke out on behalf of Republican presidential candidate Barry Goldwater, stressing themes of individual freedom, hostility to big government, and an unshakable hatred of Soviet communism. As governor of California from 1967 to 1975, he clashed with student protestors, called for restrictions on abortion, denounced welfare programs, and tried to trim the size of government. In 1980, he built a successful bid for the White House on the principles of lowering taxes, delegating power to state and local governments, and having a strong national defense. Reagan became the standard-bearer of a revived and nationally successful conservative political movement in America. Though a late-comer to politics, he possessed rare political gifts, including his personal warmth, his deft touch with the public, and his ability to give voice to the deeply held convictions of millions of Americans that government was a bloated obstacle to their own happiness.[2]

François Mitterrand, by contrast, was a lifelong politician whose convictions were not always clear or consistent. He moved even farther across the political spectrum than Reagan ever did, starting his career as a Catholic nationalist and even joining far-right antidemocratic groups in the late 1930s. Wounded in 1940 and for a time a German prisoner of war, Mitterrand escaped his German captors and served in the Vichy government briefly in 1942–1943. He eventually abandoned Vichy to work for the French resistance in the war. He was a frequent minister in French governments of the 1950s, and his political allegiances varied. He challenged Charles de Gaulle for the presidency in the mid-1960s and did surprisingly well. In 1969, after de Gaulle's resignation and at a time when the old French socialists were divided and adrift, Mitterrand helped create a new Socialist Party; by 1971, he was its leader. In the beginning, the

Socialist Party was openly hostile to capitalism, wary of the North Atlantic Treaty Organization (NATO), and opposed to the French nuclear weapons arsenal. Mitterrand narrowly lost the presidential election of 1974 to Giscard d'Estaing, a moderate conservative. But in May 1981, in a presidential rematch, Mitterrand beat Giscard by four percentage points, and the Left entered into power. Mitterrand, unlike Reagan, was an introverted, frosty intellectual, a rather austere figure whose true pleasures were to read books, browse Paris bookstores, and retreat to his weekend home deep in the southwestern countryside. He was also a serial adulterer who maintained a mistress (at government expense) from 1974 until his death in 1996, with whom he fathered a daughter out of wedlock.

These two leaders came into office in 1981 in an atmosphere of economic turmoil. The citizens of both states wished for a new start and a break with the past. Unemployment, recession, inflation, oil price spikes, malaise: in varying ways, these afflictions had hit all the economies of the West. But Reagan and Mitterrand proposed dramatically different solutions to address these problems. In his Inaugural Address on January 20, 1981, Reagan laid out his philosophy of governing quite clearly: "In this present crisis," he declared, "government is not the solution to our problem; government is the problem. . . . It is my intention to curb the size and influence of the Federal establishment. . . . Our present troubles parallel and are proportionate to the intervention and intrusion in our lives that result from unnecessary and excessive growth of government."[3] Reagan's antigovernment ideas became a rallying cry for millions of Americans and continue to echo today in our politics. In his first year in office, Reagan tried to follow through with his economic ideas by proposing legislation to cut taxes, slash entitlement spending, and at the same time increase the defense budget. Meanwhile, the US Federal Reserve Board set high interest rates in an effort to control inflation. Leave aside for the moment that these economic policies increased the deficit and were ineffective in shrinking government: the point is that Reagan came at the economic crisis as a conservative, believing that government had created America's economic problem and that free enterprise would solve it.[4]

By contrast, François Mitterrand took precisely the opposite approach. In his presidential campaign, he spoke of making government work better, making it more responsive to the needs of the public, and using the levers of government to create jobs and to provide housing, health care, transportation, and good stewardship of the nation's economy. Indeed, in the election of May 1981, Mitterrand received the support of millions of members of the French Communist Party, which provided him a crucial margin of victory in a tight race. He promised bold new government intervention in the economy to overcome the long lethargy of the 1970s, calling for nationalizing banks, raising wages, and stimulating job growth.[5]

Critics on the French right heaped scorn on the new president's proposals: France would soon slip into "totalitarian Marxism," feared the conservative newspaper editor and writer Jean d'Ormesson, and the influential centrist scholar of international affairs Raymond Aron said Mitterrand's economic ideas "can't be seriously discussed." The French stock market agreed and tanked upon the news of his election.[6] Nonetheless, Mitterrand started off in a blaze of government intervention in the economy, nationalizing the largest industrial conglomerates in France as well as thirty-six banks. He launched a new stimulus plan to create jobs, outlined a low-cost housing program to build fifty thousand new apartments, proposed spending $2 billion on new social programs and increasing the minimum wage by 10 percent, and implemented increases in social security, family allowances, and old-age pensions. To pay for this largesse, he imposed a windfall profits tax on banks and oil companies, a special wealth tax on the top one hundred thousand taxpayers in the country, and a sales tax on luxury goods.[7]

Thus, when these two leaders first met at the G-7 meeting in July 1981 in Ottawa, Canada, the atmosphere was charged with controversy. France wanted the United States to lower interest rates and ease the high value of the dollar so as to make French purchases of oil on the global market less expensive; it also wanted the United States to ease up global credit so as to trigger more investment. Above all else, Mitterrand wanted to attack unemployment (then running at 7.5 percent in France) through a government stimulus plan, and he blamed tight US monetary policy for hurting the European economies. Reagan went to Ottawa prepared to hold the line: high interest rates and a monetary squeeze were necessary to get control of inflation, he believed, and the United States would not budge. "The picture," wrote *New York Times* journalist Steven Rattner, "is one of new leaders single-mindedly pursuing policies to which they are deeply committed, leaving moderation for later."[8] At Ottawa, news reports declared that Mitterrand and German chancellor Helmut Schmidt "bluntly challenged" Reagan on US monetary policy, and Mitterrand told the press after the meeting that "sometimes brutal exchanges" had taken place behind closed doors.[9]

Economic policy was not the only source of friction in the early days. In the first year of the two presidencies, Mitterrand pressed the issue of development aid for Third World nations. This proposal was the public face of a long-running French policy to curry favor with a variety of governments, from newly independent African states to leftist regimes. By contrast, the United States was ill at ease with the delivery of aid through international organizations and in any case was hostile to aid for revolutionaries. The debate revealed a fundamental divide over how to handle the threat posed by Third World turmoil and radicalism. Should the West curry favor with newly independent—and often politically unpredictable—countries by offering them economic aid? Or should the West instead ally with often unsavory partners to wage local wars against the threat of radical movements? France favored the former approach, the United States preferred the latter, and their respective disagreements over policy toward Central America provided a clear example of their divergent policies. France urged the United States to broker a peace in the civil war in El Salvador between leftist guerillas and the military government. The United States refused and backed the military regime. In Nicaragua, too, the United States and France fell on opposing sides, with the French sympathetic to the leftist Sandinista government and the Americans backing the counterrevolutionaries, or contras. Frankly, the debate between Paris and Washington was not so much about left versus right as it was about grand strategy: Which nation had a more effective plan to manage and contain the political turmoil in the Third World? For Mitterrand and the French, Washington's policies seemed needlessly ideological and counterproductive; for Reagan, any toleration of communism was mere appeasement of the enemy.

Reagan and Mitterrand soon met again, in October 1981. The occasion was the bicentennial of the Battle of Yorktown, where French naval vessels and American colonial troops had combined to thwart the British army in Virginia during the Revolutionary War. Though the public ceremonies were intended to demonstrate two hundred years of Franco-American solidarity, a certain tension was palpable as both men used the event to restate their differing philosophies of government. Reagan gave a speech that linked the sacrifices of colonial soldiers, fighting British tyranny, to his own antigovernment ideas. Freedom and independence were "threatened," he said, "by government's bloated size and the distortions of its true functions." Just as the colonials refused to be taxed by Britain, so too did today's Americans resent their "punishing tax burden." Mitterrand, with the Third World clearly in mind, instead praised the spirit of revolution and asked the Americans to remember that "the aspirations of the peoples of the world today are just as legitimate as those of our forefathers."[10]

The Franco-American relationship was further jeopardized by a serious disruption over trade policy, known simply as the "pipeline controversy." During the last years of the Carter administration, the United States sought to punish Russia for the invasion of Afghanistan by imposing sanctions and a grain embargo. Reagan dropped the grain embargo but still wanted to pressure the West European states, which had a much higher volume of trade with the Soviets, to curtail that commerce. But this subject was very touchy: at a time of deep economic gloom, no European nation wanted to lose out on the profitable trade with the Soviets in which high-quality industrial goods were sent east in exchange for Soviet oil and natural gas. In 1980, a major pipeline project among France, Germany, and the Russians was inked, to be built with West European technology and financed by West European banks. After the imposition of martial law in Poland in December 1981, the Reagan administration called for a strict embargo on high-tech exports to the Soviets and pressured the Europeans to join it. They refused, and the issue led to a serious souring of transatlantic relations during 1982, until a new US secretary of state, George P. Shultz, had the good sense to retreat from the sanctions policy.[11]

The Franco-American relationship, it would seem, had started badly. How then to explain the fact that during the period 1982 to 1985 France arguably became America's most valuable ally in Europe? In truth, these initial policy differences, though quite real, masked one important powerful force of attraction: Reagan and Mitterrand's shared antipathy toward the Soviet Union and toward communism in particular. Here is where their shared "sense of history" paid significant dividends.

We need not spend much time here on the origins of Reagan's anticommunism. The biographer Lou Cannon has expertly described Reagan's work in the Screen Actors Guild in 1947, when as president of that organization Reagan testified before the House Un-American Activities Committee about alleged Communist infiltration of Hollywood. Reagan claimed to be naive about Communists' tactics, but he deftly positioned himself as the champion of freedom and democracy in contrast to scheming Communists who sought to control the nation's movie industry. But in assuming this position, Reagan, then still a Democrat, was hardly taking a risk: the country had turned sharply against communism at that time and was caught up in the emerging Red Scare. From his Hollywood days, Reagan developed "a resolute conspiracy theory about communists which he never abandoned."[12]

More surprising, perhaps, is the depth of François Mitterrand's hostility toward communism and the Soviets in particular. Mitterrand had a very long history with communism. The French Communist Party was routinely one of the most powerful and disciplined political organizations in postwar France, usually garnering a quarter to a third of the votes in parliamentary elections in the late 1940s and 1950s. When Charles de Gaulle became president in 1958, he used anticommunism as a binding force to create a broad coalition of center/right voters who supported Gaullist candidates, but his ascent also served to give the Communists a clear focus for their venom: a general turned president who, the Communists alleged, was more like Franco or Mussolini than a republican leader.

In this atmosphere of sharp polarization between Gaullism and communism, Mitterrand had to devise a strategy to gain political traction. In the 1960s and 1970s, his political strategy was to shore up the divided non-Communist Left, pick off the centrist parties that were mistrustful of de Gaulle, and then present himself to the Communists as a true man of the left who could lead a united left-wing movement into power. In short, though Mitterrand loathed the Stalinist and sclerotic French Communist Party, he knew he could not rise to the top without them. In his presidential bids of 1974 and 1981, he managed to secure Communist support, but it pained him to do so, and he deeply resented having to rely upon Communists for his margin of victory in 1981. His aim as president, therefore, was to create a broad-based Socialist Party that could jettison the Far Left, attract the moderate center, and consistently beat back the center–right parties. Entering into office, then, Mitterrand was already thinking about how to build the Left into a permanent majority in France.[13]

These domestic considerations are crucial in understanding Mitterrand's foreign policy in the Cold War. Mitterrand believed that to be a successful political force his party had to find a secure place between Gaullism, which was skeptical toward the United States, hostile to NATO, and eager to play off the East against the West, and the left-wing sentiments of the Communists and other fellow travelers who saw the United States as the main irritant in world affairs, wanted the United States out of Europe, wanted Europe to become neutral and united, and aimed to accommodate the Soviet Union.

Reagan was quick to perceive that he shared a basic distrust of the Soviets with Mitterrand. At their first meeting, in Ottawa in 1981, Reagan told the press that he was "a little bit surprised"—and happily so—by Mitterrand's "resoluteness with regard to the Soviet threat." Mitterrand's statements to the leaders at Ottawa about how to handle the Russians "sounded like me," Reagan chirped.[14]

And no wonder Reagan was surprised. In the 1970s, French leaders had routinely courted Soviet favor. President Georges Pompidou had visited Moscow in 1970, 1973, and 1974; Leonid Brezhnev was welcomed in France in 1971 and 1973. Giscard visited Moscow in 1975 and 1979, resisted US pleas for a boycott of the Soviet Union after the Soviet invasion of Afghanistan, and even met with Brezhnev in Warsaw in May 1980. By contrast, Mitterrand, in his election campaign in 1981, denounced the Soviet deployment of intermediate-range nuclear weapons, the SS-20s, whose target could only be western Europe, and decried the Soviet invasion of and ongoing war in Afghanistan. Once in office, he embraced NATO's decision to respond to the SS-20s with the deployment of Pershing II and Cruise missiles, despite the unpopularity of this proposal among the public in West Germany. In an equally surprising shift of French policy, Mitterrand moved to improve ties with Israel, shrugging off the Israeli attack on Iraq's nuclear reactor in June 1981 and visiting Israel in March 1982—the first French president to do so. By December 1981, when the Soviet Union demanded the imposition of martial law in Poland as a response to the growing challenge by the Solidarity movement, Mitterrand could feel vindicated in his staunch anti-Soviet attitudes.[15]

Mitterrand took sincere risks in adopting this position. Not only did he alienate his left-wing allies in France—just at a time when he was backtracking from his more radical economic reforms—but he also ran the risk of losing influence inside the Western alliance. By aligning Paris with Washington, Mitterrand gambled that he would not surrender the autonomy in East–West relations that de Gaulle had so carefully maintained and would be allowed wide freedom of action. He instead nailed his colors to the mast. He wanted the Pershing II and Cruise missiles to be deployed because he feared that if such missiles were not delivered, Washington, shielded by its own vast nuclear deterrent, would weaken its connection to Europe, and Germany would be ever more drawn into a stance of accommodation and appeasement toward Moscow.

Mitterrand was pleased in October 1982 when Helmut Kohl, the leader of the Christian Democratic Party, became chancellor of the Federal Republic of Germany, yet he remained anxious at the deep divisions inside Germany about the missile deployment. The West German peace movement was large and boisterous, and it opposed any more missiles in Europe. In January 1983, while Kohl was in the midst of a national parliamentary election, Mitterrand visited Bonn and spoke before the Bundestag. He openly warned about the prospect of decoupling Europe and the United States, and he called for "determination and solidarity" with NATO's decision to deploy the missiles. That same month he announced that France would expand its own independent nuclear weapons arsenal. His message was directed at the German Socialists and marked a striking act of solidarity with Washington.[16]

For Mitterrand, the missile debate was not one of left versus right. What guided his policy was his sense of history: every Frenchman knew that if Germany and Russia should ever join forces or even become neutral toward one another, France would be the loser. There was a word for this nightmare scenario: *Rapallo.* This was the Italian town where in 1922 Germany and Russia signed a cooperative pact that soon led to secret military cooperation between the two. It was this scenario that Mitterrand feared most. Indeed, he even invoked Rapallo the day after his famous Bundestag speech, when he praised the efforts of former chancellor Konrad Adenauer to embrace NATO and the West and to turn his back on neutralism and Rapallo.[17]

Furthermore, it was France's historic mission to tie Germany securely to the West, and this project had begun to come unraveled in the previous decade. The German Left had become deeply skeptical of Cold War structures. Ostpolitik had placed a premium on normalization of relations with the East. In such circumstances, the German public began to think that a neutral, accommodating West Germany would be a surer road to peace and stability than a Germany linked to NATO. In thinking about a Europe outside the Cold War framework, Germans had been largely encouraged by de Gaulle and even by Giscard. Mitterrand wished to put a stop to all this, for he perceived that a neutralist Germany was bad for French national security. A decoupling of the United States from Europe would embolden the Russians, which could only fulfill the long-held Soviet ambition of putting western Europe under Moscow's thumb. Mitterrand rightly saw the Euromissile debate as a new Berlin crisis or even a Cuban Missile Crisis, in which the Soviets were testing Western resolve and alliance solidarity.[18]

Mitterrand's courageous support for the NATO missile deployment, defying left-wing sentiment across Europe, made him much admired in Washington. It also made him a somewhat embarrassed bedfellow, for Reagan's own flights of rhetoric at this period were far more zealous than anything Mitterrand would have used. It was in March 1983, just as the Germans and other Europeans were hedging about the missile deployment, that Reagan invited Europeans to recall that the Soviet Union was "an evil empire." This was not Mitterrand's style, of course, but the two men had a common understanding: the Soviet Union was not a state to be trusted, and it respected only strength. In a test of wills, democracy must show its mettle. As the leading scholar of these matters has put it, France was becoming "the best pupil in the NATO class." Indeed, just a few weeks after Reagan's "evil empire" speech, France expelled forty-seven Soviet diplomats from Paris—most of them known Committee for State Security, or KGB, agents. It was a deliberate statement of France's alignment with the West in the missile stand-off.[19]

When the international scene darkened even further with the Soviet downing of Korean Air Lines Flight 007 in September 1983, both Reagan and Mitterrand could feel that their suspicions of the Soviet bear had been borne out. Mitterrand in particular, given the fierce opposition he faced to his policies, felt renewed in his campaign against the neutralist tendency. "I understand the concern that people, especially in Europe, feel about the accumulation of nuclear arms," he said in an address during a state dinner in Belgium in October 1983. "But does that mean the lessons of history should be forgotten? Or that unilateral disarmament, or accepting existing imbalances, would contribute to peace? I think not." In a memorable line, he said he "saw pacifism in the West and missiles in the East. I consider that an unequal relationship."[20] By the end of 1983, the German Parliament had voted in favor of the missile deployment. The West had not buckled but had cohered in the face of vociferous internal dissent. The Soviets took notice, and Mitterrand could take some satisfaction in having rescued the Western alliance from a signature defeat.

If Reagan and Mitterrand were brought together in their positions on the Euromissile debate by a shared "sense of history," it might be possible to suggest that it was also a sense of history that pushed them apart in the period from 1985 to the end of Reagan's presidency. Each leader in these years pursued what he considered to be a major historic achievement and legacy, but as it turned out, these two sets of goals did not align and left the Franco-American relationship in a fragile state by the time Reagan left office.

For Reagan, his greatest ambition was to move boldly toward a grand nuclear bargain with the Soviet Union that would ultimately free Europe and maybe the world of nuclear weapons. He pursued this goal along two axes: he publicly announced a new commitment to building a space-based weapons shield that would protect Americans from nuclear attack. But he also made clear his deep desire to limit and even ban nuclear weapons, starting with the very intermediate-range missiles that had just been deployed in Europe. To the French, these policy ideas were slaps in the face, for three reasons. First, the Strategic Defense Initiative (SDI) seemed to propose a decoupling of America from Europe by offering protection only to North America and leaving Europe vulnerable: a direct contradiction of postwar US policy and a nightmare scenario for Europe. Second, the French worried that America would throw into any grand bargain with the Russians France's own independent nuclear deterrent, which the French insisted they would keep out of any negotiations. And third, Mitterrand had expended enormous political capital in getting the French public as well as West Germans to believe that the intermediate-range nuclear missiles were critical to their security. Now Reagan was proposing that they be put up for auction in a deal with the Soviets. Feeling left out and burned, Mitterrand began to consider Reagan an unreliable ally. Of course, the bilateral relationship was in a sense rescued by Mikhail Gorbachev, for his willingness to take Reagan up on his proposals for a treaty regarding intermediate-range missiles and his desperate desire for a deal led to a deal in 1987 that left SDI untouched and did not affect the French nuclear deterrent. But the road to that deal, from the shocking surprise of Reykjavik in 1986 through to the last-minute negotiations, left France thinking that the United States was becoming erratic and unpredictable.[21]

But on the other side of the ledger and in some ways as a consequence of developments on the strategic front that Reagan was pursuing, Mitterrand was aiming at his own historic legacy, and his great vision left the United States out. When Mitterrand came into office in 1981, the European integration project was almost totally dead. De Gaulle had done everything to kill it off. Pompidou had let it falter. Giscard had revived it but kept the ambitions of European integration focused on narrow economic cooperation—namely, the loose linkage of European currencies through the European Monetary System, established in 1979. Mitterrand and his German counterpart, Helmut Kohl, pulled along by the diligent work of the French Socialist Jacques Delors, who became head of the European Commission in 1985, came to believe that their nations' national interest would be enhanced by transforming Europe into a single dynamic common market and creating the structures in which a new Europe could be born. The dream had been expressed in the 1950s, and America had supported it then, but for two decades the move toward a united Europe had been hampered. Mitterrand and Kohl joined forces and pushed through the Single Europe Act in early 1986, placing Europe on the path toward a unified market, shared monetary policy, and a single currency.

Mitterrand saw this process as not only desirable for French national interests but also urgent given that the rise of Mikhail Gorbachev to power in the Soviet Union seemed to signal a major thaw in the Cold War. If the division in Europe were going to be eased or even eradicated altogether, Mitterrand wanted to be sure a strong European Community would be in place to cement a once fractious and divisive continent together. He also wanted to reassert the importance of France in world affairs, not only in Europe but in areas of traditional French influence, such as North Africa. France's desire to play a role in influencing Arab politics in North Africa led to a regrettable clash with the United States in 1986. Though

Mitterrand loathed Libyan leader Muammar Gaddafi and had discussed his ouster with American officials in the early 1980s, the French did not support an American plan to bomb the home of the Libyan strongman in reprisal for his alleged support of anti-American terrorism in Europe. The French asserted that such action would make Gaddafi a martyr and boost hatred of the West in the Arab world; France wanted to play a more subtle game. Presented with an American bombing plan at the last minute, Mitterrand denied French airspace to the US F-111s, which nonetheless carried out their mission on April 15, 1986 (missing Gaddafi but killing his daughter and more than thirty others). Washington announced its deep disappointment with France following the raid, and anti-French sentiment in the United States soared.[22]

The issue pointed to a broader source of friction: France wanted to exercise power in world affairs and was actually doing so in the shaping of Europe. The United States did not perceive this change. In Washington, the movement toward a new Europe that featured not only economic but also political integration was ignored or misunderstood. The Americans expressed support but failed to grasp the enormous implications of the creation of an integrated European continent that might have as much economic weight and political clout as the United States. When the Single Europe Act came into effect in July 1987, one observer concluded, "There was little top-level attention devoted" to it in Washington. The Reagan administration "remained largely unaware and certainly unconcerned with the tectonic shifts occurring across the Atlantic."[23]

These twin developments—the easing of the nuclear arms race and the progress of European integration—reflected the ambitions of two important world leaders, Reagan and Mitterrand, and neither process could have succeeded without them. Yet these policies moved in parallel rather than in harmony. That may explain why the French and the Americans would eventually find themselves taking slightly different positions toward the events in eastern Europe from 1988 on. Again, history mattered. As the Soviet bloc unraveled and as the prospect of German unification suddenly opened up, Americans naturally viewed these developments through the lens of a long ideological struggle with Soviet communism. They could read the collapse of that system only as a victory for American values of freedom and free markets. By contrast, Mitterrand and many of his countrymen would see the collapse of communism with hope but also some anxiety, for the Soviet Union and the Cold War had effectively solved France's overriding security problem—the German threat. A united Germany, once again the hinge of Europe, able to pivot East or West as it desired—this was always France's worst nightmare. Therefore, as the process of German unification unfolded, Mitterrand would sound a note of caution, ensuring that a new united Germany be securely locked into those institutions, NATO and the European Community, that the United States and France had played such an important role in designing.[24]

France and the United States have always been especially proud of their histories. Both nations have a distinct sense of their own exceptionalism, which has always colored their foreign policies. In the 1980s, when it mattered most, their historic antipathy toward the Soviet Union proved a powerful force of attraction in the bilateral relationship. Indeed, over the course of two centuries, France and the United States, despite many serious quarrels, have usually found themselves together on the disputed barricades, joined together by common interest, common enemies, and a shared sense of history.

Notes

I thank Michael De Groot for the research assistance he provided for this chapter.

1. An excellent synthesis of Franco-American relations in the Cold War, with a very good chapter on the Reagan period, is Frank Costigliola, *France and the United States: The Cold Alliance since World War II* (New York: Twayne, 1992). See also Richard Kuisel, *The French Way: How France Embraced and Rejected American Values and Power* (Princeton, NJ: Princeton University Press, 2012), 99–150, and N. Piers Ludlow, "The Unnoticed Apogee of Atlanticism? U.S.–Western European Relations during the Early Reagan Era," in *European Integration and the Atlantic Community in the 1980s,* ed. Kiran Klaus Patel and Kenneth Weisbrode (New York: Cambridge University Press, 2013), 17–38.

2. For a complete introduction to Reagan's life, see the fine collection of materials prepared under Lou Cannon's direction by the Miller Center of Public Affairs at the University of Virginia, Charlottesville, at http://millercenter.org/president/reagan.

3. Ronald Reagan, "Inaugural Address," January 20, 1981, at http://www.presidency.ucsb.edu/ws/?pid=43130.

4. W. Elliot Brownlee and C. Eugene Steuerle, "Taxation," in *The Reagan Presidency: Pragmatic Conservatism and Its Legacies,* ed. W. Elliot Brownlee and Hugh Davis Graham (Lawrence: University Press of Kansas, 2003), 155–81.

5. "Mitterrand Beats Giscard," *New York Times,* May 11, 1981.

6. D'Ormesson and Aron quoted in "French Reaction to Mitterrand," *Wall Street Journal,* May 13, 1981; "French Franc, Stock Market Slump," *Washington Post,* May 12, 1981.

7. "Mitterrand's New Growth Plan," *Los Angeles Times,* June 23, 1981. For a detailed scholarly analysis of the type of steps Mitterrand took, see Pierre-Alain Muet and Alain Fonteneau, *Reflation and Austerity: Economic Policy under Mitterrand* (New York: Berg, 1990).

8. Steven Rattner, "Diverging on the Summit," *New York Times,* July 12, 1981. The West German chancellor Helmut Schmidt issued a statement also critical of US monetary policy ("Bonn and Paris Agree to Oppose US Rate Policy," *New York Times,* July 14, 1981).

9. Lou Cannon and Hobart Rowen, "Reagan Is Challenged at Summit," *Washington Post,* July 20, 1981; Lou Cannon, *President Reagan: The Role of a Lifetime,* paperback ed. (New York: PublicAffairs, 2000), 409–10; Mitterrand quoted in Steven R. Weisman, "Accord Viewed as Symbolic with Deep Rifts Remaining," *New York Times,* July 22, 1981.

10. Both Reagan and Mitterrand quoted in "Reagan and Mitterrand Observe 200th Anniversary of Yorktown," *New York Times,* October 20, 1981.

11. A lucid summary of the dispute is in Costigliola, *France and the United States*, 203–8.

12. Lou Cannon, *Reagan* (New York: Putnam's Sons, 1982), 86.

13. For surveys of Mitterrand's political work in this period, see David S. Bell, *François Mitterrand: A Political Biography* (Cambridge: Polity, 2005), chap. 4, and Ronald Tiersky, *François Mitterrand: The Last French President* (New York: St. Martin's Press, 2000), esp. chaps. 1–4.

14. Quoted in Hedrick Smith, "Reagan, Reflecting on Ottawa Parley, Praises Mitterrand," *New York Times,* July 23, 2014. Columnist Jim Hoagland also speculated that Mitterrand could become a close ally of Reagan ("Mitterrand's Views Could Rebuild Basis for US-French Cooperation," *Washington Post,* May 11, 2014).

15. Dominique Moisi offered an excellent contemporaneous summary of the French shift in these years: "Giscard d'Estaing was anti-communist at home and soft on the Soviet Union. Mitterrand has brought communist ministers into his government for a mixture of historical and tactical reasons but is firmly anti-Soviet. In the last six months of his mandate, Giscard had slightly toughened his position vis-à-vis the Soviet Union, but his May 1980 Warsaw trip to meet with Leonid Brezhnev after the Soviet invasion of Afghanistan, which haunted him during his campaign, remains symbolic of his seven years in office. Mitterrand and his Foreign Minister, Claude Cheysson, have lifted this veil of ambiguity by stressing unequivocally the unacceptability of a Soviet military presence in Afghanistan. Shielding himself behind France's nonparticipation in NATO's military wing, Giscard adopted an attitude of benign neglect toward the quarrel between Europe and America over placing medium-range missiles in Western Europe. Mitterrand, on

the other hand, has come out strongly in support of the West German Chancellor, Helmut Schmidt, in denouncing the Soviet buildup in medium-range missiles, thus approving the NATO decision of 1979 to counter the Soviets with US missiles on European soil. But Mitterrand has not abandoned his commitment to disarmament and arms control; he simply feels that such negotiations can only take place once a balance of power has been restored in Europe" ("Mitterrand's Foreign Policy," *Foreign Affairs* 60, no. 2 [1981–1982]: 347–57, quotation on 348–49).

16. "Mitterrand, on Bonn Visit, Warns against Efforts to Divide the West," *New York Times,* January 21, 1983. On French expansion of nuclear weapons, see John Vinocur, "French Are Planning to Bolster Their Nuclear Force," *New York Times,* January 2, 1983, and Tiersky, *François Mitterrand,* 169–76.

17. See "No Drift toward Neutralism, Kohl Tells the French," *New York Times,* January 22, 1983.

18. For background on the Euromissiles by an acute observer of European affairs, see Samuel F. Wells, "The Mitterrand Challenge," *Foreign Policy* 44 (Fall 1981): 57–69, and "Reagan, Euromissiles, and Europe," in *The Reagan Presidency,* ed. Brownlee and Graham, 133–52. See also R. E. Utley, *The French Defense Debate: Consensus and Continuity in the Mitterrand Era* (London: Macmillan, 2000), 113–22.

19. Frédéric Bozo, "Before the Wall: French Diplomacy and the Last Decade of the Cold War, 1979–1989," in *The Last Decade of the Cold War,* ed. Olav Njolstad (London: Frank Cass, 2004), 243. Speaking to a group of American evangelicals, Reagan said: "I urge you to speak out against those who would place the United States in a position of military and moral inferiority. . . . In your discussions of the nuclear freeze proposals, I urge you to beware the temptation of pride—the temptation of blithely declaring yourselves above it all and label both sides equally at fault, to ignore the facts of history and the aggressive impulses of an evil empire, to simply call the arms race a giant misunderstanding and thereby remove yourself from the struggle between right and wrong and good and evil" (Ronald Reagan, "evil empire" speech, March 8, 1983, at http://millercenter.org/president/speeches/speech-3409).

20. Quoted in John Vinocur, "Mitterrand Presses NATO to Be Firm," *New York Times,* October 15, 1983.

21. For a recent account of Reagan's policies on nuclear weapons control and SDI, see James Graham Wilson, *The Triumph of Improvisation: Gorbachev's Adaptability, Reagan's Engagement, and the End of the Cold War* (Ithaca, NY: Cornell University Press, 2014). For Mitterrand's reaction to US strategic initiatives in the 1980s, see Frédéric Bozo, *Mitterrand: The End of the Cold War and German Unification* (New York: Berghahn Books, 2009), 1–28, and Sean N. Kalic, "Reagan's SDI Announcement and the European Reaction," in *The Crisis of Détente in Europe,* ed. Leopoldo Nuti (New York: Routledge, 2009), 99–110.

22. Costigliola, *France and the United States,* 209.

23. Samuel F. Wells Jr., "From Euromissiles to Maastricht: The Policies of Rea-

gan–Bush and Mitterrand," in *The Strategic Triangle: France, Germany, and the United States in the Shaping of the New Europe,* ed. Helga Haftendorn, Georges-Henri Soutou, Stephen F. Szabo, and Samuel F. Wells Jr. (Baltimore: Johns Hopkins University Press, 2006), 301–2.

24. France's role in the end of the Cold War has occasioned a great deal of scholarship. For a review of the issue, see Frédéric Bozo, "'Winners' and 'Losers': France, the United States, and the End of the Cold War," *Diplomatic History* 33, no. 4 (2009): 927–56.

8

Navigating Choppy Waters

US-German Relations during the Last Decade of the Cold War

David F. Patton

One can hardly overestimate West Germany's strategic importance in the Cold War. Situated on the front line of the conflict, this key member of the North Atlantic Treaty Organization (NATO) hosted hundreds of thousands of Western troops (the United States alone had 250,000 troops and eight hundred military bases and outposts in the country by the mid-1980s), allowed the deployment of vast arsenals of nuclear weapons—although it was proscribed from developing or controlling them—and through its Bundeswehr featured a military of just less than a half-million soldiers.[1] Divided Berlin proved a dangerous hot spot that at times appeared capable of transforming a cold war into a very hot one. Moreover, the West German economy had emerged from the rubble of the lost war to become the largest and arguably most dynamic in all of western Europe. This "economic miracle" (*Wirtschaftswunder*) conferred upon the young Federal Republic of Germany greater stature in European and world affairs—just decades after the Third Reich's crushing defeat. For all these reasons, Washington greatly valued its close relationship to Bonn during its decades-long showdown with the Soviet Union. All the more, Moscow had an interest in driving a wedge between West Germany and the United States.

Strains in US–West German relations heightened in the 1980s and transcended party political lines, bridging the center-left government of Helmut Schmidt (1974–1982), the center-right government of Helmut Kohl (1982–1998), the Jimmy Carter administration (1977–1981), and the Ronald Reagan presidency (1981–1989). On the security front, West Germany and the United States struggled with the controversial deployment of Eurostrategic intermediate-range nuclear forces (INF). The Reagan administration's Strategic Defense Initiative (SDI)—dubbed "Star Wars"—proved contentious as well, portending in the eyes of some Germans a troubling shift in US strategy away from deterrence toward defense. On economic policy, the two allies quarreled over interest rates, trade imbalances, and budget deficits. In short, on key security and economic matters, the United States and its West German partner seemed to be reading from different scripts.

This chapter foregrounds NATO's double-track decision as a window into interconnected concerns about the Eurostrategic missile balance, SDI, and economic policies. The shifting intra-alliance balance of power, divergent positions on détente, domestic political considerations, and the role of leadership are considered. Despite their disagreements, the United States and Germany remained close and prevented tensions from worsening. Moreover, the momentous events of 1989–1990—when the Berlin Wall fell, the postwar division of Europe and Germany ended, and the death knell of Soviet communism sounded—have cast the transatlantic conflicts of the 1980s in a somewhat different light and, to some, have vindicated the choices of the Reagan administration and its West German partners.

The INF Debate in the 1980s

Helmut Schmidt, who became West Germany's chancellor in 1974, came to the job well prepared, having served as federal defense minister (he had earlier penned a book on nuclear deterrence) and as economics and finance minister. As chancellor, he was active on the global stage, responding to challenges such as the oil shocks and financial instability of the 1970s and the Soviet Union's deployment of new intermediate-range nuclear weapons. He developed a reputation for managerial competence, mastery of the issues, and political pragmatism—often in the face of left-wing opposition from within his own party, the Social Democratic Party of Germany (SPD). Recalled the journalist Dan van der Vat, "He was the most skilled, experienced and respected western statesman of his time. Unburdened by modesty, he was fully aware of the fact. He once told me, wagging his admonitory finger, that he was 'tired of educating American presidents,' being on his fourth."[2]

For more than a decade, the balance of INF in Europe would prove an especially vexing issue for policy makers in the United States and West Germany. In the mid-1970s, the Soviet Union had begun to upgrade its INF by deploying SS-20 nuclear missiles. After Chancellor Schmidt failed to convince Washington that intermediate-range nuclear weapons should be included in the Strategic Arms Limitation Treaty (SALT) II, he publicly sounded the alarm in a much-noted address at the International Institute of Strategic Studies in London.[3] Schmidt cautioned that SALT "neutralizes their [i.e., the superpowers'] strategic nuclear capabilities. In Europe this magnifies the significance of the disparities between East and West in nuclear tactical and conventional imbalance."[4] The German chancellor said that the principle of parity must "apply to all category of weapons" and that the superpowers' negotiations and agreements must not undermine the Atlantic alliance's deterrence strategy.[5] Schmidt and other West Europeans were concerned about the Soviet military threat, the possibility of political blackmail, and the credibility of extended deterrence—namely, America's willingness to counter a Soviet attack on western Europe with nuclear weapons.[6]

In December 1979, NATO members backed the double-track decision in which the United States would pursue negotiations with the Soviet Union to limit INF in Europe. If a deal, however, were not reached by 1983, then NATO would upgrade its own INF by sending Pershing II and Cruise missiles to Great Britain, Italy, and West Germany. This carrot-and-stick approach stipulated that if the Soviet Union would not accept the Western offer of INF reductions on both sides, then NATO would restore the balance on its own. With this decision, the United States and its allies showed a willingness not only to stand together in the face of the Soviet buildup but also to strengthen the credibility of extended deterrence. "Because of their range, these missiles would also allow the United States to threaten the Soviet Union without immediately subjecting its territory to an all-out nuclear war."[7] However, despite the common front among alliance members, certain asymmetries remained. The part of the plan that found public favor in West Germany, the negotiations track, would be handled bilaterally by the United States and the Soviet Union, and the element that stoked fierce grassroots resistance, the procurement and deployment track, required Bonn's explicit consent, a fraught proposition in the Federal Republic given public hostility to the stationing of nuclear weapons in the country.[8]

Complicating matters significantly for Bonn, the Soviet Union invaded Afghanistan a few weeks after the NATO decision had been taken. By early 1980, the Carter administration no longer pursued Senate ratification of the SALT II agreement, and although initial talks commenced in October, the prospects for a deal on INF were poor. The Reagan administration also showed little initial interest in negotiations. Ronald Reagan, who was staunchly anti-Communist and had campaigned against SALT II, had key arms-control advisers, among them Paul Nitze and Richard Perle, who were highly critical of US arms-control efforts. Rather than envision military parity between the superpowers, President Reagan instead pursued superiority through an ambitious nuclear and conventional arms buildup that would allow Washington to negotiate, when deemed appropriate, from a position of strength. His apparent hostility toward arms control hardly reassured Bonn in the early 1980s, which had hoped for a deal on INF reduction before the deployment deadline.[9]

In an effort to assuage its allies—among them Chancellor Schmidt, who faced a growing challenge on the double-track decision within his own party—the Reagan administration did resume talks with the Soviet Union on the Eurostrategic balance in the fall of 1981.[10] At this time, it proposed a "zero option" to eliminate the longer-range missiles. Although the Schmidt government had encouraged the United States to adopt this bargaining position, which the political scientist Thomas Risse-Kappen has described as a "German-American baby,"[11] many saw it as unrealistic and likely to reduce the chances of an accord. As the date for deployment in 1983 drew nearer, the ensuing arms negotiations brought little progress despite the outlines of a deal that Paul Nitze and Juli Kvitsinsky had arrived at during their well-known "walk in the woods"—a deal that both the Soviet Union and the United States subsequently rejected. To Helmut Schmidt's disappointment, the Reagan administration had rejected the deal without consulting its allies, who got wind of its terms only through press leaks.[12] With the Soviet Union hoping that the INF deployment would founder on European public opposition and the United States in the midst of an arms buildup, the conditions for an agreement were hardly propitious. Although at the West Germans' urging the United States had come around to an "interim solution" that would permit ceilings rather than zero Eurostrategic missiles, both sides were willing to offer only limited concessions, and the Geneva talks between the United States and the Soviet Union ended in stalemate.[13] On November 22, 1983, the German Bundestag voted to deploy by a margin of 286 to 226. The following day, Pershing II missiles started arriving in the Federal Republic, and the Soviet Union broke off negotiations in Geneva.

Yet the INF saga was far from over. Although the two superpowers did not resume arms-control talks in 1984, they did convene in Geneva in January 1985 to discuss strategic missiles, space-based defense, and INF. There was no agreement, however, despite greater flexibility on the part of the new Soviet leader, Mikhail Gorbachev, and the Reagan administration. In the course of 1986, Soviet officials made substantial concessions on INF, including acceptance of the zero option in Europe and the willingness to no longer include French and British nuclear weapons in the equation. At the Reykjavik summit in October 1986, the Soviet Union and the United States achieved a basic agreement that an INF treaty would include the zero option in Europe. However, the treaty was not finalized at the summit due to a lack of agreement in other areas, such as SDI. In effect, the Soviet Union had essentially come around to the US negotiating position of 1981, thereby vindicating NATO's double-track approach. Nonetheless, there was concern among US allies, including Bonn, that President Reagan had acted unilaterally at Reykjavik and that the Soviet conventional-force superiority remained.[14] Franz Josef Strauss, Christian Social Union (CSU) chair and minister president in Bavaria, warned in October 1986: "We must watch out like hell lest the Americans agree to solutions which do not damage their security but can work out very problematically for us."[15]

In early 1987, Gorbachev no longer insisted that INF be tied to space-based weaponry (the stumbling block in Iceland) and proposed a double-zero option that would include shorter-range INF. However, the Soviet Union stipulated that West German Pershing I missiles, equipped with US nuclear warheads, must be part of the deal. Behind the scenes, Chancellor Kohl opposed the double-zero option on the grounds that it would compromise West German security in light of the Soviet Union's conventional superiority and the many short-range battlefield nuclear forces on German soil. The option raised concerns that the Federal Republic would hold a distinct, "singularized" position within the North Atlantic alliance, captured well by the phrase "the shorter the range, the deader the Germans." The Reagan administration, however, rejected the Kohl government's efforts to remove shorter-range INF from the equation and instead made it clear that were Bonn to block the proposed treaty, then it would be asked to deploy additional shorter-range INF in West Germany. After unsuccessfully attempting to broaden the arms-control agenda to include short-range nuclear forces, the Kohl government eventually yielded and agreed to back the double-zero option and to junk the Federal Republic's Pershing I missiles.[16] In December 1987, the United States and the Soviet Union signed the INF Treaty, which was ratified by the US Senate the following spring. Writing in the late 1980s, Wolfram Hanrieder offered a harsh assessment of how the INF controversy had unfolded: "The entire issue of modernizing NATO's Eurostrategic arsenal had turned into an unrelieved nightmare for Bonn that lasted a decade: taking the missiles out proved almost as troublesome as putting them in, and the Germans had lost their own in the process. Moscow has succeeded in driving a major wedge between Washington and Bonn, abetted by an American administration singularly unconcerned about the consequences of its arms control decisions for the cohesion of the alliance."[17]

US-German Relations in the 1980s

The INF debate tested West German–American relations given its political salience in the Federal Republic and its ties to other issues, such as transatlantic disagreements over economic policies, détente, and SDI.

After World War II, the United States exercised unquestioned military and economic leadership in the non-Communist world. It established international regimes such as the International Monetary Fund, the World Bank, the Bretton Woods system of fixed exchange rates, and the General Agreement on Tariffs and Trade. As the Cold War intensified, the United States proposed the Marshall Plan and supported European integration. US economic strength and military might were highly complementary and together served as the glue that fixed the Western alliance. By the 1970s and 1980s, however, these two elements of American leadership no longer dovetailed as they once had. The United States remained unchallenged militarily among its allies, yet on the economic front, others—especially Japan and West Germany—had closed the gap with strong postwar recoveries. The economic historian Harold James identifies a "transatlantic decoupling" and the decline of the Cold War as an "integrative framework," which he traces to the US decision to abandon the Bretton Woods system of fixed currency exchange in the early 1970s and to the weakening of a multilateral free-trade regime.[18]

The Federal Republic was now less susceptible to direct US pressure.[19] As discussed later, the US–West German disagreement over a Soviet gas pipeline illustrates this development. At the G7 economic summit in Versailles in 1982, Chancellor Schmidt attempted to turn the tables when the United States pressed him on the need for tougher trade sanctions toward the Communist bloc: "At the outset of the negotiations we have told you that we think the business of East/West commerce appears secondary to us. It is much more important to strengthen the cohesion of the West, and in order to do this, you need to modify your monetary policy."[20] In the late 1980s, the historian Paul Kennedy wrote of "imperial overstretch" and viewed the Soviet Union and United States as potential candidates.[21]

Whereas the United States had lost its position of undisputed economic leadership by the 1970s and 1980s, the Federal Republic, after very high growth rates in the 1950s and 1960s, had come through the oil shocks of the 1970s quite well, maintained its export competitiveness amid a rising Deutsche Mark, and established itself as the lynchpin of the European Monetary System. By 1980, it was widely being touted as "Modell Deutschland," which bestowed upon the Schmidt government influence and prestige abroad. During the early 1980s, the Federal Republic viewed high interest rates and large budget deficits in the United States as a problem for its own economy, which was experiencing low growth and rising unemployment. Although Bonn, ever concerned about inflationary pressures, initially welcomed the Reagan administration's determination to curb inflation, the administration's reliance on monetary policy to do so, in particular very high interest rates, caused consternation as foreign capital poured into the United States. In his memoirs, Chancellor Schmidt expressed frustration that Reagan did not see that "high American interest rates had led to the omission of the investments necessary for growth and employment in the rest of the world."[22]

The Reagan administration's seeming indifference to budget deficits and the exploding federal debt ran counter to Bonn's view of what constituted responsible fiscal policy. After the Federal Republic's trade surplus with the United States had risen steeply, reaching $25 billion by 1985—fueled by the strong dollar—Washington changed course and agreed in the Plaza Accord on international monetary coordination to bring down the value of the dollar. It pressed the West Germans to do more to increase domestic consumption, cut taxes, and relax their monetary policies in order to increase the demand for US products.[23] As tensions over currency exchange rates persisted (the falling dollar was now a concern), the major industrial powers reached an agreement (the Louvre Accord) in 1987 on how to proceed. Even on the issue of free trade, in which the West German government and the Reagan administration were in general agreement, tensions arose as the US Congress grew more protectionist, assertive, and unilateral on trade issues.[24] In short, the 1980s were a time of economic friction between the United States and West Germany, and although these tensions did not preclude consensus on key security issues, they raised concerns that the two allies were drifting apart.

Arms control and the recognition of the territorial status quo in postwar Europe had together comprised integral elements of East–West détente in the early and mid-1970s. SALT had stood for the former; the Helsinki Accords represented the latter, a kind of ersatz peace treaty for World War II.[25] During the détente years, the more permissive international system allowed the Federal Republic to pursue a new foreign policy toward eastern Europe. Although Chancellor Willy Brandt and his coalition—made up of the SPD and the Free Democratic Party (FDP)—remained firmly committed to the Western bloc and still held out hope for eventual German unification, they strove to normalize Bonn's relations with the Soviet Union, Communist eastern and central Europe, and the German Democratic Republic. They negotiated treaties that rejected the use of force and recognized the Oder-Neisse line as Germany's eastern border. The Basic Treaty of 1972 for the first time established formal relations between the Federal Republic of Germany and the German Democratic Republic and paved the way for greater political, economic, and cultural ties. Likewise, the Four Power Agreement on Berlin of 1972 reduced tensions among the former wartime allies and enhanced contacts between both halves of the divided city. In short, Brandt's new foreign policy, Ostpolitik, which Chancellor Schmidt continued after 1974, proved highly beneficial for the Federal Republic, refashioning West German foreign policy toward the East along realistic and constructive lines, improving trade opportunities for West German industry, and easing restrictions on travel and cultural exchanges between the two German states. It was therefore not surprising that both the Schmidt government and the Kohl government favored continuing a policy of enhanced political, economic, and cultural links to eastern Europe.

By the late 1970s, however, superpower relations had deteriorated markedly. In the waning years of the Carter administration, the United States shifted its approach toward the Soviet Union from accommodation to confrontation. Whereas the West Germans were more inclined to see the Afghanistan invasion as a case of the Soviet Union policing its sphere of influence, the United States regarded it as evidence of renewed Soviet expansionism.[26] The Reagan administration showed little interest in arms control, embarking on a massive arms buildup and adopting a more combative tone, with Reagan speculating early in his presidency that a nuclear war could be limited to Europe, referring in March 1983 to the Soviet Union as "an evil empire," and joking on a live microphone that the bombing of Russia would commence in five minutes.[27]

At this time, the United States and West Germany held divergent views on the merits of further normalization. Unlike Washington, which felt that the Soviets had taken advantage of the thaw and so believed that it now had to pursue a harder line toward Moscow, Bonn had achieved concrete benefits that it hoped to extend. It favored arms control as a way to correct the imbalance in INF without having to deploy new weapons to West Germany and as a means of reducing Cold War tensions. This reduction in tension would, in turn, make it easier for West Germany to continue its own little détente toward the East. In short, the West Germans hoped that détente would prove "divisible"—that is, sheltered and maintained in Europe—whereas the United States regarded it as "indivisible" and conditional upon the Soviet Union's good behavior globally and its human rights record.[28] "In terms of the pendulum swings vis-à-vis the Soviet Union, while the US pendulum swung from cooperation with high hopes under Nixon–Kissinger to disappointment under Jimmy

Carter and new confrontation under Ronald Reagan, the German pendulum remained stuck in a cooperative framework."[29]

In 1980, Chancellor Schmidt had called upon the United States and the Soviet Union to impose a three-year moratorium on deploying additional INF in Europe and planned a trip to Moscow as an "interpreter" in the hope of keeping détente and Ostpolitik alive. The Carter administration feared that the West Germans might be backsliding on the double-track decision and responded strongly, thereby prompting a bitter exchange between the West German chancellor and the American president.[30] In 1981, Chancellor Schmidt pressed the new Reagan administration on resuming INF negotiations. Chancellor Kohl, as had his predecessor, valued Ostpolitik, although he made sure that Bonn's ties to Washington and its own security did not suffer.[31] The Kohl government assiduously sought to develop economic relations between the Federal Republic and the Soviet Union, even as Washington pressed Bonn to limit them.[32] For the most part, Kohl managed to square the circle between close partnership with the United States and better relations with the German Democratic Republic and the Eastern bloc.[33] This outcome likely had to do with the good will in Washington that Kohl had earned as a result of his government's vote on INF deployment and decision to participate in SDI.[34]

In the late 1970s, the Soviet Union had queried western European governments about participating in the construction of a pipeline that would deliver Russian natural gas to the West. In 1980, the Schmidt government and Moscow reached an understanding, with the Federal Republic agreeing to have its firms and banks supply turbines, pipes, and financing.[35] France, the United Kingdom, the United States, and other countries also allowed their companies to sign contracts as well. The Reagan administration, however, voiced concerns that the pipeline would increase West European energy dependence and provide the Soviet Union with much needed credit. After the imposition of martial law in Poland in December 1981, the United States placed a trade embargo on Poland and the Soviet Union that included the parts and technology necessary for pipeline construction. In June 1982, the Reagan administration upped the ante by extending sanctions to the overseas subsidiaries of American companies and to firms that held licenses from American companies.[36] If foreign companies disregarded the extended sanctions, then, according to a leading US Commerce Department official, they could be banned from buying American merchandise and information, with legal action and fines ensuing. France, West Germany, and the United Kingdom expressed outrage at this extension, and the crisis escalated into one of NATO's worst.[37]

Why did this issue prove so difficult for US-German relations? At a time of high unemployment and energy dependence on the volatile Middle East, Bonn balked at the Reagan administration's unilateral decision on sanctions. Although exports to the East were never a very high share of overall US or German trade—by 1975 they had risen to 7.2 percent of West German exports and to 2.6 percent of US exports—they remained much more important to the West German economy than to the US economy.[38] Moreover, Schmidt later pointed out that the United States was expecting economic sacrifice on the part of the Germans but was unwilling to halt its own grain exports to the Soviet Union.[39] The West German government had further concerns about détente, its sovereignty, and its contractual obligations.[40] Washington soon backed down in part because the new US secretary of state, George P. Shultz, shared Helmut Schmidt's concerns that the dispute might complicate the stationing of INF in Europe.[41]

In March 1983, President Reagan announced the SDI. To the president, space-based defense promised an alternative to the deterrence-based doctrine of mutually assured destruction. In his television address to the nation, he asked, "What if free people could live secure in the knowledge that their security did not rest upon the threat of instant US retaliation to deter a Soviet attack, that we could intercept and destroy strategic ballistic missiles before they reached our own soil or that of our allies?"[42] In short, by envisioning security for the United States that would not require the Soviet Union's consent, the Reagan administration foreshadowed a strategic shift from mutual deterrence to unilateral defense.[43] To Washington, SDI offered an alternative to détente that promised to ensure safety for the country and more independence from its allies.[44]

The Western allies, however, did not share Reagan's hostility to mutually assured destruction. Moreover, France, the United Kingdom, and the Federal Republic had doubts about SDI's implications for the Anti–Ballistic Missile Treaty of 1972, their place in the Atlantic alliance in light of their not being consulted on SDI, whether they would be more vulnerable to Soviet INF, and SDI's impact on the military balance and détente.[45]

According to Hanrieder, "From the German perspective, deterrence has always conveyed the reassuring intent to prevent the outbreak of hostilities; defense has always meant that deterrence has failed and hostilities have broken out, presumably involving the German people and German territory. Over the decades, deterrence came to signify for the Germans an antiwar or at least a prewar military posture; defense signified a wartime posture and the ultimate calamity."[46] Bonn likewise had initial concerns about SDI's implications for the singularization of the West German position, American unilateralism, and the possible decoupling of the United States from Europe.[47] The Kohl government withheld its endorsement of the initiative until it was reassured on three points: "1) Will SDI jeopardize the Geneva Arms Control Talks? 2) Can SDI lead to a decoupling of America from Europe? 3) Will SDI research result in a 'brain drain'?"[48] After two years of bilateral talks with the United States, the Federal Republic was on board with SDI, in 1985 agreeing in a memorandum and welcoming the economic opportunities presented to West Germany's industry and science community.[49] Nevertheless, just 22 percent of West Germans favored their country's involvement in SDI, according to polls conducted in late 1986 and early 1987.[50]

West German Domestic Politics: The Schmidt Government

Domestic political pressures played a significant role during the INF debate. In the early 1980s, the largely stalled arms-control negotiations and the widespread perception in West Germany that the Reagan administration was not serious about an accord with the Soviets added to the political woes of Chancellor Helmut Schmidt, who led an increasingly precarious SPD-FDP coalition government. Backed by the churches, trade unions, and the newly formed Green Party, which featured Petra Kelly and General Gert Bastian as prominent anti-NATO activists, a resurgent West German peace movement swelled in the early 1980s after the double-track policy was announced. In Bonn, an estimated three hundred thousand gathered in October 1981 to protest against INF deployment; the following June, as Ronald Reagan visited the capital, an even larger crowd rallied. In addition, several million West Germans signed the Krefeld Appeal, which rejected nuclear deployment. In terms of public

President Ronald Reagan with Chancellor Helmut Schmidt (*right*) and West Berlin mayor Richard von Weizsäcker at "Checkpoint Charlie" near the Berlin Wall, June 11, 1982. (Courtesy of the Ronald Reagan Presidential Library)

opinion, however, West Germans indicated plurality support (between 48 percent and 54 percent from 1981 to 1983) for the double-track decision, but a clear majority (57 percent to 66 percent in 1983 and 1984) were against the deployment of nuclear weapons on German soil.[51] Although most West Germans were increasingly critical of the Reagan administration, they nonetheless remained supportive of the United States, but those in the peace movement, especially its educated, younger adherents, expressed strongly anti-American views.[52]

The opposition to INF deployment extended to the SPD's left wing and endangered Schmidt's ability to implement the double-track decision. At an SPD congress in April 1982, 40 percent of members had backed disarmament. The following month, however, one-third of the delegates at an FDP congress rejected the double-track decision.[53] In May 1981, the chancellor threatened to resign unless his unruly party fell in line. Foreign Minister Hans-Dietrich Genscher issued a similar threat to his party, the FDP, that same month.[54] In short, the INF issue roiled German politics and jeopardized the Schmidt government. Throughout this period, Chancellor Schmidt cited his difficult domestic political situation when pressing Washington on the negotiations track. According to Steve Breyman, "organized West European pacifists as filtered through a Schmidt government under fire from the grass roots of the SPD" helped convince the Reagan administration to begin INF talks with the Soviets in late 1981.[55] In September 1982, the SPD–FDP coalition collapsed after the liberals shifted their support to Helmut Kohl and the Christian Democrats. The Christian Democratic Union (CDU) and the CSU had been critical of the SPD for not supporting the US negotiating stance on INF and for its attempts to have Chancellor Schmidt pressure the Reagan administration to adopt a more conciliatory approach.[56] For Kohl, the worsening of American–West German relations had provided a key reason to topple Helmut Schmidt as chancellor.[57]

West German Domestic Politics: The Kohl Government

Unlike Helmut Schmidt, who had served as an officer during World War II, his successor, Helmut Kohl, had been spared conscription into Hitler's army because of, as he poignantly phrased it, "the mercy of the late birth" (he was born in 1930). Kohl became chancellor in late 1982, after taking a quite different path to power than had his predecessor. Rather than achieve recognition as a policy expert and skilled technocrat, Kohl excelled at party politics and soon advanced in the center-right CDU—first in his home city of Ludwigshafen, then in the state of Rhineland-Palatinate, and subsequently in the federal party, when he became chair in 1973—a post he held until 1998. He was sworn in as minister president in Rhineland-Palatinate in 1969, a region with more American soldiers than any other in Europe, which afforded him the opportunity to begin to build relations with US officials.[58] Kohl's domestic critics often dismissed him as being provincial and plodding. Nonetheless, at key moments during his chancellorship he showed decisive and effective leadership, whether in advancing European integration or in forging national unification in 1990—his crowning achievement.

Chancellor Kohl came to power as the German peace movement was cresting. Yet he did not face the same vulnerabilities as Schmidt because the CDU and its Bavarian sister party, the CSU, stood much more firmly behind the double-track decision than had the divided SPD. Nonetheless, although Kohl did not conceive of Bonn as a mediator between Washington and Moscow, his administration urged President Reagan to show flexibility during INF negotiations and proposed an "interim solution" (*Zwischenlösung*) that would allow for ceilings in place of the less probable zero option. Once again, German domestic politics mattered, with federal elections slated for March 1983 and the SPD shifting leftward on the INF issue. Noted Strobe Talbott in 1984, "Thus like the 'zero option' in 1981, the catch phrase that would end up becoming American policy in 1983—the 'interim solution'—was a translation from German, and from the language of West German domestic politics."[59]

In the Bundestag election of March 1983, the Christian Democrats and Free Democrats achieved a clear victory that put their coalition on a sound footing. The SPD lost, and the pacifist Greens, staunchly opposed to missile deployment, became the first new party to enter the Bundestag in three decades. As the INF vote in the German Bundestag neared, peace movement demonstrations swelled as hundreds of thousands marched against deployment. Now out of office, the SPD held a party congress in Cologne and overwhelmingly backed a resolution opposing the missiles. In the November Bundestag vote, all SPD deputies voted against deployment. The CDU-CSU coalition and the FDP held firm as all but one of their deputies, who abstained, voted in favor of it.

A few years later it was Chancellor Kohl's turn to struggle with an internal revolt over INF that, as it had during the Schmidt chancellorship, tested transatlantic ties. Only this time, the roles were reversed, with the Reagan administration pushing for a sweeping INF settlement by 1987 (double zero) and the West German government applying the brakes. A group within the CDU-CSU coalition had long viewed the zero option with trepidation in light of the existing imbalance in conventional forces, and once it was confronted with the real possibility of a double-zero settlement, it opposed the option on the grounds that Germany would be the one to bear the full brunt of a nuclear exchange, given the many short-range tactical nuclear weapons stationed on German soil.[60]

In 1987, Washington presented Kohl with an unappetizing choice: either accept the double-zero option or deploy additional shorter-range INF. Within West Germany, those resisting the double-zero approach included the CSU, whose leader, Franz Josef Strauss, had long been critical of the zero option; the CDU's right wing (known as the Stahlhelmfraktion, or Steel Helmet Faction), headed by Alfred Dregger; and the federal Defense Ministry. Supporters of the approach included the SPD, the Green Party, and the FDP as well as, although not openly, the foreign minister, Hans-Dietrich Genscher.[61] Public opinion also favored this approach to disarmament by a large majority. Helmut Kohl hesitated as his fraying coalition questioned the double-zero proposal, as West German public opinion stood behind it, and as the Federal Republic's NATO partners sided with Washington in support of the proposed treaty terms. In mid-May, the CDU suffered election losses in Hamburg (–1.4 percentage points) and Rhineland-Palatinate (–6.8 percentage points), and the FDP gained. The CDU federal leadership attributed the party's losses to the missile controversy.[62] The Kohl government, divided at home and isolated abroad, eventually chose to back the double-zero proposal.

Soon thereafter, however, the Soviet Union demanded that the Federal Republic's Pershing I missiles be removed as well. Again, the right wing of the CDU-CSU coalition demurred, and again the Federal Republic faced potential diplomatic isolation. Once more, only this time more decisively, the Kohl government agreed to comply. Strauss and the CSU subsequently voiced disapproval of the double-zero decision, but to no avail.[63] As in 1983, the West German government in 1987 chose not to position itself against the United States and its allies. Were it to have done so, then the Kohl government would have likely paid a heavy price abroad and at home. The chancellor would have faced the prospects of yet another deployment controversy and with it the revitalization of the West German peace movement.

Final Thoughts: The Role of Leaders and Leadership

Despite serious challenges, the United States and West Germany remained close allies and together implemented difficult measures during the last decade of the Cold War. They had agreed in the late 1970s on the double-track decision, and after US-Soviet negotiations failed, the West Germans voted to deploy Pershing II and Cruise missiles. When subsequent arms-control talks were successful, they agreed on removing this class of weapons, notwithstanding significant reservations within the Kohl government. Concerns about economic policy, détente, SDI, and arms control had tried the relationship between the two partners but not taken it off track. By the end of the decade, the United States showed its commitment to German national aspirations by backing German unification early on and throughout—something that could not be said of Bonn's partners in Paris and London. Although German-American relations showed strains, they proved highly resilient.

Both Washington and Bonn recognized the importance of economic and security partnership. For the Federal Republic, the United States, as the world's leading power, remained an indispensable ally that offered security from the Soviet Union. For the United States, West Germany was a crucial frontline democracy that buttressed the Atlantic alliance, was a key economic partner, and generally served as an Atlanticist and free-trade advocate within the European Community.

Yet strong leadership maintained the close partnership. The Schmidt government, although on occasion outspoken in its criticism of US policy, nonetheless carried through on its end of the INF bargain under very difficult circumstances. Helmut Schmidt enjoyed a better personal relation with Ronald Reagan than with Jimmy Carter, against whom he had repeatedly clashed. In his memoirs, he stated his initial impression of Reagan that he was "once again dealing with a consistent and therefore reliable American president."[64] He identified three main character traits in Reagan: an ability to simplify complex material and then on that basis draw political conclusions; a firm belief in the principles that made America great; and an uncanny ability to communicate to the public in an accessible way. Although Schmidt acknowledged Reagan's sincere belief in free trade, he viewed his budget policy as disastrous.[65] For his part, Reagan appreciated the domestic pressures under which the West German chancellor stood and accommodated him on INF by resuming talks and by adopting the zero-option position. Yet the two leaders overlapped in office for less than two years and did not forge a close personal relationship. In Reagan's memoirs, Schmidt is mentioned only a few times and not in a particularly favorable light. The two had different political styles and personalities. Rather than articulating a broad vision, Schmidt favored a pragmatic approach and was comfortable dealing with technical problems. He once quipped: "Whoever has visions should go see the doctor." Reagan was less interested in the nitty-gritty and did not shy away from espousing grand principles.

Chancellor Kohl developed a good working relationship with President Reagan. Both were from center-right parties, although Kohl did not represent the conservative wing of his party and, unlike Reagan, had made his career as a consummate party man by building close ties with officials at all levels of the CDU. In light of Schmidt's poor rapport with Carter and the rise of sentiment within the SPD Left that was highly critical of the Reagan administration, Kohl and the CDU-CSU coalition came to office intent on improving relations with the United States. After meeting President Reagan in fall 1982, Kohl indicated that they had clicked right away: "We get along well together; we like each other; we are on the same wavelength." Aides on both sides reported that the "chemistry" between the two leaders was right.[66] On key issues such as INF and SDI, Chancellor Kohl generally kept his reservations private and in the end took strong pro-Washington positions. In his memoirs, Kohl praised Reagan's domestic- and foreign-policy accomplishments, in stark contrast to Schmidt's more critical tone, and wrote that he was honored to interact with a man of Reagan's stature.[67]

The Reagan administration valued Helmut Kohl as a dependable partner and appreciated his support on INF and SDI. In return, it did not complain when Kohl continued his predecessors' Ostpolitik policy. In 1984, Reagan accepted Kohl's invitation to visit the German military cemetery in Bitburg, West Germany, where they would lay a commemoratory wreath. The visit was intended to showcase German-American friendship four decades after World War II, but it turned into a public-relations disaster for the Reagan administration after it became known that Waffen SS soldiers were buried in Bitburg and that the US president had declined to visit a German concentration camp. Sharply criticized by American Jewish groups, Reagan made matters worse at a press conference when he referred to the SS men as "victims of Nazism also. . . . They were victims, just as surely as the victims in the concentration camps."[68] Despite the growing controversy, Reagan did not cancel his visit to Bitburg (but he did also go to a concentration camp) in order not to embarrass Helmut Kohl and, as he wrote later, not "to keep on punishing Germans for the Holocaust."[69] The political scientist Christian Hacke summarizes the two men's relationship: "Kohl's main interest lay in maintaining the strength of the alliance. Washington, in turn, paid greater attention to German arguments. Reagan came to value Kohl as his most important partner in Europe."[70]

With West Germany concerned about unilateralist tendencies in Washington during the 1980s, the Reagan administration sought to reassure its ally. Reagan's rhetoric and occasional loose talk, however, did cause Bonn some headaches because not a few Germans took Reagan's anti-Communist pronouncements and his musings on a nuclear war in Europe at face value, which in turn stoked anti-Americanism in the Federal Republic, especially among those in the peace movement. To Hanrieder, "The more the United States escalated its verbal assaults on the Soviet Union to levels of stridency recalling the Cold War, the more it produced in Europe and especially in Germany the opposite reaction: American bellicosity and European pacifism were interdependent."[71] In 1980, polls showed that 42 percent of West Germans agreed with US defense and security policy, and 31 percent disagreed. By 1982, only 18 percent agreed with US defense and security policy, and 62 percent disagreed with it.[72] Reagan's rhetorical flourishes (not dissimilar to George W. Bush's two decades later) did not play well among West Germans, who were quick to draw upon the cliché of the trigger-happy cowboy of the Western films Reagan had done. Even Reagan's speech at the Brandenburg Gate in 1987, in which he said, "Mr. Gorbachev, tear down this wall," and proposed ways to make West Berlin a more attractive international center, largely fell flat at a time when most West German elites preferred constructive engagement with the East to provocative language. Six months later the leading German news magazine, *Der Spiegel,* noted that Reagan's challenge to Gorbachev was a nonstarter and described his plans for West Berlin as poorly conceived, the work of dilettantes, and a dud.[73]

From a post–Cold War perspective, the US-German exertions of the Reagan era worked out very well indeed. NATO's decision to deploy Pershing II and Cruise missiles to western Europe sent a message to Moscow that the West was determined to protect its security and that that the Soviet Union would therefore either have to engage in a costly arms race or blaze another trail—such as Gorbachev's "new thinking" and the aspiration of a "common European home."[74] Likewise, Reagan's SDI, in which West Germany in the end participated, may have contributed to the crisis in Soviet communism, which could not keep up with American technology.[75] Moreover, in hindsight, President Reagan's exhortation to Gorbachev at the Berlin Wall has been taken as evidence that Reagan regarded the German Question as still open and relevant even at a time when the West German establishment had made peace with the postwar settlement.[76] To Hacke, Reagan "did not gallop backward into the 1950s, as his critics charged, but was the first man to glimpse the vision of the 1990s and to hammer on the gate for a united Germany within a united Europe."[77] Finally, it seems likely that Bonn's key role in the deployment and removal of the intermediate-range nuclear missiles generated trust and enhanced loyalty between the two allies that buttressed the George H. W. Bush administration's decision to back German unification so strongly. This support proved essential in 1989–1990, when President Bush, Reagan's former vice president, stood by Germany every step of the way as it realized its long-standing goal of national unity.[78]

Notes

1. "Fulda Gap Is Key Point in NATO Defense against Soviet Forces," Associated Press, March 1, 1987, at http://articles.latimes.com/1987-03-01/news/mn-6926_1_fulda-gap.

2. Dan van der Vat, "Helmut Schmidt obituary," *Guardian,* November 10, 2015, at http://www.theguardian.com/world/2015/nov/10/helmut-schmidt.

3. Richard C. Eichenberg, "Dual Track and Double Trouble: The Two-Level Politics of INF," in *Double-Edged Diplomacy: International Bargaining and Domestic Politics,* ed. Peter B. Evans, Harold K. Jacobsen, and Robert D. Putnam (Berkeley: University of California Press, 1993), 47–48.

4. Helmut Schmidt, "The 1977 Alastair Buchan Memorial Lecture," *Survival* 20, no. 1 (1978): 3–4.

5. Ibid.

6. Wolfram F. Hanrieder, *Germany, America, Europe: Forty Years of German Foreign Policy* (New Haven, CT: Yale University Press, 1999), 110; Helga Haftendorn, *Coming of Age: German Foreign Policy since 1945* (Lanham, MD: Rowman and Littlefield, 2006), 250.

7. Lynne E. Davis, "Lessons of the INF Treaty," *Foreign Affairs* 66, no. 4 (1988): 721.

8. Hanrieder, *Germany, America, Europe,* 112–13.

9. Ibid., 114–15.

10. See Strobe Talbott, *Deadly Gambits: The Reagan Administration and the Stalemate in Nuclear Arms Control* (New York: Knopf, 1984).

11. Thomas Risse-Kappen, *The Zero Option: INF, West Germany, and Arms Control,* trans. Leslie Booth (Boulder, CO: Westview Press, 1988), 78–85.

12. Helmut Schmidt, *Men and Powers: A Political Retrospective,* trans. Ruth Hein (New York: Random House, 1989), 246.

13. Risse-Kappen, *Zero Option,* 85–101.

14. Ibid., 109–17.

15. Quoted in Clay Clemens, *Reluctant Realists: The Christian Democrats and West German Ostpolitik* (Durham, NC: Duke University Press, 1989), 142.

16. Haftendorn, *Coming of Age,* 265–67; Hanrieder, *Germany, America, Europe,* 116–21.

17. Hanrieder, *Germany, America, Europe,* 118.

18. Harold James, "Cooperation, Competition, and Conflict: Economic Relations between the United States and Germany, 1968–1990," in *The United States and Germany in the Era of the Cold War, 1968–1990,* vol. 2: *A Handbook,* ed. Detlef Junker, Philipp Gassert, and Wilfried Mausbach (Washington, DC: German Historical Institute and Cambridge University Press, 2004), 197. See also Hanrieder, *Germany, America, Europe,* 323–28.

19. James, "Cooperation, Competition, and Conflict," 2:196.

20. Quoted in ibid., 2:197.

21. Paul Kennedy, *The Rise and Fall of the Great Powers: Economic Change and Military Conflict from 1500 to 2000* (New York: Random House, 1987).

22. Schmidt, *Men and Powers,* 272.

23. Harold James, "The Deutsche Mark and the Dollar: Domestic Price Stability and the Dollar," in *The United States and Germany in the Era of the Cold War,* ed. Junker, Gassert, and Mausbach, 2:232.

24. Andreas Falke, "American and German Trade Policy: Between Liberal Multilateralism, Neoprotectionism, and Regional Integration," in *The United States and Germany in the Era of the Cold War,* ed. Junker, Gassert, and Mausbach, 2:223–27.

25. Hanrieder, *Germany, America, Europe,* 104–5.

26. Haftendorn, *Coming of Age,* 258.

27. When asked whether he could foresee a nuclear war being limited to Europe, President Reagan responded, "I honestly don't know," and then continued: "And if you still had that kind of a stalemate, I could see where you could have the exchange of tactical weapons against troops in the field without it bringing either one of the major powers to pushing the button" (quoted in Geoffrey Godsell, "Limited Nuclear Warfare: Why Reagan Worries Europe," *Christian Science Monitor,* October 21, 1981). See also Ronald Reagan, "evil empire" speech, March 8, 1983, at http://millercenter.org/president/speeches/speech-3409.

28. Hanrieder, *Germany, America, Europe,* 211–14.

29. Geir Lundestad, "The European Role at the Beginning and Particularly the End of the Cold War," in *The Last Decade of the Cold War: From Conflict Escalation to Conflict Transformation,* ed. Olav Njølstad (London: Frank Cass, 2004), 68.

30. Haftendorn, *Coming of Age,* 260–61; Eichenberg, "Dual Track and Double Trouble," 50–51.

31. Clemens, *Reluctant Realists,* 307–8.

32. Timothy Garton Ash, *In Europe's Name: Germany and the Divided Continent* (New York: Random House, 1993), 102.

33. Clemens, *Reluctant Realists,* 277–313.

34. Klaus Schwabe, "Détente and Multipolarity: The Cold War and German-American Relations, 1968–1990," in *The United States and Germany in the Era of the Cold War,* ed. Junker, Gassert, and Mausbach, 2:8–9.

35. Wallace J. Thies, *Why NATO Endures* (Cambridge: Cambridge University Press, 2009), 244.

36. Ibid., 253.

37. Ibid., 253–57.

38. Welf Werner, "Emancipation, Regionalization, and Globalization: German-American Trade Relations," in *The United States and Germany in the Era of the Cold War, 1968–1990,* ed. Junker, Gassert, and Mausbach, 2:217–18.

39. Werner D. Lippert, "Economic Diplomacy and East–West Trade during the Era of Détente: Strategy or Obstacle for the West," in *The Crisis of Détente in Europe: From Helsinki to Gorbachev, 1975–1985,* ed. Leopoldo Nuti (London: Routledge, 2009), 196.

40. Schwabe, "Détente and Multipolarity," 2:8; Thies, *Why NATO Endures,* 254–55; Lippert, "Economic Diplomacy and East–West Trade," 197.

41. Thies, *Why NATO Endures,* 262.

42. Ronald Reagan, "Address to the Nation on Defense and National Security," March 23, 1983, at http://www.reagan.utexas.edu/archives/speeches/1983/32383d.htm.

43. Thomas C. Schelling, "What Went Wrong with Arms Control?" *Foreign Affairs* 64, no. 2 (1985–1986): 232; Hanrieder, *Germany, America, Europe,* 127.

44. Hanrieder, *Germany, America, Europe,* 128.

45. Sean N. Kalic, "Reagan's SDI Announcement and the European Reaction: Diplomacy in the Last Decade of the Cold War," in *Crisis of Détente in Europe,* ed. Nuti, 99–110, esp. 102–3.

46. Hanrieder, *Germany, America, Europe,* 123–24.

47. Ibid., 123–25.

48. Kalic, "Reagan's SDI Announcement and the European Reaction," 104.

49. Ibid., 104–5.

50. See polling data in Werner J. Feld, "The Role of the Federal Republic of Germany in NATO," in *The Federal Republic of Germany at Forty,* ed. Peter H. Merkl (New York: New York University Press, 1989), 405.

51. See polling data in Risse-Kappen, *Zero Option,* 73.

52. Harald Mueller and Thomas Risse-Kappen, "Origins of Estrangement: The Peace Movement and the Changed Image of America in West Germany," *International Security* 12, no. 1 (1987): 52–88, esp. 54–70.

53. Risse-Kappen, *Zero Option,* 75–76.

54. Robert Leicht, "1982: Wenn Kanzler kippen," *Die Zeit,* October 16, 2003, at http://www.zeit.de/2003/43/Reg'krise_1982.

55. Steve Breyman, *Why Movements Matter: The West German Peace Movement and U.S. Arms Control Policy* (Albany: State University of New York Press, 2001), 80.

56. Clemens, *Reluctant Realists,* 216.

57. Hanrieder, *Germany, America, Europe,* 116.

58. Henning Köhler, *Helmut Kohl: Ein Leben für die Politik. Die Biographie* (Cologne: Bastei Lübbe, 2014), 161–62.

59. Talbott, *Deadly Gambits,* 172.

60. See Risse-Kappen, *Zero Option,* 124–35.

61. Ibid., 132.

62. Ibid., 138.

63. Ibid., 140–43.

64. Schmidt, *Men and Powers,* 245.

65. Ibid., 247.

66. Quoted in Jürgen Leinemann, "Die Märchenwelt des 'Bitburg-Gipfels,'" *Der Spiegel,* May 6, 1985.

67. Helmut Kohl, *Erinnerungen, 1982–1990* (Munich: Droemer, 2005), 63–64.

68. Quoted in Deborah E. Lipstadt, "The Bitburg Controversy," in *American Jewish Year Book,* vol. 87 (New York: American Jewish Committee; Philadelphia: Jewish Publication Society, 1987), 26.

69. Ronald Reagan, *An American Life: The Autobiography* (New York: Simon and Schuster, 1990), 380–81.

70. Christian Hacke, "The United States and the German Question," in *The United States and Germany in the Era of the Cold War,* ed. Junker, Gassert, and Mausbach, 2:23–24.

71. Hanrieder, *Germany, America, Europe,* 216.

72. See table 5 in Mueller and Risse-Kappen, "Origins of Estrangement," 61.

73. "Berlin: Amateure am Werk," *Der Spiegel,* January 18, 1988.

74. Michael Broer, "The NATO Double-Track Decision, the INF Treaty, and the SNF Controversy: German-American Relations between Consensus and Conflict," in *The United States and Germany in the Era of the Cold War,* ed. Junker, Gassert, and Mausbach, 2:154.

75. See Beth A. Fischer, "The United States and the Transformation of the Cold War," in *The Last Decade of the Cold War,* ed. Njølstad, 227–28, and John Lewis Gaddis, *The Cold War: A New History* (New York: Penguin, 2005), 227.

76. Hacke, "The United States and the German Question," 2:24.

77. Ibid.

78. Schwabe, "Détente and Multipolarity," 2:9–14; Stephen F. Szabo, "The United States and German Unification," in *The United States and Germany in the Era of the Cold War,* ed. Junker, Gassert, and Mausbach, 2:104–5.

Part 3

Asia, Latin America, and the Middle East

9

Ronald Reagan and the Puzzles of "So-Called Communist China" and Vietnam

Michael Schaller

At a National Security Council meeting on September 20, 1983, Secretary of State George P. Shultz and a small group of advisers briefed President Ronald Reagan on recent political and economic developments in the People's Republic of China (PRC). Shultz and his colleagues spoke positively of the "headway in our relations with China" and noted progress on issues related to both trade and security. Under Deng Xiaoping's pragmatic leadership, the administration's China experts believed, many of the Cold War tensions that originated with the Communist victory in 1949 were being swept away. After listening silently for some time, Reagan suddenly interjected, "You mean our position should be 'no ticky, no laundry'?"[1] The president, who often deflected complex discussions with a humorous anecdote, limited his remarks on developments within the world's most populous nation to retelling a mildly racist ethnic joke poking fun at the limited English of immigrant Chinese laundry workers in the United States. Before and after becoming president, Reagan remained confused by the meaning of events in China and deeply ambivalent over how to deal with the PRC. In many ways, the PRC—like the Communist regime that had taken over Vietnam in 1975—remained a puzzle that failed to conform to his notion of a world divided between "free" democratic nations and "totalitarian" Communist nations.

Since beginning his long campaign for the presidency in 1976, Reagan frequently warned the American public that his Republican as well as Democratic rivals' retreat before communism in Asia was as flawed as the pursuit of détente with the Soviet Union. Both actions had betrayed the nation's allies and endangered its security. He condemned Richard Nixon's diplomatic opening to China and subsequent negotiated withdrawal from South Vietnam as moral and strategic blunders that left key Asian allies such as Japan, Taiwan, and Thailand vulnerable to Communist military and economic threats. Reagan complained that Presidents Gerald Ford and Jimmy Carter made these problems worse. Just as he faulted détente with the Soviet Union as a form of unilateral disarmament, he pledged to reverse course in Asia and heal an America whose leaders suffered from what he called the "Vietnam Syndrome," a refusal to support friendly foreign regimes or to resist Soviet threats. As president, Reagan promised, he would stand up to aggressors and stand by friends.

Both supporters and critics of Reagan's foreign policies have written surprisingly little on his approaches toward China and Vietnam. And East Asian affairs are largely absent from Reagan's own accounts of his presidency. For example, in his memoir *An American Life,* the former president recalls that in preparation for his first visit to China in 1984, he practiced using chopsticks and consulted with Richard Nixon. What did he recall of Nixon's advice? "Don't ask about the food they serve you at the big banquets, just swallow it." The president's diary account of his state visit expressed a similar travel-guide naivety about the mysterious Orient and "inscrutable" Chinese.[2]

Despite his relatively few expressed thoughts and opinions about China while in the White House, Reagan frequently criticized efforts by his three predecessors (Nixon, Ford, and Carter) to improve the US relationship with the PRC. He voiced even more criticism about Carter's tentative moves to restore contact with the Communist government in the Socialist Republic of Vietnam. Like many conservative Republicans in the 1970s, the then California governor harbored grave doubts about the wisdom of initiatives by Nixon, Ford, and Carter. He especially worried over how the dialogue with Beijing would affect America's long-standing Cold War ally Taiwan (Republic of China).

Soon after Nixon startled the nation by announcing in July 1971 his opening to the PRC, he persuaded Reagan to travel as his personal emissary to Taiwan in a bid to reassure its longtime leader Chiang Kai-Shek (Jiang Jieshi) that Washington would never "sell Taiwan down the river." Nixon also hoped to use Reagan's stature among conservatives and hard-line cold warriors to mollify the criticism coming from what remained of the so-called China Lobby, an informal network of American anti-Communist activists who had supported Taiwan since 1949 and opposed recognition of the Chinese Communist regime. Despite his own deep misgivings, Reagan agreed to deliver Nixon's message to Chiang. The purpose of his visit, he later recalled, was to explain to Chiang that Nixon and Kissinger's opening to Beijing "did not mean an abandonment of our relationship with the Republic of China." To emphasize his personal feelings on this point, while attending Taiwan's National Day celebration in October 1971, Reagan supplemented Nixon's assurance with his own public pledge of support. "We will weaken no cherished associations; we will break no promises. Our defense commitment remains in full force and we will continue to support the full participation of the Republic of China [Taiwan] in the international community."[3]

Nixon convinced a skeptical Reagan to undertake this hand-holding mission to Taiwan by assuring him that the purpose behind the China opening was primarily a tactical move to tie down and further weaken the Soviet Union. After all, he told Reagan, if the Soviets had to worry about the security of their 4,500-mile border with China, their ability to cause mischief elsewhere would be limited. Reagan explained Nixon's reasoning (and his own thoughts) in a private letter he wrote to a friend and conservative political activist during the president's historic trip to China in February 1972. Conservatives, Reagan observed, should ignore the "forgive and forget" nice words Nixon lavished on Mao Zedong and other Communist leaders. The true purpose of the trip was not to appease Chinese communism, but this information could not be publicly revealed because it would "blow the whole diplomatic game plan." Nixon, Reagan asserted, recognized that "American public opinion will no longer tolerate wars of the Vietnam type because they no longer feel a threat—thanks to the liberal press, from Communism." Ordinary Americans had unfortunately lost sight of the fact that wars like the one fought in Vietnam were "really in defense of freedom and our own country." Nixon, however, recognized the "disaffection between China and Russia, [and so] visits China, butters up the warlords, and lets them be because they have nothing to fear from us." This American pivot would force the Soviets to commit "140 divisions on the Chinese border," would increase tension between the Communist giants, and would provide "a little time and elbow room" for the United States. This "simple strategic move," Reagan held, "was a million miles removed from the soft appeasement of previous Democratic administrations." Although Nixon's goals in approaching China were neither as secret as Reagan suggested nor that different from what many Asia specialists in government and academic circles had favored ever since the creation of the PRC, Reagan clearly felt a need to justify his going along with this opening to a Communist regime by framing it primarily as an anti-Soviet scheme.[4]

Reagan's faith in Nixon's approach was soon shaken by what he saw as the administration's lackluster effort to defend Taiwan's continued membership in the United Nations (UN) and other international organizations. Nixon hoped the UN would allow Taiwan to retain a seat in its body even if it transferred representation in the General Assembly and Security Council to the PRC. But President Nixon and National Security Adviser Henry Kissinger made only token efforts to preserve Taiwan's UN seats in the fall of 1971. The UN vote to expel Taiwan infuriated Reagan. The California governor urged Nixon to go on television and denounce the UN or even to quit the world body. He insisted that, if nothing else, the administration should slash US funding for the UN. When Nixon ignored these demands, Reagan understood that Nixon had dispatched him to Taiwan as a sop to mollify fellow conservatives uneasy with the opening to China. This deception added to Reagan's growing misgivings about Nixon's domestic and foreign policies.

Although Reagan declined to challenge Nixon's renomination in 1972, he shed few tears when the disgraced president resigned in August 1974 amid the Watergate scandals. The new, unelected president, Gerald Ford, had a weak base among Republicans, and Reagan recognized his rival's vulnerability. As the leading Sunbelt conservative in a Republican Party that increasingly reflected the views of its growing southern and western base, Reagan accused Ford of continuing Nixon's misguided policy of détente abroad and social moderation at home. In June 1975, the now former California governor ridiculed President Ford for his continuing efforts to cooperate with the Soviet Union and to establish full diplomatic relations (as distinct from the existing liaison office, which was short of formal relations) with what Reagan continued to call "Red China." Ford was, in fact, pursuing pledges that Nixon and Kissinger had secretly made to Chinese leaders to move toward formal ties. In 1976, when Reagan declared his intention to seek the Republican presidential nomination, he told Ford that one of the reasons for his challenge was his opposition to any deal that called for abandoning Taiwan while normalizing relations with China.[5] The growing support of Reagan within the Republican Party and other attacks on administration policies from the right persuaded Ford to abandon efforts to normalize diplomatic relations with the PRC before the election in 1976. Although Ford narrowly beat back Reagan's quest for the Republican Party nomination, he lost the election to Democratic Party nominee Jimmy Carter.

Over the next several years, Reagan sniped at President Carter as Carter inched toward formalizing US ties with China. To demonstrate his own foreign-policy credentials in advance of the next presidential campaign, Reagan traveled to Asia during April 1978. In visits to Japan and Taiwan, he stressed their strategic importance in the Cold War. In a meeting with Taiwan's new strongman Chiang Ching-kuo (Jiang Jingguo, son of Chiang Kai-shek) and in public speeches, Reagan declared that it was "hard for me to believe than any sensible American who believes in individual liberty and self-determination would stand by and let his government abandon an ally whose only 'sins' are that it is small and loves freedom." (Taiwan, in fact, was ruled by martial law until 1987 and remained a one-party dictatorship until the 1990s.) In a warning to Carter, Reagan asserted that the administration would pay a "serious price" and lose credibility as an ally if it improved relations with China at Taiwan's expense.[6]

Ignoring Reagan's warning, on January 1, 1979, Jimmy Carter established full diplomatic relations with China. In a deal months in the making, the United States withdrew diplomatic recognition from Taiwan and abrogated the defense pact with the island that stretched back to the mid-1950s. However, the United States maintained vigorous commercial ties with Taiwan as well as de facto diplomatic relations through an ostensibly private organization staffed by retired diplomats. Chinese and American negotiators included ambiguous wording in their agreement as to whether the United States could continue to sell weapons to Taiwan. US officials interpreted the language as permitting sales for the time being, but the Chinese insisted it precluded new arms sales. Reagan condemned Carter's act of "betrayal" and warned that it risked "consigning Taiwan's 17 million people to the rule of Communism." The former governor made a quick campaign trip to Taiwan, where he again promised to stand by an ally.[7]

Although most Americans and their congressional representatives supported the normalization of relations with China, many shared at least some of Reagan's misgivings about Taiwan's security. In April 1979, Carter signed the Taiwan Relations Act, which Congress had passed by large bipartisan majorities. This law governing future informal ties with Taiwan contained security guarantees that paralleled the terms of the now cancelled Mutual Defense Treaty of 1954. Future relations with China, the law declared, would rest "upon the expectation that the future of Taiwan will be determined by peaceful means" and that "any effort to determine the future of Taiwan by other than peaceful means, including boycotts or embargoes," would be considered a "threat to the peace and security of the Western Pacific and of grave concern to the United States." The law also required the president to "provide Taiwan such defense articles and defense services in such quality as may be necessary to enable Taiwan to maintain a sufficient self-defense capability."[8]

China's new supreme leader at the time, Deng Xiaoping, felt betrayed by this wording, which appeared to continue US interference in what China considered its internal affairs. (The PRC viewed Taiwan as a renegade province, not an independent country.) But Deng's anger was outweighed by China's reliance on close ties with the United States to bolster its economic modernization, to continue to shield it from Soviet pressure, and to support it in its brief border war with Vietnam during the spring of 1979. Nevertheless, the issue of US arms sales to Taiwan remained a sore point during the Reagan administration and beyond.

During the presidential campaign of 1980, Reagan portrayed Carter's recognition of the PRC and the abrogation of the defense treaty with Taiwan as one more misguided effort to appease America's enemies by abandoning its friends, such as the shah of Iran and Nicaraguan president Anastasio Somoza. The Republican nominee linked Carter's alleged appeasement of Beijing with his supposed failure to press Vietnam for information about Americans still missing in action (MIA) from the war. In angry tones, Reagan declared that "there's one message I want to deliver more than anything in the world as president—no more Taiwans, no more Vietnams, no more betrayal of friends and allies by the U.S. government." If elected, he not only would stand by Taiwan, an "American ally," but also might restore formal diplomatic ties with its anti-Communist government. When asked if he would recognize Taiwan as an independent nation if it asserted autonomy from China, Reagan answered, "Yes, just like a lot of countries recognized the thirteen colonies when they became part of the United States." In response, Chinese officials warned that if he implemented such a policy, "it would wreck the very foundations of Sino-U.S. relations."[9]

Reagan perceived a similar pattern of weakness in how the Ford and Carter administrations buckled under to China and failed to secure a full accounting or release of American prisoners of war (POWs) and MIA service members who might remain in Vietnam. As early as 1976, he told family members of missing servicemen that if elected president he would obtain a full accounting of all POWs and MIAs during his first week in office. In 1980, as a presidential candidate Reagan told a veteran's convention that Carter had coddled the Hanoi regime, thus encouraging Communist expansion and bungling efforts to find and free possible POWs. The Vietnam War, Reagan asserted, had been a "noble cause," and those Americans who expressed "feelings of guilt" cruelly "dishonor the memory of 50,000 young Americans who died in that cause."[10]

Even as Reagan rhetorically ramped up his defense of Taiwan and celebrated the Vietnam War, several of his advisers feared that Carter might use his statements as evidence that Reagan was an ideological extremist not to be trusted as president. They worked behind the scenes to buffer Reagan's remarks concerning China and Taiwan. In August 1980, in the midst of the presidential campaign, vice presidential nominee George H. W. Bush and two of Reagan's advisers, Richard Allen and James Lilley, flew to Beijing to reassure Deng's deputies that Reagan would not actually do what he promised: restore links to Taiwan or reverse Carter's policy. But when Reagan's aides informed him of what his advisers had told the Chinese, he refused to back them up by issuing a clarifying statement. Bush and other advisers spent several tense hours pleading with Reagan before he agreed to modify his stand. He did so only after convincing himself that the Taiwan Relations Act already conferred a form of informal US recognition and protection of the island—even though he had criticized this law as inadequate.[11]

Following his victory in the election of November 1980 and inauguration as president in January 1981, Reagan maintained this strident rhetoric, especially toward the Soviet Union and its proxies active in Latin America, Africa, the Middle East, and Southeast Asia. Yet unlike the new administration's challenges to the "evil empire" in many other parts of the world, in Asia most of the "big Cold War issues" had actually been settled before Reagan became president. As Nixon perceptively observed in remarks to his staff in July 1971, the opening to China, the gradual troop withdrawal under way in Vietnam, and the economic dynamism among the arc of nations stretching between Japan and Southeast Asia largely superseded the Cold War confrontations that had dominated American-Asian relations during the 1950s and 1960s.[12]

Especially during his first term as president, Reagan and his advisers engaged in spirited verbal disputes with China over continued US arms sales to Taiwan. They also condemned Vietnam for leaving unresolved the fate of missing American service members, hinting broadly that Hanoi still held at least some Americans against their will. But in contrast to the administration's hard line toward the Soviet Union and revolutionary groups in much of the Third World, after 1981 the United States under Reagan cooperated closely with China's Communist rulers in opposing the Soviet Union in Afghanistan and moved cautiously to resolve disputes with Communist Vietnam. In many ways, the withering away of the Cold War in Asia by 1981 was prologue to the end of the Soviet-American Cold War a decade later.

Shortly after Reagan took office as president in January 1981, the China issue reemerged. Part of the problem stemmed from differences among key members of the new administration. On one side, Secretary of State Alexander Haig, a Nixon–Kissinger protégé, lobbied for closer ties with the PRC, especially as a way to pressure the Soviets. On the other side, National Security Adviser Richard Allen and Defense Secretary Caspar Weinberger voiced strong sympathy for upgrading relations and cooperation with Taiwan. Allen's consulting firm had previously received contracts from Taiwan, and both he and Weinberger recognized the emotional bond Reagan felt for the island regime.

This bickering became a major problem when Taiwan requested that the Reagan administration approve sales of an advanced fighter jet dubbed the FX. Beijing insisted that the United States was supposed to be curtailing, not expanding, the quantity and quality of arms sold to its rival. Haig proposed solving the problem by selling advanced weapons to *both* China and Taiwan. He predicted that although each side would protest, they would privately be pleased to gain access to American weapons. Through weapons sales, Haig claimed, the administration would preserve cooperation with China, enhance Taiwan's security, and yield big profits for US arms exporters, whose corporate leaders were also strong Reagan supporters.

The president authorized Haig to explore this idea quietly during the secretary of state's visit to China in June 1981. Haig instead boasted during a press conference that Washington was poised to sell China some of the most advanced weapons in the US arsenal while selling Taiwan less-lethal equipment. Reagan promptly contradicted Haig, explaining that he had not changed his feelings about Taiwan and intended to sell it, not China, advanced weapons. For its part, China condemned any US arms sales to Taiwan and threatened to downgrade its relations with Washington if such sales were to occurr.[13]

The United States and China exchanged angry accusations of bad faith during the remainder of 1981 and the first half of 1982. When the Reagan administration decided to sell Taiwan an older-model military jet, the F-5e, China, rather than accept the deal, demanded instead that the United States set a date for ending *all* military sales to the island. In his diary, Reagan voiced growing frustration with what he considered Haig's effort to "betray our pledge to Taiwan."[14] In June 1982, Haig resigned as secretary of state after mounting disputes with Reagan over policies in the Middle East, Latin America, and Asia. (Haig soon found work as a highly paid arms salesman for United Technologies, peddling weapons to a variety of nations, including China and Taiwan!) His departure opened a path to compromise. On August 17, 1982, the United States and China issued a joint communiqué in which the US government promised to gradually reduce and eventually terminate arms sales to Taiwan, but only as regional security conditions permitted. Chinese leaders were pleased to get the US government on record as accepting the principle of terminating arms sales to Taiwan even if no certain date were set. Reagan believed he had kept faith with Taiwan, even while accepting that weapons sales might cease at some future date. In a memorandum he wrote for the record, the president stated that the level and type of arms sold to Taiwan should reflect the balance of power between the island and China. If China gained strength and appeared to threaten Taiwan, the United States could increase arms sales. If relations improved, the US could exercise restraint. Reagan told himself that the "truth is we are standing with Taiwan and the P.R.C. made all the concessions." In fact, the new agreement pretty much reconfirmed the ambiguity contained in Carter's agreement normalizing US-China ties in 1979, a deal Reagan had originally condemned as a betrayal.[15]

Haig's replacement as secretary of state, George Shultz, forged a far more relaxed and productive relationship with Reagan than had Haig. Shultz, like Reagan, expressed skepticism about the value of an enhanced military relationship with the PRC, but not primarily because he shared Reagan's emotional attachment to Taiwan. Shultz simply doubted the near-term value of China's geostrategic and economic importance. The PRC, he acknowledged, could be a useful ally in stabilizing Asia and leveraging US efforts to reduce Soviet power, but it was not vital to these efforts. Simply put, the PRC was neither a great military power nor an economic power, and the United States had no need to make fundamental concessions to Beijing. America's priorities in Asia, Shultz declared in a speech delivered early in 1983 and as he later made plain in his memoirs, should remain centered on bolstering trade and military ties with its long-term ally Japan.[16]

During 1982–1983, Chinese leaders, such as the new Communist Party head, Hu Yaobang, also questioned the value of closer ties to the United States. Since 1971, the PRC had relied on the United States to counter Soviet power. But Reagan's massive arms buildup and challenge to Soviet influence in Asia, Africa, Latin America, and South Asia worried Chinese strategists, who feared that Beijing might be swept up into an unwanted armed conflict between the two superpowers. At the end of 1982, Hu told a gathering of Communist Party elders that China would follow a more even-handed foreign policy, distinct from that of either the United States or the Soviet Union.

Despite these hints of Chinese-American friction, both nations remained on relatively good terms. In China, Deng Xiaoping's modernization policy required not only continued but increased access to European, Japanese, and American technology and capital. As China industrialized, it also needed export markets in the West and Japan. (Chinese exports to the United States would surge from virtually nothing in the 1970s to about $13 billion annually by the time Reagan left office in early 1989. They remained a tiny portion of US overseas trade, but a growing one.) Deng's chief deputies, Hu Yaobang and Premier Zhao Ziyang, were, if anything, even more enthusiastic than their boss about Western economic ties. When Zhao visited the White House early in 1984, Reagan described him as a "likable fellow & a very capable one." The president expressed pleasure that Chinese communism had made "room for some private enterprise." He wrote in his diary that once he told Zhao that any use of force against Taiwan would change the Chinese-American relationship "beyond repair," he and Zhao "got along fine from then on."[17]

As indicated in Reagan's comments on the National Security Council briefing of September 1983 described earlier, the president's perception of China hinged to a large extent on reports that the country was moving toward private enterprise. He was especially impressed by a report from Treasury Secretary Donald Regan in March 1984 that the regime was "opening up to outright capitalist investment by foreign businesses and industries."[18]

In addition to his belief that China was become "more like us," Reagan also appreciated that the PRC shared his determination to oppose Soviet intervention in Afghanistan. When Soviet forces entered that unhappy land in 1979 (to prop up a tottering Communist regime that had held tenuous power for several years), the Carter administration began supporting anti-Soviet, Islamist guerrillas known as mujahedeen. Reagan, like Carter, perceived Soviet intervention in Afghanistan primarily as a thrust toward the oil-rich Middle East. In order to substantially enhance aid to the mujahedeen, the Reagan administration required Chinese cooperation. With covert funding from the Central Intelligence Agency, Chinese military planners supplied thousands of mules to transport Chinese weapons paid for by the United States, such as AK-47 assault rifles, to the Afghan resistance. This military operation proved the most successful of the Reagan administration, eventually forcing a humiliating Soviet retreat. It also had the unintended consequence of promoting the fortunes of Osama bin Laden and other Islamists, especially in Pakistan, who later turned their wrath against the United States.[19]

Despite this cooperation, the president's often unscripted but unintentionally provocative remarks drove Beijing's leaders to distraction. Several times during 1982 and 1983, Reagan called Taiwan an American ally, implying that the United States viewed it as a sovereign nation. Chinese officials considered this characterization an insult and contradiction of past promises. If Reagan continued to speak this way, China threatened, it would cancel a "good will" visit Reagan had requested to make early in 1984 as part of his reelection campaign. Chinese officials warned American diplomats, visiting businesspeople, and scholars that unless Reagan dropped his talk of an alliance with Taiwan, he would not be welcome in China. For example, in December 1983 Communist Party leader Hu Yaobang raised the subject with a visiting scholar. He asked for assistance in sending a "personal" message to the White House outside normal diplomatic channels because Reagan had ignored formal complaints made in the past. "Tell Reagan," Hu declared, that "if he wants a successful trip to China he can use to boost his reelection, he should keep his big mouth shut about Taiwan." This declaration, along with similar warnings from many sources, resulted in Reagan muting his public references to Taiwan.[20]

In April 1984, Reagan traveled to the PRC, a Communist state he had bitterly criticized since he had entered politics in the early-1960s. En route, Senator Barry Goldwater, returning from a junket to Taiwan, spoke with Reagan on Guam. Goldwater, one of Taiwan's strongest supporters, feared the president would be "selling out our friends on Taiwan." Reagan assured him that the Communist leadership there understood he would "not forsake old friends in order to make new ones."[21]

Goldwater, Taiwan, and the PRC had little to worry about. Reagan spent most of his five days in country on the tourist circuit, visiting the Great Wall, the giant pandas in the Beijing Zoo, and the recently unearthed life-size clay warriors in the city of Sian. The president thoroughly enjoyed the experience. He took Nixon's advice not to ask about what he was eating at banquets and praised his own proficiency at using chopsticks. Reagan, unlike most westerners who encountered General Secretary Hu Yaobang, found him "doctrinaire about his ideology." In his public remarks, the president criticized the Soviet Union, praised democ-

President Ronald Reagan reviews troops during his arrival ceremony at the Great Hall of the People in Beijing on April 26, 1984. Although Reagan was an opponent of Communist China before 1981, his approach toward the People's Republic of China changed dramatically during his presidency. (Courtesy of the Ronald Reagan Presidential Library)

racy, but said nothing provocative about Taiwan. His Chinese hosts similarly avoided the subject.[22] Aside from expressing enthusiasm for China's emerging markets, Reagan declined to explain then or later why a Communist Soviet Union was an implacable threat but a Communist China was a worthy partner. At least in his own mind, he appeared to resolve the contradiction by telling journalists after his departure that he had actually visited "so-called communist China,"[23] in contrast to the Soviet Union, which remained a real Communist "evil empire."[24]

During Reagan's second term as president, US relations with China remained generally positive and low key. China sent and Americans welcomed thousands of graduate students, who flocked to American universities for advanced technical training. As noted earlier, Chinese exports to American consumers grew from virtually nothing to sales of $13 billion in 1988, a modest but expanding sum. Washington and Beijing continued to cooperate closely in the shadow war against the Soviets in Afghanistan. In

1984, China and Great Britain reached an accord to return Hong Kong to Chinese control when Britain's ninety-nine-year lease on the colony expired in 1997. Since British prime minister Margaret Thatcher was Reagan's closest foreign ally, this deal eliminated a potential source of US friction with China.

Perhaps more than any other factor, economic and political reform in both China and Taiwan during the 1980s reduced tensions in the region and provided the Reagan administration breathing room on the China versus Taiwan issue. China's increased emphasis on economic growth and its gradual substitution of market forces for Communist ideology deferred its leadership's concern with recovery of Taiwan. And even without a US security treaty, Taiwan's economy surged during the 1980s. As the regime prospered, its ruling clique, led by Jiang Jingguo, relaxed many of its harsher domestic political restrictions. With both China and Taiwan experiencing rapid economic growth, the argument over continued US arms sales to the island faded in immediate importance. For Reagan, so long as China posed no imminent threat to Taiwan and cooperated with the United States in Afghanistan, it barely intruded on his thinking. He made few substantive references to China in his diary or in public speeches during the last four years of his presidency.[25]

Just as the president's policy and references to China mellowed by the end of his first term, so did his strident criticism of the Communist government of Vietnam. As noted, while a presidential candidate, Reagan had vigorously defended the Vietnam War and accused both the Hanoi regime and Presidents Nixon, Ford, and Carter of virtually abandoning the search for missing Americans in the jungles of Southeast Asia. In 1983, Reagan told a gathering of the National League of Families of MIAs and POWs that his highest priority remained seeking an accounting for the 2,200 MIAs. He also upgraded the status and resources given to the Inter-Agency Group, which coordinated the government's efforts to find those who were MIA.[26]

The Inter-Agency Group condemned Vietnamese handling of the MIA problem. The organization domestically funded private-sector speakers, who addressed public gatherings on the subject. Many of these presentations not only condemned Hanoi for holding back the remains of dead Americans but also stressed the "real possibility" that live Americans remained in captivity.[27]

But even as his administration promoted this angry and misleading public rhetoric, Reagan quietly approved the dispatch of several emissaries to Hanoi to discuss unresolved issues. In July 1984, after the Vietnamese turned over the remains of several American servicemen they had located, Reagan publicly praised Hanoi for demonstrating a new spirit of cooperation. A few months later the Vietnamese permitted a joint recovery team to explore crash sites of downed US aircraft. Despite incremental progress, self-serving activists such as Texas businessman H. Ross Perot continued to stir up members of Congress and the families of MIA soldiers by claiming that even Reagan had abandoned their loved ones.[28]

By 1987–1988, after three years of deliberate but slow progress, the thaw in US-Soviet relations, the stable ties between the United States and China, and the rise to power of reformers in Vietnam resulted in more rapid progress on the MIA problem. In 1988, Reagan sent retired US Army general John Vessey to Hanoi. Vessey, a former chairman of the Joint Chiefs of Staff, carried a personal letter from the president stating that solving the MIA issue would "finally put the war behind us." The two sides reached an agreement to cooperate more fully in the search for MIA Americans, and the Reagan administration relaxed the tight trade embargo on Vietnam by permitting American humanitarian groups to provide aid to Vietnamese agencies and individuals.[29]

In the final months of his presidency, Reagan publicly acknowledged the progress made in reaching an accord with Vietnam. During 1988, speaking to the National League of Families and while visiting the Vietnam Memorial, the president recognized the substantial progress already made in resolving the MIA issue. If this cooperation continued, he asserted, he saw the probability of restoring trade and diplomatic ties with the former enemy.[30]

The Reagan administration did criticize one Chinese government initiative—its entry into the international arms market. Although the United States was by far the world's largest arms merchant, Washington disputed the right of other nations to sell certain weapons to what it considered unstable regions or unfriendly nations. As China's military technology improved during the 1980s, it began marketing several types of short- and medium-range missiles to countries such as Iran, Pakistan, and Saudi Arabia. The Reagan administration vigorously opposed these sales and threatened trade sanctions if China continued its missile exports. China alternately denied selling these weapons or promised not to do so again. But because arms sales were so profitable and represented a path toward global influence, it continued to export weapons, as did the United States.

Reagan's policies toward both China and Vietnam underwent dramatic change during his presidency. The strident anti-Communist rhetoric and suspicion he voiced in the late 1970s and early 1980s gave way to a more relaxed relationship, especially with China. As the president did so often when he changed his mind or adopted new policies, he convinced himself that the PRC and Socialist Republic of Vietnam had done nearly all the changing, while he remained constant in his resistance to and condemnation of communism. He refused to acknowledge that his bellicose support for Taiwan nearly derailed progress in US-China relations. In fact, however, during his presidency and especially in his second term, Reagan's China policy moved steadily from the right fringe of American politics toward the center. Similarly, after years of condemning both Hanoi and Washington for "covering up" the truth about MIAs, Reagan quietly acknowledged that no evidence existed to support claims of live Americans held in captivity. By 1988, responding to Hanoi's cooperation in body-recovery searches, he told the families of MIAs that the time had nearly come to resume normal relations with the Socialist Republic of Vietnam. In personal conversations with aides and journalists during his second term, he no longer spoke of the "menace" of Red China, replacing the Cold War imagery with approving references to "so-called Communist China."

Notes

1. National Security Council Meeting, September 20, 1983, "Review of U.S.-China Relations," F99-004# 52, Ronald Reagan Presidential Library, Simi Valley, CA.

2. Ronald Reagan, *An American Life: The Autobiography* (New York: Simon and Schuster, 1990), 368; see also Ronald Reagan, *The Reagan Diaries,* unabridged ed., 2 vols., ed. Douglas Brinkley (New York: HarperCollins, 2009). Many of the Reagan diary entries can also be found on the Reagan Presidential Library website. Other than the odd anecdote and clichéd repetition of his support for Taiwan, his diary entries and letters reveal relatively little about his views or policies toward China and Vietnam. The one memoir by an administration "insider" that has much to say about China is George P. Shultz, *Turmoil and Triumph: My Years as Secretary of State* (New York: Scribner's, 1993).

3. James Mann, *About Face: A History of America's Curious Relationship with China, from Nixon to Clinton* (New York: Knopf, 1998), 37–38; Patrick Tyler, *A Great Wall: Six President's and China* (New York: PublicAffairs, 1999), 117. These two accounts by seasoned journalists, relying on both archival research and interviews, present the best overall treatment of the Reagan administration's China policy. For Reagan's description of his motives, see Ronald Reagan to "Senator," June 1980, in Ronald Reagan, *Reagan: A Life in Letters,* ed. Kiron K. Skinner, Annelise Anderson, and Martin Anderson (New York: Free Press, 2003), 206.

4. Ronald Reagan to M. Stanton Evans, n.d. (c. 1972), quoted in Tyler, *A Great Wall,* 289. For a similar letter explaining Reagan's view of Nixon's opening to China, see Reagan to Mrs. Frances Cooke, December 1971, in *Reagan: A Life in Letters,* 526.

5. For a typical statement by Reagan critical of Ford and Kissinger's approach to China and Taiwan, see "Reagan's Plan Would Cut H.E.W.," *New York Times,* January 31, 1976. Reagan asserted that any normalization of relations with China should be made conditional on Beijing's acceptance of independence for Taiwan and South Korea.

6. "Reagan Says Peking Ties Will Become a Major Issue," *New York Times,* April 21, 1978; Mann, *About Face,* 115–16; Tyler, *A Great Wall,* 214–15.

7. Ronald Reagan, "Decency for Taiwan," *New York Times,* January 28, 1979; "Carter's Vow on Taiwan Is Demanded by Reagan," *New York Times,* February 11, 1979; "Reagan Demands Taiwan Guarantees," *Los Angeles Times,* January 13, 1979; Mann, *About Face,* 95; Tyler, *A Great Wall,* 273.

8. Taiwan Relations Act, Pub. L. 96-8, 93 Stat. 14 (1979); "Unofficial U.S. Links to Taiwan Approved by House and Senate," *New York Times,* March 14, 1979; "Senate Approval 85 to 4 Sends Taiwan Bill to Carter," *Chicago Tribune,* March 30, 1979; "Carter Signs Bill Allowing Taiwan Ties," *Los Angeles Times,* April 10, 1979. In both public speeches and private letters, Reagan expressed his view that Carter had betrayed Taiwan by caving to Chinese demands. See, for example, Reagan to Norman Littell, c. late 1979; Reagan to Sam Yorty, August 18, 1980; and Reagan to Earl B. Dunckel, September 2, 1980, all in *Reagan: A Life in Letters,* 527–29.

9. Reagan's campaign speeches on China, Taiwan, and Vietnam include "The Basic Speech," *New York Times,* February 29, 1980, and "A Reporter's Notebook: Visit to Reagan Country," *New York Times,* March 29, 1980. See also Mann, *About Face,* 116, and Tyler, *A Great Wall,* 290–95.

10. "Reagan Talks of Rumors Administration Plans to Renounce Taiwan after Election," *Los Angeles Times,* May 29, 1976; "A Father Charges MIA Cover-Up," *Washington Post,* July 25, 1976; "Reagan Calls War a 'Noble Cause,'" *Los Angeles Times,* August 18, 1980.

11. "Reagan Acts to Reassure Peking on Ties," *Washington Post,* August 17, 1980; "Bush Denies That Reagan Backs Two-China Policy," *Los Angeles Times,* August 19, 1980; Tyler, *A Great Wall,* 290–95; Mann, *About Face,* 116–18.

12. Nixon quoted in Michael Schaller, *Altered States: The United States and Japan since the Occupation* (New York: Oxford University Press, 1997), 227–28.

13. "Haig Walks a Shaky Line on China Trip," *Los Angeles Times,* June 12, 1981; "Haig Says U.S. Ready to Sell Arms to China," *Los Angeles Times,* June 17, 1981; "Reporter's Notebook on Haig's Trip," *New York Times,* June 26, 1981; "Haig Remarks on China Puzzles White House Aides," *New York Times,* June 27, 1981. For a rambling and self-serving account of Haig's tenure as secretary of state, see Alexander M. Haig Jr., with C. B. Luce, *Caveat: Realism, Reagan, and Foreign Policy* (New York: Macmillan, 1984).

14. Diary entries for January 8 and 10, March 26 and 29, 1982, in Reagan, *Reagan Diaries,* 61, 75, 76.

15. Diary entry for August 18, 1982, in Reagan, *Reagan Diaries,* 98; Tyler, *A Great Wall,* 118–28; Mann, *About Face,* 306–27.

16. "U.S.-China Ties: Lower Expectations," *New York Times,* February 2, 1983; "Shultz Says U.S. Seeks Stronger Ties to China," *Washington Post,* March 6, 1983; Shultz, *Turmoil and Triumph,* 172–96.

17. Diary entry for January 10, 1984, in Reagan, *Reagan Diaries,* 211.

18. Diary entry for March 27, 1984, in ibid., 228.

19. Mann, *About Face,* 134–50.

20. Hu Yaobang, interviewed by the author, December 1983, Beijing; see also Michael Schaller, *The United States and China into the Twenty-First Century,* 4th ed. (Oxford: Oxford University Press, 2016), 181.

21. Diary entry for April 24, 1984, in Reagan, *Reagan Diaries,* 233.

22. Diary entries for April 26, 27, 28, 29, 30, 1984, in ibid., 234–36.

23. Although Reagan probably did not make the association, anti-Communist activists from 1949 through the early 1970s condemned the "China Hands," the State Department officials who had urged cooperation with Mao's forces during and immediately after World War II, for using the phrase "so-called Communists" when describing Chinese Communists. On this topic, see, for example, E. J. Kahn, *The China Hands: America's Foreign Service Officers and What Befell Them* (New York: Viking, 1975), and Michael Schaller, *The U.S. Crusade in China, 1938–1945* (New York: Columbia University Press, 1979).

24. Reagan calls the Soviet Union an "evil empire" in Ronald Reagan, remarks at the Annual Convention of the National Association of Evangelicals in Orlando, Florida, March 8, 1983, at http://www.reagan.utexas.edu/archives/speeches/1983/30883b.htm

25. Tyler, *A Great Wall,* 329–39; Mann, *About Face,* 134–54.

26. "Reagan Vows Top Priority to Accounting of Viet MIAs," *Los Angeles Times,* January 28, 1983; "Reagan Puts Top Priority on Full Accounting of MIAs," *Los Angeles Times,* January 30, 1983; "Pledge to Families: Reagan Pledges Search for Men Missing in Vietnam," *Washington Post,* January 29, 1983.

27. "Gritz Raises New Hope for MIAs, and It's Sad," *Washington Post,* March 9, 1983. The most complete treatments of these events are found in P. D. Mather, *MIA: Accounting for the Missing in Southeast Asia* (Washington, DC: National Defense

University Press, 1994), 151–65, and Robert Schulzinger, *A Time for Peace: The Legacy of the Vietnam War* (New York: Oxford University Press, 2006), 33–34.

28. "Shultz Says Vietnamese Agree to Talks on MIAs," *Washington Post,* July 19, 1984; "Laos, U.S. to Search Crash Site for MIAs," *Los Angeles Times,* July 20, 1984; Mather, *MIA,* 95–120; Schulzinger, *A Time for Peace,* 24–25.

29. Mather, *MIA,* 151–65; Schulzinger, *A Time for Peace,* 33–34.

30. "Reagan Links Diplomatic Ties, MIAs: U.S. May Normalize Relations if Vietnam Resolves Questions," *Los Angeles Times,* July 31, 1988; "Reagan Applauds Vietnam's Agreement on Search for MIAs," *Washington Post,* July 30, 1988; "Reagans Pay Emotional Visit to Vietnam Veterans Wall," *Washington Post,* November 12, 1988.

10

An Obsession

The Central American Policy of the Reagan Administration

Kyle Longley

In the classic *Saturday Night Live* skit "Mastermind," broadcast by NBC on December 6, 1986, comedian Phil Hartman plays President Ronald Reagan. In the opening, the Reagan character meets with a reporter. Acting like a doddering old man, Hartman responds to a question regarding the Iran-Contra Affair. "Well, all I can say is I didn't know," he answered. "We're trying to find out what happened because none of us know." He concludes, "I hope I answered your questions as best as I could given the very little I know." Then, when the reporter leaves the stage, the old man moves into hyperdrive, ordering his advisers into action over arming the counterrevolutionaries, or "contras," and laundering money, declaring at one point, "I am the president. I am the only one who needs to understand." He talks about buying off John Tower and drugging Edmund Muskie, the head of the Iran-Contra investigation. At another point, he concludes a long meeting with speculation of how to funnel money through the corrupt Wall Street stock trader Ivan Boesky. Ultimately, after a very long meeting, his advisers fall asleep in their chairs. At that point, Reagan says, "Just me again. I have been doing it this way for six years. Why should it change now?"[1]

The skit in many ways asks an important question that still shapes the discourse over Reagan's leadership: Was he in control, or was he a puppet of others? This chapter contends that Reagan actively directed policy, particularly when it interested him. In the case of Central America in the 1980s, it became an obsession with him, one that almost destroyed his presidency.

The US preoccupation with Central America has deep roots. Ever since the Central American nations gained independence in the 1820s, the United States has historically maintained a strong interest in the region for economic and strategic reasons. Central America's proximity near major shipping routes, the multiple locations possible for a trans-isthmian canal, and economic interests in the region led to multiple interventions starting in the 1850s with William Walker in Nicaragua.[2]

The interest intensified after the Spanish-American War in 1898. The United States moved its attentions from a possible canal route through Nicaragua and instead settled on Panama. With the construction of the canal, the region became even more important as American policy makers feared outside forces establishing bases to threaten the vital asset.[3] In addition, US economic interests led by banana, railroad, and mining companies, including United Fruit, established dominance in much of Central America, leading to the rise of a new term, *banana republic*. These companies typically supported military dictators, who provided stability and optimal business environments. When perceived threats arose to American hegemony, the American companies often pressured Washington into using military force in the region, as evidenced in Nicaragua in the 1920s.[4]

When Franklin Roosevelt took the office of the presidency in 1933, he rejected many of his predecessors' policies. Promoting the Good Neighbor Policy, he pushed for nonintervention in the affairs of Latin America and rejected dollar diplomacy of unquestioned protection of US business interests in the region. This approach paid significant dividends when the United States entered World War II in December 1941. With few exceptions, the region supported the Allies in their conflict against the Axis Powers, providing some military support and large quantities of materials, including food and strategic minerals, that helped ensure an Allied victory.[5]

US interest in Latin American intensified after World War II due to the rise of Communist paranoia in the United States. The US support of anti-Communist dictators in the region and an operation conducted by the Central Intelligence Agency (CIA) in 1954 that displaced the Arbenz government in Guatemala highlighted the American preoccupation with perceived Communist threats.[6] The rise of Fidel Castro in Cuba further fueled the fear of a Communist bloc establishing a beachhead on the US southern border.[7] The obsession with Castro and fear of his revolution extending to the region preoccupied American leaders, in particular those within the conservative movement, including Reagan.

Reagan became even more attentive to the region during the 1970s when debates arose over the Panama Canal. He vocally opposed the treaty pushed by President Jimmy Carter, arguing that it was surrendering "sovereign rights" and the US "rights of defense of the Canal."[8] Also, a prominent group of advisers, the Council for Inter-American Security, which included future US ambassador to the United Nations Jeanne Kirkpatrick, strongly influenced Reagan. The group's Santa Fe Commission Report characterized Central America as the "soft underbelly" of the Americas and pushed for more military aid to US allies in the region, regardless of their authoritarianism or human rights violations. Kirkpatrick emphasized early in 1981, "Central America is the most important place in the world for the United States today."[9]

Beyond the Council for Inter-American Security, a virulent anticommunism fervor infected those close to Reagan. Powerful advisers, including William Casey, Reagan's campaign manager in 1980 and director of the CIA from 1981 to 1987, pushed the intelligence agency to prove that the Soviets were at the heart of all terrorist activity in the world. Many conservatives at various levels of the government—especially in the National Security Council (NSC), on which Robert McFarlane and John Poindexter served—joined the chorus of those stressing Soviet culpability as well as the need to move away from détente and from the concentration on human rights of the 1970s.

From the beginning, Central America became a standard by which the White House measured its anticommunism. The political scientist William Leogrande correctly observes that Reagan and his advisers believed that "a victory in Central America would be Reagan's first foreign policy success and its ramifications would be global. By defeating the Soviet challenge in Central America, the United States would demonstrate to the Kremlin and its Cuban proxies that the new president would not tolerate Soviet adventurism in the Third World."[10]

When Reagan entered office in early 1981, the major issue facing the United States in Central America was the civil war in El Salvador. The Carter administration had grappled with the problem, especially after General Carlos Humberto Romero seized power through fraudulent elections in 1977. Leftist guerrillas, fighting under the umbrella of the Farabundo Martí Liberation Front, launched an insurgency. In response, the government and right-wing death squads viciously counterattacked opponents. The violence spiraled out of control.

The Carter administration denounced the El Salvador government's human rights violations, blocked economic aid, and continued an arms embargo first put in place in 1975 when an investigation uncovered Salvadoran arms being sold to American gangsters. Even when the military overthrew Romero, the violence continued, including the murder of the archbishop of San Salvador, Oscar Romero, who had denounced the government's armed forces. The Carter administration struggled to keep a policy characterized as KISSSS, "Keep it simple, sustainable, small, and Salvadoran." It pushed land reform and change, but the violence only intensified.[11]

As Carter neared the end of his presidency, the conditions deteriorated even further with the murder of three American nuns and a layperson. New embargoes were put into place, and the administration struggled to develop a coherent response. The Farabundo Martí Liberation Front sought to capitalize on the period of transition from one US president to another a week and half before Reagan took office. Its leaders had read the Republican platform and so called for a general uprising before "the fanatic Ronald Reagan takes over the presidency."[12] They launched a major offensive that threatened to overthrow the Salvadoran government. In response, the Carter administration unfroze funding, and the Salvadorans desperately held on while the presidential transition occurred. As Carter left office, an observer noted, "El Salvador was the stage on which Jimmy Carter would perhaps play his most anguished version of Hamlet as played by a policymaker."[13]

Thus, when Reagan entered office, the initial focus was on El Salvador. He wrote privately, "If the Soviets win in Central America, we lose in Geneva and every place else."[14] In an NSC meeting in February 1981, he told his advisers, "If the Junta falls in El Salvador, it will be seen as an American defeat. . . . We must not let Central America become another Cuba on the mainland. It cannot happen."[15]

Others echoed this fear, including Secretary of State Alexander Haig, who warned of "a well-orchestrated Communist campaign designed to transform the Salvador crisis from the internal conflict to an increasingly internationalized confrontation is under way."[16] Early on in Reagan's first term, this pugnacious Vietnam veteran and former commander of the North Atlantic Treaty Organization often led the hard-liners on Central America. Reagan's chief of staff, James Baker III, would emphasize that "if we give Al Haig his way, the next thing you know, we'll be carpet bombing Central America."[17]

Once in office, the White House published a White Paper titled *Communist Interference in El Salvador.* It argued that captured documents showed that "over the past year, the insurgency in El Salvador has been progressively transformed into a textbook case of indirect aggression by Communist Power." Blaming a broad alliance that included the Soviet Union and Cuba as well as Vietnam and East Germany, the paper noted that hundreds of tons of arms had been delivered to El Salvador, with more promised. It led White House Press Secretary James Brady to crow, "We have clear evidence of catching Communists' hands in the cookie jar."[18]

After the release of the White Paper, the White House pushed for $25 million in military assistance, to be taken from a presidential discretionary fund to circumvent congressional oversight. It also increased the number of military advisers in El Salvador and gave the CIA nearly $20 million to assist the Salvadoran government. Reagan, when queried why he pushed no social or political reforms, responded, "You do not try to fight a civil war and institute reforms at the same time. Get rid of the war. Then go forward with the reforms."[19]

Critics of the White Paper arose, especially within the press. One newspaper examined the documents and found that many of the administration's claims had no support within the evidence provided. An intelligence expert called the paper's arguments a "castle of sand," and a *Wall Street Journal* writer challenged the assertion that the Salvadoran uprising was well equipped, instead calling it "a disorganized rag-tag rebellion." Others highlighted Moscow's clear lack of interest and noted that the report failed to paint a picture of the Soviets having more than a passing interest in the Salvadoran rebels, many of whom opposed communism.[20]

Although El Salvador sucked up a lion's share of the Reagan administration's energy early on, the administration also remained clearly fixated on the Sandinistas in Nicaragua, who had come to power in 1978 after deposing dictator Anastasio Somoza-Debayle, a longtime American ally.[21] The Republican platform in 1980 had branded the Sandinistas as "Marxist" and had promised to "support the efforts of the Nicaraguan people to establish a free and independent government."[22] Reagan would write at the time, "Of course, Nicaragua is another Cuba."[23]

Reagan often appeared aloof at times, and Haig complained that the Reagan White House was "as mysterious as a ghost ship" and that it was often difficult to tell which "one of the crew had the helm."[24] One thing appeared certain: it was an administration clearly conservative, leading Reagan to joke, "Sometimes our right hand doesn't know what our far-right hand is doing."[25]

Despite the appearance of no one being fully at the helm, within a short time the administration had started operations against the Sandinistas with National Security Decision Directive 17. It called for increasing aid to the contras working out of bases in Honduras.[26] By early 1982, the CIA had received $20 million to train five hundred contras, a number that swelled into thousands over the next few years, and hundreds of millions of dollars in government and private assistance flowed to the contras. The United States actively cooperated with the Argentine military and with Manuel Noriega in Panama to train and arm the contras.

In response, the Sandinistas defiantly challenged the Reagan administration. The Sandinista minister of agrarian reform Jaime Wheelock declared, "Nicaragua has never been a country with real sovereignty or national independence. Nicaragua has been an appendage of the United States. . . . Our function was to grow sugar, cocoa, and coffee for the United States; we served the dessert at the imperialist dinner table. . . . We have to be against the United States in order to reaffirm ourselves as a nation."[27] He articulated a long-standing anti-Americanism that dated back more than a century to the invasion by William Walker and continued with the multiple interventions by the United States from 1911 to 1934.

Ultimately, the attacks by the contras and the Reagan administration further strengthened the hard-liners in the Sandinista government, who fought for peasant support by pushing land reform and cracked down on their political opponents, including those in the press and opposition parties. More important, they increasingly moved into the sphere of Castro and the Communists, who began sending large quantities of economic and military aid.

Central America would remain a constant fixation for the Reagan administration, particularly within the NSC. In April 1982, a secret paper emphasized that the United States must prevent "the proliferation of Cuba-modeled states which would provide platforms for subversion, compromise vital sea lanes and pose a direct military threat at or near our borders." The writers worried, "This [proliferation] would undercut us globally and create economic dislocation and a resultant influx to the US of illegal immigrants."[28]

The Reagan administration, led by the president, launched a major public-relations campaign to support its efforts in Central America. Reagan went so far as to characterize the contras as "freedom fighters" and the "moral equivalent of our Founding Fathers."[29] He would later emphasize that if the contras suffered defeat and the Sandinistas stayed in power, "a privileged sanctuary for terrorists and subversives [would be] just two days' driving time from Harlingen, Texas."[30]

Yet, early on, strong domestic opposition developed in relation to Reagan's policies in Central America. Memories of Vietnam still haunted many Americans, and Representative Clarence Long (D–MD) chastised the president for "gunboat diplomacy all over again," adding, "I wish to God presidents would read a few books. If Johnson had read some, we wouldn't have been in Vietnam. If Reagan would read some, we wouldn't be here now."[31]

The debates flowed into the streets, where groups such as the Sanctuary Movement, Committee in Solidarity with the People of El Salvador, Americas Watch, and North American Congress on Latin America criticized US support for the repressive government in El Salvador and the contras. Although decentralized, the overall movement employed many different tactics, such as lobbying Congress, questioning the fallacies of the administration's arguments, picketing outside of the White House, and providing asylum to political refugees. In fact, sixty thousand people signed a pledge to disrupt government operations if the United States were to attack Nicaragua.[32]

The Reagan administration's responses to these opposition groups ranged from disdain to paranoia, accusing them of being Communist puppets. Reagan signed Executive Order 12333, which allowed the Federal Bureau of Investigation to wiretap and conduct surveillance on more than 138 organizations opposed to his policies in Central America. The bureau's operatives broke into the groups' offices as well as into churches allied with the movement. They desperately sought but failed to make connections between the groups and known Communists.[33] The obsession led to direct violations of US citizens' civil liberties and was an outright abuse of power by Reagan and his advisers.

As the general public mobilized, Congress remained a central place for debate. Many Democrats and some Republicans challenged the basic assumptions on which Reagan and his advisers built their policies. Leaders emerged in presenting the challenge, including Senators Christopher Dodd (D–CT) and Tom Harkin (D–IA) as well as Representatives Steve Solarz (D–NY) and Michael Barnes (D–MD). They sought to restrict economic and military assistance to the Salvadoran and Guatemalan militaries, highlighting their long-standing horrible human rights records.

Over time, these leaders of the opposition on Capitol Hill also increasingly focused on the contras and their continued buildup in bases in Honduras. Harkin echoed the feelings of many when he called the contras "vicious cutthroat murderers . . . remnants of the evil, murderous National Guard. In the name of all that is right and decent, we should end our involvement with this group."[34] Congressman Thomas Downey (D–NY) stated that many of his colleagues "have transited the last 30 years without learning very much about American diplomatic history." To him, the Reagan administration appeared to be preparing a "land version of the Bay of Pigs, with the 10,000 thugs, brigands, and thieves" in Nicaragua. He predicted failure and underscored, "It remains our adherence to ideals, and not our abandonment of them, that offers our most successful strategy for competing with our adversaries."[35]

Reagan often looked on Congress with contempt when any of its members opposed him, once characterizing the body as a meddlesome "committee of 535."[36] Nonetheless, he was not without his supporters in that body. Representative Bob Dornan (R–CA) responded to Harkin's critique, "What is Mr. Harkin's terrorist is my freedom fighter, and what is his freedom fighter is my terrorist."[37]

Over time, Democrats restricted contra funding. The first major effort occurred in 1982 with the Boland Amendment to the House Appropriations Bill of 1982. Although Harkin and his allies called for a complete prohibition on Defense Department and CIA funding and training of the contras, the chairman of the House Intelligence Committee, Edward Boland (D–MA), fashioned a compromise that limited the government agencies only to assisting efforts to interdict arms from Nicaragua to El Salvador. Reagan signed the appropriations bill that contained the amendment, but he and his advisers showed little interest in following the letter (or intent) of the law.[38]

Opponents of the Reagan administration's policies became even more alarmed at the direction the White House was taking in 1983. The military undertook Operation Big Pine II, with more than four thousand troops doing maneuvers that included amphibious landings and bombing exercises in Honduras. The US military also built advance bases there and left behind materials for the Honduran military and the contras, all of which escaped congressional oversight.[39]

Reagan had approved the operation, worrying, "The security situation in Central America is deteriorating" due to a lack of "adequate resources." At first, he and the hard-liners purposely left Secretary of State George Shultz in the dark because he represented a more moderate and transparent path. A Defense Department official admitted, "We're playing a little cat-and-mouse game with them [the Sandinistas], putting a little squeeze on, making them wonder what's going to happen next."[40]

In a strange twist, the White House tried some damage control by sending Shultz to Capitol Hill to testify and meet with prominent senators and representatives. He acknowledged the White House's failure to consult with Congress on Operation Big Pine II, but he never admitted that he had not been informed about it either. He promised that the United States had no plan of attack and that if the Hondurans or Nicaraguans initiated hostilities, US forces would immediately withdraw. He ignored Secretary of Defense Caspar W. Weinberger's admonitions to "ignore Congress," and when one of Weinberger's aides spoke negatively of Congress, Shultz reminded him that the legislative branch "is provided for in the Constitution."[41]

A concerned Congress immediately questioned Big Pine II. Powerful Speaker of the House Tip O'Neill complained that Reagan "thinks he's John Wayne. He thinks he can go down there and clean the place out." Others in Congress complained that the operation violated the War

Powers Act of 1973, and so they sought to pass legislation prohibiting the administration from sending additional troops to Central America without congressional approval.[42]

If Big Pine II alarmed some Americans as well as the Sandinistas, what transpired in October 1983 proved even more ominous. The Reagan administration, reeling from the suicide bombing of the marine barracks in Beirut, Lebanon, on October 23 that claimed 241 American lives, decided to invade Grenada, ostensibly to protect the lives of American medical students on the island.[43] Although some planners of the invasion considered using only a small group of Special Forces to land and extricate the Americans, others prevailed, and Operation Urgent Fury began.[44]

On October 25, 1983, nineteen hundred US marines stormed ashore on Grenada. Administration officials kept the media in the dark. For six days, these US troops (with an additional four thousand dispatched over time) battled members of the Grenadian military and Cuban security forces. Finally, the resistance collapsed, allowing President Reagan to crow, "I can't say enough in praise of our military . . . Army Rangers and paratroops, Navy, Marine and Air Force personnel, those who planned a brilliant campaign and those who carried it out."[45]

Debates raged in Congress and the American public as Congressman Downey grumbled, "This is an administration that shot first and asked questions later." Prominent senator Patrick Moynihan (D–NY) demanded that the administration answer questions on how the invasion accorded with international laws and treaties. He complained that the administration had committed an act of war and stressed, "I don't know that you restore democracy at the point of a bayonet."[46]

Despite a domestic and international outcry, the Reagan administration proudly heralded the triumph as many Americans savored the first victory of American troops since the Vietnam War. Reagan would later write in his autobiography, "I probably never felt better during my presidency than I did that day."[47] Shultz also later described Grenada as the "shot heard round the world by usurpers and despots of every ideology. . . . Some Western democracies were again ready to use the military strength they had harbored and built up over the years in defense of principles and interests."[48]

Many argued that the invasion also served as a reminder of US military power to the Sandinistas in Nicaragua as well as to Castro. The president and his supporters argued that the victory in Grenada signified the resurgence of US power and ability to rollback Communist threats, including those in Central America and the Caribbean.[49]

By 1984, Congress responded to military posturing in Big Pine II and the invasion of Grenada as well as to the perceived lies and misrepresentations, which included the secret mining of Nicaraguan harbors by CIA-sponsored commandos.[50] In October, with the Boland Amendment II, Congress ended funding "for the purpose of which would have the effect of supporting, directly or indirectly, military or paramilitary operations in Nicaragua by any nation, group, organization, movement, or individual."[51] Congressman Tom Foley (D–WA) noted, "No one appears to have had any doubt about the [Boland] amendment's meaning. It meant the end of United States assistance to the contras."[52]

Despite the defeat, the White House reacted quickly to the Boland Amendment II. The act infuriated Reagan, who called it "irresponsible," and others in the administration dismissed it as "partisan politics." When it passed, Reagan told National Security Adviser Robert McFarlane, "I want you to do whatever you have to do to help these people keep body and soul together."[53] A showdown appeared on the horizon.

With Reagan pushing hard, the White House, especially in the NSC, started formulating plans to circumvent congressional restrictions. One group, which included Vice President George H. W. Bush, supported working through third parties to fund lethal assistance to the contras.

The most serious efforts would revolve around taking funds from a secret sale of arms to Iran that was done in an effort to free hostages and then diverting the funds to the contras. This discussion unfolded despite the fact that Reagan had said in a speech, "America will never make concessions to terrorists—to do so would only invite more terrorism. Once, we head down that path, there would be no end to it."[54]

The idea of trading of arms for hostages had alarmed many officials in the White House since it had first developed. Weinberger vigorously opposed the deal, stressing that it was probably illegal.[55] Shultz cautioned that circumventing Congress possibly constituted "an impeachable offense."[56]

Reagan ignored the warnings. On July 27, 1985, he called National Security Adviser Robert McFarlane and told him, "I wanted to find a way to do this." A couple of weeks later the president met with Bush, Shultz,

President Ronald Reagan with contra leader Adolfo Calero and Colonel Oliver North, US Marine Corps, in Robert McFarlane's office, April 4, 1985. The Iran-Contra Affair nearly destroyed the Reagan presidency. (Courtesy of the Ronald Reagan Presidential Library)

Weinberger, and McFarlane and called for a "go slow" strategy. Shultz and Weinberger interpreted the statement as stopping the trade of arms for hostages. However, only a few days later Reagan met with McFarlane and stated, "Well, I've thought about it . . . and I want to go ahead with it. . . . I believe it's the right thing to do."[57]

Not long thereafter, war materials, including aircraft replacement parts and tube-launched, optically tracked, wire-guided (TOW) missiles, headed to Iran through Israeli and Iranian intermediaries. The administration did everything possible to evade congressional oversight and publicly denied trading arms for hostages. However, Reagan would later admit in his diary, "I agreed to sell TOWs to Iran."[58]

The arms-for-hostages arrangement generated millions of dollars of revenue that went into Swiss bank accounts. Poindexter and NSC staffer Marine Corps colonel Oliver North began siphoning money from this ready spigot to fund the contras, a clear violation of the Boland Amendment II. Such actions built off operations already in place. CIA director William Casey and North had begun raising funds from foreign governments, including Saudi Arabia, Taiwan, and Brunei as well as from organizations such as the World Anti-Communist League, led by retired US Army general John Singlaub. Conservative donors such as Joseph Coors and Ellen Garwood poured money into a fund to provide arms to the contras.[59]

In Washington and various capitals around the world, rumors abounded about the arms for hostages and the transfer of money to the contras. When Congress heard of the efforts and requested documents from the White House, the administration stonewalled by claiming executive privilege.[60]

The whole arms-for-hostages diversion of funds to the contras unraveled in October 1985 when the Sandinistas shot down a cargo plane en route to resupply the contras. They captured pilot Eugene Hasenfus, an American who reported that he had been working with CIA operatives. Soon after that, a Lebanese magazine, *al-Shiraa,* broke the news on the arms-for-hostages agreement. The dominoes began to fall.[61]

While North and Poindexter shredded large quantities of evidence as the news broke, Reagan tried damage control. On November 13, he went on national television and tried to convince people that he had wanted to use the arms to open a diplomatic door to the Iranians and to counter Soviet efforts. He filled his speech with lies and half-truths, telling his audience that the spare parts "could easily fit into a single cargo plane." He emphasized, "We did not—repeat, did not—trade weapons or anything else for hostages, nor will we." Few people bought his story of events; one poll showed only 14 percent of Americans believed him.[62]

More administration efforts followed to put in place a flawed timeline that distorted the truth. Casey and Poindexter lied in front of the House and Senate Intelligence Committee, saying that no one in the government knew about the shipments. In a nationally televised press conference on November 19, Reagan again misled the people by criticizing the media for undermining the efforts to ensure the release of more hostages. When a reporter queried why Reagan did not just admit the "mistake" and move on, Reagan responded, "I don't think a mistake was made. It was a high-risk gamble, and it was a gamble that . . . I believe the circumstances warranted."[63]

On the defensive, Reagan began even more damage control. On November 25, the president accepted Poindexter's resignation and fired

North, someone he later characterized as a "national hero." The next day he agreed to the creation of a special investigating committee headed by former senator John Tower (R–TX). Two weeks later he asked for a special independent counsel and ultimately appointed Lawrence Walsh to lead the review.

For a year, Walsh, congressional committees, and the Tower Commission investigated the arms-for-hostages exchange as well as the diversion of funds. In one meeting on January 26, 1987, Reagan talked with members of the Tower Commission. To the astonishment of his advisers, including White House counsel Peter Wallison, Reagan admitted to approving the first sales of arms as well as subsequent ones, supporting the timeline that McFarlane had given to the Senate Foreign Relations Committee only a few days earlier.[64]

For a follow-up commission meeting, Wallison and Bush had prepped Reagan on a different timeline. They wanted Reagan to note his surprise to learn of the shipment of arms so that his testimony would coincide with testimony given by Chief of Staff Donald Regan. As the interview unfolded, Reagan asked for a memorandum that Wallison had prepared. To Wallison's dismay, Reagan read the memo verbatim to the committee: "If the questions comes up at the Tower Board meeting, you might want to say that you were surprised." The shocked commission members stopped the interview. Tower Commission cochair Senator Edmund Muskie (D–ME) afterward expressed his frustration that the president obviously had often asked about the hostages and had thought "over this thing every day, and yet he can't remember anything about it. My God!"[65]

To some, the president's performance highlighted memory problems, something that the later diagnosis of Alzheimer's seemed to reinforce. However, Reagan seemed perfectly lucid at the time when discussing issues related to Gorbachev and the Soviet Union. More likely, the poor memory related more to not wanting to remember or to selectively blocking out negative ideas, which he seemed to do often. A close political adviser, Stuart Spencer, emphasized, "The key to the whole thing is he can remember. There are some things he remembers very poorly, but I think he wants to remember them very poorly. He really has a good memory."[66] North wrote afterward, "The president didn't always know what he knew."[67]

With the release of the Tower Commission Report in late February

1987, the president's leadership came under fire. The report found "the arms transfers to Iran and the activities of the NSC staff in support of the contras are case studies in the perils of policy pursued outside the constraints of orderly process." Critically, it added, "The Iran initiative ran directly counter to the administration's own policies on terrorism, the Iran/Iraq war, and the military support to Iran. The inconsistency was never resolved. . . . The result taken as a whole was a U.S. policy that worked against itself."[68]

In response, Reagan went on television to note, "A few months ago I told the American people I did not trade arms for hostages. My heart and my best intentions still tell me that's true, but the facts and the evidence tell me it is not."[69] This backhanded acknowledgment of culpability helped deflect some of the criticism, but many continued to believe that the president knew much more than he let on.

While Poindexter shielded Reagan from direct ties to the schemes, shielding that was aided by Casey's death in 1987, the final congressional committee report found "enough is clear to demonstrate beyond doubt that fundamental processes of governance were disregarded and the rule of law was subverted."[70] It also stressed, "If the President did not know what his National Security Advisers were doing, he should have."[71]

After a thorough investigation, Walsh indicted some members of President Reagan's inner circle, including Poindexter, Assistant Secretary of State Elliott Abrams, and Weinberger. Walsh secured the convictions on lying, obstruction, and other crimes for several primary people, including Poindexter, North, Abrams, and Weinberger. However, presidential pardons and technicalities ultimately swept away most of the convictions.

Walsh released his final report in 1994. He found that Reagan's actions "fell well short of criminality to be successfully prosecuted." But he emphasized, "President Reagan created the conditions which made possible the crimes committed by others by his secret deviations from announced national policy as to Iran and hostages and by his own determination to keep the contras together 'body and soul.'" In conclusion, Walsh underscored that Reagan's actions should still have given pause to Congress and that impeachment should have been discussed.[72]

Although the president was not indicted and convicted, his leadership took a hit. If he did not know, as he claimed, then he lacked oversight over his protégés even though at the same time he appeared very much in control of the efforts to engage the Soviet Union. At the very least, as Walter LaFeber notes, the scandal constituted a "dangerous threat" as "unelected and unaccountable military officers in the NSC worked with key State Department personnel to defy U.S. laws. . . . They dragged the Constitution, U.S. policies in Central America, American reputations and credibility around the world through the mud."[73]

Reagan's obsession with Central America nearly destroyed his presidency in the Iran-Contra Affair. He and his advisers clung to their ideology, which made them feel as if they answered to a law higher than that of the land. The president dangerously pushed people to circumvent the Boland Amendment with schemes that undermined US policy in the Middle East as well as in Central America. The diversion of funds clearly violated the law. The insular nature of the NSC activities created significant problems with oversight by Congress and other watchdogs, clearly undermining the balance of powers envisioned by most Americans, including the Founding Fathers, and written into the Constitution.

Although Reagan escaped the Iran-Contra Affair without impeachment, the affair defanged his administration's plans in Central America, especially efforts to displace the Sandinistas. Ironically, while the investigations were taking place and years before the final report was released, that very thing occurred instead through efforts made by Costa Rican president Oscar Arias, who took office in 1986. Concerned about Costa Rica's role as a southern front in the contra war, Arias immediately denounced contra aid, the Sandinistas, and other warring parties. He instead called for a peace plan that would include cease-fires, democratic elections, dialogues between the governments and "unarmed opposition," and the creation of commissions for national conciliation.[74]

Most of the Reagan administration, outside of Secretary of State Shultz and special envoy to Central America Philip Habib, immediately opposed the Arias plan. One former NSC staffer warned, "This is it! The Arias plan . . . that will be used for this year's run at a false political statement. . . . Its fatal flaw is that it would have the Nicaraguan armed resistance dismantled today in return for Sandinista promises to have democratic elections in 1990."[75]

Reagan and his advisers responded by not sending Vice President George H. W. Bush to Arias's inauguration.[76] The administration also significantly reduced economic aid to Costa Rica.[77] Then it tried direct pressure by dispatching Casey on a huge transport plane to talk to Arias secretly about the peace process. Arias rebuffed Casey by refusing to go to the airport to meet him and instead dispatched his chief of staff and foreign minister. Not long after that, during the Costa Rican president's visit to Washington, DC, Casey asked Arias to visit CIA headquarters at Langley. Arias declined and instead invited Casey to the Westin Hotel, where he was staying. Once the CIA director arrived, Arias refused to dismiss his entourage. Within thirty minutes, Casey stormed out of the room.[78]

The Costa Ricans recognized the opposition. One of Arias's top aides commented, "The [US] administration is very angry with Oscar, and Reagan will continue to be very tough." Another Costa Rican diplomat emphasized, "The Reagan administration is blind, obsessed with Nicaragua. But they are not going to succeed in overthrowing the Sandinistas. In the end they are going to destroy Costa Rican democracy instead."[79]

Congressional supporters of Arias responded enthusiastically to the announcement of his plan. In February 1987, Senator Terry Sanford (D–FL) pushed a Senate resolution that stated that "the Congress strongly supports the initiative and looks forward to the summit meeting in Esquipulas, Guatemala . . . as the next phase in this historic effort of the Central American heads of state to forge a firm and lasting peace in Central America." The measure passed ninety-seven to one.[80]

Others in the media and general public in the United States supported the plan. In June 1987, a *New York Times* editorial emphasized, "If President Reagan wanted an honorable and sensible resolution of conflicts in Central America, he would grab for the peace plan put forward by Costa Rica's President, Oscar Arias." It added, "Mr. Reagan's own policy of backing the Nicaraguan rebels and driving the Sandinistas out of Nicaragua is at a dead end. The Arias plan, whatever its flaws, has promise and wide support."[81]

To try to take some momentum away from Costa Rica, Reagan and his advisers invited Arias to the White House that same month. In the meetings, administration officials tried to focus on their continued support of the contras and what they considered to be weaknesses in Arias's plan. The Costa Rican stood firm, however, and succeeded in changing the emphasis in the meeting to why the contras were part of the problem, not a solution. One observer recalled that as Arias talked, Reagan kept looking to his advisers as if to ask, "Who let this midget in here?"[82]

Some mixed messages on the peace process went out as Reagan vacillated, owing largely to the pressures exerted by his new chief of staff, the moderate Howard Baker, and to the defensiveness created by the Iran-Contra Affair. Throughout the summer, Habib promoted peace while nevertheless maintaining support for the contras, working to close perceived loopholes, and pushing a plan put forth by Speaker of the House Jim Wright (D–TX) and Reagan.[83]

There was quite a bit of skepticism to the Wright–Reagan plan. Some speculated, however, that one of the proponents of the plan, National Security Adviser Frank Carlucci, wanted to create unreasonable demands on the Sandinistas so that they would refuse and thus make it easier for the Reagan administration to push forward a $270 million contra aid program.[84] When the plan was finally released, it appeared on regular paper without any indication that it was an official document.[85] Wright eventually abandoned the plan after growing aggravated with the White House and in turn threw his full support behind the Arias template.

Making a last-minute effort to undermine Arias's peace plan, the White House put pressure on the president of El Salvador, José Napoleon Duarte, to subvert the plan. Wright personally intervened at this point and pressured the El Salvadoran president. In response, Duarte commented, "Remember that Ronald Reagan is only President for sixteen more months. Jim Wright is going to be Speaker for the next ten years."[86] Despite the administration's effort, the various parties signed the agreement in August 1987.

Reagan privately categorized the Arias plan as "fatally flawed," and Abrams complained, "Communists win these kind of negotiations."[87] The *Wall Street Journal* characterized the plan as "Ronald Reagan's Bay of Pigs," but the *Washington Times* warned that it was a "peace proposal trap."[88]

Wright and others in Congress continued to support Arias, redoubling their efforts after the signing of the accords. Despite White House opposition, Arias spoke in front of a joint session of Congress on September 22. After receiving a standing ovation, Arias encouraged his audience, "Let us restore faith in dialogue and give peace a chance."[89] He avoided the contra issue but in an interview afterward emphasized, "The military support to the contras has been the main excuse for the Sandinistas to do all they have done in the past—to abolish individual freedoms, to abolish pluralism, to make of Nicaragua a more dictatorial state." He stressed, however, the need to give the Sandinistas the opportunity "to comply with all the provisions of the Guatemalan accord."[90]

In the aftermath of Arias's visit in September, the administration and its conservative allies continued to characterize the Esquipulas II Accords as a defective process. Even when the Sandinistas began implementing elements of the pact, the administration remained pessimistic. After the Sandinistas allowed the reopening of the newspaper *La Prensa* and Radio Católica, Reagan called the moves "window dressing" and "a sham." State Department spokesperson Phyllis Oakley added, "We are not encouraged by what appears to be cosmetic gestures of compliance."[91] To accentuate the point, Reagan promised at an October meeting of the Organization of American States that he would "speak and work, strive and struggle" for aid to the contras.[92]

The international community also strongly supported Arias's efforts. He received a major boost when he was awarded the Nobel Peace Prize. *Time* magazine concluded, "The prize both enhances the credibility of the fragile peace process and augments Arias' moral authority as an arbiter of peace" while further handicapping "the Reagan's administration's attempts to secure $270 million in new aid for the Contra rebels." The *Time* article quoted one administration official, who admitted, "This complicates everything we're trying to do in Central America."[93] The *Washington Post* noted, "With his peace plan and laurels, Arias has put the Reagan administration's passionate policy of support for the war waged by the Nicaraguan rebels, or contras, into checkmate."[94]

Although Shultz and Reagan publicly congratulated Arias, the conservatives criticized the selection of him for the Nobel Prize.[95] A State Department official complained bitterly, "He won the prize for defunding the Contras and taking an anti-American stance."[96] One of Abram's closest top aides complained to reporters that "all of us . . . reacted with disgust, unbridled disgust."[97] Congressman Jack Kemp (R–NY) argued, "They ought to save the peace prize until they see what happens in the future," and House Minority Leader Bob Michel (R–IL) stated, "I don't know that the Norwegians got all that much to say about what goes on in Central America."[98]

With newfound moral authority, Arias pushed hard, and the Reagan administration's opposition to the peace process continued until it left office. To justify continued aid to the contras, the administration tried to focus the debate on Nicaragua's noncompliance. Despite a report by an independent commission that found "Nicaragua has been the country in which the greatest change has occurred under the terms and timetables of the accord," the administration pressured the Central Americans with some success to declare the Sandinistas in violation of the accords.[99]

Nonetheless, the plan appeared to be progressing forward into 1988, although sometimes slowly. Glitches developed as the Sandinistas created problems by suppressing internal dissension. However, the most significant event of early 1988 was a congressional vote on aid to the contras. Before the vote took place, Arias had continued to call on Congress to deny any assistance to the contras, including nonlethal aid. His efforts and those of others succeeded. On February 3 and March 3, 1988, Congress rejected Reagan's request for additional military assistance to the contras.[100]

Soon after those votes, the contras went to the negotiating table under the guidance of a Nicaraguan reconciliation commission. On March 23, 1988, they signed a sixty-day cease-fire, an accord that ultimately granted amnesty to former contra members and moved the Sandinistas toward an open political system. Although the cease-fire broke down in the summer, the process started with the Arias plan helped in large part to ensure that the contras would return to the bargaining table until the final agreements were reached.

Obstacles developed along the way, but Arias and his allies fought back most of the Reagan administration's efforts to continue funding the contras. The election of George H. W. Bush in 1988 caused US attentions to shift, especially as the Soviet Union crumbled. By the time Bush took office in early 1989, the Reagan policy in Central America was dead. The United States committed itself to enhancing the peace process rather than to hindering it. Numerous administration officials emphasized that they supported the peace process and would not seek any additional assistance for the contras. The decline of the Soviet Union and the end of Soviet subsidies to the Sandinistas and Cubans enhanced the process as the Sandinistas proved more willing to compromise.

In both cases, the changes heartened those Central Americans who backed the peace plan. This heartening further facilitated a return to more stability in the region as the peace process picked up momentum throughout 1989 and 1990. As Arias had predicted, the removal of the contra threat, on top of the years of dictatorial rule by the Sandinistas, resulted in a change in power in 1990. The Sandinistas participated in free elections, which they lost. The political situation in El Salvador and Guatemala improved over time as national reconciliation committees secured cease-fires and elections. By 1991, the region had comparative peace for the first time in more than a decade.

The irony of the Reagan administration's opposition to the Arias peace plan was that the plan accomplished the goal of removing the Sandinistas and further helped to stabilize the situation in El Salvador, Guatemala, and Honduras. Although some Reagan supporters later stressed that his policy led to the changes, in reality it was the Central Americans, led by Arias, who changed the trajectory of the situation and brought more stability to the region.

Reagan's obsession with Central America ultimately ensured a set of negative outcomes for the administration. First, the overarching desire to fund the contras in the face of congressional restrictions nearly destroyed the presidency and at a minimum tainted it. Reagan bounced back because of the improving economy and, more important, the breakthrough with the Soviet Union that opened up under Mikhail Gorbachev. Yet the blemish of indictments, the brazen disregard for the Constitution, the trampling of civil liberties, and the association with authoritarian governments and groups were blots on the Reagan's presidency. His forceful leadership on the matter of Central America created conditions that cost him and the country dearly.

Notes

1. "Mastermind," *Saturday Night Live,* December 6, 1986, NBC, at https://screen.yahoo.com/president-reagan-mastermind-000000075.html.

2. Stephen Dando-Collins, *Tycoon's War: How Cornelius Vanderbilt Invaded a Country to Overthrow America's Most Famous Military Adventurer* (New York: DaCapo Press, 2009); Robert May, *Manifest Destiny's Underworld: Filibustering in Antebellum America* (Chapel Hill: University of North Carolina Press, 2004); Frederic Rosengarten Jr., *Freebooters Must Die! The Life and Death of William Walker, the Most Notorious Filibuster of the Nineteenth Century* (New York: Haverford House, 1976).

3. David McCullough, *The Path between the Seas: The Creation of the Panama Canal, 1870–1914* (New York: Simon and Schuster, 1978); Walter LaFeber, *The*

Panama Canal: The Crisis in Historical Perspective (New York: Oxford University Press, 1990).

4. Jason M. Colby, *The Business of Empire: United Fruit, Race, and U.S. Expansion in Central America* (Ithaca, NY: Cornell University Press, 2013); Paul Dosal, *Doing Business with the Dictators: A Political History of United Fruit in Guatemala, 1899–1944* (Lanham, MD: Rowman and Littlefield, 1995).

5. Frederick Pike, *FDR's Good Neighbor Policy: Sixty Years of Generally Gentle Chaos* (Austin: University of Texas Press, 1995); Bryce Wood, *The Making of the Good Neighbor Policy* (New York: Columbia University Press, 1961); David Green, *The Containment of Latin America: A History of Myths and Realities of the Good Neighbor Policy* (New York: Quadrangle Books, 1971).

6. Richard Immerman, *The CIA in Guatemala: The Foreign Policy of Intervention* (Austin: University of Texas Press, 1982); Stephen Schlesinger and Stephen Kinzer, *Bitter Fruit: The Story of the American Coup in Guatemala,* rev. and exp. ed. (Cambridge, MA: Harvard University Press, 2006); Stephen Rabe, *Eisenhower and Latin America: The Foreign Policy of Anticommunism* (Chapel Hill: University of North Carolina Press, 1988).

7. Dan Bohning, *The Castro Obsession: U.S. Covert Operations against Cuba, 1959–1965* (Lincoln, NE: Potomac Books, 2006); Thomas J. Paterson, *Contesting Castro: The United States and the Triumph of the Cuban Revolution* (New York: Oxford University Press 1995).

8. Adam Clymer, *Drawing the Line at the Big Ditch: The Panama Canal Treaties and the Rise of the Right* (Lawrence: University Press of Kansas, 2008); Reagan quoted in Kiron Skinner, Bruce Bueno de Mesquita, Serhiy Kudelia, and Condoleezza Rice, *The Strategy of Campaigning: Lessons from Ronald Reagan and Boris Yeltsin* (Ann Arbor: University of Michigan Press, 2007), 147.

9. Quoted in Walter LaFeber, *Inevitable Revolutions: The United States and Central America,* 2nd ed. (New York: Norton, 1993), 271.

10. William Leogrande, *Our Own Backyard: The United States in Central America, 1977–1992* (Chapel Hill: University of North Carolina Press, 1998), 81.

11. Robert D. Ramsey, *Advising Indigenous Forces: American Advisors in Korea, Vietnam, and El Salvador* (N.p.: CreateSpace, 2012), 85.

12. Hal Brands, *Latin America's Cold War* (Cambridge, MA: Harvard University Press, 2010), 200.

13. Karen DeYoung, "El Salvador: Where Reagan Draws the Line," *Washington Post,* March 9, 1981.

14. Quoted in Richard Reeves, *President Reagan: The Triumph of Imagination* (New York: Simon and Schuster, 2005), 152.

15. NSC meeting, February 11, 1981, in *The Reagan Files: Inside the National Security Council,* ed. Jason Saltoun-Ebin (N.p.: CreateSpace, 2010), at http://www.thereaganfiles.com/19810211-nsc-2.pdf.

16. Quoted in "Excerpts from Haig's Briefing about El Salvador," *New York Times,* February 21, 1981.

17. Quoted in Bob Schieffer and Gary Paul Gates, *The Acting President* (New York: Dutton, 1989), 125.

18. Quoted in Leogrande, *Our Own Backyard,* 86.

19. Quoted in ibid., 90.

20. This criticism of the White Paper is covered and quoted in ibid., 87–88.

21. For a concise overview of the administration's strategy for Latin America, see John Pitts, "Reagan Doctrine: Strategy for Latin America," August 2006, US Southern Command, Miami.

22. Roger Peace, "The Anti-contra-war Campaign: Organizational Dynamics of a Decentralized Movement," *International Journal of Peace Studies,* Spring–Summer 2008, 67.

23. Diary entry for February 4, 1982, in Ronald Reagan, *The Reagan Diaries,* ed. Douglas Brinkley (New York: HarperCollins, 2007), 67.

24. Quoted in Bernard Gwertzman, "Books of the Times," *New York Times,* April 18, 1984.

25. Quoted in Mark Gilderhus, *The Second Century: U.S.–Latin American Relations since 1889* (Wilmington, DE: Scholarly Resources, 2000), 223.

26. Federation of American Scientists, "National Security Decision Directive on Cuba and Central America," January 4, 1982, at http://fas.org/irp/offdocs/nsdd/nsdd-17.pdf.

27. Quoted in *Sarasota Herald-Tribune,* August 28, 1983.

28. Quoted in LaFeber, *Inevitable Revolutions,* 271.

29. Quoted in *Washington Post,* June 10, 2004.

30. Quoted in *Los Angeles Times,* March 4, 1986.

31. Quoted in Leogrande, *Our Own Backyard,* 96.

32. Christian Smith, *Resisting Reagan: The U.S. Central American Peace Movement* (Chicago: University of Chicago Press, 1996); Clare Weber, *Visions of Solidarity: U.S. Peace Activists in Nicaragua from War to Women's Activism and Globalization* (Lanham, MD: Lexington Books, 2006); Sharon Erickson Nepstad, *Convictions of the Soul: Religion, Culture, and Agency in the Central American Solidarity Movement* (New York: Oxford University Press, 2004).

33. Michael Linfield, *Freedom under Fire: U.S. Civil Liberties in Times of War* (Cambridge, MA: South End Press, 1990), 164–65.

34. Quoted in Leogrande, *Our Own Backyard,* 303.

35. Quoted in Robert David Johnson, *Congress and the Cold War* (New York: Cambridge University Press, 2006), 277.

36. Quoted in Thomas M. Kane, *Theoretical Roots of US Foreign Policy: Machiavelli and American Unilateralism* (New York: Routledge, 2006), 117.

37. Quoted in Johnson, *Congress and the Cold War,* 267.

38. Ibid., 267–68.

39. Leogrande, *Our Own Backyard,* 316–17. See also General Paul Gorman, interviewed by Nicholas R. Hassell, May 26, 2014, John A. Adams '71 Center for Military History and Strategic Analysis, Virginia Military Institute, Lexington.

40. Both Reagan and the Defense Department official quoted in Leogrande, *Our Own Backyard,* 316–17.

41. Quoted in ibid., 319.

42. Ibid., 318.

43. M. Shahabudden, *The Conquest of Grenada: Sovereignty in the Periphery* (Georgetown, Guyana: University of Guyana Press, 1986), 173–77.

44. Ivan Musicant, *The Banana Wars: A History of United States Military Intervention in Latin America from the Spanish-American War to the Invasion of Panama* (New York: Macmillan, 1990), 375–81.

45. Quoted in ibid., 389. The United States ultimately spent more than $75.5 million on the Grenada operation, which cost 18 American lives and 116 wounded. A comparable number of Cubans died as well as nearly 50 members of the Grenadian military. The United States soon expelled all Eastern Bloc and Cuban officials, declared victory, and installed a pro-US government. The new government received significant amounts of foreign assistance from the Reagan administration over several years. For more on the operation, see Mark Adkin, *Urgent Fury: The Battle for Grenada* (Lexington, MA: Lexington Books, 1989).

46. Quoted in Reynold A. Burrowes, *Revolution and Rescue in Grenada: An Account of the U.S.-Caribbean Invasion* (New York: Praeger, 1988), 88. Also see James Baker III, with Thomas DeFrank, *The Politics of Diplomacy: Revolution, War, & Peace, 1989–1992* (New York: Putnam, 1995), 334–35.

47. Ronald Reagan, *An American Life: The Autobiography* (New York: Simon and Schuster, 1990), 457.

48. George P. Shultz, *Turmoil and Triumph: My Years as Secretary of State* (New York: Scribner's, 1993), 447.

49. Kai P. Schoenhals and Richard A. Melanson, *Revolution and Intervention in Grenada: The New Jewel Movement, the United States, and the Caribbean* (Boulder, CO: Westview Press, 1985), 165–77.

50. *Los Angeles Times,* March 5, 1985; *New York Times,* January 29, 1997.

51. Quoted in Kyle Longley, *In the Eagle's Shadow: The United States and Latin America,* 2nd ed. (Malden, MA: Wiley-Blackwell, 2009), 314.

52. Quoted in Cynthia Aronson, *Crossroads: Congress, the President, and Central America, 1976–1993* (University Park: Pennsylvania State University Press, 1993), 179. During the debates over the Boland Amendment, the White House supporters in Congress attacked the Democrats for acting like Neville Chamberlain at Munich. Representative Bob Livingston (R–LA) called the act "an abomination" and questioned the patriotism of the opposition, asking why his colleagues ignored the calls for freedom in Central America: "Is it naivete? Is it isolationism? Is it partisan politics? Or is it worse?" The pugnacious and confrontational Newt Gingrich (R–GA) stressed that severing the act amounted to showing the division "between radicals who want unilateral disarmament and the rest of us." He charged that some in the opposition party "believe the CIA is more dangerous than the KGB" (both Livingston and Gingrich quoted in Leogrande, *Our Own Backyard,* 321).

53. Quoted in Michael W. Flamm, "The Reagan Presidency and Foreign Policy: Controversies and Legacies," in *Debating the Reagan Presidency,* ed. John Ehrman and Michael W. Flamm (Lanham, MD: Rowman and Littlefield, 2009), 144.

54. Quoted in Lawrence E. Walsh, *Firewall: The Iran-Contra Conspiracy and Cover-Up* (New York: Norton, 1997), 4.

55. Robert McFarlane, with Zofia Smardz, *Special Trust* (New York: Cadell and Davis, 1994), 31.

56. Quoted in Don M. Coerver and Linda Biesele Hall, *Tangled Destinies: Latin America and the United States* (Albuquerque: University of New Mexico Press, 1999), 167.

57. Quoted in McFarlane, *Special Trust,* 34.

58. Quoted in Lou Cannon, *President Reagan: The Role of a Lifetime* (New York: Simon and Schuster, 1991), 638. For more on the Iranian side of the story, see David Crist, *The Twilight War: The Secret History of America's Thirty-Year Conflict with Iran* (New York: Penguin, 2012).

59. Gary Thatcher, "Private Donors to Contras 'Misled' on 'Overhead' Costs," *Christian Science Monitor,* May 22, 1987, at http://www.csmonitor.com/1987/0522/apanel.html.

60. Malcolm Byrne, *Iran-Contra: Reagan's Scandal and the Unchecked Abuse of Presidential Power* (Lawrence: University of Kansas Press, 2014); Walsh, *Firewall*; Theodore Draper, *A Very Thin Line: The Iran-Contra Affairs* (New York: Hill and Wang, 1991).

61. James F. Siekmeier, "Iran-Contra Affair and the Reagan Administration's Leadership Style," paper presented at the conference "The Enduring Legacy: Leadership and National Security Affairs during the Ronald Reagan Era," November 2–4, 2014, Virginia Military Institute, Lexington.

62. Cannon, *President Reagan,* 683.

63. Quoted in ibid., 689–90.

64. Ibid., 708–9.

65. Quoted in ibid., 710–11.

66. Quoted in ibid., 711.

67. Quoted in Schaller, *Reckoning with Reagan,* 154.

68. "Excerpts from the Tower Commission's Report," *New York Times,* February 27, 1987, quoting Lee Hamilton and Daniel Inouye, *Report on the Congressional Committees Investigating the Iran-Contra Affair* (Washington, D.C.: Government Printing Office, 1987).

69. Ronald Reagan, "Address to the Nation on the Iran Arms and Contra Aid Controversy," March 4, 1987, in *Public Papers of the Presidents of the United States: Ronald Reagan, 1987* (Washington, DC: US Government Printing Office, 1989), 209.

70. Hamilton and Inouye, *Report on the Congressional Committees Investigating the Iran-Contra Affair,* 11.

71. Quoted in William E. Pemberton, *Exit with Honor: The Life and Presidency of Ronald Reagan* (Armonk, NY: M. E. Sharpe, 1997), 191.

72. Quoted in ibid., 191–92.

73. LaFeber, *Inevitable Revolutions,* 338.

74. Longley, *In the Eagle's Shadow,* 322.

75. Quoted in Constantine C. Menges, *Inside the National Security Council: The True Story of the Making and Unmaking of Reagan's Foreign Policy* (New York: Simon and Schuster, 1988), 321.

76. Shultz, *Turmoil and Triumph,* 952.

77. Richard Walton, "Costa Rica: Back from the Brink?" *The Nation* 243 (December 20, 1986): 699.

78. Mary McGrory, "Reagan's Last Hope: Ortega," *Washington Post,* October 11, 1988.

79. Both quoted in Martha Honey and Tony Avirgan, "Leaning on Arias," *The Nation* 245 (September 12, 1987): 220, 221.

80. 133 Cong. Rec. S4357 (February 26, 1987). In March 1987, Representative Jim Slattery (D–KS) successfully secured the support of 110 of his colleagues. They sent a letter to Reagan urging him to support a ninety-day cease-fire as well as an end to both US aid to the contras and Soviet assistance to the Sandinistas. They also called for bilateral talks between the United States and Nicaragua and between the Sandinistas and the internal opposition. The administration tried unsuccessfully to draft a response, but internal divisions prevented it (Linda Robinson, "Peace in Central America?" *Foreign Affairs* 66, special issue [1988]: 593).

81. "Explore Peace in Nicaragua," *New York Times,* June 18, 1987.

82. *Washington Post,* October 11, 1987; "one observer" quoted in LaFeber, *Inevitable Revolutions,* 343. Shultz would emphasize that Reagan's "blind spot—an unwillingness to recognize the importance of pressure from the Contras to spur the Nicaraguans to the negotiating table—always baffled me. But I never doubted his sincerity of purpose" (*Turmoil and Triumph,* 952).

83. On August 5, Reagan and Wright issued a joint statement that outlined US security concerns and called for an immediate cease-fire in Nicaragua with verification by the Organization of American States, an end to foreign aid, and the withdrawal of foreign military advisers. The proposal called for, after completion of the initial requirements, the creation of an independent multiparty electoral commission to monitor elections and the Sandinistas' acceptance of a plan of national reconciliation that would provide amnesty to the contras. Once these steps were concluded, negotiations would follow to reduce the region's military forces and restore a military balance. Finally, the plan promised an end to the US embargo if the Nicaraguans complied with the conditions of the Wright–Reagan plan. Shultz also later emphasized that the "thrust [of the Esquipulas II Accords] was similar in general terms to the Wright–Reagan plan, but the language was looser and with less attention given to enforcement mechanisms. . . . The Wright–Reagan proposal had created an important and helpful pressure" (*Turmoil and Triumph,* 957–59; see also Jim Wright, *Worth It All: My War for Peace* [Washington, DC: Brassey's, 1993], 268–70).

84. Dario V. Moreno, *The Struggle for Peace in Central America* (Gainesville: University Press of Florida, 1994), 84.

85. Ibid., 88–89.

86. Quoted in ibid., 89.

87. Reagan quoted in Edward A. Lynch, *The Cold War's Last Battlefield: Reagan, the Soviets, and Central America* (Albany: State University of New York Press, 2011), 241; Abrams quoted in Longley, *In the Eagle's Shadow,* 322.

88. "Reagan's Bay of Pigs," *Wall Street Journal,* August 11, 1987; *Washington Times,* August 11, 1987.

89. Quoted in "Speaking His Peace: Mr. Arias Comes to Washington, but Not Everybody Cheers," *Time,* October 5, 1987.

90. Quoted in John M. Goshko, "Costa Rican Opposes Reagan Bid for Aid during Talks," *Washington Post,* September 23, 1987.

91. Reagan and Oakley quoted in "Speaking His Peace."

92. Quoted in Aronson, *Crossroads,* 223.

93. Jill Smolowe, "Central America: Golden Opportunity for Don Oscar," *Time,* October 26, 1987.

94. *Washington Post,* October 11, 1987.

95. Arias stated in an interview, "President Reagan and Secretary Shultz sent me kind messages of congratulations about the prize. But I wonder what is in their hearts. I suspect un poco de mixed feelings" (quoted in *Washington Post,* October 11, 1987). An editorial in the *Washington Post* criticized the administration for an "inadequate" response to the prize announcement: "Far from praising him for unlocking a door it had been unable to open on its own for nearly seven years, the American government acts as though the award would only complicate its life in Central America," the editorial emphasized. "It took several hours for the administration to compose a response gracious enough to match this great honor to a man and his country. Even then the impression was left that Costa Rica has a lightheaded policy for a suspect 'peace' while the United States pursue[s] a separate, serious policy to remove the Sandinistas from power" ("Toward Peace in Central America," *Washington Post,* October 15, 1987).

96. Quoted in "Undermining Arias?" *Commonweal* 115 (October 7, 1988): 517.

97. Quoted in LaFeber, *Inevitable Revolutions,* 343–44.

98. Quoted in "Blessed Are the Peacemakers," *America* 157 (October 31, 1987): 283.

99. Moreno, *The Struggle for Peace in Central America,* 99.

100. Arias stated on December 9, "I've been asking Mr. Reagan in Washington that he should stop all economic support to the contras. . . . As long as there is that aggression, you cannot ask Nicaragua to democratize" (quoted in *Central American Update,* December 11, 1987). Arias earlier had angered contra supporters when he ordered the contra military leaders and soldiers to leave Costa Rica by November 7 to fulfill terms of the peace plan (*La Prensa Libre,* August 12, 1987).

11

Toward an Ecological Frontier

Environmental Policy, Economic Development, and US-Mexican Relations during the Reagan Presidency

Evan R. Ward

On January 3, 1986, Ronald Reagan and Mexican president Miguel de la Madrid Hurtado met in the most unlikely of sites for their annual meeting—Mexicali, Mexico, situated in close proximity to farm fields, maquiladoras, and the border-defining All-American Canal.[1] Previous and future presidential meetings took place in more desirable climes, but the four-hour meeting in northern Baja California's burgeoning capital city symbolized progress achieved in US-Mexican economic integration and environmental cooperation during the previous decades. *New York Times* correspondent William Stockton described the meeting as one in which "nothing dramatic occurred" and where "there were no sharp disagreements or clashes."[2] It stood in sharp contrast to the scene in front of the US consulate in Mexicali two decades earlier. In 1963, hundreds of Mexican protesters, carrying placards with inflammatory anti-American rhetoric, decried the pollution of the Colorado River by US farmers, whose pumping of highly saline drainage water from their fields had adversely affected agricultural production in the Mexicali Valley.[3]

To be sure, it would be wrong to characterize the Reagan presidency as a time of significant progress in environmental policies. Many would claim that Ronald Reagan's secretary of the interior, James Watt, overlooked the forest *and* the trees. In this context, academic environmental studies multiplied against the backdrop of dwindling regulatory statutes.[4] And yet international obligations agreed upon by President Reagan's predecessors, including Franklin Roosevelt, Richard Nixon, and Jimmy Carter, regarding division and management of water resources in the Colorado River and Rio Grande basins promised the possibilities for a modicum of environmental collaboration with Mexico in the border region between 1981 and 1989.

Identifying significant moments in US-Mexican presidential relations in the post–World War II era proves rather illusive. There is, of course, the indelible image of President Harry S. Truman placing a wreath at the monument to the fallen cadets near the Castle of Chapultepec in Mexico City during his visit in March 1947. In recent memory, George W. Bush's appeal to Latino voters during the presidential election of 2000, followed by warm *abrazos* with newly elected Mexican president Vicente Fox in the wake of their victories in 2001, may stand out as the most immediate image of US-Mexican rapprochement. Yet the intensified East–West orientation of US foreign policy toward the Middle East, particularly in the wake of the events of September 11, 2001, as well as the rise of populist leaders in Venezuela and Bolivia—extending their own *abrazos* toward *el comandante* in Havana—in many senses obscured the contemporary relevance of cooperation between Mexico and the United States during the 1980s that contributed to the further economic and political integration of the North American neighbors.

This essay focuses in particular on the achievements of the US Department of State and the International Boundary and Water Commission (IBWC), created in 1889 to regulate the shared natural resources that flow across the international border, as well as on the shifting territorial nature of the border itself, Reagan's personal investment in his relationship with his professional counterparts to the South—José López Portillo from 1981 until 1982, Miguel de la Madrid from 1982 until 1988, and Carlos Salinas Gortari during the final months of the Reagan presidency in 1988—added personal authenticity to less-publicized cooperation on natural-resource management amid more contentious problems, including drug trafficking, immigration, and postures toward political upheaval in Central America. The high degree of cultural, social, and demographic interdependence between the two countries—an ongoing process accelerated after World War II—influenced policy choices in directions that might not have been possible in other circumstances.

The history of US-Mexican environmental diplomacy since World War II suggests that during the Reagan presidency modest gains were made toward a truly bidirectional, collaborative approach to questions of ecology along the shared border. During World War II, with the world's attention riveted on Asia and Europe, President Franklin D. Roosevelt recognized the contributions of Mexican soldiers to the Allied war effort through participation in combat side by side with US soldiers as well as the contributions made by the braceros working in the fields of the southwestern United States. Under some pressure to acknowledge the ambiguity of existing international water law regarding waterways that crossed sovereign boundaries, such as in the Colorado River and Rio Grande basins, as well as to emphasize the Good Neighbor policy, Roosevelt assented to guarantee Mexico a percentage of the water from those two rivers in the Mexican Water Treaty of 1944. Although the terms of the agreement favored interests in the United States (which received approximately 90 percent of the water resources in the two river basins), the treaty vouchsafed the viability of industrial, urban, and agricultural development along Mexico's northern border, at least through the twentieth century.[5]

Some seventeen years later, in 1961, when highly saline water deliveries in fulfillment of that treaty devastated cotton and truck-crop farms in Baja California, Mexican officials demanded that the quality as well as the quantities of water meet standards sufficient for their intended uses.[6] At the time, both countries turned to their own scientific specialists and engineers to justify their respective positions on the question—reports commissioned by the United States justified the status quo ante, and studies commission by Mexico demanded remediation. In 1974, despite dogged local and state opposition in the western United States, Herbert Brownell, whom President Richard Nixon had appointed to find a solution to the impasse, put forth a successful proposal to build a costly desalinization plant near Yuma, Arizona, to purify polluted water destined for farms and homes in Mexico.

Resolution of the Colorado River salinity crisis in 1974 illustrated the potential diplomatic sensitivity of international issues that crossed borders and affected residents on both sides of the border. It should be noted that by the mid-1960s manufacturing plants known as maquiladoras contributed to the stew of domestic, industrial, and agricultural runoff that flowed northward in the New River from Mexico into Imperial County, California, on its way to the man-made Salton Sea.[7] In both cases, the IBWC, tasked with arbitrating such disputes, offered an institutional setting for conflict resolution that the historian Oscar Martinez argues characterized binational relations after 1920.[8] By the close of the Jimmy Carter presidency, the two countries, through the IBWC, agreed to closer collaboration on questions of water quality along the border.

Crisis, however, precipitated even closer cooperation during the early Reagan presidency. During the winter of 1983, abnormally high levels of snowfall in the Rockies, occasioned by an El Niño event, portended a spring of heavy runoff. In December 1982, for example, snowfall reached 112 percent of its historical norms. At the same time, releases from Hoover Dam increased, filling up the reservoir behind Davis Dam. Riverside residents complained about the damage caused by these excess waters, and the US Bureau of Reclamation (USBR) subsequently reduced release amounts below Hoover Dam. Mexican officials, however, petitioned the IBWC to inform them of changes in water releases, particularly in light of the increased precipitation.[9]

As a result of meetings between Mexico's Comisión Internacional de Límites y Aguas and the IBWC during the winter of 1983, the two nations improved communication regarding water-release levels. In April, IBWC commissioner Joseph Friedkin noted that unusually strong storms in March 1983 had raised snowpack levels from 96 percent to 109 percent of the historical average for snowfall. He also observed that snow runoff had exceeded earlier predictions and would remain heavy throughout the rest of the year. According to Friedkin, "about 2,500,000 acre-feet of water needs to be released before January 1, 1984 in order to provide needed flood control space, in addition to the releases for scheduled water uses in the United States." At the same time, Mexican officials feared that as a result of the increased precipitation there would be fewer requests for Colorado River water from farmers in the Imperial Valley, so excess waters would subsequently be delivered to Mexico.[10]

Abnormal weather conditions continued through June 1983. Snowstorms pummeled the Rockies at the end of May. Warm weather in mid-June quickly turned the frozen blanket of snow into mountain streams that filled the upper Colorado River and its tributaries. The USBR subsequently released large amounts of water from the dams on the Colorado River during the first week of July out of fear that water might spill over the top of Hoover Dam or break through Glen Canyon Dam. When these "controlled" releases reached the delta, however, traveling at many times their normal speed, they flooded farmlands in Yuma County and Mexicali Valley. Although water was diverted through the All-American Canal to the Salton Sea to alleviate pressure on the main channel of the river, John A. Bethel, a member of the Yuma County Sheriff's office, expected water levels to rise another one to two feet. As a result of the flood, five people were killed in Mexico. Later congressional hearings confirmed that three thousand acres of Mexican farmland (inside the protective dikes) were also damaged in the floods. Groundwater that seeped beneath the protective dikes also threatened farms located on the river.[11]

US news magazines focused on the causes of the flooding. An article in *Time* noted that the destruction caused by the floods in California, Mexico, and Arizona could not be termed a "natural disaster." As one victim noted to correspondent Kurt Anderson, "This is a man-made disaster, and there's no excuse for it. . . . It's just plain stupidity." Although the article in *Time* did not attribute the disaster explicitly to the USBR's failure to carry out its flood-control responsibilities before protecting water-storage capacity and maintaining optimal levels of electricity production, it did note the complexity of controlling the river. USBR commissioner Robert Broadbent observed in retrospect, "Our estimates were wrong. The flows this year just didn't fit into that computer model. It was winter clear up to the 20th of May, and then all of the sudden in turned to summer." Contrasting the disaster on the Colorado River to active volcanoes in Hawaii and tornadoes in the Midwest that did not claim any lives, *Time* journalist Kurt Anderson noted that these latter events were "not good news, but not disasters either: if those were acts of God, at least he pulled his punches."[12]

In a *Newsweek* article titled "The Colorado: Man-Made Flood," published in June 1984, correspondents noted that "for the first time in decades, nature took the upper-hand, filling the dams and reservoirs that regulate the river's flow . . . to the bursting point with a massive and largely unpredicted influx of late-spring rain and rapidly melting winter snow." As a result, the USBR was forced to release water, an event known as a "controlled disaster." By the first week in July, the correspondents reported, additional water would have forced the bureau to relinquish control of the river to nature. They also noted the political fallout from the floods throughout the river basin. The long-standing love–hate relationship between delta residents and the USBR continued. As one Arizona resident noted, "We trusted the bureau and their dams. . . . We don't trust them anymore."[13]

A year later *Sports Illustrated* published an article by James Kirshenbaum titled "Rising Waters and Mismanagement on the Colorado," which accused the USBR and individual states in the Colorado River basin of giving water storage and electricity production a higher priority than flood control. Furthermore, Kirshenbaum observed, such patterns of water use altered water levels below the dams as much as fifteen feet in twenty-four hours. "At times the Colorado is practically bone-dry downriver," he noted, "with harmful consequences for fish and other wildlife; at other times heavy flooding is the problem." Kirshenbaum also noted the political implications of these geoenvironmental disconnections between those living in the delta and conditions upstream. Although Interior Secretary James Watt was justifiably ecstatic that flooding did not recur close to the dams in the spring of 1984, the reporter noted, "People as far away as Yuma. . . . didn't join in the huzzahs. The bureau had dumped water on them with virtually no advance notice."[14]

The floods of 1983, together with national press coverage of and congressional hearings on the floods, raised important issues related to water management in the Colorado River basin that went beyond the principles that had sustained the irrigated agribusiness there during the preceding decades. The floods ultimately provided additional momentum for the environmental movement. In the wake of the Teton Dam break in 1976, environmentalists wanted to emphasize not only dams' potential harm to human communities but also their deleterious effects on surrounding landscapes, flora, and fauna. Scholars would later link the effects of Colorado River dams to the socioeconomic challenges faced by the Cocopah natives in the lower Mexican delta. Ecologists also argued that dams upstream physically disconnect various segments of the riparian plane and riverbed from each other, ultimately increasing erosion and decreasing the diversity of organisms in the riparian plain.[15]

Ronald Reagan's election in 1980 also coincided with the hemorrhaging of Mexican debt in the wake of the decision by the Organization of Petroleum Producing Countries to lift its oil embargo, effectively devaluing the one resource on which Mexico had staked so much of its social and economic developmental promise. When Presidents López Portillo and Reagan conducted their first meeting in 1981, they formalized the creation of the US-Mexico Binational Commission, whose mandate included periodic meetings between officials of both countries and acknowledgment of the border region's unique role in the relationship between the two countries. López Portillo and Reagan's conversations centered on economic questions and likely served as preliminary executive soundings for structural shifts in Mexico's economy toward free trade that would be elaborated two years later in the Baker Plan. But those early meetings also encompassed discussions, at times fractious, regarding US concerns that Mexico allowed its border rivers that ran north into the United States—the New River and Tijuana River in Baja California—to endanger public health in the United States.

When Reagan met subsequently with President de la Madrid in August 1983 at the city of La Paz in southern Baja California, he and the Department of State capitalized on the opportunity to press Mexico for greater cooperation on persistent border problems that reflected broader economic integration as well as on more substantive questions related to the viability of the Mexico's global financial stability.

As had been the case in other negotiations regarding economic integration of the border region, local leadership leveraged diplomatic action between the two countries. Beginning in the 1960s, Mexico pursued a strategy of attracting US corporations across the border by offering attractive incentives to locate factories, or maquiladoras (an epithet referring to the value added by grinding wheat into flour), there. With the promise of new jobs along the border, northern Mexico subsequently experienced exponential industrial growth as well as an influx of Mexican citizens. Industrial and human waste multiplied, overwhelming existing sewage facilities and sending toxic refuse into the United States in plain sight of citizens in southern California near San Diego in the case of the Tijuana

River as well as in Calexico and the Imperial Valley adjacent to the New River.

Californians clamored in protest of what had once been merely an irritant but now posed the potential threat of encephalitis outbreaks as well as adverse impacts on regional flora and fauna. For eighteen years, Arthur Swajian, executive officer of the Regional Water Quality Control Board, had appealed to the existing US agency tasked with monitoring water-quality issues arising between the two countries, the IBWC, for redress of the growing problem. After failing to elicit an effective response from US officials at the commission, Swajian turned to political channels to elevate local concerns to international importance. Media attention, gubernatorial pressure, and appeals to then secretary of state Cyrus Vance in the waning years of the Carter presidency raised environmental issues to the fore in US-Mexican relations.[16]

Mexico's economic implosion emboldened Reagan and the Department of State to press for environmental protections and economic reforms, even if the new president had not been the initial impetus behind those efforts.[17] When the existing framework for resolving border environmental issues, which were now of national and international concern, proved ineffectual, the new administration pressed for a new framework for conflict resolution. As a result of the international consequences of regional water problems as well as other environmental issues, Presidents Reagan and de la Madrid officially agreed during their meetings in August 1983 to even closer collaboration on issues related to their shared rivers, signing the accord Cooperation for the Protection and Improvement of the Environment in the Border Area, informally known as the La Paz Agreement. This agreement required both countries to "undertake, to the fullest extent practical, to adopt appropriate measures to prevent, reduce and eliminate sources of pollution in their respective territory which affect the border area of the other."[18] The problems—including controlled flooding, the prospect of untreated sewage from Tijuana drifting northward onto San Diego beaches, and high levels of selenium concentrated through intensive use along the northern stretches of the Colorado River in the United States—flowed in both directions, as both the floods of 1983 and the sewage problems in the New River attested.[19] In addition, the Reagan administration empowered the Environmental Protection Agency to mediate with the Mexican government all US concerns regarding binational environmental issues "that impact public health and the environment of both nations."[20]

The two nations also established "a coordination team composed of both US and Mexican federal officials . . . for each of the areas of water pollution, air quality control and hazardous waste management . . . and were given the ability to communicate directly with their counterparts without using the formal, cumbersome diplomatic route."[21] In spite of many Americans' skepticism as to the likelihood of Mexican compliance with the new accords, Swajian hailed the La Paz Agreement as a significant achievement. "We're very pleased now to note that the coordination role in the United States has been given to the Environmental Protection Agency," he testified in a state congressional hearing. "We think that it's a new show; a new ball game. And, you know, maybe something will come from that."[22]

In President Reagan's personal recollections—recorded on a daily basis while he was in office, according to the historian Douglas Brinkley, in the five leather-bound volumes of his diaries for the ostensible purpose of his and Nancy's own reflection but most assuredly for broader consumption and legacy shaping—Mexico remains on the margins, a status reflective, perhaps, of what one analyst of Reagan's foreign-policy record in Latin America, David Ignatius, observed when he wrote at the end of the Reagan presidency: "American policy towards Mexico—the real strategic prize in the region—was subordinated to the make-believe war against the Sandanistas."[23] The content of Reagan's diaries does suggest that strategic partnerships with Mexico targeted his broader aims of thwarting Communist political and economic influence in Central America. On January 23, 1983, for example, Reagan wrote that civil war in El Salvador might lead to "a general revolution aimed at all of Central [America] and yes, Mexico."[24] Five years later, regarding his meeting with President de la Madrid in 1988 in the decidedly more attractive environs of Mazatlán, Reagan noted that his exchanges with his Mexican counterpart were "good" and focused on "our mutual drug problem, on trade and on the threatened increase of Soviets in Mexico." Ever vigilant against Communist infiltration along the border, even as perestroika loomed on the horizon, Reagan expressed satisfaction with de la Madrid's cooperation in "[refusing] to allow [the Soviets] to set up consulates along our border."[25]

Paradoxically, the last visible manifestation of socialist sympathies along the US-Mexico border probably took place in 1963 in Mexicali during the aforementioned Colorado River salinity crisis.[26]

It is certain that during the meeting in Mexicali in 1986 Mexico's resistance to walking in lockstep with the United States in the latter's public pronouncements regarding Nicaraguan politics and the recent death of US agent Enrique Camarena in the hemispheric war on drug trafficking were surely on Reagan's mind, but he also had a personal interest in Mexico since the devastating earthquakes that had rocked Mexico City in September 1985.

"[The] evening news brought word of a gigantic earthquake that caused incalculable damage in Mexico," Reagan wrote in his diary entry for Thursday, September 19, 1985. "[The] [f]irst TV shots were horrible." "The news was full of the horror of Mexico," he recorded the next night.[27]

And for the weekend of September 21 and 22, he noted with evident compassion: "Another quake hit Mexico City, the death toll is climbing into the 1000s. Late Sat. night I got through to [President] de la Madrid by phone. We're mustering all the help we can. Nancy is going to go to California by way of Mexico City to emphasize our concern and cooperation."[28]

By the time the two presidents met in Mexicali some three and a half months later, Reagan's mind had turned to questions of economic development in Mexico. "In the meetings I tried to sell him the idea of opening his country up to outside investors," he remarked in his diary. "My pitch was that Baja could be one of the world's great resort areas."[29] At lower levels, State Department officials worked through the contentious high-profile issues of drug trafficking and immigration issues. Only Paul Knox, correspondent for the Canadian-based periodical the *Globe and Mail* noted, however, that at the department level officials from the two countries discussed environmental issues, including questions related to the "irrigation of crops in the Southwestern United States [that] . . . lowered water levels in several Mexican regions"—a clear reference to the high levels of salinity that flowed from American farms in Arizona across the border into Baja California—as well as the question of "sewage from Tijuana [that] polluted beaches in San Diego." Some twenty-five years earlier, similar problems had threatened to sour US-Mexican relations between 1961 until 1972, yet by the time of Reagan and de la Madrid's meetings and largely through the IWBC's cooperative efforts, Knox reported, "both sides say progress has been made on environmental questions in department-level talks, and these points are not expected to be contentious."[30]

Yet President Reagan's personal responsiveness to Mexico's need for greater collaboration in the face of flooding in 1983 as well as the collaborative accomplishments achieved by the IWBC invite a modest reconsideration of the intersection between US domestic environmental policies and the legacy of environmental diplomacy in the broader context of US-Mexican relations. International policy directives issued during the 1980s suggest that bidirectional aspects of institutional efforts aimed at greater cooperation contributed in some measure to the inclusion of environmental aspects of the North American Free Trade Agreement, including the Border Environmental Commission and the North American Development Bank, which coordinated funding and oversight for resolution of complicated transborder ecological problems.[31]

Eight months after his Mexicali encounter with President de la Madrid, President Reagan jotted in his leather journal, "We're getting good cooperation on the drug problem but their economic woes are very serious." One step was to pledge to help raise $4 billion toward Mexico's staggering $90 billion foreign debt following the implosion of the oil market, but it was clearly not enough. "I'm going to approach him on things he could do to open Mexico to outside investment and more entrepreneurship," Reagan continued.[32] The creation of the North American Free Trade Agreement was still somewhere in the near future—for better or for worse—but the fact that border environmental questions no longer headlined US-Mexican diplomatic relations, as they had during the 1960s and 1970s, suggested that Reagan and the IBWC played a crucial role in offering a forum and format for conflict resolution in advance of the more comprehensive and complex trade agreement in 1994.

Notes

1. William Stockton, "A Show of Unity along the Border," *New York Times,* January 5, 1986.

2. Ibid.

3. Evan R. Ward, *Border Oasis: Water and the Ecology of the Colorado River Delta, 1940–1975* (Tucson: University of Arizona Press, 2003), passim.

4. Jeffrey K. Stine observes, "Policies relating to natural resources and the environment never received high priority during the Ronald Reagan presidency except to the extent that they advanced the administration's broader political objectives of reducing the overall size of federal government and diminishing industrial regulation. . . . Toward this end, Reagan sought to expand the reliance on market forces and lessen the role of the federal government. This structural framework, he contended, would meet more of society's needs, without causing undue harm to the natural environment and public health" ("Natural Resources and Environmental Policy," in *The Reagan Presidency: Pragmatic Conservatism and Its Legacies,* ed. W. Elliot Brownlee and Hugh Davis Graham [Lawrence: University Press of Kansas, 2003], 233).

5. See April R. Summitt, *Contested Waters: An Environmental History of the Colorado River* (Boulder: University of Colorado Press, 2013).

6. See Norris Hundley, *Water and the West: The Colorado River Compact and the Politics of Water in the American West,* 2nd ed. (Berkeley: University of California Press, 2009).

7. IBWC, Minute Number 264, "Recommendations for Solution of the New River Border Sanitation Problem at Calexico, California—Mexicali, Baja California Norte," August 26, 1980, all minutes archived at http://www.ibwc.gov/Treaties_Minutes/Minutes.html.

8. Oscar J. Martinez, *Troublesome Border,* rev. ed. (Tucson: University of Arizona Press, 2006), 8.

9. "Minuta de la reunión celebrada en Yuma, Arizona, a las 13.00 hrs. del día 10 de enero de 1983," Fondo Consultativo Técnico, Caja 15, Archivo Historico del Agua (AHA), Mexico City. Recent scholarship has attributed the increased rainfall and flooding to an El Niño event and climate change. See Norman Edilberto Rivera Pazos and Enriqueta Salazar Ruiz, "Analisis de modificaciones den caudal en el rio Colorado debido al cambio climatico, y repercusiones en el valle de Mexicali," paper presented at the Fifteenth Congreso Internacional de Ingeniería de Proyectos Huesca, July 6–8, 2011, at http://www.aeipro.com/files/congresos/2011huesca/CIIP11_1035_1049.3320.pdf.

10. J. F. Friedkin to Joaquin Bustamante R., Comisión Internacional de Límites y Aguas commissioner, April 5, 1983, Fondo Consultativo Técnico, Caja 15, AHA.

11. "Colorado River Flooding Peaks," *Engineering News-Record,* July 7, 1983, 13. Comments on losses in Mexicali Valley are located in US House of Representatives, Committee on Interior and Insular Affairs, *Hearings on Colorado River Management,* 98th Cong., 1st sess., September 7–8, 1983, Serial no. 98-20 (Washington, DC: US Government Printing Office, 1983), 18. Dr. Fernando J. Gonzalez Villarreal also discusses the impact of the summer floods in Mexicali Valley with Daniel Diaz Diaz, subsecretary of infrastructure for the secretary of communications and transportation in a letter on August 30, 1983 (Fondo Consultativo Técnico, Caja 15, AHA). He notes that Imperial Valley's lack of need for water deliveries during the summer sent increasingly large amounts of water to Mexicali Valley at an aver-

age rate of 950 cubic meters per second and a maximum rate of 1,110 cubic meters per second. These floodwaters accelerated erosion near the Federal Railroad Bridge Number 2 in San Luis Rio Colorado, Sonora. He also pointed out that mainly marginal lands had been affected.

12. Kurt Anderson, "Somber Prelude to the Fourth: A Faulty Bridge and an Untamable River Claim Eight Lives," *Time,* July 11, 1983.

13. Tom Morgantau, Darby Junkin, and Linda Prout, "The Colorado: Man-Made Flood," *Newsweek,* July 11, 1983.

14. James Kirshenbaum, "Rising Waters and Mismanagement on the Colorado," *Sports Illustrated,* June 11, 1984.

15. Patrick McCully, *Silenced Rivers: The Ecology and Politics of Large Dams* (London: Zed Books, 1996), 29–31. Also see Sasha Nemecek, "Frankly, My Dear, I Don't Want a Dam: How Dams Affect Biodiversity," *Scientific American,* October 1997.

16. For a discussion of Arthur Swajian's direct and indirect role in the politicization of water-quality issues in the border region in the 1970s and early 1980s, see Robert D. Tomasek, "Colorado River Salinity and New River Sanitation: Environmental Issues in U.S.-Mexican Relations," *Universities Field Staff International Reports,* no. 32 (1982): 1–8, at http://www.icwa.org/wp-content/uploads/2015/11/RDT-2.pdf. Tomasek argues that Swajian "adopted a three-pronged go-for broke strategy," including placing pressure on then California governor Edmund Brown's office to resolve the problem, appealing to the Department of State, and eliciting mainstream attention from *Time* magazine and the *New York Times* regarding the gravity of pollution levels in the New River.

17. Maxwell A. Cameron and Brian W. Tomlin argue that the economic downturn in Mexico in the early 1980s forced Mexican officials to entertain US overtures that its southern neighbor open its economy by signing the General Agreement on Tariffs and Trade, for instance. "When oil prices began to decline in the early 1980s and interest rates shot up," write Cameron and Tomlin, "Mexico found itself vulnerable to U.S. trade remedy actions at a time when it needed to generate hard currency through nonoil exports" (*The Making of NAFTA: How the Deal Was Done* [Ithaca, NY: Cornell University Press, 2000], 58). I contend that this bargaining power spilled over to environmental issues, which cannot be separated from the increasing integration of the two economies.

18. IBWC, Minute No. 270, "Recommendations for the First Stage Treatment and Disposal Facilities for the Solution of the Border Sanitation Problem at San Diego, California—Tijuana, Baja California," Ciudad Juarez, Chihuahua, April 30, 1983.

19. In his seminal overview of the US-Mexico border region, Oscar J. Martinez notes that an institutional framework for resolution of binational problems followed in the wake of the Mexican Revolution. Although this medium of conflict resolution was often contentious, as evidenced by the more than decade-long diplomatic impasse represented by the salinity crisis in the 1960s and early 1970s, the

two countries, by way of the IBWC, transitioned to collaborative identification, definition, and resolution of shared sanitation issues in 1979 (*Troublesome Border,* 121–26; see also IBWC, Minute 261, "Recommendations for the Solution to the Border Sanitation Problems," El Paso, Texas, September 24, 1979). During Reagan's presidency, joint attention was paid to sanitation issues in the San Diego–Tijuana metropolitan areas (see note 18) and to similar problems at Naco, Arizona, and Naco, Sonora (see IBWC, Minute 273, "Recommendations for the Solution of the Border Sanitation Problem at Naco, Arizona–Naco–Sonora," El Paso, Texas, March 19, 1987). Water-quality concerns in the Imperial Valley–Mexicali Valley region of the Colorado River Delta were addressed with a jointly funded project (see IBWC, Minute No. 274, "Joint Project for Improvement of the Quality of the Waters of the New River at Calexico, California—Mexicali, Baja California," Ciudad Juárez, Chihuahua, April 15, 1987). And a joint report was issued on sanitation problems in the twin cities Nogales, Arizona, and Nogales, Sonora (see IBWC, "Joint Report of the Principal Engineers Concerning the Conveyance, Treatment, and Final Disposal of Sewage from Nogales, Arizona and Nogales, Sonora, Exceeding the Capacities Allotted to the United States and Mexico at the Nogales International Sewage Treatment Plant in Conformance with Minute No. 227," Ciudad Juárez, Chihuahua, July 25, 1988). Stephen P. Mumme and Kimberly Collins have more recently explored the impact of the La Paz Agreement in "The La Paz Agreement 30 Years On," *Journal of Environment and Development* 23, no. 3 (2014): 1–28, doi: 10.1177/1070496514528801.

20. Frank Covington, director, Water Management Division, US Environmental Protection Agency, written testimony, Assembly Select Committee on International Water Treatment and Reclamation, "New River Border Pollution," Sacramento, California, May 9, 1984, at http://digitalcommons.law.ggu.edu/caldocs_assembly, 79.

21. Covington, written testimony in ibid., 81.

22. Arthur Swajian, testimony, in ibid., 9.

23. David Ignatius, "Reagan's Foreign Policy and the Rejection of Diplomacy," in *The Reagan Legacy,* ed. Sidney Blumenthal and Thomas Byrne Edsall (New York: Pantheon Books, 1988), 189. In the context of broader US foreign policy, Ignatius wrote the following during the second term of Reagan's presidency: "The Middle East was the clearest example of the Reagan administration's incapacity in foreign policy, but it wasn't the only one. The competence problem affected even the area that seemed to matter most to Reagan—Central America. . . . The survival of the contras—the 'freedom fighters,' as the president and his men called them—became a sentimental goal that overshadowed America's actual strategic goals in Central America. American policy toward Mexico—the real strategic prize in the region—was subordinated to the make-believe war against the Sandinistas" (190–91).

24. Diary entry for January 23, 1983, in Ronald Reagan, *The Reagan Diaries,* ed. Douglas Brinkley (New York: Harper Collins, 2009), 162.

25. Diary entry for March 13, 1988, in ibid., 578.

26. Ward, *Border Oasis,* 78–85.

27. Diary entries for September 19 and 20, 1985, in Reagan, *The Reagan Diaries,* 354.

28. Diary entry for September 21–22, 1985, in ibid., 354–55.

29. Diary entry for January 3, 1986, in ibid., 381.

30. Paul Knox, "Real Problems Lurk behind Smiles; Reagan, Mexican Leader Pushing 'Equals' Image," *Globe and Mail,* January 3, 1986.

31. Maxwell A. Cameron and Brian W. Tomlin discuss the context for environmental provisions included in the North American Free Trade Agreement in *The Making of NAFTA*, 180–208, passim; James Baker III discusses the conceptual origins of a free-trade agreement in his memoir, written with Thomas M. DeFrank, *The Politics of Diplomacy: Revolution, War, and Peace, 1989–1992* (New York: Putnam's, 1995), 606.

32. Diary entry for August 11, 1986, in Reagan, *The Reagan Diaries,* 431.

12

Stranger in a Dangerous Land

Reagan and Lebanon, 1981–1984

Charles F. Brower IV

The call from National Security Adviser Robert C. McFarlane to the president's military aide came shortly after 2:00 a.m. on Sunday, October 23, 1983: there had been a suicide attack with a truck laden with explosives on the marine barracks in Beirut, and the casualties were high and climbing. McFarlane wanted me to awaken the president so that he and Secretary of State George P. Shultz could inform the president of the devastating news.

By the time I slipped into the president's bedroom in the Eisenhower Cottage on the grounds of the Augusta national golf course about thirty minutes later, the previous twenty-four hours had already been unusually complicated. Shultz and McFarlane had met with the president at 5:15 a.m. on October 22 to discuss the invitation received from the Organization of Eastern Caribbean States for the United States to restore peace and stability on Grenada, and Reagan had directed the vice president to convene a Special Security Group to develop contingency plans. Air Force One had been alerted to be prepared for an early return to Washington in the event the press got wind of these developments. In the meantime, to avoid arousing suspicions and thus truncating planning time and freedom of action, it was decided that the president's schedule would proceed as planned. However, that afternoon's round of golf with Shultz, Treasury Secretary Donald Regan, and former US senator Nicholas Brady had been interrupted when a bearded gunman had crashed his truck through the country club's gates and taken hostages in the clubhouse. Secured by the Secret Service in an armored limousine off the sixteenth fairway until the threat was properly categorized and later returned by motorcade rather than golf cart to the Eisenhower Cottage, the president had a quiet dinner with Mrs. Reagan, and they had retired for the evening.

With Mrs. Reagan eyeing me in disbelief as I entered around 2:30 a.m., I wakened the president and led him to the sitting room, where Shultz and McFarlane waited with the horrific news of the disaster in Beirut and casualty reports that in just thirty minutes had now risen to nearly two hundred. "Surely they're not all dead," I recall the president saying. "How bad is it? How could this have happened? Who did it?"

Shultz and McFarlane, both former marines, were visibly stricken, McFarlane later writing that it felt as if he "had been stabbed in the heart."[1] Reagan was ashen-faced and clearly in a state of grief. He would later call October 23, 1983, "the saddest day of my presidency, perhaps the saddest day of my life."[2] After a long reflective moment to himself, he looked up at us. "Let's go back to Washington." On Air Force One during the return flight, the grim news sharpened in terms of both rising American casualties, which would ultimately total 241 dead marines and other US servicemen, and the report of a companion terrorist attack on the French contingent in Lebanon. Speaking without notes in the rain after arrival on the South Lawn, Reagan denounced this "despicable act of bestial enemies" and called for Americans to be "more determined than ever" that the United States could not be driven from that "vital and strategic part of the earth."[3] In fact, by February 1984 the marines had been redeployed—not withdrawn, the administration was quick to emphasize—and the administration's Lebanon policy lay in ruins.

How did Lebanon, in which the United States had no vital interests and whose problems preoccupied so few officials in the new Reagan administration, come to play such a dominant role in the administration's foreign policy in the president's first four years in office? Why did the Reagan administration's Lebanon policy so disastrously collapse? In short, why did Ronald Reagan and his administration find themselves from 1981 to 1984 in the uncomfortable role of a stranger in a dangerous land?

Following its inauguration, the new Reagan administration shaped its foreign policy principally in terms of its global containment of the Soviet

Union and communism and thus viewed regional conflicts in Cold War terms. In the Middle East, its preoccupation was the promotion of a "strategic consensus" among nations such as Israel, Egypt, Jordan, and Saudi Arabia to deal with the threat of the expansion of Soviet influence. In this context, Secretary of State Alexander Haig was especially suspicious that the Soviet Union would see Lebanon as an opportunity for using its regional allies and proxies, Syria and the Palestinian Liberation Organization (PLO), as agents for advancing its interests and influence in the region.[4] This ideological prism, the defining of Lebanon's difficulties in terms of the influence of foreign forces rather than in terms of its own complex and profound internal disarray, would distort the administration's understanding of the Lebanon crisis and foreshadow the failure of its policy.

The Lebanese Context

The nation that first drew the Reagan administration into the Middle East was one of the region's most complex. Lebanon's carefully drawn borders after World War I had left a majority Maronite Christian enclave concentrated on Mount Lebanon and in East Beirut, surrounded by a patchwork of sixteen competing ethnoreligious sects, few of whom thought of themselves as Lebanese. An oral agreement in 1943 known as the National Pact established an independent Lebanon. Based on a census arrived at in 1932 whose demographic validity had long since been overcome by a Muslim tide, the National Pact reserved the presidency for the Maronites, awarded the prime ministry to a Sunni, and left the fastest-growing sect, the Shi'ites, with fewer meaningful positions in government.[5] As a result, Jonathan Randal has explained, the Maronites publicly kept pretending that they were in the majority while privately acting like the minority they had become.[6]

In 1970, external factors further complicated Lebanon's delicate confederation when King Hussein forcibly expelled the PLO from Jordan. Some twenty thousand PLO fighters solidified a Palestinian presence in southern Lebanon and Muslim West Beirut and soon generated a multisect civil war that at its core was a bloody struggle between the Maronites and the PLO. The Lebanese army fractured along religious lines, and in 1975 Lebanon's president invited Syria's president Hafiz al-Assad to intervene to restore order. Mediation by Secretary of State Henry Kissinger secured Israel's tacit acquiescence to Syrian intervention in return for Syrian acceptance of some Israeli limits on the scope of the intervention. By June 1976, Syrian–Maronite operations had brought the PLO to the edge of humiliation. Arab leadership directed by Saudi Arabia and Kuwait then formalized Syria's new role in Lebanon by establishing a thirty-thousand-strong and mostly Syrian Arab Deterrent Force under the nominal authority of Lebanon's president and financed by the oil-producing states.[7]

The pieces were now in place for the Lebanon into which the United States would be drawn during the first Reagan administration. The Lebanese state exerted authority only over a small part of Beirut; the Lebanese army, riven by sectarian fractures, remained ineffective. Syria controlled northern Lebanon, the Bekaa Valley, and Lebanon's Shi'ite Muslim population. The Maronite Lebanese Front operated autonomously north of Beirut; Druze Muslims feuded with Christians in the Shouf Mountains overlooking Beirut; Palestinians and their Nationalist Front Lebanese allies controlled the area south of the capital; and pro-Israeli militias vied for power with the PLO and Shi'ite militias along the Israeli border.[8]

This instability, Syria's claimed special role in Lebanon, and the increased salience of the PLO's presence in a swath stretching from West Beirut south and east to the Litani River and then on to the Syria border led to heightened Israel interest and involvement. Moreover, the longer Syria remained in Lebanon, the more the Maronite-dominated and pro-Israel Lebanese Front, now led by the charismatic Bashir Gemayel, became suspicious of Assad's hegemonic ambitions for what he openly called "Greater Syria." The civil war's Syrian-Maronite alliance against the PLO and the Lebanese Left had been an artificial one, and subsequent Syrian-PLO fence mending forecast clashes that would risk a dangerous Syrian-Israeli war.

In April 1981, Gemayel's efforts to establish a presence in Zahle in the Bekaa Valley, an area regarded vital to defense of Damascus, sparked a strong Syrian response. Assad launched a massive bombardment and airlifted commandoes into the Maronite heartland. In defense of its ally, Israeli warplanes downed two Syrian helicopters. Syria then deployed surface-to-air missiles to the Bekaa and moved longer-range missiles to the Syrian side of the Lebanese border. Both moves seemed to anticipate a future Israeli-Syrian conflict. The government of Israeli prime minister Menachem Begin then threatened to destroy the missiles if they were not removed.

Reagan Diplomacy: The Habib Mission

The Reagan administration did not relish the prospect of a Middle Eastern war, and on April 30, 1981, Reagan announced that he was sending Philip C. Habib, a retired diplomat and gifted negotiator, to the region as his special envoy to defuse the crisis.[9] Although Habib quickly papered over the issues underlying the missile crisis, for two weeks in July the Israelis struck PLO concentrations in Beirut and southern Lebanon, and the PLO relentlessly shelled settlements in northern Galilee. The Reagan administration again intervened, and Habib brokered a cease-fire with the help of Saudi Arabia. But the July cease-fire did not alleviate the problem; it merely froze it. All parties understood that the PLO had the capacity to shell northern Israel and that the Begin government was determined to put an end to its capacity to do so.[10]

Reagan's conventional diplomacy had defused the crisis, but Habib warned the president in late July 1981 that although "the situation is not too bad, we have to keep our fingers crossed for the future." He worried about groups in the PLO independent of Yasser Arafat who would seek to provoke the Israelis and undermine the cease-fire. In a meeting with the president, Habib explained that he had stressed to Begin the need to bring a sense of proportion to his decisions. The president then suggested optimistically that "if the cease-fire held, it might be possible to proceed in steps toward a greater Middle East peace." Haig reinforced the hopeful theme, indicating the intent to "build upon these steps so that over the long term the basic Lebanese problem could be resolved." However, Habib's more cautious reminder that "the Palestinian problem in Lebanon was serious" failed to slow the meeting's optimistic course as Haig recommended against decoupling Habib from his mission prematurely, and Reagan agreed that Habib's diplomacy was "an on-going process."[11]

Despite the development of a plan of action in the State Department that sought to build on the Habib cease-fire, Habib went back to playing golf in his retirement, and the administration passively slipped Lebanon into the background as the imminent Israeli return of the Sinai to Egypt in April 1982 persuaded the administration to proceed slowly on Lebanese issues relating to the PLO.[12]

By November, after learning from Begin that Israel had begun contingency planning for a major move into southern Lebanon against the PLO, Haig was ready to send Habib back to the region. "If you move, you move alone," Haig claims he told Begin. "Unless there is a major, internationally recognized provocation, the United States will not support such an action."[13]

It was thought that Habib's diplomacy and peacemaking talents might help to forestall such an Israeli move. "Our underlying—but unspoken—objective," Haig wrote to Reagan, "should be to defuse Israeli interests in exercising the military option in Lebanon while [Habib] works with the Saudis and the Syrians to bring about basic changes in the political and security situation."[14] Reagan and Haig were clearly worried that an Israeli invasion would scuttle the final transfer of the Sinai to Egypt, thus unraveling the Camp David Israeli-Egyptian relationship so vital to the strategic consensus needed to counter the expansion of Soviet influence in the region.[15]

Habib plunged into his mission, shuttling between Lebanon and Israel in December. In Lebanon, he consulted with a broad cross-section of governmental and political leaders, stressing the importance for all Lebanese factions to sustain the cease-fire. He further emphasized the significance of a peaceful national reconciliation among the important Lebanese national groups, given the factional confrontations that would inevitably be stirred by the upcoming Lebanese presidential election in 1982. For their part, the Lebanese leaders worried about "Israeli impatience," "Syria's heavy-handed tactics," a Bashir Gemayel military challenge of Syrian efforts to install a puppet in the elections, and, worse, a unilateral Gemayel move to carve out a separate Maronite Lebanon.[16]

Habib's meeting with Israeli minister of defense Ariel Sharon on December 4, 1981, raised a prominent red flag about Israeli intentions. Sharon combatively lectured Habib that the US goal should be to establish a central Lebanese governmental authority "capable of exercising its influence throughout the country, associated with the free world, and at peace with Israel." As long as the Syrians occupied Lebanon, he ominously noted, this objective could not be realized. Free elections in Lebanon might be possible if the Syrians were confined to the Bekaa Valley;

however, the present arrangement of a large Syrian sector and a highly reduced Christian-controlled area was unacceptable. Moreover, armed "Arab Terrorists [*sic*]" in the southern region threatened Israel's northern areas and were a mortal threat to the cease-fire. As long as they remained, Sharon flatly asserted, Lebanese elections could not be held. Finally, he pointed out, the forward-deployed Syrian missiles prevented adequate Israeli photo reconnaissance of key Syrian military dispositions and thus had to go. Sharon's line of argument alarmed Habib, who warned Washington by secure phone about Sharon's plans, taking care to note that he did not think Begin was part of the plan.[17]

US ambassador to Israel Samuel Lewis reiterated these warnings on February 4, 1982, when he reported to Haig about his own meeting with Sharon. Despite the ambassador's caution to Sharon about Israel's "growing [and bellicose] image problem abroad," Sharon emphasized that no "legitimate" Lebanese government could be established as long as the Syrians controlled large areas of Lebanon and "flourishing terrorist organizations" remained. "We want the Syrians and the Terrorists [*sic*] out and a friendly and peaceful government in," he said. "Israel had saved the Maronites," he added, "and helped them to have a normal life in their area of Lebanon. We did our part and they know it. If our help is [now] a barrier, [the United States] should take over."[18]

This cable stimulated a flurry of activity in Washington, with Haig warning Reagan on February 6 that Begin and Sharon were convinced that further Palestinian terror attempts would require "a major assault into Lebanon to try to destroy the PLO infrastructure there." His analysis shone through a Cold War lens: "It appears clear to me that the Soviets, Syrians and the PLO are working together to provoke just such an Israeli military move—confident that we and Israel would emerge the big strategic and political losers in the Middle East and beyond." The invasion would be "large-scale," he warned the president, and would advance to the southern suburbs of Beirut. Israel would seek to avoid conflict with Syria, but Begin "admits this could not be ruled out." A general regional war might be avoided, but the United States would "find our Middle East policy gravely discredited and our relations with moderate Arabs undermined. . . . Internationally, we would find ourselves isolated with Israel on this issue [and] it could fatally poison the Camp David peace process." Haig emphasized the urgent need to forestall such an Israeli action and especially to clarify that Washington would not give a "green light" to the Israeli invasion. He informed the president that he was sending Begin a message to that effect and instructing Lewis to ensure that Begin understood the US message clearly. He explained that there was no need for the president to involve himself directly at that point, but if Begin and Sharon were not dissuaded by these diplomatic efforts, the president's direct intervention might be required. Finally, he indicated that he was alerting Habib that his services might be again required.[19]

Habib's new marching orders came directly from the president: to demonstrate the US reaffirmation of the importance of the cease-fire and provide "a fresh reading of Lebanon, the 'sick man of the Middle East,' while reasserting that the sovereignty and integrity of Lebanon was [*sic*] still a major US objective." It was essential that the Israeli invasion not proceed—"the Arab world would go up in smoke," Habib told the president. The administration had been successful in "putting on the brakes now," but he warned that Sharon wanted "a way of cleaning up the PLO completely and solving the Lebanese problem, and not simply as a plan of action in response to a provocation." His frustration showing, Reagan stressed the need for Israeli patience. If the United States were to be a "good catalyst" in the Middle East peace process, "this can only be true if we have a satisfactory relationship with Israel. . . . What is needed now is for Begin to provide the world evidence of Israel's basic patience and peaceful nature. There is a limit to how many times we can be confronted with a new Israeli step which we are forced to criticize; then, after we go back to our previous position, bang comes another step."[20]

In mid-March, after two and a half weeks of intensive diplomacy involving trips to Lebanon, Israel, Syria, Jordan, and Saudi Arabia, Habib reported to Haig that the likelihood of an early breakdown of the cease-fire had been reduced, and he underlined the need for the United States to reinvigorate its policy of "strengthening a united, integral Lebanon, sovereign within its traditional borders." He predicted that the forthcoming Lebanese elections would be a chancy affair but indicated that he was "more than ever convinced that the Lebanese themselves have the capacity to handle the situation." The Lebanese "'genius for compromise' might help to produce an outcome satisfactory to U.S. interests," he noted, but otherwise "there is plenty of room for contingency planning in the event things get out of hand." He offered one discomforting conclusion: "Assad remains convinced we are trying to destabilize his regime, despite my categorical denials authorized by you and the President."[21]

But the storm of war continued to gather. During an official visit to Washington, DC, in May 1982, Sharon revealed to Haig and his staff, including Habib, the expansiveness of the impending Israeli operation in Lebanon. Sharon's presentation was unambiguous: "We see no alternative to entering and destroying the terrorist bases" but "don't want war with Syria," the official note taker recorded him saying. "Tomorrow or three weeks, we just don't know. . . . I see no alternative." Haig's response seems to have left the door open for American acquiescence to the decision: "I thought you intended a deep lasting attack. Now I sense a departure from that. We can't tell you not to defend your interests. But we are living with perception. *Must be a recognizable provocation.* . . . Hope you'll be sensitive to the need for provocation to be understood internationally. Make every effort to avoid it. We want Syria out of Lebanon more than you. It is a Soviet proxy." Sharon understood Haig. "We are aware of your concern about size. Our intent is *not a large operation.* [We will] *try to be as efficient as possible.*" "Like a lobotomy," Haig summarized.[22]

In advance of the Sharon visit, Ambassador Lewis had warned Haig that the United States was "skating on extremely thin ice" because of a "growing sense of inevitability" in Israel that an invasion was "only a matter of time." If Sharon were to conclude that the American reaction would be "merely verbal and short-lived," that perception would be "a dangerous signal" that Israel could do whatever it must do about the PLO and could do so "without lasting damage to U.S.-Israeli relations." Lewis's summary was blunt: "Don't allow Sharon to leave Washington with any illusion about the degree to which a major move into Lebanon would affect the course of U.S.-Israeli relations, if indeed it would have those consequences."[23]

Historians continue to debate over whether Haig gave Sharon a "green light" for the Israeli invasion.[24] Haig has always insisted vehemently that he did not, and it is fair to consider that perhaps he did not do so intentionally. This was Habib's interpretation at the time.[25] But nuance was not Sharon's strong suit, and it was clear Haig had not resisted firmly enough even a more limited Israeli operation—and we are reminded that even limited military operations, like lobotomies, are susceptible to frequent and serious side effects.

The Israeli Invasion of Lebanon, Habib's Tour de Force, and the Multinational Force

A week after Haig's meeting with Sharon, on June 6, Israeli Defense Forces (IDF) launched Operation Peace for Galilee, which smashed into Lebanon, advancing in three days to the southern suburbs of Beirut and on June 9 humiliating the Syrian air force by shooting down more than twenty warplanes and destroying the Syrian surface-to-air missile batteries in the Bekaa Valley.[26] Shrugging off an American-instigated cease-fire on June 13, Israeli forces began what would become a brutal ten-week siege of the PLO in Beirut that threatened to escalate into a broader Israeli-Syrian war, strained US standing in the Arab world, compromised US-Israeli relations, and contributed to the replacement of Haig with George P. Shultz. Through Habib's skillful negotiations, however, the siege ended with the peaceful PLO evacuation of Beirut in October. The invasion also stimulated a major Reagan Middle East initiative on September 1 calling for a "fresh start" in the peace process that would "reconcile Israel's legitimate security concerns with the legitimate rights of the Palestinians."[27] The initiative was, according to King Hussein of Jordan, "the most courageous stand taken by an American administration since 1956." Begin was less effusive.[28] Reagan only briefly mentioned Lebanon and ignored Syria in his televised address to the nation on US policy on peace in the Middle East on September 1.[29] The president's assumption that the Lebanon crisis was largely resolved was sadly premature.

Reagan surely deserves important credit for facilitating the diplomatic tour de force by Habib that engineered the evacuation of Yasser Arafat's PLO fighters from Beirut. Reagan admired and trusted Habib's instincts and judgment, and it was Habib's arguments that persuaded the president in early July 1982 that US participation in a non–United Nations multinational force (MNF) offered the possibility of closing the evacuation negotiations. US participation would ease the Lebanese government's fears that it did not possess the capacity to handle the complex evacuation, and it was prepared to request an MNF composed of US and French forces. More importantly, US participation was essential if Israeli observance of the cease-fire were to be maintained and the Israelis' assault on West Beirut avoided. Without US participation, Habib argued, the French were unlikely to go alone, and it would be manifestly more difficult to persuade other nations to participate if the United States would not. He acknowledged that a US role would not guarantee success, but "the absence of US participation would doom it." US participation in the MNF was "the clincher."[30] Reflecting on the negotiations many years later, Shultz provided the broader context: with the PLO out of Lebanon, the administration could then turn to getting the Syrian and Israeli armies out of Lebanon and thus allow Lebanon to start the process of its peaceful national reconciliation and begin to stand on its own.[31]

The Department of Defense concurred with the proposal but without any enthusiasm and noted its concern about "the strong possibility of US involvement in hostilities." It suggested instead exploring the use of troops from Tunisia, Egypt, India, Indonesia, and Norway. Nonetheless, Secretary of Defense Caspar Weinberger did acknowledge that "anything that could remove the PLO was a good thing to do." The MNF would get that "volatile unpredictable group" out of Beirut and would also "remove any excuse the Israelis ha[ve] for moving into Beirut." It was a "first step and a necessary step to take," Weinberger argued. It would thus be a way station to a stable Lebanon and a narrowly proscribe role for the US forces.[32]

In California for the Fourth of July weekend and in the midst of changing secretaries of state, Reagan quickly accepted Habib's arguments and approved US participation in the MNF for a comparably brief period of time. Habib was also thinking that the MNF would be needed for a brief period of time but envisioned some responsibilities for it after the PLO evacuation. Arafat feared for the safety of the PLO's families and Palestinian refugees who would remain in Beirut after his fighters were evacuated, and Habib recognized that it would take some time for the government to reassert its control.[33] That the MNF would be needed to play an important stabilizing role in that transitional environment was not clear in the way Habib framed the decision for Reagan, however, and that ambiguity would come to haunt the administration.[34]

In the seven weeks between when Reagan approved in principle US participation in the MNF and the arrival of the first marines in Lebanon on August 25, Sharon's steady escalation of his siege of Beirut finally got Reagan's attention. Shultz, Habib, and other members of the president's inner circle, especially Deputy Chief of Staff Michael Deaver and National Security Adviser William C. Clark, urged the president to confront Begin directly about the escalating numbers of killed and wounded noncombatants in the urban fighting. As the president's envoy, Habib felt no reservations about speaking with Reagan directly, and he sometimes communicated his outrage about the Israeli excesses with the sound of explosions audible over the telephone.[35] In a personal appeal to Begin on August 4 calling for restraint, the final section of which Reagan rewrote during the National Security Council (NSC) meeting that day, the president vowed that "the relationship between our countries is at stake" unless Israel reestablished and maintained the cease-fire until the PLO left Beirut.[36] His message was answered dismissively the next day. A week later, on August 12, a seven-hour Israeli air bombardment of the city prompted Deaver to walk into the Oval Office and emotionally implore that Reagan intervene: "You're the one person who can stop it. . . . All you have to do is tell Begin you want it stopped."[37]

In Reagan's words, the result was "an angry demand for an end to the bloodletting," a testy and harsh telephone conversation with Begin that illustrated how strained the relationship between the two allies had become. The bombing—this "Holocaust," a name the president deliberately employed because he knew it would have special effect on Begin—had to stop, Reagan insisted, "or our entire future relationship [will be] endangered." Twenty minutes later Begin called to say that he had ordered Sharon to stop.[38] A tough cable from Reagan reinforced the message the following day: "I cannot stress enough to you how seriously I regard this situation. Ambassador Habib must be enabled to fulfill these last steps in his mission. The cease-fire must be kept. Our entire relations are at stake if this continues."[39] Begin most likely did not like the message or its tone but was prepared at this moment to respect US power.

Over the remainder of August, Habib pulled together the loose strands of the plan to evacuate Arafat's fighters and Syrian troops from Beirut and to secure Israeli acceptance of an MNF composed of US, French, and Italian forces that would supervise the evacuation. In the midst of the evacuation, Maronite leader Bashir Gemayel was elected president of Lebanon. Arafat left Beirut on August 30, and on September 1, the same day that Reagan announced his plan for a "fresh start" in the Middle East peace process, the last PLO shipload departed. All told, by shipload and overland convoys, more than 15,000 fighters were evacuated from Beirut, including more than 3,600 Syrian troops.[40] On Weinberger's order, the US Marine Corps contingent of the MNF redeployed to its ships between

September 10 and September 16; the French and Italians left soon after. Although Shultz, Habib, and many in the NSC had misgivings about such a quick withdrawal, Weinberger acted decisively, and Reagan characteristically did not referee. Habib worried especially about the thousands of Palestinians left behind at the tender mercies of the Christian Phalangist militias and the Israelis. He had envisioned multiple missions for the MNF, both supervising the evacuation of the PLO and protecting the civilians in the transition period that followed. He also recognized that Weinberger's more narrow definition of the mission was the dominant voice in Washington, at least in part because of Habib's own failure to explain the Lebanese environment clearly enough to Shultz and Reagan.[41]

Habib's accomplishments were heroic and rightfully celebrated. Reagan awarded him the nation's highest civilian honor, the Presidential Medal of Freedom, recognizing his role in resolving the Beirut Crisis as "one of the unique feats of diplomacy in modern times." The lead editorial in the *Washington Post* on September 8 lauded Habib's "imagination, toughness, and perseverance"; it also complimented Reagan for seeking to coordinate "the use of American power in its various dimensions to shape a political accommodation." The editors noted that the careful calibration of diplomacy, military force, economic power, and moral suasion was needed for "the larger quest" in the Middle East that Reagan now sought.[42] The celebrations were surely premature, however. The dangerous cancer of the PLO had been removed, but Israeli and Syrian forces remained, and until they were gone, the most complex and daunting American objectives—the establishment of a strong central Lebanese government with control over all its territory, good relations with Israel, and the promotion of peaceful national reconciliation among the national groupings within Lebanon—really could not be addressed in a substantive fashion.

"Lebanon is a harsh teacher," one of America's preeminent Middle East experts reminds us,[43] and the Reagan administration had little time to savor its apparent success. Bashir Gemayel was assassinated on September 14, and the next day Sharon, with Begin's approval, ordered the IDF into West Beirut ostensibly to prevent "intercommunal strife and massacres." On September 16, the fig leaf of Israel's military presence allowed Lebanese Phalangist forces to enter the Shatila and Sabra Palestinian refugee camps in search of some two thousand PLO fighters that Sharon believed had stayed behind in violation of the evacuation agreement. Over the next two days, these Phalangist forces massacred more than seven hundred unarmed men, women, and children.[44]

Shatila and Sabra horrified Reagan and his advisers. Relying on Israeli and Lebanese promises, Habib had assured Arafat that those Palestinians who were left in the camps would be protected. "The brutal fact is," Shultz told his deputy, "we are partially responsible. We took the Israelis and the Lebanese at their word." Geoffrey Kemp, the NSC's senior director for Near East and South Asian affairs, later made the point more vividly: "We had promised to protect the Palestinian civilians, [but] it was our allies, the Israelis, who permitted the massacre to happen, and it was our boy Bashir Gemayel's troops that did the killing."[45]

Within twenty-four hours, Reagan signaled that he wanted to take strong action that would demand Israeli withdrawal from Beirut, initiate the process for withdrawal of all foreign forces from Lebanon, and join in a reconstituted MNF. Weinberger and the Joint Chiefs of Staff were skeptical and thought a limited Beirut mission "too risky" and undefined.[46] Shultz and NSC deputy McFarlane were more eager to find ways to use US military power in conjunction with diplomacy and other instruments of national power to further Reagan's aims. For his part, Shultz seemed to be envisioning a phased approach to the military element of the Lebanon policy: an initial phase involving a "limited MNF presence in Beirut," followed by a surely more robust phase dealing with the "larger issues of Lebanon."[47] McFarlane favored an even more full-bodied "large force option." The "deployment of the MNF was a political, not a military act," Shultz recalled him saying, "and if we didn't do it, we would lose credibility in the Middle East and any hope with the president's peace initiative."[48] His concept was grand in the extreme: "Get all of the foreign forces out of the country and move our forces in, to provide security as we worked toward establishing a stable Lebanese government and building up an integrated Lebanese military capable of preserving the security of Lebanon's borders with its neighbors."[49]

By September 19, the president had decided to send the MNF back to Beirut for about sixty days. The following day in a televised address to the nation, he announced that decision and its aim of helping bring "the long nightmare of Lebanon's agony . . . to an end." The MNF's mission was not for internal security or policing purposes, he assured the nation, "but to make it possible for the lawful authorities of Lebanon to discharge those duties themselves." Basic national objectives remained unchanged—"the restoration of a strong and central government" in Lebanon and the withdrawal of all foreign forces—and "the place to begin this task is in Beirut." The accomplishment of these objectives was requisite to the success of the basic peace process and the resolution of the Palestinian people's legitimate needs and desires in a manner consistent with Israel's security interests. "I am especially anxious to end the agony of Lebanon," the president concluded, "because it is both right and in our national interest. But I am also determined to press ahead on the broader effort to achieve peace between Israel and its Arab neighbors. The events in Beirut of last week have served only to reinforce my conviction that such a peace is desperately needed and that the initiative we took on September 1st is the right way to proceed."[50]

By the end of September, Habib was back in the region with the mission of negotiating the removal of all foreign forces from Lebanon, presumably within the MNF's short sixty-day mandate. McFarlane's assessment of the political effect of the MNF's return at first seemed prescient. Bashir's brother, Amin Gemayel, was elected president of Lebanon on September 20, and many Lebanese factions seemed inclined to see what he could do to rally Lebanese unity. Both Syria and Israeli were temporarily quiescent; Assad was licking his wounds after the Israeli drubbing in the Bekaa; and the Begin government was chastened by the Beirut massacres.[51]

The Reconciliation of Force and Diplomacy Begins

The fall of 1982 began to slip away in the face of Israeli and Syrian intransigence and disagreement within the Reagan administration among the State Department, Defense Department, and the NSC over the issue of how best to reconcile the use of force in diplomacy to resolve the Lebanon problem. However, in late October a more muscular US policy emerged for accomplishing the fundamental objective of having all foreign forces—Syrian, Israeli, and the remaining PLO—out of Lebanon by the end of the year. It was anticipated that the withdrawal process would proceed in two steps: first, the initial disengagement of the Israeli-Syrian forces along the Beirut–Damascus highway and, second, their joint withdrawal to their respective frontiers. The poor state of training and readiness of the Lebanese Armed Forces (LAF) would necessarily require an expanded MNF during both step one and step two, and the MNF would also most likely be needed for up to a year following the withdrawal of the Syrians and Israelis. In step one, the MNF was to ensure disengagement and withdrawal by occupying key positions so that neither force gained tactical advantage. In step two, it would assist the LAF's anti-infiltration role against Palestinian forces seeking to cross the frontier.[52]

Reagan signed National Security Decision Directive 64 (NSDD-64), titled "Next Steps in Lebanon," on October 28. It signaled the US willingness to expand the size of the MNF and to broaden its role as part of a series of "bold and timely initiatives" aimed at forcing the withdrawal of foreign forces from Lebanon. Such actions were deemed essential if Lebanon were to "become once more a sovereign, independent country" and if the Reagan Plan were to succeed. Reagan, emphasizing the sense of urgency and importance he attached to the mission, directed Shultz and Weinberger to develop a diplomatic strategy and plans for the "quickest, orderly withdrawal" of foreign forces and the rebuilding of the LAF to improve the Lebanese government's ability to assume its responsibilities. He further accentuated that the United States must be prepared to contribute additional forces to the MNF. "I recognize that there are substantial risks in these undertakings. . . . However, mindful of the recent tragic history of this traditionally friendly country and the opportunity which now exists to further the cause of peace between Israel and its neighbors, we cannot let this historic moment pass."[53]

The NSC cover letter for the directive highlighted the essence of the president's decision: "The analysis should be premised on the understanding . . . that we will probably need to agree to the expansion of the MNF and that it may have to be deployed into any of several areas in Lebanon (northern, central or southern). While we should generally seek to broaden international participation, we must accept that the measure of U.S. leadership relies on our willingness to contribute."[54]

NSDD-64's major effect was that it expanded the area of the MNF presence mission into East Beirut and established a date for the removal of the foreign forces. However, Habib's negotiations went nowhere, frustrated by Israeli and Syrian intransigence, internal disagreement among the members of the Reagan national security team, and the daunting challenges posed by the weaknesses of the Gemayel government and the LAF. The Syrian factor was further complicated in the fall when the Soviet Union began a massive effort to resupply the materiel the Syrians had lost in the battles with Israel the previous summer. This improved military posture made Assad an even more difficult diplomatic opponent for Habib.[55]

Shultz and the May 17 Agreement

In April 1983, Habib informed Shultz that his negotiations had reached a critical point. "We can either push forward to bring [the negotiations] to an early conclusion," Shultz explained for the president on April 21, "or accept the prospect of an impasse followed by protracted negotiations." For Shultz, the choice was clear: US interests required "some new impetus to force the pace of decision." What Shultz had in mind was his personal engagement in breaking the logjam. If Reagan agreed, Shultz would fly to the Middle East as soon as possible, secure an agreement on the withdrawal of all foreign troops from Lebanon, and generate real progress on the Reagan Plan.[56]

Reagan's quick decision was formalized on April 27 when he signed NSDD-92, "Accelerating the Withdrawal of Foreign Forces from Lebanon." Reagan directed Shultz to complete Habib's efforts to secure an agreement between Israel and Lebanon that would leave "no overt residual Israeli military presence in Lebanon." If successful, then Shultz was to travel to other Arab capitals in search of an agreement for the withdrawal of Syrian and PLO forces.[57]

NSDD-92 reflected continuity with Reagan's general strategy that the sequential keys to his larger Middle East initiative would lead initially to ridding Lebanon of foreign forces, starting with Israel. The logic was that because Syria's priority was to see Israel leave Lebanon, the brokering of a reasonable deal that resulted in Israel's departure would be in Syria's best interest, and thus Shultz might be able to secure the Syrians' acceptance of the deal and the withdrawal of both its forces and those of its PLO and Iranian allies. The administration believed that withdrawal of the foreign forces was a necessary precondition for Lebanese security, stability, and political reconciliation and that a stable Lebanon was a precondition for the success of the larger Middle East peace process envisioned in the Reagan Plan.[58] But the assumption that ridding Lebanon of the foreign forces was attacking the real source of Lebanese instability was never seriously debated. Moreover, the intervention of the nation's senior foreign-policy official into the negotiations further committed the administration's prestige and credibility to the resolution of the crisis in Lebanon.

But NSDD-92 also reflected how frustrated the Reagan administration was with Israel's obstructionism. Shultz was to make it clear to Begin that it was Reagan's "strong wish" to restore and deepen the US-Israeli relationship, but he was also to make it equally clear that Reagan saw two courses of action before him: either the restoration and enhancement of the relationship or "a fundamental reappraisal of the entire US-Israeli relationship." "We clearly prefer the former course, but we are also committed to obtaining the withdrawal of foreign forces from Lebanon," Shultz was to tell Begin.[59]

Over the next three weeks, Shultz shuttled among Lebanon, Israel, Syria, Jordan, and Saudi Arabia, seeking a document that addressed both the security of Israel's northern border and the maintenance of Lebanon's Arab character.[60] Leveraging the Israelis' increasing worries about the souring of their relationship with the Americans as well as growing Israeli domestic opposition to the dangerous quagmire and some courageous statesmanship by Amin Gemayel, Shultz had by May 6 secured approval by Lebanon and Israel of an agreement that committed the Israelis to withdraw, provided for the security of Israel's northern border, and established the conditions for normalized relations between Israel and Lebanon.[61] By accepting an important Israeli side letter, Shultz acknowledged that the Begin government would not withdraw its forces unless the Syrians did so as well. But he expected to finesse the "simultaneous withdrawal" requirement by persuading Assad that a closely conjoined removal of Israeli and Syrian forces from Lebanon, whatever the sequence, would constitute "simultaneous withdrawal" for prestige purposes. He also planned to use Saudi influence and financial incentives as leverage. An Israeli withdrawal would be in Syria's national interest, not the least because it would help Assad avoid another painful military clash with the Israelis.[62]

On May 7, 1983, Shultz flew to Damascus to work his magic with Assad. His memoir account not only correctly acknowledges Assad's cool negativity toward the agreement but also masks the Syrian president's firm rejection, which Shultz apparently interpreted as a bargaining tactic rather than a statement of policy: "[Assad] did not say no, and he invited me to return for further discussion. The discussion had gone as well as I could have expected. The real tests lay ahead."[63]

Underestimating Syria was a theme of Shultz's Middle Eastern diplomacy. Syria was not significant in the Reagan Plan, and Shultz failed to appreciate the effects of the recent Soviet rearmament of Syria. In a White House meeting in October 1982, Reagan, with Shultz at his side, had told Israeli foreign minister Yitzhak Shamir that the United States and Israel should "leave the Syrians on the outside looking in." Neither Shultz nor Reagan (nor most of the American intelligence community) had appreciated the broader hazards to the United States of Assad's reversal in the summer of 1982 regarding his prohibition against allowing Iranian elements into Lebanon or the subsequent dangers represented by the addition of those Iranian Revolutionary Guard units in the Bekaa Valley. Moreover, the US embassy in Damascus had regularly reported to Shultz Assad's reservations about Syria's support of any Israeli-Syrian agreement—without apparent effect, however. Finally, in the shuttle diplomacy leading to the May 17 agreement, Shultz left Assad outside the negotiations until after the Israeli-Lebanese agreement had been largely hammered out.[64] Shultz explained later that the Syrians were left out of the negotiations because they thought of Lebanon as part of "Greater Syria." He quotes Assad as saying, "We don't have an embassy in Lebanon [just as] you don't have an embassy in Chicago."[65] Emboldened by his rearmament by the Soviets, blinded by his belief in a "Greater Syria," and offended by American treatment of him as a secondary factor in the region, Assad thus acquired both the capability and the inclination to veto the May 17 agreement.

Geoffrey Kemp observed a few years later that Reagan's diplomatic strategy in Lebanon had by May 1983 acquired an inflexible momentum. "So much human capital and so many egos had been invested in the Israeli-US-Lebanese negotiations that any alternative policy approach was ruled out by the State Department as 'counterproductive,' even though most U.S. Middle East specialists were convinced that the Syrians would never accept the agreement."[66]

Kemp was bemoaning what he saw as the lost opportunities of the fall and winter of 1982–1983 and the notion that better reconciliation of force and diplomacy by Reagan would have yielded a better outcome. But as the Lebanon case so persuasively illustrates, distinctions between vital and peripheral interests can be quickly blurred, and an alternative approach that more rigorously assesses the relationship between policy and available power suggests a different interpretation: that American interests in this case were not vital ones; that the Americans' ability to influence the withdrawal of foreign troops from Lebanon on US terms was narrow; that the Americans' ability to influence political reconciliation and state building in Lebanon was even more proscribed; and that the US marines in the MNF were at increasing risk of being caught in the crossfire between the conflicting parties in Lebanon or, worse, becoming a specific target as they were more and more associated with the Gemayel government.

The deadliest attack in history on a US diplomatic mission occurred on April 18, 1983, in Beirut, adding another bloody player to the tragedy of Lebanon. A delivery van stocked with two thousand pounds of high explosives, driven by a Lebanese Shi'ite, crashed through the US embassy's front door and into the lobby. An enormous explosion pancaked the center of the crescent-shaped structure, killing 63 people—17 Americans, 32 Lebanese employees, and 14 visitors or passersby—and wounding 120, many with lifetime injuries.[67]

US intelligence investigators found the fingerprints of the Iranian Foreign Ministry and the Iranian Republican Guard Corps all over the evidence they uncovered relating to the attack. National Security Agency intercepts led to the Iranian embassy in Damascus. There was less agreement, with strong positions on both sides of the debate, about whether Syria helped with the attack or even knew about it in advance. What was known was that in the aftermath of the Israeli invasion in 1982, Assad had reversed his previous prohibition and allowed Iranian Revolutionary Guard units into the Bekaa Valley. They served as a link for Iran to the most radical elements of the burgeoning and underrepresented Shi'ite population in Lebanon, most notably Hezbollah.[68] Although the evidence about Syria's specific role in the bombing was inconclusive and circumstantial, most of the major decision makers in the Reagan administration believed that the Syrians were at the very least the not-so-silent accomplices of the Iranians. Indeed, on May 4, as Shultz was making final arrangements to meet with Assad on the Israeli-Lebanese agreement, he received a report that "Syria had been involved in the bombing of the American embassy in Beirut on April 18." Both he and Reagan, however, vowed not to be deterred from their search for peace in the Middle East in the face of this terror attack.[69]

Israel and Lebanon signed the painstakingly negotiated Agreement on Withdrawal of Troops from Lebanon on May 17. Assad promptly rejected the agreement and simultaneously declared Habib persona non grata, calling him "one of the most hostile American officials to the Arabs and their causes."[70] Assad then encouraged the Druze militia, a Shi'ite branch centered in the Shouf Mountains overlooking Beirut, to increase military pressure on the government of Lebanon, a move that put the IDF forces in the Shouf in the middle and raised potential dangers for the marines located in the Beirut airport below.[71]

Over the remainder of the summer and into the fall of 1983, the Shouf Mountains would be the major battleground in Lebanon, involving the Israelis, who had occupied the area after the invasion in 1982; the Druze, whose homeland it had historically been but who were now increasingly viewed as Syria's proxies; the Christian Phalangist militia, which Israel had encouraged to come into the area as a countervailing force to the Syrians even before the invasion; and forces from Gemayel's national army. This struggle for the Shouf would inexorably draw the United States and the MNF into the deadly vortex of the Lebanese Civil War. The Begin government's decision to withdraw the IDF from the Shouf to more defensible positions in southern Lebanon, a result of strong domestic dissatisfaction with the war in Lebanon and its draining casualties, initiated the pull into that vortex. August and September would paradoxically find Reagan personally pleading with Begin to keep the IDF in the Shouf.[72]

McFarlane's More Aggressive Diplomacy

On July 21, Reagan appointed Robert C. McFarlane to replace Habib as his personal representative to the Middle East. As the former counselor to the State Department before joining the White House staff as deputy assistant to the president for national security affairs in 1982, a position he would continue to hold in addition to his duties as Middle East emissary, McFarlane had become deeply critical of Habib's lack of results in Lebanon. "We had wasted eight months dithering in Lebanon," he wrote later, "and nothing had changed." Habib may have had a "giant reputation as a skilled diplomat" in Asian affairs, but "he had no experience dealing with Arabs or Israelis, nor had he ever been a man with strategic breadth, able to analyze American issues regionally, not just in Lebanon."

In fact, Habib had misread everything that had followed the Israeli invasion, McFarlane concluded, and, worse, had fed Reagan "a pointless line." Syria had not wanted to talk with Habib for eight months, which was why Habib worked so hard to enlist Saudi help in securing Syrian withdrawal. To McFarlane, this was the most damning criticism of Habib's diplomacy. "At a time with Syria so vulnerable to external pressure, Habib should have stepped aside . . . and given us a chance to get someone else in there to talk to Assad."[73]

McFarlane thought he was just the man for that job. "Over the last eight months, Syria has managed to position itself as the arbiter of inter-Arab politics," he wrote to the president on July 27, 1983, and "the Syrians will continue to be difficult to get out of Lebanon unless new pressures can be brought to bear." Assad saw the correlation of forces as favorable to Syria—growing domestic opposition in Israel, increasing internal strife in Lebanon threatening the unraveling of the Gemayel government consensus and credibility, and a rebuilt Syrian military. That correlation had persuaded Assad not to withdraw but to "wreck the Lebanon-Israel agreement by waiting out the Israelis, bringing down Gemayel, and undermining US influence with the other Arabs."[74]

McFarlane faced three problems: the inevitability of a partial Israeli withdrawal; continued communal violence, especially in the Shouf, which was undermining the Gemayel government; and Syrian intransigence. The fighting involving the Druze and Lebanese factions had to be halted, and the Lebanese Shi'ites in southern Lebanon had to be reassured that the Israeli partial withdrawal was not a harbinger of the partition of southern Lebanon. McFarlane's strategy emphasized first ensuring that the Israeli withdrawal be creatively shaped as a "partial withdrawal . . . conducted in the context of interim steps toward complete withdrawal," with the last phase linked to Syrian withdrawal. The casting of this partial withdrawal as "a step in the right direction" was essential, for if the Israeli move were interpreted as a permanent occupation of southern Lebanon and de facto partition, it would be disastrous for the Gemayel government, and the Syrians would never leave. Easing fears of partition would also assist with the national reconciliation efforts, as would an increase in US economic and military assistance, especially support for training and equipping the LAF. An increase in the $15 million foreign military sales program for Lebanon was one element of the strategy.[75]

McFarlane's strategy for dealing with Syrian intransigence, couched in worst-case scenario terms, favored more aggressive pairing of diplomatic and military power by the United States. Reflecting on this point after he had made his initial on-the-ground assessment in the region, he identified the "central factor in the Lebanon conflict" as Assad's intent "to maintain an enduring influence" over Lebanon. He also concluded that "absent major third country military intervention on behalf of Lebanon, [Syria] can achieve her goal." In sum, given the power realities in Lebanon, the Reagan administration's current inclination to expand the MNF's force presence only gradually "could be at best irrelevant, and at worst catastrophic, unless applied in the context of a specific strategy designed to bring about an early positive change in Syrian behavior. On the other hand, we believe that a strategic escalation—in both political and military terms—could achieve the desired result."[76]

The political terms of the McFarlane case envisioned a quadripartite (United States, United Kingdom, France, Italy) call for an immediate cease-fire in place, minor LAF redeployments in Beirut, commencement of a process of immediate withdrawal of foreign forces over an indeterminate period, and "an agreement in principle on the extension of Lebanese sovereignty through the country via gradual LAF presence in evacuated areas." No country would be allowed to subvert this process, and to that end the MNF units would control strategic locations, such as the passes westward from the Bekaa Valley along the Beirut–Damascus highway. McFarlane judged optimistically that "the four flags accompanied by modest forces" would sufficiently deter Syrian and PLO infiltration from the east.[77]

McFarlane believed that a joint US-UK-French-Italian démarche to Syria, accompanied by parallel Saudi and other moderate Arab pressure, could result in Syrian withdrawal. He warned that the Reagan administration was "falling into a trap of incremental escalation which will ultimately be exposed as a bluff." Coordinated collective action entailed risks with respect to US relations with Israel, the US Congress, and the Soviet Union, he acknowledged, but in his view the "enormous strategic stakes" in the eastern Mediterranean and the Near East "justified the possible use of American military power." Reagan's handwritten notation on the cable indicated that McFarlane had struck a responsive chord: "I consider this very important. R.R."[78]

The NSC thus took the McFarlane "worst-case scenario" cable very seriously and began an accelerated high-level review of the strategy for dealing with Syrian intransigence. Marine casualties from Druze artillery and mortar fire had begun in late August, and the situation had worsened as the Israeli withdrawal from the Shouf commenced in September. When Marine artillery replied to bombardment on August 29, the MNF began to be sucked into the civil war. Marine casualties made for a skittish Congress and led to questions about whether the War Powers Act of 1973 should be in effect. This domestic political backdrop introduced an important cautionary note into the NSC debate.

The result of the deliberations, NSDD-103, "Strategy for Lebanon," signed by the president on September 15, 1983, expanded the "presence" mission that had guided the MNF's purpose since its reintroduction to the area the previous September to one of "aggressive self-defense against hostile or provocative acts from any quarter." This guidance also envisioned that the activities of the MNF contingents and supporting naval, tactical air, intelligence, and reconnaissance activities should be coordinated. The battleship USS *New Jersey* was also ordered to the Mediterranean, and Reagan directed Weinberger and Chairman of the Joint Chiefs of Staff General John W. Vessey to notify him if conditions warranted the warship's deployment in support of the MNF. The issues of US actions against Syrian forces, the extension of the MNF's perimeter beyond Beirut and the reinforcements required to do so, and "a strategy which will help to restore Lebanon over the longer-term in a global context" were deferred for further analysis.[79]

On September 11, an urgent "action message" from McFarlane recommended that the president modify the rules of engagement to allow the US destroyers offshore to fire in support of LAF forces in the Shouf, who were in danger of being overrun by "Palestinian forces commanded by Syrian officers . . . directly controlled by the [Syrian General Staff.] In short, this represents foreign aggression against Lebanon." In a claim belied by the cable's dramatic prose, McFarlane wrote: "I do not say this to be melodramatic, but make it clear that the GOL [Government of Lebanon] is threatened with impending takeover by an uncivilized foreign force." McFarlane creatively sought to stretch the logic of "aggressive self-defense" by arguing that the collapse of the LAF in the high ground overlooking the marines at Beirut International Airport would position an enemy force so that it would be a direct threat to the marines' security, which would thus justify the use of "aggressive self-defense" measures.[80]

Reagan directed that the rules of engagement be modified later the same day.[81] The historian Gail Yoshitani explains in her reappraisal of the Weinberger Doctrine that Reagan sought to use the naval gunfire to signal American resolve to Syria in order to move Syria toward accepting the May 17 agreement and to withdraw from Lebanon. But the administration was actually deeply divided on this application of US military force to the Lebanon equation. Shultz and McFarlane supported the decision, though McFarlane probably saw it only as a way station to his "worse-case scenario" option. Shultz supported the general thrust of a more aggressive defense by the MNF and the need to take actions to strengthen the Gemayel government's ability to defend Beirut, but he also took a more cautionary line about the escalatory thresholds and the need for careful assessment of gains and losses before those thresholds were crossed.[82] Weinberger and Vessey were skeptical that the naval gunfire support would have any effect on the Shouf battles or Assad's behavior and worried that it would instead expose the marines to retaliation, which the lightly armed peacekeeping force was ill equipped to deal with. Their reservations were reflected in the order transmitting the president's decision, which noted that "nothing in this message shall be construed as changing the mission for the US multinational force."[83]

But many of the Lebanese factions and the Syrians would clearly view gunfire from a US battleship in support of the LAF for what it was—the United States taking sides, supported by its French MNF partner. A series of US and French airstrikes in the Shouf, the positioning of the USS *New Jersey* off the Lebanese coast, and Congress's extension of the MNF mission for eighteen months ratcheted up the pressure on Assad, who signed a cease-fire with Gemayel on September 26, and the warring factions agreed to meet for negotiations in Geneva. The international airport reopened and was by early October averaging thirty-five flights a day. The American show of force in September seemed to have produced results, and Reagan, Shultz, and especially McFarlane eagerly grasped at the wispy sign of progress. The cease-fire was, as Shultz characterized it for the president, "a major achievement of our diplomacy."[84]

A careful reading of McFarlane's reporting in the weeks following the cease-fire reveals how little progress had really been made in the region, despite the cease-fire. All three of the regional players worried about what sort of role Syria and Israel would play in Lebanon during and after the political reconciliation process. McFarlane concluded that US firmness and diplomacy had "lessened Assad's willingness to undertake a military solution," but he also noted that Syrian forces were still a threat to Gemayel and a counter to Israel as well as a way for Damascus to influence the reconciliation talks and the broader peace process. Assad still sought to be "the dominant leader in the Arab world," he wrote to Shultz.[85]

The "palpable fear" in the Israeli camp was that the May 17 agreement would be "tossed aside," which the Israelis were quick to remind McFarlane would directly affect their withdrawal decision and the larger Middle East peace process. Indeed, Israel's real concern was that the United States was prepared to pressure Lebanon and Israel to accept a Syrian role that they could not tolerate. As for the Lebanese reconciliation process, McFarlane warned that the road ahead would be long and hard. "The history of our efforts in Lebanon demonstrates that our estimates of the time required to accomplish the milestones are too short," he ruefully admitted. The United States should "accept from the beginning that the process will be one with disagreements, difficulties and probably some violence as well as spurts of progress." "I suppose we should be heartened by Arab and Israeli confidence that the United States can do anything," he noted candidly. "They don't realize how circumscribed our freedom of maneuver is."[86]

These forebodings notwithstanding, McFarlane left Beirut in October on a high note, feeling that "we had carried the day" and stabilized the situation, at least temporarily. There was at this point a "glimmer of hope that the cease-fire would hold and the Lebanese would get their domestic act together," Geoffrey Kemp wrote later. On October 17, soon after McFarlane's return to Washington, Reagan appointed him national security adviser, replacing Clark, who became secretary of the interior. McFarlane found the pace of events in the White House "as frantic and frenetic" as ever as he coordinated the interagency process to determine what the next steps for the United States would be for building on the cease-fire in Lebanon.[87]

In the West Basement's Situation Room, Shultz and Weinberger were at it again over the MNF's role. According to Shultz, the basic underlying problem in Lebanon, even with the cease-fire, was the shift in the balance of forces caused by the unilateral Israeli pullback to southern Lebanon:

"This has created a vacuum, which *we* have been drawn into to sustain the Gemayel government" because we had "committed our prestige" to that government. Syrian aims sought the cancellation of the May 17 agreement, the withdrawal of the MNF, and the installation of a Lebanese government more friendly to Syria than to the United States or Israel. Such Syrian success would humiliate the United States, Shultz warned, and would tilt the balance of forces in the Middle East in favor of the radicals and rejectionists while weakening moderate Arab friends. A satisfactory outcome to the Lebanese political reconciliation negotiations should thus be our "priority object, since so much depends upon it—our standing in the Middle East and our prospects for bringing the Marines home in honorable circumstances."[88]

Thus, for Shultz, ensuring a tolerable outcome required maintaining the balance of forces so that Syria could not "steamroll the conference." Doing so required active US involvement behind the scenes as well as actions to avoid any signal of a unilateral reduction of US forces, including the USS *New Jersey,* because such a signal would have harmful repercussions in the negotiations. In fact, Shultz recognized that the Syrian threat to break the cease-fire was a powerful weapon for the Syrians in the Lebanese talks and that such a rupture would create "complicated problems" for the United States with the MNF partners and Congress, so in a memo to the president on October 13 he argued for a broadening of the rules of engagement for the MNF, "more of a sense that we are still there to be reckoned with if the cease-fire should break down."[89]

Weinberger attacked Shultz's memorandum like a piece of red meat thrown to the wolves. Emphasizing "the fragility of the current situation" rather than the diplomatic triumph of the cease-fire, Weinberger argued that the United States should keep its options open for alternate employment of the MNF because of the unsettled environment. "The static position of the Marines ashore presents an extremely difficult defensive position," he emphasized. Additional US defensive actions might be required, or "it might be necessary and desirable to reduce or eliminate US ground presence in Beirut and keep our forces offshore, perhaps bolstered by additional naval gunfire support." Such a stratagem "would not be weakening our commitment" but actually "strengthen[ing] it in terms of firepower." He flatly waved off any idea of expanding the employment of the MNF or their rules of engagement as "premature," deleterious to the cease-fire and reconciliation process, and risky because it might encourage Gemayel to be less flexible in the current talks.[90]

McFarlane's strong belief that the MNF presence was essential to the preservation of the cease-fire and any chance for success in the reconciliation talks as well as his certainty that American firmness had facilitated his recent diplomatic success meant that he was in the Shultz camp. Reagan was clearly influenced by the Shultz–McFarlane line of argument, and so the last chance to avoid catastrophe for the marines passed.[91]

The Bombing of the Marine Barracks and the Withdrawal of the MNF

The disastrous suicide attack on the Beirut marine barracks on October 23, 1983, revealed just how illusory the claims of American progress in Lebanon truly were. Reagan's instinct was to stand firm. "This is an obvious attempt to run us out of Lebanon," the president told his national security team on October 23. That same day, the nation's intelligence agencies were directed to identify those responsible for planning, conducting, and supporting the attack, and the Department of Defense was ordered to develop options for attacking known terrorist elements threatening our forces in Lebanon.[92] On October 28, echoing Shultz and McFarlane's logic before the attack, Reagan expanded the rules of engagement, which had previously been restricted only to the Shouf, to allow the marines to support LAF positions controlling any strategic arteries to Beirut that were in danger of being overrun.[93]

However, the loss of the marines and other servicemen had poleaxed the Reagan administration and the nation and had dealt a mortal blow to the administration's Lebanon policy. Although Reagan and Shultz reflexively—and sincerely—resisted for fifteen long weeks the growing pressure from Congress, the public, Weinberger, and the Joint Chiefs to completely withdraw the marines from Lebanon, one gets the sense that the final outcome was never in doubt. Although public opinion briefly rallied in support of the administration's Lebanon policy after a speech by the president on October 27 that skillfully conjoined the shooting down of Korean Air Lines Flight 007 by the Soviet Union, the marine barracks attack, and the Grenada operation as evidence of the dangerous and uncertain world confronting America, support soon headed south again.[94]

In addition to growing congressional and public support for withdrawal of the marines that was accelerating weekly, three other factors seem to have been instrumental in changing Reagan's mind so that he decided to redeploy the marine MNF contingent. First, an abortive punitive airstrike against Syrian positions in the Bekaa Valley in December resulted in the shooting down of two US Navy aircraft; one pilot was killed, and another bombardier was captured, so there was no "eye-for-an-eye" satisfaction.[95] Second, on December 23 Weinberger delivered to the president the report of the Department of Defense Commission, which had been tasked with investigating the attack on the marine barracks (referred to as the Long Commission). Its findings faulted "the *entire* operational chain of command" for failing to ensure the security of the US contingent of the MNF in light of the deteriorating situation in Lebanon, and it made specific recommendations for addressing the failings by the NSC, the Central Intelligence Agency, and the Joint Chiefs of Staff in what was "tantamount to an act of warfare using the medium of terrorism." The criticism of the NSC hit closest to the mark. The commission recommended that the NSC "undertake a reexamination of alternative means of achieving US objectives in Lebanon, to include a more vigorous and demanding approach to pursuing diplomatic alternatives." It was a pointed criticism of Shultz and McFarlane's efforts to add more military firmness to what they viewed as an unduly diplomatic approach to early Reagan policy in Lebanon.[96] The final straw was the virtual disintegration of the Lebanese army in February 1984, when Druze and Shi'ite leaders persuaded large numbers of their sects to desert—a major blow to the Gemayel government, which had clung to power in the face of Shi'ite and Druze calls for the abrogation of the May 17 agreement, a purge of his Phalangist Party supporters from key positions, and a power-sharing reorganization of the government. The Gemayel government subsequently collapsed, and Reagan's Lebanon policy was in tatters.[97]

The denouement occurred when Shultz, the sole remaining supporter of a US military presence in Lebanon, was on a trip to Central and South America. By this time, McFarlane had concluded that Lebanese political conciliation was a chimera and that it was time to bow to the inevitable.[98] In a curious bit of symmetry, on February 7, 1984, Reagan pulled the plug on the MNF while he was in California, where twenty months earlier he had agreed to its redeployment. Pulling the MNF would mean, as he had told the *Wall Street Journal* five days earlier, "the end of Lebanon . . . and also means the end of any ability on our part to bring about an overall peace in the Middle East." With these words, he dictated the epitaph of his administration policy on Lebanon and the Middle East.[99]

On February 17, Reagan approved the interagency plan for the phased deployment of the Marine Amphibious Unit at Beirut. The redeployment was to take place as expeditiously as possible consistent with maintaining security and tactical unit integrity and was to be completed by March 15. In fact, the last elements of the US MNF contingent left Beirut on February 26. Within minutes of the marines' departure, Shi'ite militia units began occupying their positions.[100]

"Our troops left in a rush amidst ridicule from the French MNF and utter disappointment and despair from the Lebanese," Shultz bitterly complained in his memoirs, and America's "precipitous departure" promised to raise future questions about the "staying power of the US under pressure—and not just in the Middle East."[101]

The Reagan administration's political aims in Lebanon were ambitious and unobjectionable in terms of intention: the withdrawal of all foreign forces, including the Syrians, the Syrians' Iranian associates, and the Israelis; the establishment of a strong central Lebanese government with control over all its territory and good relations with Israel; and encouragement of a peaceful national reconciliation among the important national groupings within Lebanon. It is a relatively simple exercise to find plentiful evidence of the consistency and clarity of these aims in the administration's public announcements and secret deliberations. Even in retrospect, few would doubt that the deliverance of Lebanon was a worthy cause.

However, the Reagan administration never systematically evaluated the linkage of these aims to US interests or the commitment of national will and power the United States would need to accomplish these national aims. The administration simply never made the supreme calculation—a careful and systematic determination of the precise significance of Lebanon in terms of US national security interests.[102] Neither could the administration adequately settle whether instability in Lebanon was principally a function of the presence of foreign forces or instead an endemic curse—that is, as much from the administration's own profound internal disarray as from external forces. Finally, the evidence reveals that the Reagan administration never undertook a comprehensive analysis of the resources and sacrifices that the accomplishment of these aims would entail for the nation.

The Israeli invasion of Lebanon in June 1982 drew the Reagan administration into Lebanon like a strong magnet. The dangerous land represented by a state and political system exerting authority over only part of Beirut; an ineffective Lebanese army riven by sectarian fractures; the control of large sections of the countryside by Christian, Druze, Palestinian, and Shi'ite militias; and entrenched foreign forces within Lebanon's borders should have given the administration pause, but it did not. The well-intended but ill-considered introduction of the MNF in August 1982 led the administration into a situation from which there was no good way out. It committed American prestige to securing the withdrawal of the PLO without thinking beyond that task to the requirements of the larger aims. When Philip Habib successfully brokered the PLO's withdrawal, the administration announced the Reagan Plan and too quickly shifted its gaze from Lebanon to the larger Middle East peace process. Its decision to quickly withdraw the MNF left the way clear for Israel's Phalangist allies to perpetuate the massacres at Sabra and Shatila.

In its haste—and likely with some guilt over the earlier, premature MNF withdrawal—the administration reintroduced a larger MNF on September 20, 1982, a decision that upped the ante for the United States in Lebanon without serious thought about the marines' mission or the full extent of Lebanon's problems. Diplomatic efforts by Habib and later by Secretary of State George Shultz to negotiate the withdrawal of all foreign forces from Lebanon culminated in the May 17 agreement, which committed the Israelis to withdraw, provided for the security of Israel's northern frontier, and established conditions for normalized relations between the two nations. But Shultz underestimated his ability to translate an Israeli withdrawal into a mutual Syrian and Israeli withdrawal, and Hafez al-Assad promptly vetoed Shultz's agreement.

The United States had little ability to influence the withdrawal of foreign troops and even less capacity to influence political reconciliation in the fractious and dangerous environment that was Lebanon. A stiff debate in the highest levels of the US national security team over the role of military force in support of Lebanon policy paired McFarlane and Shultz, who favored more aggressive use of diplomatic and military power, against Weinberger and the Joint Chiefs of Staff, who did not. Neither McFarlane nor Shultz was satisfied with their partial victory in expanding the marines' mission from "presence" to "aggressive self-defense" and in subsequently extending the rules of engagement to allow marine support of the Lebanese Armed Forces in the Shouf Mountains overlooking Beirut. The Shouf was now far more dangerous terrain because of the unilateral withdrawal of the Israelis and the presence of increasingly radicalized Lebanese Shi'ite sects and Iranian terrorists bent on striking the Americans hard. The administration misread the significance of the bombing of the US embassy in Beirut in April 1983, and by October the marines were in the terrorists' crosshairs.

On October 27, 1983, four days after the marine barracks bombing, President Reagan addressed the nation on the events in Lebanon and Grenada. At one point in the speech, he told how he had ordered a marine contingent sailing on its way to Lebanon to shift course and head for Grenada. That little detail revealed the vast gap that existed between the US mission worldwide, as defined by the president, and the capacity to fulfill that mission. "We're a nation of global responsibilities," Reagan said. "We're not somewhere else in the world protecting someone else's interests; we're there protecting our own." Relating that point to Lebanon, the president sought to answer the question why the United States was there: "The answer is straightforward—to help bring peace to Lebanon and stability to the vital Middle East." But in describing the marines' operational mission, Reagan sketched very modest goals: "To secure a piece of Beirut, to keep order in their sector and to prevent the area from becoming a battlefield."[103]

Few would argue that a quantum leap would be required from that limited assignment to the wider goal of stabilizing the Middle East. Indeed, the gap between ends and means was enormous. "The world has changed," Reagan nonetheless continued. "Today, our national security can be threatened in faraway places. It's up to all of us to be aware of the strategic importance of such places and to be able to identify them."[104]

President Reagan should have heeded his own advice. Accomplished policy makers and strategists understand the nature of the strategic environment in which they are operating; they understand the need for congruence between means and ends; and they understand the imperative of reconciling policy with available power. They recognize that a great superpower must have an appreciation for the limits of its power, that hierarchies of interest—establishing distinctions between vital, important, and peripheral interests—are crucial to successful policy and strategy making. Sadly, in his Lebanon policy from 1981 to 1984, neither the president nor his national security team performed any of these vital assessments.

Writing to the conservative columnist William F. Buckley Jr., his friend, in a year-end letter over Christmas in 1983, the president commented: "Bill, the Middle East is a complicated place—well not really a place, it's more a state of mind." Upon reflection, he added, sadly: "A disordered mind."[105] President Reagan was indeed a stranger in a dangerous land.

Notes

1. Robert C. McFarlane, with Zofia Smardz, *Special Trust* (New York: Caddell and Davies, 1994), 262.

2. Ronald Reagan, *An American Life: The Autobiography* (New York: Simon and Shuster, 1990), 437.

3. Quoted in Lou Cannon, *President Reagan: Role of a Lifetime* (New York: PublicAffairs, 2000), 388–89.

4. Alexander M. Haig, *Caveat: Realism, Reagan, and Foreign Policy* (New York: Macmillan, 1984), 169–71, 319.

5. Itamar Rabinovich, *The War for Lebanon, 1970–1985,* rev. ed. (Ithaca, NY: Cornell University Press, 1985), 17–26; John Boykin, *Cursed Is the Peacemaker* (Belmont, CA: Applegate Press, 2002), 42–43; David C. Martin and John Walcott, *Best Laid Plans: The Inside Story of America's War against Terrorism* (New York: Touchstone, 1988), 85–86.

6. Jonathan Randal, *The Tragedy of Lebanon* (London: Chatto and Windus, 1983), 52.

7. Rabinovich, *The War for Lebanon,* 43–59.

8. Ibid., 57–59.

9. Haig, *Caveat,* 180.

10. Ze'ev Schiff and Ehud Ya'ari, *Israel's Lebanon War* (New York: Simon and Schuster, 1984), 29–37; Rabinovich, *The War for Lebanon,* 118–20; Boykin, *Cursed Is the Peacemaker,* 46–47; Haig, *Caveat,* 186.

11. Memo of Conversation of the President's Meeting with Ambassador Habib, July 28, 1981, Box 90493, Geoffrey Kemp Files, Ronald Reagan Presidential Library (RRL), Simi Valley, CA.

12. Richard V. Allen to the President, memo, "Plan of Action for the Lebanese-Israeli Situation," August 26, 1981, Box 90494, Kemp Files, RRL.

13. Haig, *Caveat,* 326–27.

14. Alexander M. Haig Jr. to the President, memo, "The Next Habib Mission," November 11, 1981, Box 90493, Kemp Files, RRL.

15. William B. Quandt Jr., "Reagan's Lebanon Policy: Trial and Error," *Middle East Journal* 38, no. 2 (1984): 238–39.

16. Philip Habib to Secretary of State, cable 010735Z, "Habib Mission: Lebanese View of the Evolving Situation," December 1981, Habib Lebanon Late 1981 Folder, John Boykin Correspondence (JBC), National Security Archive (NSA), George Washington University, Washington, DC.

17. Deputy Chief of US Mission in Tel Aviv William Brown to Alexander Haig, cable 051155Z, "Habib Mission: Meeting with Defense Minister Sharon," December 1981, Habib Lebanon Late 1981 Folder, JBC, NSA.

18. Samuel Lewis to Alexander Haig, cable 021430Z, "Habib Mission: Meeting with Minister of Defense Sharon," February 1982, Habib Lebanon Early 1982 Folder, JBC, NSA.

19. Haig to the President, memo, "Possible Israeli Move against PLO in Lebanon," February 6, 1982, Habib Lebanon Early 1982 Folder, JBC, NSA.

20. Department of State Memo of Conversation, "Ambassador Habib's Consultations with the President and Secretary Haig," February 22, 1982, Habib Lebanon Early 1982 Folder, JBC, NSA.

21. Habib to Haig, cable 112001Z, "Habib Mission: Summing-up Report," March 1982, and Acting Secretary of State Walter J. Stoessel Jr. to the President, memo, "Result of the Habib Mission," March 15, 1982, Habib Lebanon Early 1982 Folder, JBC, NSA.

22. Memo of Conversation, "The Secretary's Meeting with Israeli Defense Minister Sharon," May 25, 1982, Habib Lebanon May 1982 Folder, JBC, NSA; Charles Hill, notes of meeting between Ariel Sharon and Haig and his staff, May 25, 1982, Notebook no. 17, emphasis in original, Charles Hill Papers, Box 76, Hoover Institution Archives, Palo Alto, CA; Boykin, *Cursed Is the Peacemaker,* 54–55.

23. Lewis to Haig, cable 151805Z, "Sharon Visit and Lebanon," May 1982, Habib Lebanon May 1982 Folder, JBC, NSA.

24. See Ze'ev Schiff, "The Green Light," *Foreign Policy* 50 (Spring 1983): 73–85.

25. Haig, *Caveat,* 335; David Crist, *The Twilight War: The Secret History of America's Thirty-Year Conflict with Iran* (New York: Penguin, 2012), 109; Boykin, *Cursed Is the Peacemaker,* 56. See also Nicholas Veliotes to Haig, action memo, "Letter to Prime Minister Begin on Israeli Military Action in Lebanon," May 28, 1982, Habib Lebanon May 1982 Folder, JBC, NSA.

26. Rabinovich, *The War for Lebanon,* 121–43; Schiff and Ya'ari, *Israel's Lebanon War,* 195–229.

27. George P. Shultz, *Turmoil and Triumph: My Years as Secretary of State* (New York: Scribner's, 1993), 96–98.

28. For Hussein's comment, see Cannon, *President Reagan,* 355; for Begin's reaction, see Shultz, *Turmoil and Triumph,* 98.

29. Ronald Reagan, "Address to the Nation on United States Policy for Peace in the Middle East," September 1, 1982, https://reaganlibrary.archives.gov/archives/speeches/1982/90182d.htm.

30. Acting Secretary of State Walter J. Stoessel Jr. to the President, memo, "An International Force for Beirut," July 2, 1982, Habib Lebanon July 1982 Folder, JBC, NSA.

31. Shultz, *Turmoil and Triumph,* 52.

32. Quoted in Martin and Walcott, *Best Laid Plans,* 93. See also Gail Yoshitani, *Reagan on War: A Reappraisal of the Weinberger Doctrine, 1980–1984* (College Station: Texas A&M University Press, 2012), 70–71.

33. Boykin, *Cursed Is the Peacemaker,* 137.

34. Lou Cannon's conclusion is that Reagan's agreement was "a tactical decision engineered by a hard-pressed diplomat who was desperately trying to negotiate a cease-fire before a weak and divided Lebanese government disintegrated" (*President Reagan,* 348).

35. Reagan, *An American Life,* 425.

36. Minutes of NSC Meeting on Lebanon Situation, August 4, 1982, Box 91284, Executive Secretariat NSC: Meeting Files, RRL.

37. Michael K. Deaver, *A Different Drummer: My Thirty Years with Ronald Reagan* (New York: Harper Collins, 2001), 101–2.

38. Reagan, *An American Life,* 427–28.

39. Quoted in Shultz, *Turmoil and Triumph,* 70–71.

40. Boykin, *Cursed Is the Peacemaker,* 263.

41. Robert McFarlane described Weinberger's order to rapidly redeploy the MNF as "criminally irresponsible" and "treacherous" (*Special Trust,* 209).

42. The Reagan remarks at the Presidential Medal of Freedom ceremony and the *Washington Post* editorial are reprinted in Shultz, *Turmoil and Triumph,* 83–84.

43. Quandt, "Reagan's Lebanon Policy," 237.

44. An Israeli national commission of inquiry, the Kahan Commission, published the results of its investigation in February 1983. It faulted several members of the Begin government and the IDF, including the prime minister himself, and called for the dismissal of Minister of Defense Sharon, the director of military intelligence, and others. Sharon resigned but soon rejoined the cabinet in the capacity of minister without portfolio. See Chaim Herzog, *The Arab-Israeli Wars: War and Peace in the Middle East from the War of Independence through Lebanon,* rev. and updated (New York: Vintage Books, 1984), 353–54; Rabinovich, *The War for Lebanon,* 144–45, 154; and Shultz, *Turmoil and Triumph,* 112–13.

45. Shultz, *Turmoil and Triumph,* 105; Kemp quoted in Martin and Walcott, *Best Laid Plans,* 95.

46. Caspar Weinberger, *Fighting for Peace: Seven Critical Years in the Pentagon* (New York: Time Warner Books, 1991), 151–53.

47. Shultz, *Turmoil and Triumph,* 108.

48. Ibid.

49. McFarlane, *Special Trust,* 212.

50. Ronald Reagan, "Address to the Nation Announcing the Formation of a New Multinational Force in Lebanon," September 20, 1982, and [George Shultz], Department of State Background Briefing, Box 90493, Kemp Files, RRL.

51. Cannon, *President Reagan,* 357–58.

52. Geoffrey Kemp and Philip Dur to Robert C. McFarlane, memo, "Next Steps in Lebanon: Basic Issues," October 23, 1982, Box 91286, Executive Secretariat NSC, RRL.

53. NSDD-64, "Next Steps in Lebanon," October 28, 1982, Box 91286, Executive Secretariat NSC, RRL.

54. Judge William P. Clark to the Vice President, Secretary of State, Secretary of Defense, Director of CIA, Chairman, Joint Chiefs of Staff, and Administrator of the United States Agency for International Development, memo, "NSDD-64: Next Steps on Lebanon," October 28, 1982, Box 91286, Executive Secretariat NSC, RRL.

55. Geoffrey Kemp, "Lessons of Lebanon: A Guideline for Future U.S. Policy," *Middle East Insight,* Summer 1988, 60–61; Quandt, "Reagan's Lebanon Policy," 242.

56. George Shultz to the President, memo, April 21, 1983, Box 91306, Executive Secretariat NSC: Records, National Security Planning Group, RRL; Shultz, *Turmoil and Triumph,* 196.

57. NSDD-92, "Accelerating the Withdrawal of Foreign Forces from Lebanon," April 27, 1983, Box 91290, Executive Secretariat NSC: NSDD, RRL.

58. Shultz, *Turmoil and Triumph,* 196–99; Boykin, *Cursed Is the Peacemaker,* 300–301.

59. NSDD-92.

60. Shultz, *Turmoil and Triumph,* 211.

61. Ibid., 201–16. On May 5, Shultz told Reagan that Amin Gemayel had been "a real stand-up guy" (ibid., 214).

62. On the side letter, see Shultz, *Turmoil and Triumph,* 221; Boykin, *Cursed Is the Peacemaker,* 306; and Yoshitani, *Reagan on War,* 103. On the Saudi role, see Shultz, *Turmoil and Triumph,* 218–19, and Boykin, *Cursed Is the Peacemaker,* 306.

63. Shultz, *Turmoil and Triumph,* 217.

64. Kathleen Christianson, "The Arab-Israeli Policy of George Shultz," *Journal of Palestinian Studies* 18, no. 2 (1989): 33.

65. George Shultz, interviewed by Lou Cannon, April 6, 1989, cited in Cannon, *President Reagan,* 361 n. 58.

66. Kemp, "Lessons of Lebanon," 61.

67. Yoshitani, *Reagan on War,* 103.

68. Martin Kramer, "Hizbullah in Lebanon," in *The Oxford Encyclopedia of the Modern Islamic World,* 4 vols. (New York: Oxford University Press, 1995), 2:130–33.

69. Martin and Walcott, *Best Laid Plans,* 105–6; Cannon, *President Reagan,* 358–59; Shultz, *Turmoil and Triumph,* 213; Reagan, *An American Life,* 443.

70. "Damascus Rejects Appeal by Reagan to Leave Lebanon," *New York Times,* May 19, 1983.

71. Shultz, *Turmoil and Triumph,* 220–21.

72. Yoshitani, *Reagan on War,* 103. On Reagan's role in seeking to slow the IDF withdrawal, see "Telephone Call with Prime Minister Menachem Begin," September 3, 1983, Box 91306, Executive Secretariat NSC: Records, National Security Planning Group, RRL.

73. McFarlane, *Special Trust,* 240–41.

74. McFarlane to the President, memo, "Proposed Strategy for My Middle East Mission," July 27, 1983, Box 53, Executive Secretariat NSC: Subject File, RRL.

75. Ibid. See also Assistant Secretary of State for Near East Affairs Nicholas A. Veliotes to Shultz, memo, "Next Steps in Lebanon," July 21, 1983, Box 54, Executive Secretariat NSC: Subject File, RRL.

76. McFarlane to Clark, Shultz, Caspar Weinberger, and John Vessey, cable 090104Z, "Worst Case Strategy for Lebanon," September 1983, Box 91285, Executive Secretariat NSC: Meeting Files, RRL.

77. Ibid.

78. Ibid.

79. NSDD-103, "Strategy for Lebanon," September 10, 1983, Box 91291, Executive Secretariat NSC: NSC Meeting Files, RRL.

80. McFarlane, *Special Trust,* 250–51.

81. Addendum to NSDD-103 on Lebanon of September 10, 1983, September 11, 1983, Box 91291, Executive Secretariat NSC: NSC Meeting Files, RRL.

82. Yoshitani, *Reagan on War,* 110–11; Cannon, *President Reagan,* 369; Shultz, *Turmoil and Triumph,* 226.

83. Shultz to Clark, memo, "Comments on Lebanon Draft NSDD," September 8, 1983, Box 91291, Executive Secretariat NSC: NSC Meeting Files, RRL.

84. Cannon, *President Reagan,* 384; Shultz to the President, memo, "Our Strategy in Lebanon and the Middle East," October 13, 1983, Box 91291, Executive Secretariat NSC: NSC Meeting Files, RRL.

85. McFarlane to Shultz and Clark, cable 051829Z, "Thinking about What's Next," October 1983, Box 55, Executive Secretariat NSC: Subject File, RRL.

86. Ibid.

87. McFarlane, *Special Trust,* 254, 257; Kemp, "Lessons of Lebanon," 64.

88. Shultz to the President, memo, "Our Strategy in Lebanon and the Middle East," October 13, 1983, Box 91291, Executive Secretariat NSC: NSC Meeting Files, RRL, emphasis in original.

89. Ibid.

90. Weinberger to McFarlane, memo, "US Policy in Lebanon and the Middle East," October 21, 1983, Box 90753, Donald R. Fortier Files, RRL.

91. Cannon, *President Reagan,* 384.

92. NSDD-109, "Responding to the Lebanon Crisis," October 23, 1983, Box 91782, Crisis Management Center, Executive Secretariat NSC: NSC Records, RRL.

The intelligence community linked Iranian agents at the Iranian Revolutionary Guard's Sheik Abdullah Barracks in Baalbek, Bekaa Valley, with the radicalized Lebanese Shi'ites who had attacked the marines (Crist, *Twilight War,* 127–48).

93. NSDD-111, "Steps toward Progress in the Middle East," October 28, 1983, Box 91291, Executive Secretariat NSC: NSC Meeting Files, RRL.

94. Michael Baroody, "President's Speech Receives Strong Support," summary, October 27, 1983, Lebanon/Grenada, "RR's Speech 10/27 [1983]" Folder 1 of 5, Michael Baroody Files, RRL.

95. Martin and Walcott, *Best Laid Plans,* 144.

96. Weinberger to the President, memo, "Long Commission Report on October 23 Bombing," December 23, 1983, emphasis in original, and McFarlane to the President, "Long Commission Report," December 23, 1983, Box 90753, Fortier Files, RRL.

97. Thomas Friedman, "Rebels Capture West Beirut," *New York Times,* February 7, 1984. As it became clear that the departure of the US marines was imminent, the Amin Gemayel government came under increasing pressure from Syria and its Muslim Lebanese allies to abandon the May 17 accord. On March 5, ten days after the marines departed, the Lebanese government canceled the agreement.

98. McFarlane, *Special Trust,* 273.

99. Ronald Reagan, interviewed by Robert L. Bartley and Albert R. Hunt, *Wall Street Journal,* February 2, 1984, at http://www.reagan.utexas.edu/archives/speeches/1984/20284j.htm.

100. McFarlane to Shultz and Weinberger, memo, "Plan for the Deployment of the USMNF Contingent," February 17, 1984, Box 90753, Fortier Files, RRL; Martin and Walcott, *Best Laid Plans,* 152.

101. Shultz, *Turmoil and Triumph,* 231.

102. Undersecretary of State for Political Affairs Lawrence Eagleburger came to this conclusion (cited in Martin and Walcott, *Best Laid Plans,* 153).

103. Ronald Reagan, "Address to the Nation on Events in Lebanon and Grenada," October 27, 1983, at http://www.reagan.utexas.edu/archives/speeches/1983/102783b.htm.

104. Ibid.

105. Quoted in Edmund Morris, *Dutch: A Memoir of Ronald Reagan* (New York: Random House, 1999), 505.

13

Researching Reagan

A Guide for Scholars of National Security Policy during the Ronald Reagan Presidency

Ryan Carpenter

When the Ronald Reagan Presidential Library opened in November 1991, the former president, Ronald Reagan, had a great deal to be happy about. The Berlin Wall, long a symbol of the tension between East and West, fell in November 1989, less than a year after he left office. In early 1991, the US military needed only one hundred hours to defeat the Iraqi army with equipment acquired mainly during the Reagan administration, the largest peacetime military buildup in US history. Then a month after the library opened, the Soviet Union collapsed. These and other developments raised important questions: Was this the beginning of a new era in international relations? Were these significant international developments a legacy of the Reagan administration policy or of some larger dynamic? The former president believed the library would serve as a platform for answering these and other questions. "It is my hope that the Reagan Library," he said at its opening, "will become a dynamic intellectual forum where scholars interpret the past and policy makers debate the future."[1] For historians interested in the Reagan administration's national security policy, Reagan's speech is a call to action. Today, sufficient time has passed—and archival material released—for historians to begin investigating the Reagan administration in new ways. Indeed, the next ten years will transform the scholarship on the Reagan presidency as historians engage new sources to reassess, rethink, and revise our understanding of the past.

Much like public opinion during the 1980s, students, scholars, and former Reagan administration officials are divided on the meaning of Reagan's legacy. The memoirs of the men and women who served during the Reagan administration expose these disagreements. Across time, many cabinet officials from both Democratic and Republican administrations have written accounts of their service, but the sheer number of cabinet-level and Reagan appointees who have penned books draws attention to the deep divisions within the Reagan government. Viewed through a critical lens, these memoirs illuminate the administration's many divergent, sometimes contradictory policies. Personal accounts of meetings and conversations compliment primary-source research and can be critical to historians researching the administration's policy-making process.[2]

Beginning at the cabinet level, memoirs by Ronald Reagan, George P. Shultz, Alexander Haig, and Caspar W. Weinberger help students develop an understanding of significant events during the Reagan years. Reagan's memoir, *An American Life,* is most useful when read in tandem with his diaries, compiled in *The Reagan Diaries.*[3] Reagan is the only president to faithfully journal his experiences while in office, so these books are a useful tool to understand his thinking about the Soviets, arms control, his relationships with those in his administration, and the occasional trip to the dentist. Although his memoir is filled with justifications for his actions as president, his diary grounds the memoir to the everyday challenges of presidents, thus giving historians a sense of change over time. Al Haig wrote his memoir, *Caveat,* as he was contemplating his own run for the presidency.[4] From outside the Reagan inner circle, Haig offers a unique perspective on the White House during the 1980s. He constantly (and justifiably) felt as though he were being undermined by the Reagan faithful, and he had an adversarial relationship with most of the cabinet members. George Shultz's memoir *Turmoil and Triumph* is an exhaustive one-thousand-page tome that includes many insider details to some of the most important events of the late Cold War.[5] It is important to note that for most onlookers, Shultz represents the balancing of Reagan's cabinet from one predominantly stocked with hard-liners to one more moderate in its approach to foreign policy, a view Shultz perpetuates in his memoir. Although it is true that Shultz preferred engaging with the

Soviets to keeping them at a distance, he also pushed for the deployment of troops to Lebanon and generally preferred military intervention as the solution to international crises. It is important to note that Shultz's memoir and Weinberger's memoir, *Fighting for Peace,*[6] were written after the collapse of the Soviet Union. Both books contain insight into the Reagan administration's approach to handling the Soviet Union in the late Cold War. Whereas Shultz clearly preferred engagement with Soviets and Third World left-wing dictators, Weinberger favored a defense buildup with limited military intervention to solve crises and preferred indirect confrontation by increasing the number of US allies as well as by improving the capabilities of those who were antagonistic to the Soviet Union in order to pressure the Soviets into strategically unfavorable situations. Weinberger's memoir emphasizes Reagan's strong anti-Communist rhetoric and unwavering devotion to the expansion of the military as two significant factors that led to the collapse of the Soviet Union. Both memoirs contain keen insights into Reagan's character.

The memoirs of significant noncabinet officials are also useful for students of the Reagan presidency. As the director of the White House's Office of Management and Budget, David Stockman was charged with implementing Reagan's competing vision of a limited government, lowered taxation, and an increased defense budget. This seemingly impossible goal was compounded by the intransigence of Weinberger, a former director of the Office of Management and Budget, on cuts to the proposed increases in the defense budget and by Reagan's aloof management style. Stockman's memoir, *The Triumph of Politics,* predictably reveals his deep dissatisfaction with the Reagan White House.[7] John Lehman Jr.'s book *Command of the Seas* is an excellent example of both the great asset and the limitation that memoirs can be.[8] The idea of a six-hundred-ship navy came from Lehman's time with the Republican National Convention, and he was the leading proponent of an enlarged navy during the Reagan administration. Reagan came out specifically in favor of the six-hundred-ship navy as a way to protect the United States and effectively project its power overseas. Lehman is able to give deep insight into the interworking of the navy while he was in office as someone who held sway with Caspar Weinberger and was a vocal advocate of the US Navy in the Defense Resources Board meetings. The gatherings were chaired by Deputy Secretary of Defense Frank Carlucci, who also favored Lehman, and were meant to connect the policy and strategy debates with the budget debates in order to justify and effectively advocate for the Reagan defense buildup. On the down side, Lehman's memoir gets bogged down in some of the minute details of naval weapon systems, and because it is a memoir, it is limited to his perspective without consideration of the other services. Other memoirs, such as Colin Powell's *My American Journey,* Paul Nitze's *From Hiroshima to Glasnost,* and Robert Gates's *From the Shadows,* are authored by men who had also served in previous administrations.[9] They offer keen but sometimes contradictory insights into Reagan's place in the larger Cold War story. They also compare and contrast the Reagan presidency with previous Republican administrations. Thus, memoirs alone cannot sufficiently tell the story of the Reagan years. Indeed, scholars must engage the ever-growing body of primary source material.

The Reagan Presidential Library, located in Simi Valley, California, grants researchers a picturesque view of southern California as well as a rich set of sources on the Reagan administration. The library is administered by the National Archives and Records Administration and contains all of Ronald Reagan's public papers, including records from his time as governor of California, as well as the papers of many officials who worked under him during his eight years in the White House. For diplomatic or military historians, the Executive Secretariat files are essential to any study. These files are split into different categories, but the most important boxes are meeting files containing material created by the National Security Council (NSC) staff for dissemination. The NSC meeting files also contain some of the most important material for researchers. These materials include memos sent to cabinet members from the NSC staff, talking points, policy studies drafted by members of the NSC staff, and, most importantly, the minutes of NSC meetings. In some instances, handwritten notes were later typed and polished for the public and can give glimpses into the personalities at the meeting table. The National Security Planning Group (NSPG) meeting files, which include all of the material created for the NSPG, are equally important because the NSC and NSPG meetings performed similar functions. The NSPG meetings were supposed to be a place where the principals hashed out differences so as to reach decisions in NSC meetings, but the opposite occurred. Rather than decide matters, the NSPG and NSC meetings extended policy debates and served to prolong rather than resolve policy disputes. Major policy decisions coming out of the NSC were called National Security Decision Directives (NSDD), and these memos are also included in the Executive Secretariat files. NSDD files contain all of the material generated by the NSC staff, including memos, and the meeting minutes relevant to major policy decisions. Most of the NSDDs have been digitized and uploaded to the Reagan Library's website (https://www.reaganlibrary.gov). These directives gauge the progression of Reagan's national security policies from the beginning of his tenure as president, but their frequency tends to fade near the end of his second administration. Similarly, National Security Study Directives (NSSD) were issue papers commissioned by the president to flush out major policy issues and to help organize the policies agreed upon at NSC meetings. They are also included in the Executive Secretariat files. The chronological files, part of the Executive Secretariat series, are a smattering of national security documents collected by different White House staffers. Arranged by date, the chronological files include memos, studies, and some routine administrative work by the NSC staff. Researchers should examine the finding aids for the Reagan Library before making the trip to Simi Valley. They should also be aware that items listed in bold type on the finding aid are considered open to the public, but some material even in "open" boxes is withheld from public view. One must trust but verify that desired material is indeed available for review.

Researchers at the Reagan Library will inevitably discover that some files are not publically available, and it is important to consider the process of submitting a Freedom of Information Act (FOIA) request. Each box from which classified material was removed has a withdrawal sheet at the front of the box outlining what has not been declassified, including a brief description of each such item. If the researcher deems it necessary to view the classified contents, he or she can scan the withdrawal sheet and highlight the material he or she would like to see. Library archivists encourage researchers to submit all FOIA and Mandatory Declassification Review (MDR) requests at the end of a research trip. For more information on ordering material through the FOIA or on utilizing the MDR process at the Reagan Library, the researcher should consult the room attendant or the archivist assigned to him or her during a research trip.

It is important to consider the material available before planning a research trip to the Reagan Library. Terrorism, particularly in Lebanon and Libya, is a rich topic to explore. The Terror Incident Working Group was a panel of cabinet members and NSC staffers established to combat the rise of violent nonstate actors. Related files are located in the chronological files. The available resources on Central America, an important region for Reagan national security policy makers, are abundant. Those interested in El Salvador, Nicaragua, Cuba, Grenada, and Honduras should explore the Country files and in particular the NSC files. Indeed, Central America consumed a great deal of time and effort by the Reagan administration; the region was discussed at length in NSC and NSPG meetings and was a major subject for both NSDDs and NSSDs. The Reagan Library also houses material related to the alliance between Great Britain and the United States as well as concerning the personal relationship between Margaret Thatcher and Ronald Reagan. Finally, arms-control issues, in particular summits and agreements from the second Reagan administration, are readily available for researchers in the NSC, NSPG, NSDD, and NSSD files as well as in the NSC Subject Files. In fact, the Reykjavik summit, the Vienna summit, the Intermediate-Range Nuclear Forces Treaty, and the Strategic Arms Reduction Treaty (which began during the Reagan administration but was signed under the George H. W. Bush administration) generated significant paperwork.

When one is planning a trip to the Reagan Library or conducting preliminary research for a project, one should consider the library's website as a starting point. For example, the Reagan Library has a complete set of the *Public Papers of the Presidents of the United States: Ronald Reagan, 1981–1989,* that is available to the public as well as a search function that allows a researcher to quickly identify topics that Reagan spoke about during his time as president. The Reagan Library also houses more than 1.5 million photos that were taken by White House photographers from 1981 to 1989. A thorough finding aid is included on the website, and scholars can request digital copies of contact sheets of photos described in the finding aid and, for a price, order photos online from the archive staff. The "Reference" section is a useful snapshot of some important moments in the Reagan administration; it lists important officials and the dates that they served, including all the members of the Joint Chiefs of Staff and all White House staff. It also lists Reagan's foreign and domestic travel and, most importantly, the NSSDs and NSDDs produced by the Reagan administration. A trip to Simi Valley is well worth the travel for those seeking to do in-depth studies of the Reagan period.

Like the Reagan Library, the Hoover Institution is located in California on the Stanford University campus and houses the personal papers of key members of Reagan's inner circle. Richard Allen, Reagan's first national security adviser, donated his files from the presidential campaign of 1980 as well as some papers, memos, and correspondence from his time in the Reagan White House. Fred Iklé, Reagan's undersecretary of defense for policy and a close adviser to Secretary of Defense Caspar Weinberger, donated his papers to Hoover as well. Last, for those historians interested in the development of strategic thinking in the late 1970s and early 1980s, the papers of the Committee on the Present Danger (CPD) are also available to researchers. Launched days after Jimmy Carter was elected president, the CPD was a bipartisan collection of foreign-policy hawks who exerted pressure on the Carter administration to adopt more hard-line policies, and when the CPD lent its support to the Reagan campaign, many members were rewarded with high-level jobs in his administration. In fact, Reagan was a member. The CPD was a short-lived advocacy group, but scholars should not overlook its influence on the Reagan administration—or on the contemporary conservative movement in the United States. The CPD's papers include outgoing correspondence, memos, financial bookkeeping, issue papers, and most of its publications.

The West Coast is not the only haven for Reagan researchers. The Library of Congress in Washington, DC, is the repository for the personal papers of two of the most important cabinet members in the Reagan administration: Caspar Weinberger and Alexander Haig. Both collections are limited because of classification restrictions, and Weinberger's collection requires the family's permission to access it. Neither barrier, however, should serve as a deterrent to scholars because the material that is available and will be available is too valuable not to explore. The recent lifting of the family permission requirement on the Haig papers should allow new research that sheds light on Haig's tenure during the Reagan period, his extensive career as deputy national security adviser and chief of staff in the Nixon and Ford administrations, and on his service as the supreme Allied commander in Europe. For those studying the Pentagon during the Reagan administration, the papers of William Howard Taft IV, Secretary of Defense Weinberger's general counsel, deputy secretary of defense, and trusted adviser, were donated to the Library of Congress. With his family's permission, researchers can look through his outgoing correspondence and daily records. In addition to the Weinberger and Haig Papers, the Library of Congress also has an impressive collection of oral histories of former Reagan officials.

Unfortunately, the National Archives in College Park, Maryland, have yet to process most of the Reagan period in its collections. The typical go-to record groups (RGs) for diplomatic and military historians have not reached the Reagan administration. The Records of the Department of State (RG 59) are organized up to 1979 and are the closest to materials from the Reagan years available for researchers. Records of the Joint Chiefs of Staff (RG 218) and the Records of the Office of the Secretary of Defense (RG 330) are disappointing and yield little to those in search of records from the 1980s on. However, the long-term prospects of research in the Reagan period are bright. The National Archives team is working to process RG 59 and will, it is hoped, begin completing the records of the Reagan administration in the near future. The National Archives website has four interviews of White House staffers who helped transition the Reagan administration both into and out of the White House.

Although the Library of Congress and the National Archives are two of the premier research locations for Reagan scholars, it is important to note that Reagan research is not exclusive to those locations. George H. W. Bush's vice presidential papers are kept at the George H. W. Bush Presidential Library on the campus of Texas A&M University at College Station. In addition to Bush's personal papers, the vice presidential material includes the papers of his chiefs of staff, correspondence, the files of the Office of National Security Affairs, the White House Office of Records Management Subject Files, and the files of the Appointments and Schedules Office. James Baker III served as Ronald Reagan's first chief of staff, and his papers are housed at Seeley G. Mudd Library at Princeton University. In addition to serving Reagan as his chief of staff, Baker also aided the Reagan campaigns and served as secretary of the treasury during Reagan's second term. His files include correspondence from his office, transition material from the Carter administration, senior staffing files, and the Subject Files of his tenure. Access to the Baker papers requires personal permission from James Baker. Last, the US Declassified Documents Online website (http://gdc.gale.com/products/declassified-documents-reference-system/)—or, as it is commonly known, the declassified documents reference system digital archive—releases recently declassified documents and is word searchable. Although the archive requires a fee to access the documents, it is available to some researchers who have access to a university library that owns a subscription to the website.

This essay is devoted mainly to repositories in the United States, but scholars should know that there are important international collections bearing on the Reagan presidency, notably files of the two foreign leaders most closely associated with Ronald Reagan: Margaret Thatcher and Mikhail Gorbachev. If one desires to examine the transatlantic relationship with Great Britain, the Margaret Thatcher website (http://www.margaretthatcher.org) offers a collection of material gathered in both England and the United States that highlight the "special" relationship between Margaret Thatcher and Ronald Reagan and between their respective governments. The website claims to have every statement made by Thatcher from 1945 to 1990, and researchers interested in getting a copy of her public statements can order one from the website or visit a list of 1,600 campuses that have a copy of the CD. The Thatcher website also holds digital copies of a massive amount of her papers, and scholars can search her files by subject, or if they know the date of the material they need, they can search her daily diary for her schedule and the documents related to each day. In addition to her personal papers, the creators of the website also digitized declassified communications between Reagan and Thatcher, a total of 127 items. For scholars who can travel, the International Foundation for Socio-economic and Political Studies, also known as the Gorbachev Foundation, is located in Moscow and holds a great deal of Mikhail Gorbachev's papers from his time as head of the Communist Party as well as the papers of his closest advisers, Anatoly Chernyaev, Georgy Shakhnazarov, and Valentin Zagladin. For those who cannot travel to Moscow, the Gorbachev Foundation website is also available (http://www.gorby.ru/en/archival/archive_library/).

In addition to the primary-source research that requires a trip to a brick-and-mortar archive, the Office of the Historian at the US Department of State publishes the *Foreign Relations of the United States* (*FRUS*) series. The official documentary record of US foreign policy, the *FRUS* volumes date back to the beginning of the Civil War. They are compiled and edited by historians, who are usually the first to fight the battle of declassification for researchers, a grueling process that is a struggle for most historians of the recent past. In 2015, the State Department released the first *FRUS* volume on the Reagan administration, *FRUS, 1981–1988,* volume 13, *Conflict in the South Atlantic, 1981–1984.* Forty-eight other volumes on his administration are in various stages of production, signaling the beginning a new phase in Reagan research as more documents become available to historians (see the website https://history.state.gov/historicaldocuments/reagan). For researchers of the early Reagan years, numerous volumes have already been complied and published on the Carter administration, which will also shed light on the issues that faced the Reagan administration upon entering office. Many of the *FRUS* volumes are also available online or can be downloaded for free onto electronic readers.

The State Department is not the only organization working to make available digital resources for Reagan scholars. The National Security Archive is a great resource for those interested in national security issues during the Reagan period. Founded in 1985, the National Security Archive is a nonprofit organization whose main purpose is to submit "directed Freedom of Information (FOIA) and declassification requests," and once the requests are granted and returned, scholars and journalists who work for the National Security Archive publish the declassified documents to the archive website (http://www2.gwu.edu/~nsarchiv/nsa/the_archive.html) as "electronic briefing books." For Reagan scholars, the briefing books "Iran-Contra Revisited," "The Shevardnadze File: Late Soviet Foreign Minister Helped End the Cold War," "The 1983 War Scare: The Last Paroxysm of the Cold War," and "Reagan, Gorbachev, and Bush at Governor's Island" offer deep insight into the most important national security issues during the 1980s. For example, the briefing book on the Iran-Contra Affair includes eight documents, seven of which are minutes from NSPG meetings, and commentary on the context of each document. Also useful for researchers is the in-depth guide to submitting a FOIA request or an MDR to its respective agency, which can be found on the National Security Archives website. For diplomatic or military historians, it is imperative that they become familiar with both hard-copy and digital research in order to maximize the material available and to receive material in a timely fashion. Also on the website is a helpful beginner's guide to interpreting diplomatic and military documents. This guide includes a glossary of terms, a list of key areas of note for scholars and advanced scholars, as well as a key for understanding diplomatic cables, whose shorthand abbreviations can give even the most seasoned historian troubles. Unfortunately, the National Security Archives do not have the staff to respond to public inquiries; however, the reading room is open weekdays from 10:00 a.m. to 5:00 p.m. and allows researchers to scan and copy documents requested on site.

For those interested in service-specific studies, each of the service historical offices or archives offers valuable primary-source resources. The Naval History and Heritage Command has the papers of John Lehman, most of which are about his time as secretary of the navy and which contain valuable information about budget, policy, and naval strategy issues that he played a role in resolving. The newly rebuilt Naval History and Heritage Command website (http://www.history.navy.mil/) also includes extensive ship command operation logs that date back to the Reagan period. These logs can prove invaluable to those looking to conduct operational histories, or, because of the extensive log of material and manpower included with each ship's log, they could prove valuable to researchers looking to research the effects of the Reagan buildup of the navy. Although the Center for Military History does not house the US Army's archival material, its website (http://www.history.army.mil/index.html) includes online publications that were produced by historians employed by the center. In particular, the "General Reference" section includes subjects that extensively cover the army during the Reagan period. The US Army Heritage and Education Center at Carlisle Barracks, Pennsylvania, also houses useful primary and secondary material related to the US Army during the 1980s. Likewise, the US Air Force Historical Office website (http://www.afhso.af.mil/index.asp) has online publications produced by office historians that cover the Reagan period. For archival experience, the Air Force Historical Research Agency is located on Maxwell Air Force Base in Alabama and has the personal papers of prominent air personnel who served during the Reagan period, including US Air Force chief of staff General Charles Gabriel, who served from 1982 to 1986.

As a nonpartisan affiliate housed on the campus of the University of Virginia, the Miller Center of Public Affairs at the University of Virginia, Charlottesville, contains one of the most exhaustive oral history collections in its Presidential Oral History Project (http://millercenter.org/oralhistory). The Miller Center specializes in presidential studies and has almost forty interviews with former Reagan administration officials, including the transcript of a special roundtable about the Falklands War that included Jeanne Kirkpatrick, Caspar Weinberger, and the defense leadership of the time. Oral histories can serve to settle scores between interagency rivals, but, like memoirs, they can also give valuable insight that documents cannot. Because all of these interviews occurred after the collapse of the Soviet Union, each interviewee usually gives his or her opinion on the role of the Reagan administration at the end of the Cold War. Also, each individual's perspective of Reagan provides valuable insight into his management style and the power of personality in deciding important issues. Scholars would be wise to consider these interviews. Jason Saltoun-Ebin's self-published book *The Reagan Files* is a collection of material he personally gathered at the Reagan Library and posted to a website (http://www.reaganfiles.com).[10] There is a surprising amount of material available in this volume, including NSC minutes, NSPG meeting minutes, and transcripts of other high-level discussions that took place in the Reagan White House. Although the book does not serve as a substitute for good primary research at the Reagan Library, it can provide a complement to a scholar's work.

Historical work on the Reagan administration is both timely and relevant. The Republican Party's belief in the relevance of Reagan's foreign policy as a guiding principal for today's world highlights the importance of the historian. As more documents come to light, the memory of Reagan and his policies will continue to shade the political debate in America. Although there has been significant progress in the Reagan historiography, more work can be done in at least two different areas. First, historians point to the military buildup in Reagan's first administration as a sign of how serious he was in his goal to balance the strategic imbalance between the US and Soviet militaries, but they rarely explain the significance of the buildup on the policy-making process or its long-term impact on later administrations. They fail to do so in part because they roughly break the Reagan administration into two parts: the hard-liner years, dominated by advisers such as Caspar Weinberger and National Security Adviser William Clark, and the dove years, heavily influenced by George Shultz. Although it is true that replacing advisers around any president can have a significant impact on policy, Reagan also trusted his instincts on policy decisions, and more can be done to find continuity between the two Reagan administrations. Another area of study is the Reagan administration's focus on Asia. Japan's rise as an economic power in the region at the time raised serious questions about America's role in defending Japan. South Korea, a major recipient of US aid and military hardware, played a role in the Reagan administration's attempt to secure footing on the Asian continent. The Philippines under Ferdinand Marcos was another region that the Reagan administration became deeply involved in and is a topic that could use much more work. Historians might also do more on Afghanistan, covert operations, counterillicit trafficking in the Americas, environmental history, and other neglected international security topics of the 1980s. In sum, this is an exciting time to study the Reagan presidency. Capitalizing on the increasingly rich body of available primary sources, scholars are poised to produce a significant body of new scholarship that will certainly broaden and deepen our understanding of the Reagan presidency and its enduring legacy for the contemporary world.

Notes

1. Ronald Reagan, speech at the opening of the Ronald Reagan Presidential Library, April 11, 1991, at http://www.planbproductions.com/postnobills/reagan1.html.

2. For more on memoirs from members of the Reagan administration, see Robert McMahon's review essay "Making Sense of American Foreign Policy during the Reagan Years," *Diplomatic History* 19, no. 2 (1995): 367–84. The memoirs mentioned here are cited in subsequent notes.

3. Ronald Reagan, *An American Life: The Autobiography* (New York: Simon and Schuster, 1990); Ronald Reagan, *The Reagan Diaries,* ed. Douglas Brinkley (New York: HarperCollins, 2007).

4. Alexander Haig, *Caveat: Realism, Reagan, and Foreign Policy* (New York: Macmillan, 1984).

5. George P. Shultz, *Turmoil and Triumph: My Years as Secretary of State* (New York: Scribner's, 1993).

6. Caspar Weinberger, *Fighting for Peace: Seven Critical Years in the Pentagon* (New York: Time Warner, 1990).

7. David Stockman, *The Triumph of Politics: The Inside Story of the Reagan Revolution* (New York: Avon Books, 1987).

8. John Lehman Jr., *Command of the Seas,* 2nd ed. (Annapolis, MD: Naval Institute Press, 2001).

9. Colin Powell, with Joseph E. Persico, *My American Journey* (New York: Ballantine, 1995); Paul Nitze, with Ann M. Smith and Steven L. Rearden, *From Hiro-*

shima to Glasnost: At the Center of Decision (New York: Grove Press, 1989); and Robert Gates, *From the Shadows: The Ultimate Insider's Story of Five Presidents and How They Won the Cold War* (New York: Simon and Schuster, 1996).

10. Jason Saltoun-Ebin, ed., *The Reagan Files: Inside the National Security Council* (N.p.: CreateSpace, 2010).

Contributors

Charles F. Brower IV is a professor emeritus of international studies at the Virginia Military Institute. He is a graduate of the United States Military Academy and the Naval War College and holds a doctorate in diplomatic and strategic history from the University of Pennsylvania. He served as the US Army aide to President Ronald Reagan from 1982 to 1984. He is the author of *World War II in Europe: The Final Year* (1998) and *Defeating Japan: The Joint Chiefs of Staff and Strategy in the Pacific War* (2012).

Archie Brown is emeritus professor of politics at Oxford University and an emeritus fellow of St. Antony's College, Oxford University. His books include *The Gorbachev Factor* (1997), *Seven Years That Changed the World: Perestroika in Perspective* (2009), and *The Myth of the Strong Leader: Political Leadership in the Modern Age* (2014). He has served as a visiting professor of political science at Yale University, the University of Connecticut, Columbia University, and the University of Texas at Austin and was distinguished visiting fellow at the Kellogg Institute for International Studies, University of Notre Dame.

Ryan Carpenter currently works as the oral historian at the Historical Office in the Office of the Secretary of Defense. He is a PhD candidate at the Catholic University of America, where he is writing a dissertation on defense policy during the Carter–Reagan years. His interests include Cold War history, military history, the Reagan presidency, and contemporary national security affairs. He earned an MA in applied history from Shippensburg University in 2010.

Bradley Lynn Coleman is the director of the John A. Adams '71 Center for Military History and Strategic Analysis at the Virginia Military Institute. He graduated from the Virginia Military Institute, Temple University, and the University of Georgia. Between 2007 and 2012, he served as command historian at US Southern Command, the US Department of Defense headquarters for US forces in Latin America and the Caribbean. He is the author of *Colombia and the United States: The Making of an Inter-American Alliance, 1939–1960* (2008).

James Cooper is a senior lecturer in history at Oxford Brookes University in the United Kingdom. He earned his doctorate at Aberystwyth University in 2010. Cooper is the author of *Margaret Thatcher and Ronald Reagan: A Very Political Special Relationship* (2012). His current research focuses on transnational aspects of contemporary US political history.

Beth A. Fischer is the coordinator of the Woodsworth ONE program at the University of Toronto. A specialist in US foreign policy and international relations, she was previously on the faculty of the Munk School of Global Affairs (Toronto) as well as of the Norman Paterson School of International Affairs (Ottawa). Fischer is the author of *The Reagan Reversal: US Foreign Policy and the End of the Cold War* (1997) and *Triumph: Ronald Reagan's Legacy and American Politics Today* (forthcoming). In 2002, she was awarded a Nobel Fellowship for her work on conflict management and the end of the Cold War.

Ronald J. Granieri is the executive director of the Center for the Study of the Americas and the West at the Foreign Policy Research Institute in Philadelphia. He is a specialist in contemporary German and international history, with degrees from Harvard University and the University of Chicago. Before joining the Foreign Policy Research Institute, he worked in the Historical Office of the Office of the Secretary of Defense, where he studied the tenure of Secretary of Defense Caspar Weinberger. Granieri is the author of *The Ambivalent Alliance: Konrad Adenauer, the CDU/CSU, and the West, 1949–1966* (2003) and *The Fall and Rise of German Christian Democracy, from Détente to Reunification* (forthcoming).

William I. Hitchcock is professor of history at the University of Virginia and the Randolph P. Compton Professor at the Miller Center of Public Affairs, a nonpartisan affiliate of the University of Virginia that specializes in presidential scholarship, public policy, and political history. Hitchcock earned a BA from Kenyon College and a PhD from Yale University, where he worked under the supervision of Paul Kennedy. He is the author of *France Restored: Cold War Diplomacy and the Quest for Leadership in Europe* (1998); *From War to Peace: Altered Strategic Landscapes in the 20th Century,* coedited with Paul Kennedy (2000); *The Struggle for Europe: The Turbulent History of a Divided Continent, 1945–Present* (2002); and *The Bitter Road to Freedom: A New History of the Liberation of Europe* (2008), which was a finalist for the Pulitzer Prize, a winner of the George Louis Beer Prize, and a *Financial Times* best seller.

James R. Locher III has more than twenty-five years of experience in both the executive and legislative branches of the federal government. He graduated from the US Military Academy in 1968, received an MBA from Harvard Business School in 1974, and was awarded an honorary Doctor of Laws degree from Hampden-Sydney College in 1992. Locher joined the Senate Committee on Armed Services as a professional staff member in 1978. He directed the bipartisan staff effort that resulted in the Goldwater–Nichols Defense Reorganization Act of 1986 and served as the senior staffer for the special operations and low-intensity conflict reform legislation known as the Cohen–Nunn Amendment. He later served as assistant secretary of defense for special operations and low-intensity conflict and as acting undersecretary of defense for policy. He is the author of *Victory on the Potomac: The Goldwater–Nichols Act Unifies the Pentagon* (2002).

Kyle Longley is the Snell Family Dean's Distinguished Professor in the School of Historical, Philosophical, and Religious Studies and the School of Politics and Global Studies at Arizona State University and an affiliate in the School of Transborder Studies, the Center for the Study of Religion and Conflict, and the Center for Law and Global Affairs in the Sandra Day O'Connor College of Law. He is also a faculty associate at the Strauss Center of the Lyndon B. Johnson School of Public Affairs. His books include *The Sparrow and the Hawk: Costa Rica and the United States during the Rise of José Figueres, 1942–1957* (1997); *Senator Albert Gore, Sr.: Tennessee Maverick* (2004); *Grunts: The American Combat Soldier in Vietnam* (2008); *In the Eagle's Shadow: The United States and Latin America* (2009); and *The Morenci Marines: A Tale of Small Town America and the Vietnam War* (2013).

David F. Patton is professor of government and international relations at Connecticut College, New London, where he teaches classes on European politics. He received a BA from Swarthmore College and a PhD in government from Cornell University. As a graduate student living in West Berlin, he witnessed the fall of the Berlin Wall and German unification. Patton's publications include *Out Cold War Politics in Postwar Germany* (1999) and *of the East: From PDS to Left Party in Unified Germany* (2011).

Michael Schaller is the Regents Professor of History at the University of Arizona. He is the author of numerous books and articles on US history and US foreign relations, including *The American Occupation of Japan* (1985), *Right Turn: American Life in the Reagan–Bush Era* (2007), and *The United States and China: Into the 21st Century* (2015). He served on the US Department of State Historical Advisory Committee from 1995 to 2000.

Evan R. Ward is a visiting fellow at the Wheatley Institution and associate professor of history at Brigham Young University. He is a graduate of Brigham Young University (BA, 1995) and the University of Georgia (MA, 1997; PhD, 2000). His research interests include economic history, Latin American history, natural-resource policy, and tourism development. Ward has traveled, worked, and studied around the world. He is the author of *Border Oasis: Water and the Political Ecology of the Colorado River Delta, 1940–1975* (2003) and *Packaged Vacations: Tourism Development in the Spanish Caribbean* (2008).

James Graham Wilson works in the Office of the Historian at the US Department of State. In the spring of 2014, he served as a shift lead on the Ukraine–Russia Coordination Team in the Bureau of European Affairs. A graduate of Vassar College and the University of Virginia, Wilson is the author of *The Triumph of Improvisation: Gorbachev's Adaptability, Reagan's Engagement, and the End of the Cold War* (2014). He is the editor of the forthcoming *Foreign Relations of the United States* documentary history of US policies toward the Soviet Union during the Reagan administration.

Index

Page numbers in italics refer to illustrations.

Studies in Conflict, Diplomacy, and Peace

Series Editors: George C. Herring, Andrew L. Johns, and Kathryn C. Statler

This series focuses on key moments of conflict, diplomacy, and peace from the eighteenth century to the present to explore their wider significance in the development of US foreign relations. The series editors welcome new research in the form of original monographs, interpretive studies, biographies, and anthologies from historians, political scientists, journalists, and policy makers. A primary goal of the series is to examine the US engagement with the world, its evolving role in the international arena, and the ways in which the state, nonstate actors, individuals, and ideas have shaped and continue to influence history, both at home and abroad.

Books in the Series

Truman, Congress, and Korea: The Politics of America's First Undeclared War
Larry Blomstedt

The Gulf: The Bush Presidencies and the Middle East
Michael F. Cairo

Reagan and the World: Leadership and National Security, 1981–1989
Edited by Bradley Lynn Coleman and Kyle Longley

American Justice in Taiwan: The 1957 Riots and Cold War Foreign Policy
Stephen G. Craft
Diplomatic Games: Sport, Statecraft, and International Relations since 1945
Edited by Heather L. Dichter and Andrew L. Johns
Nothing Less Than War: A New History of America's Entry into World War I
Justus D. Doenecke
Aid under Fire: Nation Building and the Vietnam War
Jessica Elkind
Enemies to Allies: Cold War Germany and American Memory
Brian C. Etheridge
Grounded: The Case for Abolishing the United States Air Force
Robert M. Farley
The American South and the Vietnam War: Belligerence, Protest, and Agony in Dixie
Joseph A. Fry
Obama at War: Congress and the Imperial Presidency
Ryan C. Hendrickson
US Presidential Elections and Foreign Policy: Candidates, Campaigns, and Global Politics from FDR to Bill Clinton
Edited by Andrew Johnstone and Andrew Priest
The Conversion of Senator Arthur H. Vandenberg: From Isolation to International Engagement
Lawrence S. Kaplan
Nixon's Back Channel to Moscow: Confidential Diplomacy and Détente
Richard A. Moss
The Currents of War: A New History of American-Japanese Relations, 1899–1941
Sidney Pash
Eisenhower and Cambodia: Diplomacy, Covert Action, and the Origins of the Second Indochina War
William J. Rust
So Much to Lose: John F. Kennedy and American Policy in Laos
William J. Rust
Foreign Policy at the Periphery: The Shifting Margins of US International Relations since World War II
Edited by Bevan Sewell and Maria Ryan
Lincoln Gordon: Architect of Cold War Foreign Policy
Bruce L. R. Smith

Made in United States
Cleveland, OH
20 February 2025

14522762R00196